MW01633000

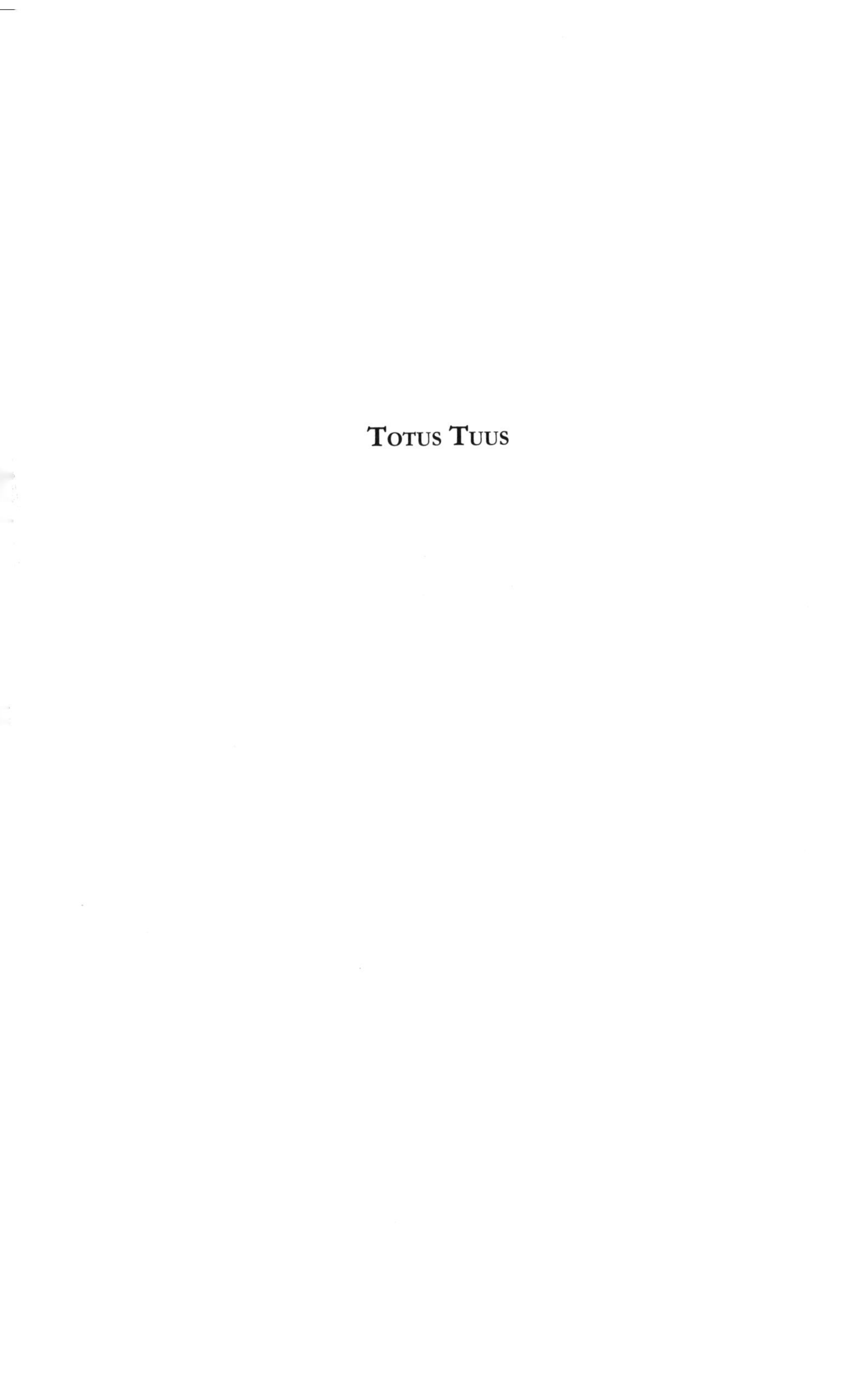

Totus Tuus

STUDIES AND TEXTS - NO. 1

TOTUS TUUS

Pope Saint John Paul II's Program of Marian Consecration and Entrustment

by ARTHUR BURTON CALKINS

ACADEMY OF THE IMMACULATE
NEW BEDFORD, MA

Totus Tuus is a book prepared for publication by the Academy of the Immaculate [academyoftheimmaculate.com], POB 3003, New Bedford, MA 02741-3003.

Second edition.

The Libreria Editrice Vaticana has granted permission to reproduce a selection of quotes from Pope John Paul II's Magisterium for the second edition of this book.

© Academy of the Immaculate 2017
All rights reserved

Nihil Obstat

Peter Damian Fehlner, O.F.M. Conv.
Censor Librorum

Imprimatur

✠ Edgar Moreira da Cunha, S.D.V., D.D.
Bishop of Fall River, Massachusetts
October 17, 2017

The nihil obstat and imprimatur are official declarations that a book or pamphlet is free from doctrinal or moral error. No implication is contained therein that those who grant the nihil obstat or imprimatur agree with the contents or statements expressed.

ISBN Print: 978-1-60114-077-7

ISBN Kindle: 978-1-60114-377-8

ISBN EPUB: 978-1-60114-577-2

Cover: Altarpiece with *La Vierge de Miséricorde* (Virgin of Mercy), detail of the the central panel, by Jean Miralhet, Chapelle de la Miséricorde (Chapel of Mercy), Nice, France. Design layout by Mary Flannery, Flannery Studios.

Table of Contents

Abbreviations

AA	*Apostolicam Actuositatem* (Vatican II Decree on Apostolate of Lay People)
AAS	*Acta Apostolicæ Sedis* (1909 –)
Africa Ap	*Africa: Apostolic Pilgrimage* (Boston: St. Paul Editions, 1980)
Africa Land	*Africa: Land of Promise, Land of Hope* (Boston: St. Paul Editions, 1982)
AG	*Ad Gentes* (Vatican II Decree on Church's Missionary Activity)
Argentina	*Pope John Paul II in Argentina* (Boston: St. Paul Editions, 1983)
ASC	*Alma Socia Christi: Acta Congressus Mariologici-Mariani Romae Anno Sancto MCML Celebrati* (Rome: Pontificia Academia Mariana Internationalis, 1953)
ASS	*Acta Sanctæ Sedis* (1865–1908)
Brazil	*Brazil: Journey in the Light of the Eucharist* (Boston: St. Paul Editions, 1980)
BSFEM	*Études Mariales: Bulletin de la Société française d'Études Mariales*, Paris
Carlen 2	Claudia Carlen, I.H.M., *The Papal Encyclicals 1878–1903* (Raleigh, N. C.: McGrath Publishing Co., "Consortium Book," 1981)

Carlen 3	*The Papal Encyclicals 1903–1939* (Raleigh, N. C.: McGrath Publishing Co., "Consortium Book," 1981)
CCC	*Catechism of the Catholic Church*, second edition (Washington, D.C.: United States Conference of Catholic Bishops, 1997)
CD	*Christus Dominus* (Vatican II Decree on the Pastoral Office of Bishops in the Church)
"Cons"	Stefano De Fiores, "Consacrazione," Stefano De Fiores, S.M.M. and Salvatore Meo, O.S.M., eds. *Nuovo Dizionario di Mariologia* (Milan: Edizioni Paoline, 1985) 394–417
D-H	Heinrich Denzinger, *Compendium of Creeds, Definitions, and Declarations on Matters of Faith and Morals*, 43rd Edition edited by Peter Hünermann for the bilingual edition and for the English edition by Robert Fastiggi and Anne Englund Nash (San Francisco: Ignatius Press, 2012)
DSp	Marcel Viller, S.J., et al., *Dictionnaire de Spiritualité Ascétique et Mystique* (Paris: Gabriel Beauchesne et Ses Fils, 1937 – 1995)
DV	*Dei Verbum* (Vatican II Dogmatic Constitution on Divine Revelation)
Far East	*The Far East: Journey of Peace and Brotherhood* (Boston: St. Paul Editions, 1981)
Flan	Austin Flannery, O.P., ed., *Vatican Council II: The Conciliar and Post Conciliar Documents* (Collegeville, Minn.: Liturgical Press, 1975)

France	*France: Message of Peace, Trust, Love and Faith* (Boston: St. Paul Editions, 1980)
Germany	*Germany: Pilgrimage of Unity and Peace* (Boston: St. Paul Editions, 1981)
GS	*Gaudium et Spes* (Vatican II Pastoral Constitution on the Church in the Modern World)
Inseg	*Insegnamenti di Giovanni Paolo II*, I-XXVIII (1978–2006) (Vatican City: Libreria Editrice Vaticana, 1979–2006)
Ireland	*Ireland "In the Footsteps of St. Patrick"* (Boston: St. Paul Editions, 1979)
LG	*Lumen Gentium* (Vatican II Dogmatic Constitution on the Church)
Maria	Hubert du Manoir, S.J., ed., *Maria: Études sur la Sainte Vierge*, 8 vols. (Paris: Beauchesne et Ses Fils, 1949–1971)
Mariology	Juniper B. Carol, O.F.M., ed., *Mariology*, 3 vols. (Milwaukee: Bruce Publishing Co., 1955–1961)
Messages	*Messages of John Paul II: Servant of Truth* (Boston: St. Paul Editions, 1979)
MotL	Pontifical International Marian Academy, *The Mother of the Lord: Memory, Presence, Hope.* Trans. Thomas A. Thompson, SM (Staten Island, NY: St Pauls, 2007)
MSS	Maria in Sacra Scriptura: *Acta Congressus Mariologici-Mariani Anno 1965 in Republica*

	Dominicana Celebrati 5: De Beata Virgine Maria in Evangelio S. Ioannis et in Apocalypsi (Roma: Pontificia Academia Mariana Internationalis, 1967)
NCE	*New Catholic Encyclopedia*, 15 vols. (New York: McGraw-Hill Book Co., 1967)
NDM	Stefano De Fiores, S.M.M. e Salvatore Meo (eds.), *Nuovo Dizionario di Mariologia* (Milan: Edizioni Paoline, 1985)
OL	*Our Lady: Papal Teachings*, trans. Daughters of St. Paul (Boston: St. Paul Editions, 1961)
Omelie	Karol Wojtyła, *Maria: Omelie*, trans. Janina Korzeniewska (Vatican City: Libreria Editrice Vaticana, 1982)
OR	*L'Osservatore Romano*, daily Italian edition. Roman numeral = volume; first Arabic numeral = number; second Arabic numeral = page.
ORE	*L'Osservatore Romano*, weekly edition in English. First number = cumulative edition number; second number = page.
PC	*Perfectæ Caritatis* (Vatican II Decree on the Up-to-Date Renewal of Religious Life)
PG	J.-P. Migne, *Patrologiæ Græcæ Cursus Completus* (Paris:1857–1866)
PL	J.-P. Migne, *Patrologiæ Latinæ Cursus Completus* (Paris:1844–1855)
PO	*Presbyterorum Ordinis* (Vatican II Decree on the Ministry and Life of Priests)

Poland	*Pilgrim to Poland* (Boston: St. Paul Editions, 1979)
Portugal	*Portugal: Message of Fatima* (Boston: St. Paul Editions, 1983)
RSV	*Revised Standard Version of the Holy Bible*
SC	*Sources Chrétiennes* (Lyons)
ST	*Summa Theologiæ*
Talks	*Talks of John Paul II* (Boston: St. Paul Editions, 1979)
Theotokos	Michael O'Carroll, C.S.Sp., *Theotokos: A Theological Encyclopedia of the Blessed Virgin Mary* (Wilmington: Michael Glazier, Inc.; Dublin: Dominican Publications, 1982)
TPS	*The Pope Speaks*, 1 – (1954 –)
Unger	Dominic Unger, O.F.M. Cap., ed. & trans., *Mary, Christ and the Church* (Bayshore, N.Y.: Montfort Publications, 1979)
U.S.A.	*U.S.A. – The Message of Justice, Peace and Love* (Boston: St. Paul Editions, 1979)
V.I.	Virgo Immaculata: Acta Congressus Mariologici-Mariani Romæ Anno MCMLIV Celebrati

Foreword

In his book, *Gift and Mystery*, written to commemorate the fiftieth anniversary of his priestly ordination, Pope Saint John Paul II reflects on what he calls the "Marian Thread" of his Christian life and, in particular, of his priestly vocation.[1] He tells how he developed a particular spiritual intimacy with the Mother of God through the devotions practiced in his home and in his parish from the time of his childhood. He mentions, for example, the devotion to Our Lady of Perpetual Help in his home parish, the investiture with the Scapular of Our Lady of Mount Carmel promoted by the Carmelite Friars at their monastery in his home town of Wadowice, and the spiritual help provided by the Carmelite Friars, especially in the Sacrament of Penance.[2]

In particular, he writes about the growth of his love of the Blessed Virgin Mary through his participation, as a young man, in the "Living Rosary" group in the Salesian parish in Cracow, where there was, in accord with the Salesian charism, a strong devotion to Mary, Help of Christians, and of how he came to understand not only that Mary leads us to Christ, her Divine Son, but that also Christ Himself leads us to His Mother.[3] He tells of a certain doubt about his Marian devotion which he experienced at the time, wondering whether a strong love of the Mother of Christ could compromise the worship owed to

1 "… filo mariano." Karol Wojtiła/Giovanni Paolo II, *Dono e Mistero. Diario di un Sacerdote* (Città del Vaticano: Libreria Editrice Vaticana, 2011), p. 42. [Hereafter, DM]. English translation: *Pope John Paul II, Gift and Mystery: On the Fiftieth Anniversary of My Priestly Ordination* (New York: Doubleday, 1996), p. 27. [DMEng].

2 Cf. DM, pp. 42-43. English translation: DMEng, pp. 27-28.

3 Cf. DM, p. 43. English translation: DMEng, p. 28.

Christ alone. It was Saint Louis-Marie Grignion de Montfort, by his book, *Treatise on True Devotion to the Blessed Virgin*, who helped him to understand that the Virgin Mary, by her unique role in the mystery of the Redemptive Incarnation, always leads us to Christ, "provided that we live her mystery in Christ."[4] Our Lady's unique participation "in the greatest event to take place in human history"—the Incarnation of God the Son in her immaculate womb—as the saintly Pontiff reflects, is underlined in the Church's praying of the Angelus three times each day.[5]

The significance of Saint Louis-Marie Grignion de Montfort in the life of Pope Saint John Paul II is evident in the choice of his episcopal motto: *Totus Tuus*, words taken from a prayer composed by the Saint.[6] They reflect the total gift of one's heart to the Sacred Heart of Jesus through the Immaculate Heart of Mary. As Pope Saint John Paul II understood so well, uniting his heart totally to the Immaculate Heart of Mary was the way to place his heart totally and forever, with hers, into the glorious pierced Heart of Jesus.

On the occasion of the twenty-fifth anniversary of his election to the See of Peter, Pope Saint John Paul II wrote his Apostolic Letter on the Holy Rosary, published on October 16, 2002, underlining once again how his whole Christian life and, in particular, his years of service as the Successor of Saint Peter had been lived in the Heart of Jesus through the Immaculate Heart of Mary, the Mother of Divine Grace. The prayer of the Holy Rosary gives powerful expression to our participation in the Mystery of Faith, the Mystery of Christ's Redemptive Incarnation, through His Mother whom He gave to us as our

4 ... a condizione che si viva il suo mistero in Cristo." DM, p. 43. English translation: DMEng, p. 29.

5 "... evento più grande che abbia avuto luogo nella storia dell'umanità." DM, p. 44. English translation: DMEng, p. 29.

6 Cf. *God Alone: The Collected Writings of St. Louis Marie de Montfort* (Bay Shore, NY: Montfort Publications, 1988), p. 515.

Mother when He accomplished the work of our eternal salvation by His death on the cross at Calvary.[7]

In the Apostolic Letter on the Holy Rosary, Pope Saint John Paul II, commenting on the great attention given to the Rosary by his predecessors, wrote:

> I myself have often encouraged the frequent recitation of the Rosary. From my youthful years this prayer has held an important place in my spiritual life. I was powerfully reminded of this during my recent visit to Poland, and in particular at the Shrine of Kalwaria. The Rosary has accompanied me in moments of joy and in moments of difficulty. To it I have entrusted any number of concerns; in it I have always found comfort. Twenty-four years ago, on 29 October 1978, scarcely two weeks after my election to the See of Peter, I frankly admitted: "The Rosary is my favourite prayer. A marvellous prayer! Marvellous in its simplicity and its depth. [...]. It can be said that the Rosary is, in some sense, a prayer-commentary on the final chapter of the Vatican II Constitution *Lumen Gentium*, a chapter which discusses the wondrous presence of the Mother of God in the mystery of Christ and the Church. Against the background of the words *Ave Maria* the principal events of the life of Jesus Christ pass before the eyes of the soul. They take shape in the complete series of the joyful, sorrowful and glorious mysteries, and they put us in living communion with Jesus through—we might say—the heart of his Mother. At the same time our heart can embrace in the decades of the Rosary all the events that make up the lives of individuals, families, nations, the Church, and all mankind. Our personal concerns and those of our neighbour, especially those who are closest to us, who are dearest to us. Thus the simple prayer of the Rosary marks the rhythm of human life."
>
> With these words, dear brothers and sisters, I set *the first year of my Pontificate* within the daily rhythm of the Rosary. Today, *as I begin the twenty-fifth year of my service as the*

7 Cf. Jn 19:26-27.

> *Successor of Peter*, I wish to do the same. How many graces have I received in these years from the Blessed Virgin through the Rosary: *Magnificat anima mea Dominum!* I wish to lift up my thanks to the Lord in the words of his Most Holy Mother, under whose protection I have placed my Petrine ministry: *Totus Tuus*![8]

In fact, it can be rightly said that perhaps the greatest gift of the immensely spiritually rich pontificate of Pope Saint John Paul II is the devotion to the Immaculate Heart of Mary as the irreplaceable way to living always in Christ, to resting one's heart totally and always in His glorious pierced Heart. That

8 "Nos praeterea Ipsi nullam omisimus opportunitatem quin ad crebram Rosarii recitationem incitemus. Iam inde ab iuvenilibus vitae annis precatio haec Nostra in spiritali vita praecipuum locum habuit. Huius memoriam recreavit recens Nostrum in Poloniam iter maximeque salutatio apud Sanctuarium Kalvariae. Temporibus enim laetitiae sicut et tristitiae Nos est corona haec precatoria comitata, cui tot commendavimus sollicitudines, in qua magnam semper repperimus consolationem. Viginti quattuor abhinc annos, die XXIX mensis Octobris anno MCMLXXVIII, duabus vix hebdomadis ab electione Petri ad Sedem, aperientes animum fere Nostrum sic sumus elocuti: "Carissima Nobis precatio Rosarium est. Oratio mirabilis! Miranda nempe sua in simplicitate atque etiam altitudine [...]. Dici quodammodo potest Rosarium commentatio et oratio extremi capituli Constitutionis *Lumen gentium* Concilii Oecumenici Vaticani II, quae singularem Matris Dei praesentiam pertractat tum Christi in mysterio tum Ecclesiae. Etenim post *Ave Maria* sonitum ante oculos animi principales vitae Iesu Christi transeunt eventus. Colliguntur enim in summa mysteriorum gaudiosorum, dolorosorum et gloriosorum nosque consociant vivo modo cum Iesu ipso per Matris Eius Cor—si ita loqui licet—. Eodem autem tempore concludere potest animus noster in has Rosarii decades cuncta eventa quae vitam singulorum hominum et familiae, nationis ipsius, Ecclesiae et totius hominum generis constituunt: uniuscuiusque hominis eventus tum etiam proximi atque praesertim eorum qui nobis proximi sunt magisque sunt cordi. Simplex igitur Rosarii precatio eundem ictum ac vitae humanae pulsat." Fratres et sorores carissimi, hisce vocibus ipsis in cursum cotidianum Rosarii inseruimus *Pontificatus Nostri annum primum*. Hodie, *anno ineunte XXV ministerii Nostri tamquam Petri Successoris*, tantundem efficere gestimus. Quot his superioribus annis per Rosarium Nos a Virgine Sancta accepimus gratias: *Magnificat anima mea Dominum*! Gratum sic animum Nostrum Domino testari cupimus Ipsius Sanctissimae Matris vocabulis, cuius tutelae Petrinum Nostrum ministerium concredidimus: *Totus tuus*!" Ioannes Paulus PP. II, Littera Apostolica *Rosarium Virginis Mariae*, "De Mariali Rosario data," 16 Octobris 2002, *Acta Apostolicae Sedis* 95 (2003), 6, n. 2. English translation: "Apostolic Letter *Rosarium Virginis Mariae* of the Supreme Pontiff John Paul II to the Bishops, Clergy and Faithful on the Most Holy Rosary," in Pope John Paul II, *Apostolic Letters* (Trivandrum, Kerala, India: Carmel International Publishing House, 2005), pp. 50-51, no. 2.

devotion finds its fullest expression in the act of consecration and entrustment, which Pope Saint John Paul II first faithfully lived and then tirelessly taught.

For that reason, I am particularly pleased to introduce to you the new and revised edition of Monsignor Arthur B. Calkins' *Totus Tuus: Pope Saint John Paul II's Program of Marian Consecration and Entrustment*. It is a work which has engaged Monsignor Calkins for well over thirty years in terms of his research and writing. It began as a licentiate thesis in theology at the Marian Research Institute in Dayton, Ohio, in 1986 and was further developed into a doctoral dissertation at the Pontifical Faculty of Saint Bonaventure, popularly known as the Seraphicum, in Rome in 1990, written under the direction of Father Peter Damian M. Fehlner, O.F.M. Conv., among the most respected of contemporary scholars in Mariology. Monsignor Calkins edited his doctoral dissertation for publication, and it was published in 1992 by the Academy of the Immaculate in Libertyville, Illinois.

But Pope John Paul II continued to shepherd the flock of Christ for another thirteen years until his death on April 2, 2005, exemplifying and teaching the consecration and entrustment. Monsignor Calkins faithfully continued to study the teaching of Pope John Paul II and is now able to offer to us an overview of the Marian teaching of the entire pontificate of Pope Saint John Paul II with particular reference to the reality known as consecration or entrustment to Our Lady.

It is no secret that the years since the conclusion of the Second Vatican Council on 8 December 1965 have been tumultuous years for the Catholic Church. All too often, the documents of the Council have been misrepresented and misinterpreted in ways that minimize their clear intent. During the last years of his pontificate, Blessed Pope Paul VI was clearly profoundly troubled by the way in which the Conciliar reforms had been implemented. For instance, one thinks of his homily on the occasion of the Solemnity of Saints Peter and Paul, during which, reflecting upon the situation of the Church in the world, he spoke of his sense that "through some fissure the smoke of Satan has entered into the temple of God."[9] He spoke of a pervasive doubt, uncertainty, restlessness, dissatisfaction and dissent, and of a loss of trust in the Church, coupled with a ready placement of trust in secular prophets who speak through the press or social movements, seeking from them the formula for a true life.[10] He noted how, also in the Church, the state of uncertainty prevailed, observing that, after the Second Vatican Ecumenical Council, it was believed that "a day of sunlight had dawned upon the Church," while, in fact, "a day of clouds, storms, darkness, wandering and uncertainty" had arrived.[11]

The pontificate of Pope Saint John Paul II can be described as a call to a new evangelization by means of the faithful implementation of the teaching of the Second Vatican Council. In setting forth the mission of the Church in our time, in his Post-Synodal Apostolic Exhortation on the Laity, *Christifideles Laici*, he declared that to remedy the situation of indifferentism, secularism and a kind of practical atheism in our time "a mending of the Christian fabric of society is urgently needed in all parts of the world."[12] He hastened to add that, if the remedy is to be achieved, the Church herself must be evangelized anew.

9 "… da qualche fessura sia entrato il fumo di Satana nel tempio di Dio." Paulus PP. VI, "Per il nono anniversario dell'Incoronazione di Sua Santità: "Resistite fortes in fide," 29 giugno 1972, in *Insegnamenti di Paolo VI* (Città del Vaticano: Tipografia Poliglotta Vaticana, 1973), Vol. 10, p. 707. English translation by author.

10 Cf. *Ibid.*, pp. 707-708.

11 "… una giornata di sole per la storia della Chiesa…una giornata di nuvole, di tempesta, di buio, di ricerca, di incertezza." *Ibid.*, p. 708. English translation by author.

12 "… consortium humanum spiritu christiano ubique denuo imbuendum est." Ioannes Paulus PP. II, Adhortatio Apostolica *Christifideles Laici*, "De vocatione et missione Laicorum in Ecclesia et in mundo," 30 Decembris 1988, *Acta Apostolicae Sedis* 81 (1989), 455, n. 34. [Hereafter, CL]. English translation: "Post-Synodal Apostolic Exhortation *Christifideles Laici* of His Holiness John Paul II on the Vocation and the Mission of the Lay Faithful in the Church and in the World," in Pope John Paul II, *Apostolic Exhortations* (Trivandrum, Kerala,

Fundamental to understanding the radical secularization of our culture is to understand also how much the secularization has entered into the life of the Church herself. In the words of Pope John Paul II, "[b]ut for this [the mending of the Christian fabric of society] to come about what is needed is to *first remake the Christian fabric of the ecclesial community itself* present in these countries and nations."[13]

Pope Benedict XVI addressed the failure of the implementation of the Conciliar teaching in his now famous address to the Roman Curia on 22 December 2005:

> The question arises: Why has the implementation of the Council, in large parts of the Church, thus far been so difficult?
>
> Well, it all depends on the correct interpretation of the Council or—as we would say today—on its proper hermeneutics, the correct key to its interpretation and application. The problems in its implementation arose from the fact that two contrary hermeneutics came face-to-face and quarreled with each other. One caused confusion, the other, silently but more and more visibly, bore and is bearing fruit.
>
> On the one hand, there is an interpretation that I would call "a hermeneutic of discontinuity and rupture"; it has frequently availed itself of the sympathies of the mass media, and also one trend of modern theology. On the other, there is the "hermeneutic of reform," of renewal in the continuity of the one subject-Church which the Lord has given to us. She is a subject which increases in time and develops, yet always remaining the same, the one subject of the journeying People of God.

India: Carmel International Publishing House, 2005), p. 895, no. 34. [Hereafter, CLEng].

13 "... [i]d [consortium humanum spiritu christiano imbuendum] tamen possible erit, si *christianus communitatum ipsarum ecclesialium contextus*, quae his in regionibus et nationibus degunt, *renovetur*." CL, 455, n. 34. English translation: CLEng, p. 895, no. 34.

The hermeneutic of discontinuity risks ending in a split between the pre-conciliar Church and the post-conciliar Church. It asserts that the texts of the Council as such do not yet express the true spirit of the Council. It claims that they are the result of compromises in which, to reach unanimity, it was found necessary to keep and reconfirm many old things that are now pointless. However, the true spirit of the Council is not to be found in these compromises but instead in the impulses toward the new that are contained in the texts....

In a word: it would be necessary not to follow the texts of the Council but its spirit. In this way, obviously, a vast margin was left open for question on how this spirit should subsequently be defined and room was consequently made for every whim.

The nature of a Council as such is therefore basically misunderstood. In this way, it is considered as a sort of constituent that eliminates an old constitution and creates a new one. However, the Constituent Assembly needs a mandator and then confirmation by the mandator, in other words, the people the constitution must serve. The Fathers had no such mandate and no one had ever given them one; nor could anyone have given them one because the essential constitution of the Church comes from the Lord and was given to us so that we might attain eternal life and, starting from this perspective, be able to illuminate life in time and time itself.[14]

---

14 "Emerge la domanda: Perché la recezione del Concilio, in grandi parti della Chiesa, finora si è svolta in modo così difficile? Ebbene, tutto dipende dalla giusta interpretazione del Concilio o—come diremmo oggi—dalla sua giusta ermeneutica, dalla giusta chiave di lettura e di applicazione. I problemi della recezione sono nati dal fatto che due ermeneutiche contrarie si sono trovate a confronto e hanno litigato tra loro. L'una ha causato confusone, l'altra, silenziosamente ma sempre più visibilmente ha portato e porta frutti. Da una parte esiste un'interpretazione che vorrei chiamare "ermeneutica della discontinuità e della rottura"; essa non di rado si è potuta avvalere della simpatia della mass-media, e anche di una parte della teologia moderna. Dall'altra parte c'è l'"ermeneutica della riforma," del rinnovamento nella continuità dell'unico soggetto-Chiesa, che il Signore ci ha donato; è un soggetto che cresce nel tempo e si sviluppa, rimanendo però sempre lo stesso, unico soggetto del Popolo di Dio in cammino. L'ermeneutica della discontinuità

The sad fact is that the "hermeneutic of discontinuity and rupture" is far from dead and has been a source of confusion and division in the Church since the conclusion of the Council. Even the salutary words of Pope Benedict have not dispelled it.

In the troubled times in which we find ourselves the Marian magisterium of Saint John Paul II provides us a sure point of reference. Monsignor Calkins is a firm believer that his Marian magisterium is the saintly Pontiff's greatest single contribution to the entire Church. I fully share his conviction, even though Pope John Paul II's teaching on so many aspects of the Church's life, on sacred worship, on doctrine regarding faith and morals, and on the various states in life and vocations continues to be an enormous magisterial patrimony for the Church.

In the course of his extensive study Monsignor Calkins ably presents the thought of this great and saintly Pope within the perspective of the constant teaching and practice of the Church and then expounds it in all of its richness. It is truly amazing that every time John Paul returned to topics like consecration to Mary, the theology of entrustment, her spiritual maternity,

rischia di finire in una rottura tra Chiesa preconciliare e Chiesa postconciliare. Essa asserisce che i testi del Concilio come tali non sarebbero ancora la vera espressione dello spirito del Concilio. Sarebbero il risultato di compromessi nei quali, per raggiungere l'unanimità, si è dovuto ancora trascinarsi dietro e riconfermare molte cose vecchie ormai inutili. Non in questi compromessi, però, si rivelerebbe il vero spirito del Concilio, ma invece negli slanci verso il nuovo che sono sottesi ai testi.... In una parola: occorrerebbe seguire non i testi del Concilio, ma il suo spirito. In tal modo, ovviamente, rimane un vasto margine per la domanda su come allora si finisca questo spirito e, di conseguenza, si concede spazio ad ogni estrosità. Con ciò, pero, si fraintende in radice la natura di un Concilio come tale. In questo modo, esso viene considerato come una specie di Costituente, che elimina una costituzione vecchia e ne crea una nuova. Ma la Costituente ha bisogno di un mandante e poi di una conferma da parte del mandante, cioè del popolo al quale la costituzione deve service. I Padri non avevano un tale mandato e nessuno lo aveva mai dato loro; nessuno, del resto, poteva darlo, perché la costituzione essenziale della Chiesa viene dal Signore e ci è stata data affinché noi possiamo raggiungere la vita eterna e, partendo da questa prospettiva, siamo in grado di illuminare anche la vita nel tempo e il tempo stesso." Benedictus PP. XVI, Allocutio "Ad Romanam Curiam ob omina natalicia, 22 Decembris 2005, *Acta Apostolicae Sedis* 98 (2006) 45-46. English translation: *L'Osservatore Romano Weekly Edition in English*, 4 January 2006, p. 5.

commentary on John 19:25–27, Mary's active collaboration in the work of the Redemption and her mediation of all graces, he never merely repeated himself, but constantly revealed unexpected facets of the question under discussion with ever new and fresh insights. All of this Monsignor Calkins has illustrated at length, providing us with texts which few of us would ever find elsewhere. While Saint John Paul II did not write a treatise on Marian consecration, Monsignor Calkins has carefully traced out the remarkable consistency of his thought and its development, which effectively provides for us a highly organized theology of consecration and entrustment to Our Lady according to the late Pontiff, even a manual of piety.

For almost twenty-five years there has been an ongoing debate in Marian circles—and indeed in the wider Church—about Our Lady's active collaboration in the work of the Redemption, that is, about the sense in which she is the New Eve, the helpmate of Jesus, the New Adam.[15] For over five hundred years the term Coredemptrix has been used to express the concept that Mary, while not being equal to Jesus, but a mere creature totally dependent on Him, secondary and subordinate to Him, nonetheless united herself with Him and joined in offering Him to the Father for our salvation on Calvary. The expression of this truth of our Faith constituted the single most contentious debate during the sessions of the Council and in the drafting of chapter eight of *Lumen Gentium*, the Second Vatican Council's fundamental document on Our Lady.[16] Ultimately, the Council did clearly teach about Mary's active collaboration in the work of Redemption in numbers 56–68 and 60–62, but did not use the word Coredemptrix out of fear that it would be misunderstood by Protestants. Our Lady's mediation of

15 Cf. Rom 5, 12-21; 1 Cor 15, 22. 45.

16 Cf. Serafino M. Lanzetta, *Il Vaticano II, un concilio pastorale. Ermeneutica delle dottrine conciliari* (Siena: Edizioni Cantagalli, 2014), pp. 369-419, 476-479. English translation: Serafino M. Lanzetta, *Vatican II, A Pastoral Council: Hermeneutics of Council Teaching*, tr. Liam Kelly (Leominster, Herefordshire: Gracewing, 2016), pp. 363-419, 452-453.

grace flows from her role as Coredemptrix. The battle raged especially fiercely on this matter and the word, Mediatrix, was used once in *Lumen Gentium* 62 with the appropriate insistence that "it neither takes away anything from nor adds anything to the dignity and efficacy of Christ the one Mediator."[17] She is Mediatrix with the Mediator, and this had already been taught in very clear language by nineteenth and twentieth century Popes. It has also been taught by the post-conciliar Popes.

Recent years have seen a strong movement in favor of recognizing Mary's role as Coredemptrix, Mediatrix and Advocate with a solemn papal definition. A commission was convened very briefly at the Mariological-Marian Congresses held in Częstochowa, Poland in August of 1996 to offer the Holy See advice on this matter. One of its counsels was that further study was needed.[18] That continues to be done by a number of competent theologians, including Monsignor Calkins, who shares his wealth of knowledge on this matter in this volume and further highlights Our Lady's role as Coredemptrix and Mediatrix of all graces as this pertains to her function as our spiritual Mother to whom we consecrate ourselves so as to belong ever more completely to Christ, her Divine Son. Two of the greatest modern teachers of Marian consecration, Saint Louis-Marie Grignion de Montfort (1673–1716) and Saint Maximilian Maria Kolbe (1894–1941), base their teaching on consecration to Mary very explicitly on Mary's mediation of the graces of the Redemption to us.

I am particularly pleased to recommend this excellent volume, which is not only a work addressed to scholars, but also to God's little ones, the very ones who instinctively appreciate the

17 "... ut dignitati et efficacitati Christi unius Mediatoris nihil deroget, nihil superaddat." Sacrosanctum Concilium Oecumenicum Vaticanum II, "Constitutio Dogmatica de Ecclesia, *Lumen gentium*," 21 Novembris 1964, *Acta Apostolicae Sedis* 57 (1965), 63, n. 62. English translation: *Vatican Council II: The Conciliar and Post Conciliar Documents*, ed. Austin Flannery, rev. ed. (Northport, NY: Costello Publishing Company, 1992), p. 419, no. 62.

18 Cf. *L'Osservatore Romano Weekly Edition in English*, 4 June 1997, 12.

goodness of putting their lives into the hands of Mary in order to belong ever more completely to Jesus. In fact, while earlier I stated that this work is the fruit of the studies which Monsignor Calkins undertook at the Marian Research Institute in Dayton, Ohio, and at the Pontifical Faculty of Saint Bonaventure or Seraphicum in Rome, in truth, as he acknowledges in the Preface, it began with his own personal consecration to the Mother of God on the Solemnity of her Immaculate Conception, December 8th, in 1978, during the first months of the pontificate of Pope Saint John Paul II. Monsignor Calkins has a gift for writing about profound matters in a way that is accessible to every reader. But what is more, he studies deeply and writes about what he himself has experienced in giving his heart totally to the Immaculate Heart of Mary, so that, with her, he may be totally and always solely for Christ. Living in union with Mary is a great key to growing in our knowledge and love of Christ. The Mother of Divine Grace never draws us to herself for her own sake, but always in order to lead us ever more closely to Christ.

Before concluding, I express my great personal pleasure in presenting the important work of a long-time friend. My friendship with Monsignor Calkins traces all the way back to August of that fateful year of 1968, when I entered the Theological College of The Catholic University of America to begin my studies in philosophy there, while Monsignor Calkins was continuing his studies in theology at the same university. Our friendship deepened during our years together at the Villa Stritch in Rome, the residence for United States priests serving in the Roman Curia, while we were both engaged in the service of the Apostolic See.

From the first time that I met Monsignor Calkins, I was impressed with his love of Our Lord and of His Mystical Body, the Church, a love which was clearly Marian. The tumultuous post-Conciliar years of the fierce battle between the "hermeneutic of reform" in continuity and the "hermeneutic of discontinuity and rupture"—the beginning of which is symbolically identified with the year 1968, the year of the cultural revolution signaled by the Paris student riots—was experienced in all of its ferocity during the seminary years which I shared with Monsignor Calkins. It was clear to me that Our Blessed Mother was guiding and protecting him in the midst of so much confusion and error. His friendship was and continues to be a blessing. It is my hope that, in reading his book, you will also discover a spiritual friend who leads you closer to the Mother of God who will unfailingly lead you to her Divine Son with the maternal counsel which she gave to the wine-stewards at the Wedding Feast of Cana: "Do whatever he tells you."[19]

It only remains to thank Monsignor Calkins for his most thorough, helpful and inspiring study and to ask that God grant to all those who take this book in hand the grace of an enriched knowledge and love of Christ, His Divine Son, through Mary, Mother of Christ and Mother of the Church. Instructed through the teaching of Pope Saint John Paul II may each reader be led to pray with him, in the words of Saint Louis-Marie Grignion de Montfort: *Totus tuus ego sum et omnia mea tua sunt. Accipio te in mea omnia. Præbe mihi cor tuum, Maria* ["I belong entirely to you, and all that I have is yours; I take you for my all. O Mary, give me your heart"].

Raymond Leo Cardinal Burke
15 August 2017
Solemnity of the Assumption of the Blessed Virgin Mary

19 Jn 2:5.

Preface

The theme of consecration to Mary came to the fore in my life virtually simultaneously with the beginning of the pontificate of Pope Saint John Paul II. The day I made my personal consecration to the Mother of God in 1978, the Solemnity of the Immaculate Conception, was also the day when the Pope launched what I refer to as his "program of Marian consecration and entrustment" from the Patriarchal Basilica of Saint Mary Major. On that day he said:

> The Pope, at the beginning of his episcopal service in St. Peter's Chair in Rome, wishes to entrust the Church particularly to her in whom there was accomplished the stupendous and complete victory of good over evil, of love over hatred, of grace over sin; to her of whom Paul VI said that she is "the beginning of the better world," to the Blessed Virgin. He entrusts to her himself, as the servant of servants, and all those whom he serves, all those who serve with him. He entrusts to her the Roman Church, as token and principle of all the churches in the world, in their universal unity. He entrusts it to her and offers it to her as her property.[1]

Curiously, I was not aware when I made that act of consecration to Mary in Warwick Neck, Rhode Island, that a major feature of the papal service of John Paul II was being established, propelling the whole Church in the same direction that I, too, had by God's grace deliberately taken that day. In a relatively short period of time, I became conscious of a new dimension in my life, a new confidence in God's providence,

1 *Inseg* I (1978) 313; *Talks of John Paul II* (Boston: St. Paul Editions, 1979) 424 (hereafter cited as *Talks*).

a new freedom; I sensed the gentle, maternal, yet powerful presence of Mary.

Perhaps not so strangely, because of my initiation into the formal discipline of theology in those stormy years (1966–1970) immediately following the Second Vatican Council, even though I felt drawn to put my life entirely in Mary's hands, I was also hesitant. Would such an act not stand in the way of my relationship with Jesus? The late Father George Kosicki, C.S.B. (1928–2014), then coordinator of Bethany House of Intercession for Priests, made two comments to me, which I have never forgotten. The first was an accommodation of the text of Matthew 1:20: "Do not fear to take Mary to yourself because that which is conceived in her is of the Holy Spirit."[2] The second was in the nature of a personal testimony made by Cardinal Leo Josef Suenens (1904–1996) to this effect: "If God has entrusted a special role to His Mother in our salvation, who are we to tell Him that He can't?"[3] Both of these reflections helped me over my theological hurdles and providentially smoothed the way for me to make the total gift of myself to Mary in order to belong ever more completely to Jesus.

When the time was made available for me to do further graduate work in theology with a specialization in Mariology, I was already deeply convinced of the value of Marian consecration for leading the Christian life and wanted to illustrate why this is necessarily so. Through much reading and discussions with Father Théodore Koehler, S.M. (1911–2001), the then Director of the International Marian Research Institute at the University of Dayton and Curator of the University's Marian Library, I came to the subject of the program of the Marian consecration and entrustment of Pope John Paul II. Could one discover a

2 Cf. George W. Kosicki, C.S.B., *Born of Mary: Testimonies, Tensions, Teachings* (Stockbridge, Ma.: Marian Press, 1985) xiii, 6–7.

3 Cf. ibid., 6.

theological rationale in the homilies, addresses and writings of John Paul II? I wanted to find out.

Besides recognizing my debt of gratitude to Fathers George Kosicki, C.S.B., and Théodore Koehler, S.M., for guiding me along a rich and fruitful path, I would also like to acknowledge the never-failing encouragement I received from Father Peter Damian M. Fehlner, O.F.M. Conv., who arranged for the publication of the licentiate thesis which I had written under Father Koehler's direction in *Miles Immaculatæ*[4] and subsequently became the moderator of this doctoral study. His help has been unstinting, positive and generous in every phase of this work—even beyond the defense. Would that every doctoral student could have such a director! I also remain grateful to the late Father Giovanni Iammarrone, O.F.M. Conv., then President of the Pontifical Faculty of Theology of Saint Bonaventure (more commonly known as the Seraphicum), for his welcoming me into the academic community of the Pontifical Faculty of Saint Bonaventure and the interest he showed in my work, and to the late Father Maurizio Wszołek, O.F.M. Conv., for his helpful comments regarding the methodology and organization of this work.

While I cannot name all those to whom I am indebted for their support in the course of these past six years, I cannot neglect to mention their Excellencies, the Most Reverend Philip M. Hannan (1913–2011), Archbishop of New Orleans from 1965 to 1988, and his successor, the Most Reverend Francis B. Schulte (1926–2016), Archbishop of New Orleans from 1988 to 2002, who allowed me to undertake and continue this study. I am also pleased to acknowledge my debt of gratitude to the late Most Reverend Constantino Luna, O.F.M. (1910–1997), Bishop of Zacapa, Guatemala, from 1955 to 1980, and International President of the World Apostolate of Fatima, whose encouragement and fatherly kindness were a constant source of

4 "John Paul II's Consecration to the Immaculate Heart of Mary: Christological Foundation," *Miles Immaculatæ* 23 (1987) 88–116, 364–417.

support to me since I first met him in 1984. It is also my happy task to acknowledge with deep appreciation the kindness and generosity of the late Father Herman J. Schnurr (1912–2006), a faithful priest for over half a century and a fervent lover of the Mother of God, whose generous benefactions made it possible for me to spend 1989 as a year of research and writing in Rome along with the inestimable benefit of my library and computer.

It was also a great privilege for me to benefit from the priestly example and paternal concern of Paul Augustin Cardinal Mayer, O.S.B. (1911–2010), first President of the Pontifical Commission, "Ecclesia Dei," during the time of the writing of this thesis; and I was especially grateful to His Eminence for having graced its defense with his presence.

I must also thank all of those who were "behind the scenes" at the time of the original publication: my mother, Frances C. Calkins (1923–2014); Shirley Kopf; Deborah Ann DeDuck; Father James McCurry, O.F.M. Conv.; the Discalced Carmelite Nuns of Erie, Pennsylvania, Flemington, New Jersey, and Regina Carmeli in Rome; the Colettine Poor Clares of Barhamsville, Virginia; and my many friends in North America and in Rome whose names remain *in pectore*.

Finally, I must bring my readers up to date. I began this study during my time as chaplain at the World Apostolate of Fatima's Shrine of the Immaculate Heart of Mary in Washington, New Jersey, from 1984 to 1988. As I indicated above, it began as a thesis for the licentiate in Sacred Theology, which I defended at the International Marian Research Institute in Dayton, Ohio, in 1986. It was expanded into a doctoral study, which I defended at the Seraphicum in Rome in 1989, and subsequently published as the first volume of the newly established Academy of the Immaculate in 1992. In the course of the time since then I have undertaken and published many studies on Our Lady, almost all of them with the collaboration and reassurance of Father Peter Damian M. Fehlner, O.F.M. Conv. He is chief among those who have consistently encouraged me to prepare a second edition of this work that would bring my original doctoral study up to the conclusion of the extraordinarily prolific pontificate of Pope Saint John Paul II. In the course of the intervening years, I continued to chronicle the enormous Marian output of the Polish Pontiff and to write research papers on his Mariology and other areas related to the evaluations which I have made in this present edition. In a sense, I can say that this second revised and enlarged edition of *Totus Tuus* is the fruit of thirty-two years of research, reflection and scholarly work. After duly acknowledging the debt of gratitude that I owe first of all to the Most Holy Trinity, to Jesus, the Incarnate Word, to the Most Holy Mother of God, and then to the great Marian Pontiff, Saint John Paul II, I would also like to acknowledge here what I owe to Father Peter Damian, whose counsel during all of these years and through this second edition has been invaluable.

Introduction

The theological problem

The placing of oneself in the hands of Mary, the gift of oneself to her, is, as we shall see, an ancient tradition in the Church, attested to in every era of her life. Yet, at the same time, this custom raises a "theological problem": How can one give, entrust or consecrate oneself to a human person when only God is the ultimate goal of our lives? Has the "tradition" of the Church in this regard actually been a "corruption" which needs to be purged of impure elements that divert our full attention from Christ, who is the only "way" to the Father (cf. Jn. 14:6)? As a young theology student in the years immediately following the Second Vatican Council, I was inclined to think so.

It seemed obvious that the goal of the Council was to bring us back to our roots, to sweep away unnecessary accretions, to reset our goals. From this perspective, consecration to Mary seemed to be missing the mark. Why consecrate oneself to Mary? Why not simply go straight to Jesus? Why multiply expendable "go-betweens"? The question continues to be asked today.

Happily, the history of Catholic theology provides answers to these questions, as we shall see in our survey of Marian consecration in the spiritual journey of the Church. Two great protagonists and theorists of this practice come readily to mind, although they are far from being the only ones: Saints Louis-Marie Grignion de Montfort and Maximilian-Maria Kolbe. Although their veneration for Mary was very great and they called themselves respectively her "slave" and her "possession and property," they cannot in justice be accused of "Mariolatry" because, in their vision, Jesus is never eclipsed by His Mother.

Nonetheless, from a "negative" perspective it is still useful in every era to ask the crucial questions again, because they are perennial and we gain in understanding as we work our way through them. Not only that, but there are many Catholics today who fear that the gift of oneself to Mary is at best an indirect way to Jesus, or at worst an obstruction or aberration. Further, there are many of our separated Christian brothers and sisters for whom the very idea of consecrating or entrusting oneself to Mary appears as a disturbing deviation from Gospel Christianity. Indeed, is there a Christological foundation for such a practice?

From the "positive" perspective as well, there is value in raising the question anew. What is the hidden spiritual dynamism, which explains the phenomenal growth of movements like the Legion of Mary and Maximilian Kolbe's Niepokalanów, which can topple oppressive regimes in places as disparate as Poland and the Philippines? Why was John Paul II so doggedly persistent in entrusting every local church and country as well as the universal Church to the Mother of God? Is there a Christological perspective which justifies such deportment?

The purpose of this study

Hence, the explicit purpose of this study is to analyze the act of consecration or entrustment to Mary in order to discover its basis in the mystery of Christ the Incarnate Word and in the eternal plan of God—and to do so explicitly in terms of the teaching and practice of one of the Church's supreme pastors, Pope Saint John Paul II.

From the moment of his election to the papacy on 16 October 1978, he never hesitated to bring the role of Mary to the forefront of Catholic life and thought. The newly elected

Pope John Paul II, speaking spontaneously from the central loggia of Saint Peter's Basilica on the occasion of his first public appearance as Pope, said these words:

> I was afraid to accept this nomination, but *I did it in the spirit of obedience to our Lord Jesus Christ and of total confidence in His Mother, the most holy Madonna* ... I present myself to you all to confess our common faith, our hope, *our confidence in the Mother of Christ and of the Church*, and also to start anew on this road of history and of the Church, with the help of God and with the help of men.[1]

Not only did the newly elected Supreme Pontiff break with precedent in addressing himself to the estimated throng of 200,000 who had gathered in Saint Peter's Square that evening to discover the identity of the 263rd successor of Peter and to receive his first blessing, but he also sounded one of the most persistent notes of his pontificate: *total confidence in Mary*.

This had been signaled already twenty years before with his episcopal coat of arms, whose primary feature is a cross "which does not correspond to the customary heraldic model,"[2] but which is "enough off center to make room for the initial of Mary, symbolically standing at the foot of the Cross of her Son,"[3] thus underscoring her unique role in the redemption. In iconographic language the statement cannot be missed—even if it may be a source of chagrin to experts in ecclesiastical heraldry. But if the symbolism were not enough, the motto would clearly bring the matter home with the simple words "Totus tuus," the beginning of a longer prayer, which he adapted, abbreviated and transposed from the Latin prayers composed by Saint Louis-Marie Grignion de Montfort: *Tuus totus ego sum, et omnia mea tua sunt. Accipio te in mea omnia. Præbe mihi cor tuum, Maria*

1 *Inseg* I (1978) 3 [*Talks* 48–49] (emphasis mine).

2 Cf. *Talks* 47.

3 George Huntston Williams, *The Mind of John Paul II: Origins of His Thought and Action* (New York: The Seabury Press, 1981) 279.

["I belong entirely to you, and all that I have is yours; I take you for my all. O Mary, give me your heart"].[4] The first sentence is attributed to Saint Bonaventure.[5] The last two sentences are adaptations of John 19:27 and Proverbs 23:26. He took *Totus tuus* as his motto as bishop and pope.

Indeed it cannot be doubted that Pope John Paul II brought the figure of Mary and her maternal relationship with the followers of her Son to the fore in the course of his pontificate in ways that surpass those of all his predecessors. And chief among the ways in which he accomplished this were the unprecedented and constantly multiplying acts of consecration or entrustment to Mary, which he made and commented upon. Pope John Paul's declaration of the second Marian Year in the history of the Church on 1 January 1987,[6] and the subsequent celebration of that special time of grace[7] for the Church from Pentecost of 1987 to the Feast of the Assumption in 1988 with the issuance of the Encyclical Letter, *Redemptoris Mater*,[8] further created the context in which to study his understanding of the relationship which the Lord Jesus willed between His Mother and His followers. Again, towards the end of his long pontificate he proclaimed the "Year of the Rosary" from October 2002 to October 2003 with the issuance of the Apostolic Letter, *Rosarium Virginis Mariæ*[9],

---

4 These Latin sentences come from the beginning and the last sentence of #266 in the *Treatise on True Devotion*. Cf. *Œuvres complètes de saint Louis-Marie Grignion de Montfort* (Paris: Éditions du Seuil, 1982) 666–667. *God Alone: The Collected Writings of St. Louis Mary de Montfort* (Bay Shore, N. Y.: Montfort Publications, 1987) 375–376. He explained his adoption of this terminology in *Gift and Mystery: On the 50th Anniversary of My Priestly Ordination* (Nairobi, Kenya: Paulines Publications, Africa, 1996) 42–43.

5 *Psalt. Majus, cant. Ad instar illius Moïsis*, Ex. 15 (*Opera Omnia*, Vivès, Parisiis 1868, 221 b).

6 *Inseg* X/1 (1987) 6–7[*ORE* 969:5].

7 René Laurentin in the title of his book on the topic describes the Marian Year *as A Year of Grace with Mary*. The English edition translated by Msgr. Michael J. Wrenn was published by Veritas, Dublin, 1987.

8 *Inseg* X/1 (1987) 678–744 [*Mother of the Redeemer: on the Blessed Virgin Mary in the Life of the Pilgrim Church* (Boston: St. Paul Editions, 1987)].

9 Cf. *Inseg* XXV/2 (2002) 486–521.

on 16 October 2002, the 24th anniversary of his election to the See of Peter.

The unprecedented and constantly multiplying acts of consecration and entrustment to Mary which I alluded to above constitute what I will refer to throughout this study as the Holy Father's "program of entrustment." "If the last popes have spoken in positive terms of Marian consecration," said Stefano De Fiores, "John Paul II has made of it one of the characteristic programmatic points of his pontificate,"[10] "a programmatic point of spiritual life and pastoral practice."[11]

The present state of research

While this "program of entrustment" was duly noted early in the pontificate by any number of commentators and scholars such as Father De Fiores, no one undertook a systematic study of it. Thus far, the most detailed inquiry would seem to be that of Padre Angel Luis, C.Ss.R., "La consagración a María en la vida y doctrina de Juan Pablo II," which appeared in *Estudios Marianos* (51:77–112) in 1986; and while that essay is helpful in signaling some fundamental texts and their magisterial precedents, it rather exposed the topic than treating it thoroughly.

Hence, what I wish to present in this study is an in-depth analysis of the papal magisterium of Pope John Paul II with regard to the question of Marian consecration based on his published statements, which occur in homilies, addresses, official documents and prayers.[12] For the sake of assessing the continuity and consistency of his thought, I have also had recourse to Italian

10 "Cons" 406 (my translation).

11 Stefano De Fiores, S.M.M., "Questi tuoi figli o Madre," *OR* 9–10 dicembre 1981, p. 2 (my translation).

12 The principal source for these is the *Insegnamenti di Giovanni Paolo II* published by the Libreria Editrice Vaticana. In the case of English translations I depend almost entirely on the translations provided by the weekly English edition of *L'Osservatore Romano* or convenient collections of those (St. Paul Editions), published by the Daughters of St. Paul in the United States.

and English translations of his pre-papal writings and homilies.[13] Without a doubt there are further riches to be mined in the corpus of his works produced as priest and bishop in Krakow and further studies to be undertaken, but I have limited myself primarily to his papal teaching, which is most important for the life of the universal Church.

The sources

Since his first papal visit to the Patriarchal Basilica of Saint Mary Major on the Solemnity of the Immaculate Conception in 1978, John Paul hardly passed up an opportunity of placing the Church and her destiny in the hands of Mary.[14] In virtually every country he visits and every region of Italy to which he travels as its Primate he seeks out a Marian sanctuary in which to renew his entrusting of the Church Universal and the local church of that place to the Madonna. And his "habitual acts of entrustment" to Our Lady in addresses to the faithful, in Angelus messages, in pontifical documents and especially in his fraternal discourses to Bishops on the "ad limina" visit are simply legion. Documenting these references has, indeed, been a major preoccupation for me since the autumn of 1984. I am indebted to the late Don Domenico Bertetto, S.D.B., for his indefatigable work of chronicling the Pope's Marian teaching for the first six years of the pontificate in his six volumes entitled *Maria nel Magistero di Giovanni Paolo II* (Rome: Libreria Ateneo Salesiano, 1980–1986). While I never had the privilege of meeting Don Bertetto, his work initiated me into the study of the *fontes* and provided helpful orientation.

13 Cf. the Bibliography where I list pre-papal works.

14 The beautiful book, *Affido a Te, O Maria*, a cura di Sergio Trasatti e Arturo Mari (Bergamo: Editrice Velar, 1982), just began to chronicle the principal Marian consecrations of the Pope from 8 December 1978 to 7 June 1981. Father Bogumil Lewandowski, in his book, *Tutti consacrati alla Madonna* (Rome, 1988) 48–149, provides some of the major national texts up to the entrustment of the United States in Los Angeles on 16 October 1987.

The method

The method that I utilize in this study is an analysis of the major themes, which I have found to be immediately related to the topic of Marian consecration in the thought of the Pope, without attempting to superimpose any category on them. I do point out in the historical section how the Pope is at home with the terminology of virtually every major period in the Church's long tradition of Marian consecration; and I attempt as well to signal for special notice springs which seem to have contributed particularly to his formation, such as the thought of de Montfort, Kolbe and Wyszyński; but the major divisions of part two, the heart of this study, have emerged from a steady pondering of the texts themselves.

Following the fundamental work of expository analysis, I consider in the third part the teaching of John Paul II on Marian consecration vis-à-vis the contemporary theological context. There, I have simply striven to compare the theological synthesis, which I have extracted from the corpus of his papal teaching, with representative contemporary theological thought on the subject of Marian consecration. From this comparison I highlight what I consider to be the primary contributions of John Paul II to the theology of Marian consecration—and these contributions continued to develop until the end of his life. Finally, it was necessary to take into consideration the changing position of mariologists regarding Marian consecration.

Framework of the Pope's program of entrustment

Within the framework of this "program of entrustment" there were certain acts which emerged as particularly solemn and paradigmatic. The first is the text of 7 June 1981. It was made by previous recording for Pentecost Sunday, 7 June 1981,[15] in conjunction with the celebration of the 1600th anniversary of the First Council of Constantinople and the 1550th anniversary

15 *Inseg* IV/1 (1981) 1241–47 [*ORE* 688:7, 10].

of the Council of Ephesus. The event itself had been planned well in advance by the Pope. The double observance had been the object of a Pontifical Letter, *A Concilio Constantinopolitano I*, addressed to the bishops of the world,[16] in which he spoke of Mary's divine maternity as establishing a "permanent link with the Church" (*perpetuum vinculum maternum cum Ecclesia*).[17] His more active participation in the festivities marking the observance of these two great Councils and culminating on Pentecost Sunday, however, was precluded by an assassin's bullet on 13 May 1981. The circumstances of this act of entrustment to Mary, which addressed her as "entrusted to the Holy Spirit more than any other human being" and "linked in a profound and maternal way to the Church," [18] were particularly poignant, then, and may also be reckoned as the plea of a stricken father on behalf of his family. The very same act was renewed again on the Solemnity of the Immaculate Conception in 1981 before the icon of the *Salus Populi Romani* in St. Mary Major's.[19]

The above-cited act of entrustment became the archetype of two subsequent acts, closely modeled upon it, which gained

16 *Inseg* IV/1 (1981) 815–28 [*ORE* 678:6–8].

17 *Inseg* IV/1 (1981) 824 [*ORE* 678:7].

18 *Inseg* IV/1 (1981) 1245 [*ORE* 688:10].

19 *Inseg* IV/1 (1981) 1245–47 [*ORE* 688:10]. But for one alteration, the text as it appears in *Inseg* IV/2 (1981) 876–79 is identical with the earlier text, except that it uses fewer exclamation points and italics (perhaps merely a matter of the type-setter's discretion). A new English translation was also rendered by the staff of the English language edition of *L'Osservatore Romano*; it seems to differ from the earlier one in only minor stylistic variations; cf. *ORE* 714:12. The one alteration in the text occurs in the seventh paragraph. In the prior version the Pope said: "Embrace with the love of the Mother and Handmaid of the Lord those who most await this embrace, and also those whose act of dedication you too await in a particular way" (*ORE* 688:10). [*Abbraccia con l'amore della Madre e della Serva del Signore coloro che questo abbraccio più aspettano, e insieme coloro il cui affidamento Tu pure attendi in modo particolare. Inseg* IV/1 (1981) 1246.] In the version he used on this date he said: "Embrace with the love of the Mother and the Handmaid of the Lord the peoples who await this embrace the most, and likewise the peoples whose consecration you, too, are particularly awaiting" (*ORE* 714:12). [*Abbraccia con l'amore della Madre e della Serva del Signore i popoli che questo abbraccio più aspettano, e insieme i popoli il cui affidamento Tu pure attendi in modo particolare. Inseg* IV/2 (1981) 878.]

considerably more public notice. The first of these was made on 13 May 1982, the Feast of Our Lady of Fatima, in that humble village in Portugal where Our Lady had first appeared sixty-five years earlier. It was also the first anniversary of the near-fatal attempt on his life. These two events remained closely linked in the mind of the Holy Father as he himself told the people of Portugal:

> I come here today because on this very day last year, in St. Peter's Square in Rome, the attempt on the Pope's life was made, in mysterious coincidence with the anniversary of the first apparition at Fatima, which occurred on May 13, 1917.
>
> I seemed to recognize in the coincidence of the dates a special call to come to this place. And so, today I am here. I have come in order to thank divine Providence in this place which the Mother of God seems to have chosen in a particular way. *Misericordiæ Domini, quia non sumus consumpti* ["Through God's mercy we were spared," Lam. 3:22.], I repeat once more with the prophet.[20]

> I had already intended for some time to come to Fatima, as I have already had occasion to say upon my arrival in Lisbon. But after the well-known attempt on my life a year ago in St. Peter's Square, on regaining consciousness, my thoughts turned immediately to this sanctuary to place in the heart of the heavenly Mother my thanks for having saved me from danger. I saw in everything that was happening—I never tire of repeating it—a special motherly protection of our Lady. And in the coincidence—there are no mere coincidences in the plans of divine Providence—I also saw an appeal and, who knows, a reminder of the message which came from here 65 years ago, through three children, children of simple country people, the little shepherds of Fatima, as they became known throughout the world.[21]

20 *Inseg* V/2 (1982) 1569 [*Portugal* 74].

21 *Inseg* V/2 (1982) 1537–1538 [*Portugal* 49–50].

The importance of this event had been previously signaled to the Bishops of the world by a letter of 19 April 1982,[22] addressed to each of them by the late Cardinal Agostino Casaroli (1914–1998), Secretary of State of His Holiness, informing them that he intended "in spiritual union with all the Bishops of the world, to renew the two acts whereby Pope Pius XII entrusted the world to the Immaculate Heart of Mary." The Pope also announced his intentions to the faithful in the course of his Regina Cæli message of 9 May 1982.[23] The act itself was preceded by a finely wrought homily[24] on Mary's role in the Christian life, her spiritual maternity and the meaning of consecration to her, and was renewed again on 16 October 1983 after the Canonization Mass of Saint Leopold Mandić of Castelnovo (1866–1942)[25] in the presence of all the bishops who were attending the Synod on Reconciliation and Penance.[26]

The second of the acts deriving from that of Pentecost Sunday 1981 was given more advance publication and, correspondingly, more emphasis was placed on the collegial nature of the act. It was announced in a Pontifical Letter to all the bishops of the world, dated from the Vatican on 8 December 1983, but only published on 17 February 1984.[27] It was intended to be one of the crowning acts of the Holy Year of the Redemption, which began on 25 March 1983 and concluded on Easter Sunday, 22 April 1984. John Paul presented the rationale to his brother bishops in this way:

> In the context of the Holy Year of the Redemption, I desire to profess this [infinite salvific] power [of the Redemption] together with you and with the whole Church. I desire to

22 Secretariat of State No. 85685.

23 *Inseg* V/2 (1982) 1460–1461 [*ORE* 734:2].

24 *Inseg* 1567–77 [*Portugal* 72–85].

25 Cf. Matthew and Margaret Bunson, *John Paul II's Book of Saints* (Huntington, IN: Our Sunday Visitor Publishing Division, 2007) 98–99.

26 *Inseg* VI/2 (1983) 793–96 [*ORE* 735:5–12]. This was done with the omission of paragraphs 2–7 of number 1.

27 *Inseg* VII/1 (1984) 416–418 [*ORE* 823:2].

> profess it through the Immaculate Heart of the Mother of God, who in a most particular degree experienced this salvific power. The words of the Act of consecration and entrusting which I enclose, correspond, with a few small changes, to those which I pronounced at Fatima on 13 May 1982. I am profoundly convinced that the repetition of this Act in the course of the Jubilee Year of the Redemption corresponds to the expectations of many human hearts, which wish to renew to the Virgin Mary the testimony of their devotion and to entrust to her their sorrows at the many different ills of the present time, their fears of the menaces that brood over the future, their preoccupations for peace and justice in the individual nations and in the whole world.
>
> The most fitting date for this common witness seems to be the Solemnity of the Annunciation of the Lord during Lent 1984. I would be grateful if on that day (24 March, on which the Marian Solemnity is liturgically anticipated, or on 25 March, the Third Sunday of Lent) you would renew this Act together with me, choosing the way which each of you considers most appropriate.[28]

The Pope carried out the act itself on Sunday 25 March 1984, in St. Peter's Square before the statue of Our Lady of Fatima, which ordinarily occupies the site of Mary's appearances at the Cova da Iria in Fatima, Portugal, and which was especially flown to the Vatican for this occasion. The Act of Entrustment[29] was recited by the Pope after the Mass commemorating the Jubilee Day of Families.

---

28 *Inseg* VII/1 (1984) 417–18 [*ORE* 823:2].

29 *Inseg* VII/1 (1984) 774–77 [*ORE* 828:9–10]. The text is exactly the same as that earlier transmitted to all the Bishops of the Church [*Inseg* VII/1 (1984) 418–421; *ORE* 823:2, 12] with this exception: that the Pope inserted between the two sentences of the last paragraph of number 2 these additional words when he recited it in St. Peter's Square: "Enlighten especially the peoples whose consecration and entrustment by us you are awaiting" (*ORE* 828:10); [*Illumina specialmente i popoli di cui tu aspetti la nostra consacrazione e il nostro affidamento. Inseg* VII/1 (1984) 776].

These number among the great acts of consecration and entrustment in the pontificate of John Paul II; and on the vigil of the Solemnity of the Annunciation in 2004, which would be his last celebration of that solemnity on this earth, he reminisced about them, but first he explained their Christological and Marian significance:

> Tomorrow we will celebrate the Solemnity of the Annunciation that leads us to contemplate the Incarnation of the Eternal Word made man in Mary's womb. The Virgin's "yes" opened the doors to the implementation of the heavenly Father's saving plan, a plan of redemption for all men and women.
>
> If this feast, which this year falls in the middle of Lent, takes us back, on the one hand, to the beginnings of salvation, it invites us, on the other, to turn our gaze to the Paschal Mystery. Let us look at the crucified Christ who redeemed humanity, obeying the will of the Father to the very end. On Calvary, in the last moments of his life, Jesus entrusted Mary to us as Mother and gave us to her as children.
>
> Since she is associated with the Mystery of the Incarnation, Our Lady shares in the Mystery of the Redemption. Her *fiat*, which we will commemorate tomorrow, echoes that of the Incarnate Word. In close harmony with the *fiat* of Christ and of the Virgin, each one of us is called to say our own "yes" to the mysterious designs of Providence. Indeed, that joy and true peace which all ardently hope for even in our times only springs forth in full acceptance of the divine will.
>
> On the eve of this feast which is both Christological and Marian, I am thinking back to several significant moments at the beginning of my Pontificate: to 8 December 1978, when I entrusted the Church and the world to Our Lady at St Mary Major's; and to 4 June the following year, when I renewed this entrustment at the Shrine of Jasna Góra. I am thinking in particular of 25 March 1984, the Holy Year of the Redemption. Twenty years have passed since that day in St Peter's Square when,

> spiritually united with all the Bishops of the world who had been "convoked" beforehand, I wanted to *entrust all humanity to the Immaculate Heart of Mary* in response to what Our Lady asked at Fatima.[30]

As we shall see, this statement introduces us to many of the themes that we will find in his teaching about Marian consecration and entrustment.

But besides the great and solemn public acts referred to above, there were literally hundreds of others. For instance, on 13 May 1991, the tenth anniversary of the attempt on his life, the Pope went to Fatima to thank Our Lady for her powerful intervention in sparing his life and to renew once more the consecration of the world to her. The text of this act of entrustment was quite independent of those of 1982 and 1984 from a literary point of view and considerably briefer. In the course of this prayer of dedication he spoke personally to the Virgin as "*My Mother* for ever, and especially on 13 May 1981, when I felt your helpful presence at my side" while addressing her also as "Mother of Christ and of the Church," "Mother of all people," "Mother of the nations" and "Mother of life." Concluding this invocation he declared:

> In Collegial union with the pastors, in communion with the entire People of God spread to the four corners of the earth, today I *renew* the filial entrustment of the human race *to you. With confidence we entrust everyone to you.*[31]

These great events, which stand out in the pontificate of Pope John Paul II must not be seen as isolated acts, but rather as special moments in continuity with his whole "program of entrustment." Here is how he spoke of his "program" without calling it such in his address to the College of Cardinals at the end of 1979, his first full year as Pope:

30 *Inseg* XXVII/1 (2004) 358–359 [*ORE* 1837:4].

31 *Inseg* XIV/1 (1991) 1238 [*ORE* 1191:7].

> All this *per Mariam*. I entrusted the beginning of my Pontificate to her, and I brought to her in the course of the year the expression of my filial piety, which I learned from my parents. Mary was the star of my way, in her most famous or most silent sanctuaries: Mentorella and St. Mary Major, Guadalupe and Jasna Gora, Knock and the national Sanctuary of Mary Immaculate at Washington, Loreto, Pompei, Ephesus. I entrust myself to her. To her I entrust the whole Church, now ending a year and awaiting the dawn of the new one.[32]

Again he spoke thus to the Roman Curia on the Vigil of the Feast of Saints Peter and Paul in 1982:

> This year, in a special way, after the attempt on my life which by coincidence occurred on the anniversary of the apparition of the Virgin at Fatima, my conversation with Mary has been, I should like to say, uninterrupted. I have repeatedly entrusted to her the destiny of all peoples: beginning with the act of consecration of 8 December (1981), feast of the Immaculate Conception, to the consecration to the Virgin of the countries visited: of Nigeria at Kaduna, of Equatorial Guinea at Bata, of Gabon at Libreville, of Argentina at the Sanctuary of Lujan. I remember the visits to the Italian sanctuaries of Our Lady of Montenero in Livorno, and of Our Lady of St. Luke in Bologna; culminating in the pilgrimage to Fatima in Portugal, "Land of St. Mary," which was a personal act of gratitude to Our Lady, almost the fulfillment of a tacit vow for the protection granted me through the Virgin, and a solemn act of consecration of the whole human race to the Mother of God, in union with the Church through my humble service.[33]

There was no veering from the path of this "program of entrustment" from the beginning of the pontificate, nor any suggestion that he considered it finished. For instance, he solemnly consecrated Poland to its Queen on his first return

32 *Inseg* II/2 (1979) 1497 [*ORE* 615:13].

33 *Inseg* V/2 (1982) 2442–2443 [*ORE* 744:6].

visit as Pope on 4 June 1979,[34] but he also did so again with less external pomp but no less explicitly on 19 June 1983.[35] Again on the Solemnity of the Assumption in 1991, he led a huge international throng of youth in an act of entrustment to Our Lady at Jasna Góra as a major feature of the Sixth World Youth Day.[36] Likewise, he entrusted the United States to Mary on 7 October 1979 in Washington, D.C.,[37] and also again in Los Angeles on 16 September 1987.[38] It would be possible to adduce many other such instances at great length while what I have referred to as the "habitual" entrustments number in the hundreds every year according to the texts supplied in *L'Osservatore Romano* and in the *Insegnamenti*. On the basis, then, of this large body of John Paul's consistent teaching, we will analyze the theological question of Marian consecration.

34 *Inseg* II/1 (1979) 1416–1419; [*Poland* 110–115].

35 *Inseg* VI/1 (1983) 1595–1600 [*ORE* 791:9–10].

36 *Inseg* XIV/2 (1991) 257–259 [*ORE* 1204:7].

37 *Inseg* II/2 (1979) 683–684; [*U.S.A.* 250–253].

38 *Inseg* X/3 (1987) 593–595 [*ORE* 1007:14]

PART ONE

MARIAN CONSECRATION IN THE SPIRITUAL JOURNEY OF THE CHURCH

CHAPTER ONE

Historical Forms

While it seems indisputable that Pope Saint John Paul II gave enormous impetus to the promotion of consecration or entrustment to Mary from the outset of his pontificate to its conclusion, it is equally clear that this practice is very ancient in the Church. Further on in this study, we will consider the Scriptural bases for this practice so deeply rooted in the Church; but for the moment, let us look at some of its principal expressions in the life of the Church.

The Patristic Period

It does not seem presumptuous to see the first adumbrations of the tradition, which would come to be known as Marian consecration in the Church in the most ancient recorded prayer to the Mother of God, the *Sub tuum præsidium.*[1] Up until the early last century, this prayer, which was known to exist in all of the liturgical families in the Church, was thought to be medieval.

1 Discovered in 1917, an Egyptian papyrus now kept in the John Rylands Library in Manchester, England contains the text of this Marian prayer, which makes it the oldest invocation of the Mother of God which has thus far been found. Cf. Gerard S. Sloyan, "Marian Prayers," *Mariology* 3:64–68; I. Calabuig, O.S.M., "Liturgia," *NDM* 778–779; Théodore Koehler, S.M., "Maternité Spirituelle, Maternité Mystique," in *Maria* VI:571–574; Gabriele Giamberardini, O.F.M., *Il culto mariano in Egitto*, Vol. I: *Secoli I-VI* (Jerusalem: Franciscan Printing Press, 1975) 69–97; Achille M. Triacca, "*Sub tuum præsidium*: nella *lex orandi* un'anticipata presenza della *lex credendi*. La *teotocologia* precede la *mariologia*?" in *La mariologia nella catechesi dei Padri (età prenicena)*, ed. Sergio Felici (Rome: Libreria Ateneo Salesiano "Biblioteca di Scienza Religiosa," no. 88, 1989) 183–205; R. Iacoangeli, "*Sub tuum praesidium*. La più antica preghiera mariana: filologia e fede," ibid. 207–40; Mother M. Francesca Perillo, F.I., "*Sub Tuum Præsidium*: Incomparable Marian Præconium," in *Mary at the Foot of the Cross – IV: Acts of the Fourth International Symposium on Marian Coredemption* (New Bedford, MA: Academy of the Immaculate, 2004) 138–169.

Subsequently, it was discovered in Greek on an Egyptian papyrus dating from the third or fourth century. It is the filial prayer of Christians who know Mary's motherly mercy (*eusplangchnía* in the Greek text) and, therefore, do not hesitate to have recourse to her protection (*præsidium* in the Latin text). If it does not speak directly of belonging to Mary, it speaks of finding refuge under her protection.

The late redoubtable Marian researcher, Father Michael O'Carroll, C.S.Sp. (1911–2004), renders this ancient and venerable prayer according to the reconstruction of Father Gabriele Giamberardini, O.F.M.: "Under your mercy, we take refuge, Mother of God, do not reject our supplications in necessity. But deliver us from danger. [You] alone chaste, alone blessed."[2] This Marian troparion, used in almost all the Rites of the Church and cited in the Marian chapter of *Lumen Gentium*,[3] is ordinarily rendered into English after the Latin version: "We fly to thy patronage, O holy Mother of God, despise not our petitions in our necessities, but deliver us from all danger, O ever glorious and blessed Virgin."[4]

This ancient Marian invocation is of capital importance from many perspectives. First, it constitutes a remarkable witness to the fact that prayer was already explicitly addressed to Mary as *Theotókos* or "Mother of God" long before the Council of Ephesus, which vindicated the use of this title in 431. Secondly, it may well reflect an oral tradition even older than the third century, the era from which many scholars believe the Egyptian papyrus dates, going all the way back to the apostolic period. Thirdly, while this antiphon (called a "troparion" according to Byzantine liturgical usage) does not explicitly call Mary "our Mother," it does so in equivalent and very expressive terms.

---

2 *Theotokos* 336.

3 *LG* #6.

4 *Theotokos* 336.

About this justly famous and most ancient of Marian prayers, Father Quéméneur makes this careful observation:

> Here we do not yet have a consecration properly so called, but we already discern the fundamental elements that characterize Marian consecrations. The *Sub tuum* recognizes the patronage of the Mother of God; it is a spontaneous gesture of recourse to Mary. Originating in Egypt, the *Sub tuum*, with slight variations, will soon be taken up by the other churches; starting with the sixth century, it is inserted into the Byzantine, Ambrosian, and Roman liturgies. We can say that it is the root from which the formulas of other Marian prayers will arise.[5]

It is in the light of the biblical connotation of the Greek root, *euspla* – [6] that the late Father Jean-Marie Salgado, O.M.I. did not hesitate to translate the beginning of the *Sub tuum*: "We take refuge in your merciful heart" or "We have recourse to your merciful heart." It seems highly significant that the living tradition of the Church testified to by its early liturgies in both East and West provides further support for rendering *euspla[gchnian]* as heart.[7] If such a rendition of this prayer can be justified—and I believe that the whole tradition seen in its remarkable continuity may well bear this out—then it would seem that the *Sub tuum* provides a foundation not only for consecration to Mary, but even more specifically for consecration to her Immaculate Heart.

Significantly, and very conscious that he was standing in the most ancient stream of the Church's tradition, Saint John Paul II framed the first part of his great acts of entrustment in 1982

5 M. Quéméneur, S.M.M., "Towards a History of Marian Consecration," trans. Bro. William Fackovec, S.M. *Marian Library Studies* 122 (March 1966) 4. (This excellent article originally appeared as "La consécration de soi à la Vierge à travers l'histoire," *Cahiers Marials* no. 14 [1959] 119–28.)

6 The remainder of the word is missing on the papyrus.

7 Cf. K. Koester's article "*splángchnon, splangchnízomai, 'eúsplangchnos*" in Gerhard Friedrich (ed.), *Theological Dictionary of the New Testament* (Grand Rapids, MI: Wm. B. Eerdmans Publishing Company, 1971) 548–57; and Jean-Marie Salgado, O.M.I., "Aux Origines de la Découverte des Richesses du Cœur Immaculé de Marie: Du IIIè au XIIè Siècle," *Divinitas* 31 (1987) 187–188, 229–232.

and 1984 with the words of this antiphon: "We have recourse to your protection, holy Mother of God."[8] Likewise for the Sixth International World Youth Day celebrated at Częstochowa on the Solemnity of the Assumption in 1991, he began the act of entrustment to Our Lady with the first Latin words of the *Sub tuum* and recited the entire Latin text in the course of the prayer.[9] Also on the Solemnity of the Immaculate Conception in 1991, at the traditional ceremony in the Piazza di Spagna, he invoked Our Lady saying: "Under your protection we take refuge once again, at the end of this year, this century, this millennium."[10]

He further alluded to or quoted this ancient prayer on numerous other occasions: in a Regina Caeli address in 1982,[11] in his Marian Encyclical, *Redemptoris Mater*,[12] and quoted from it in the final paragraph of his Encyclical, *Sollicitudo Rei Socialis.*[13] He referred to it in his commentary on the doctrine of the *Theotókos* in the course of his Christological catecheses,[14] and made it his own prayer for various groups upon whom he had invoked Our Lady's protection in 1988.[15] He quoted it in a meditation for the Italian Bishops, which he wrote from the Gemelli Polyclinic in Rome on 13 May 1994,[16] in his Angelus

8 *Inseg* V/2 (1982) 1586, 1587 [*ORE* 735:5, 12]; *Inseg* VII/1 (1984) 774, 775. He also utilized the words "we take refuge under your protection" in the Act of Entrustment of Colombia to Mary on 3 July 1986, *Inseg* IX/2 (1986) 93 [*ORE* 948:5].

9 *Inseg* XIV/2 (1991) 257–259 [*ORE* 1204:7].

10 *Inseg* XIV/2 (1991) 1345 [*ORE* 1220:5]. On that occasion the Pope prayed: "*Sotto la Tua protezione ci rifugiamo* ..." which is almost exactly the same as the beginning of the ancient prayer in the standard Italian translation: "*Sotto la tua protezione cerchiamo rifugio*..."

11 *Inseg* VI/1 (1983) 1057 [*ORE* 782:2].

12 *Inseg* X/1 (1987) 717 [St. Paul edition 45].

13 *Inseg* X/3 (1987) 1611–12 [*ORE* 1028:13].

14 *Inseg* XI/1 (1988) 642 [*ORE* 1031:1].

15 To a group of clergy from Novara on 11 March 1988, *Inseg* XI/1 (1988) 615 [*ORE* 1032:10]; to the youth of Bolivia in Cochabamba on 11 May 1988, *Inseg* XI/2 (1988) 1321 [*ORE* 1043:13]; on the occasion of the *Moleben* in honor of the Mother of God during the celebration of the Millennium of Christianity in Ukraine on 9 July 1988, *Inseg* XI/3 (1988) 64 [*ORE* 1051:4].

16 *Inseg* XVII/1 (1994) 1063 [*ORE* 1343:4].

address of New Year's Day 1996,[17] in his Angelus address of 14 August 1996,[18] in his homily at Vespers on 7 November 1996;[19] and in his general audience address of 27 November 1996, he quoted this classic Marian prayer in the context of entrustment to the Mother of God:

> Already in the third century, as can be deduced from an ancient written witness, the Christians of Egypt addressed this prayer to Mary: "We fly to thy patronage, O holy Mother of God: despise not our petitions in our necessities, but deliver us from all evil, O glorious and blessed Virgin" (from the *Liturgy of the Hours*).
>
> Following the example of the ancient Christians of Egypt, let the faithful entrust themselves to her who, being the Mother of God, can obtain from her divine Son the grace of deliverance from evil and of eternal salvation.[20]

In 1997, he would explicitly cite the prayer twice in the course of his general audience catecheses on Our Lady: on 24 September 1997[21] and on 5 November of the same year.[22] In his address to Catholic Patriarchs of the East on 29 September 1998, he introduced this prayer as "an ancient Coptic hymn, which later became part of the devotion of the Byzantine and Latin Churches";[23] and in #14 of *Incarnationis Mysterium*, his Bull of Indiction of the Great Jubilee Year of 2000 on 29 November 1998, he made a clear allusion to it.[24] On 16 June 1999, in his hometown of Wadowice, he used the ancient prayer as a framework for his own as he had done at Częstochowa on the Solemnity of the Assumption in 1991:[25]

17 *Inseg* XIX/1 (1996) 6 [*ORE* 1423:3].

18 *Inseg* XIX/2 (1996) 172 [*ORE* 1454:2].

19 *Inseg* XIX/2 (1996) 654 *ORE* [1466:3].

20 *Inseg* XIX/2 (1996) 762, 764 [*ORE* 1469:11].

21 *Inseg* XX/2 (1997) 382–383 [*ORE* 1510:11]..

22 *Inseg* XX/2 (1997) 737 [*ORE* 1516:11].

23 *Inseg* XXI/2 (1998) 593 [*ORE* 1561:4].

24 *Inseg* XXI/2 (1998) 1117 [*ORE* 1569:4].

25 *Inseg* XIV/2 (1991) 257–259 [*ORE* 1204:7].

> *Sub tuum præsidium ...*
>
> We fly to your protection, O Mary. To your protection we entrust the history of this town, of the Church of Kraków and the whole country. To your maternal love we entrust the lives of each individual, of our families and of society as a whole. *Despise not our petitions in our need, but deliver us always from every danger.* Mary, obtain for us the grace of faith, hope and love, so that following your example and guidance, we may carry into the new millennium our witness to the Father's love, to the redeeming Death and Resurrection of the Son and to the sanctifying work of the Holy Spirit. Be with us at all times! *O glorious and blessed Virgin, Our Lady, Our Advocate, Our Mediatrix, Our Consolatrix, Our Mother!* Amen.[26]

In his Jubilee pilgrimage to St. Catherine's Monastery on Mount Sinai on 26 February 2000, the Pope made mention of this ancient prayer, stating: "As early as the third century Egyptian Christians appealed to her with words of trust: We have recourse to your protection, O Holy Mother of God! *Sub tuum præsidium confugimus, sancta Dei Genetrix!*"[27] Subsequently, in his Jubilee Act of Entrustment united with the Bishops of the World, of whom a good number were present with him on 8 October 2000, he prayed:

> Here, then, are your children, gathered before you at the dawn of the new millennium. The Church today, through the voice of the Successor Peter, in union with so many Pastors assembled here from every corner of the world, *seeks refuge in your motherly protection* and trustingly begs your intercession as she faces the challenges, which lie hidden in the future.[28]

26 *Inseg* XXII/1 (1999) 1395 [*ORE* 1599:8].

27 *Inseg* XXIII/1 (2000) 269 [*ORE* 1632:2].

28 *Inseg* XXIII/2 (2000) 564 [*ORE* 1663:7] (italics my own).

In his New Year's Day homily of 2001, he quoted the famous prayer again with this preface: "On this first day of 2001, we entrust to you the expectations and hopes of all humanity."[29]

John Paul II's last recorded reference to this prayer occurred on the liturgical memorial of Our Lady of Lourdes in 2004, the World Day of the Sick, which he himself had inaugurated. As one bent under extreme infirmity, he prayed:

> "*Sub tuum præsidium …*," as we prayed at the beginning of our meeting. "Under your protection we seek refuge," Immaculate Virgin of Lourdes, who present yourself to us as the perfect model of creation according to God's original plan. To you we entrust the sick, the elderly, the lonely: soothe their pain, dry their tears and obtain for each one the strength they need to do God's will.[30]

From all of these texts, it may be seen how Saint John Paul II had integrated this venerable Marian antiphon into his own spirituality and frequently employed it as a way of putting himself and others into the hands of the Mother of God.

If the *Sub tuum praesidium* testifies to the Christian's child-like tendency to take refuge under the protection of the *Theotókos*, history will illustrate this truth many times over in the course of the centuries. The first such recourse of which we are aware that involves an entrustment to the Mother of God was made by the Byzantine Emperor Heraclius in 626, according to Saint Germanus of Constantinople. When the city on the Bosphorus was in imminent danger, the Emperor confided it to God and to the Virgin Mother, and it was spared.[31] This is

29 *Inseg* XXIV/1 (2001) 6–7 [*ORE* 1674:3].

30 *Inseg* XXVII/1 (2004) 175 [*ORE* 1831:11].

31 Cf. Angelo Cardinal Mai (ed.), *Nova Patrum Bibliotheca*, Vol. VI, *Pars Secunda* (Rome: Typis Sacri Consilii Propagando Christiano Nomini, 1853) 423–437 (esp. nos. 1, 5, 6, 7, 9, 12, 16); A. Wenger, "L'Intercession de Marie en Orient," *BSFEM* 23 (1966) 58; J. Marangos, S.J., "Le Culte Marial Populaire en Grèce," in *Maria* 4:810–811; Gabriele Roschini, O.S.M., *Maria Santissima nella Storia della Salvezza* Vol. IV: *Il Culto Mariano* (Isola del Liri: Tipografia Editrice M. Pisani, 1969) 84–85; Stefano De Fiores, *Maria, Nuovissimo Dizionario* 1 (Bologna; Edizioni Dehoniane, 2006) 361.

one of several incidents which would lead to the establishment of the Byzantine feast of the Protection of the Holy Mother of God (*Pokrov*) who stretches out her mantle over the peoples;[32] and Father Joseph de Sainte-Marie, O.C.D., did not hesitate to see in this the first known collective Marian consecration in history.[33]

Father O'Carroll informs us that his confrere, Father Henri Barré, C.S.Sp., had found evidence for the title, *servus Mariæ*, in African sermons from the fifth and sixth centuries which indicate a personal attitude of belonging to Mary.[34] Father Stefano De Fiores, S.M.M., also points to the use of this term in Saint Ephrem the Syrian (+ 373) and Pope John VII (+ 707), but indicates that these instances cannot compare to the consistent usage and fervor of Saint Ildephonsus of Toledo (+ 667).[35] Ildephonsus is usually considered the first major representative of the spirituality of "Marian slavery"[36] which eventually develops into what is now known as Marian consecration.[37]

Pope Saint John Paul II himself, in his homily in Saragossa on 6 November 1982, immediately prior to the Entrustment of Spain to Our Lady, reviewed what is for us the most relevant information about this Benedictine Abbot who became the Archbishop of Toledo:

> Saint Ildephonsus of Toledo, the most ancient witness of that form of devotion that we call slavery to Mary, justifies our attitude of being slaves of Mary because of the singular

32 Cf. S. Salaville, A.A., "Marie dans la Liturgie Byzantine ou Gréco-Slave," in *Maria* I:280; cf. also Quéméneur 4 and *Redemptoris Mater* # 33.

33 *Teologia e Spiritualità della Consacrazione a Maria* (Rome: Pontificio Istituto di Spiritualità del Teresianum, dispensa, n.d.) I-13.

34 *Theotokos* 107.

35 "Cons" 400. Cf. also De Fiores, *Maria, Nuovissimo Dizionario* 1:361–363. In the case of Pope John VII one might profitably consult the testimony presented in Roschini, *Maria Santissima* IV:97–98.

36 Cf. the excellent article by Théodore Koehler, S.M., "Servitude (saint esclavage)" in *DSp* 14:730–745.

37 Cf. Patrick J. Gaffney, S.M.M., "The Holy Slavery of Love," in *Mariology* 3:143–146; Roschini, *Maria Santissima* IV:85–86.

relation she has with respect to Christ. "For this reason I am your slave, because your Son is my Lord. Therefore you are my Lady because you are the slave of my Lord. Therefore, I am the slave of the slave of my Lord, because you have been made the Mother of my Lord. Therefore I have been made a slave because you have been made the Mother of my Maker" [*De virginitate perpetua Sanctæ Mariæ*, 12: *PL* 96, 108].

As is obvious, because of these real and existing relationships between Christ and Mary, Marian devotion has Christ as its ultimate object. The same Saint Ildephonsus saw it with full clarity: "So in this way one refers to the Lord that which serves his slave. So, what is delivered up to the Mother redounds to the Son; thus passes to the King the honor that is rendered in the service of the Queen" [c. 12: *PL* 96, 108]. Then one understands the double employment of the desire expressed in the same blessed formula, speaking with the most Holy Virgin: "Grant that I may surrender myself to God and to you, to be the slave of your Son and of you, to serve your Lord and you" [c. 12: *PL* 96, 105].[38]

The next major witness to the development of the tradition is the great Doctor of the Church, Saint John Damascene (+ c. 750).[39] The last of the great Eastern Fathers of the Church interprets the name of Mary according to Syriac etymology to mean "lady" or "mistress."[40] In his *Exposition of the Orthodox Faith* he says of Mary: "Truly she has become the Lady ruler of every creature since she is the Mother of the Creator."[41] In

38 *Inseg* V/3 (1982) 1179–1180 (translation by Debra Duncan).

39 Cf. De Fiores, Maria, Nuovissimo Dizionario 1:361.

40 On the rich background of Syriac mariology of which St. John was the heir cf. Cuthbert Brogan, O.S.B., "Mary and the Eucharist in the Syriac Fathers," in *Mary at the Foot of the Cross – VI: Marian Coredemption in the Eucharistic Mystery. Acts of the Sixth International Symposium on Marian Coredemption* (New Bedford, MA: Academy of the Immaculate, 2007) 95–113.

41 Cited in Valentine Albert Mitchell, S.M., *The Mariology of Saint John Damascene* (Kirkwood, MO: Maryhurst Normal Press, 1930) 76, cf. also 214.

his first homily on the Dormition of the Mother of God, he consequently prays:

> We are present before you, O Lady [*Despoina*], Lady I say and again Lady, binding our souls to our hope in you, and as to a most secure and firm anchor [cf. Heb. 6:9], *to you we consecrate* [*anathémenoi*] *our minds, our souls, our bodies* [cf. I Th. 5:23], *in a word, our very selves*, honoring you with psalms, hymns and spiritual canticles [cf. Eph. 5:19], insofar as we are able—even though it is impossible to do so worthily. If truly, as the sacred word has taught us, the honor paid to our fellow servants testifies to our good will towards our common Master, how could we neglect honoring you who have brought forth your Master? … In this way we can better show our attachment to our Master.
>
> Turn your gaze on us, noble Lady, Mother of the good Master, rule over and direct at your discretion all that concerns us; restrain the impulses of our shameful passions; guide us to the tranquil harbor of the divine will; make us worthy of future blessedness, of the beatific vision in the presence of the Word of God who was made flesh in you.[42]

One notes how, in language which is redolent with Scriptural overtones, Saint John makes the total gift to Our Lady of himself and of those who are joined with him—of all that they have and are. He deliberately used the Greek term *anathémenoi* in order to indicate that "consecration" means "setting aside for sacred use." What is literally signified, according to the use of this word in Leviticus 27:28 and in other places in the Old Testament, is that this "giving of oneself to Mary" is so exclusive, absolute and permanent that one who would revoke the gift would be "cut off" (i.e., *anathema*) from God and his people. In analyzing this

42 *PG* 96, 720C-D, 721A-B; *SC* 80, 118 (my translation made with reference to *Theotokos* 199 and Georges Gharib et al (ed.), *Testi Mariani del Primo Millennio* Vol. 2: *Padri e altri autori bizantini* (Rome: Città Nuova Editrice, 1989) 519–520) (italics mine). It is fascinating that Saint Louis-Marie de Montfort would quote the text on Our Lady as "a most secure and firm anchor" in his *Treatise on True Devotion* #175.

text, Father José María Canal, C.M.F., makes three major points: (1) Damascene's deliberate use of the term "consecration" which pertains to setting aside for sacred use; (2) the comprehensiveness of this act which excludes nothing; and (3) its basis in Mary's unique relationship to her Divine Son by virtue of the Divine Maternity.[43]

The Medieval Period

In the feudal setting of the early Middle Ages we find the custom of "patronage" (*patrocinium*) becoming widespread. In order to protect their lives and possessions, freemen would vow themselves to the service of their overlords; in exchange for the assurance of protection and the necessities of life, the client would place himself completely at the disposal of his protector. Here is a description of a traditional ceremony by which a vassal would put himself under the patronage and at the service of a suzerain, by the well-known liturgical scholar, Josef Jungmann, S.J.:

> He put his hands in the enfolding hands of the master, just as is done today by the newly ordained priest when he promises honour and obedience to his bishop at the end of the ordination Mass. The act is also called commendation: *se commendare, se tradere, in manus* or *manibus se commendare (tradere)*, and also *patricinio se commendare (tradere)*. From the side of the overlord there was the corresponding *suscipere, recipere, manus suscipere* and the like.[44]

Not surprisingly, in those ages of faith this relationship of vassalage would provide a way of describing one's relationship to Mary. If Jesus is one's Lord, as we have already seen Saint John Damascene reason, then it is only logical that Mary becomes

43 P. José María Canal, C.M.F., "La Consagración a la Virgen y a Su Corazon Inmaculado," *V.I.* XII:234–235. Cf. also Joseph de Sainte-Marie I-14, I.T-2.

44 J. A. Jungmann, S.J., *Pastoral Liturgy* (New York: Herder and Herder, 1962) 298.

one's Lady. Fulbert of Chartres (+ 1028)[45] provides us with a beautiful prayer in which he underscores that his consecration to Christ in Baptism also makes of him another "beloved disciple" (cf. Jn. 19:26–27) "committed" to Mary:

> Remember, O Lady, that in Baptism I was consecrated to the Lord and professed the Christian name with my lips. Unfortunately I have not observed what I have promised. Nevertheless I have been handed over [*traditus*] to you and committed to your care [*commendatus*] by the Lord, the living and true God. Watch over the one who has been handed over to you [*traditum*]; keep safe the one who has been committed to your protection [*commendatum*].[46]

Likewise, a freeman who was in debt or otherwise not prospering in his affairs might present himself to an overlord "a rope around his neck, a sign that [he] was to become a serf, engaging his person, his family and his goods."[47] This, too, could be transferred into the spiritual realm and appropriated to one's relationship to Our Lady as we see in the case of St. Odilo, Abbot of Cluny (+1049)[48] who, as a young man, consecrated himself to Our Lady by going to a church dedicated to her and presenting himself at her altar with a rope around his neck and praying:

> O most loving Virgin and Mother of the Savior of all ages, from this day and hereafter take me into your service and in all my affairs be ever at my side as a most merciful advocate. For after God I place nothing in any way before you and I give myself over to you for ever as your own slave

45 Cf. *Theotokos* 150–151.

46 Henri Barré, C.S.Sp., Prières Anciennes de L'Occident à la Mère du Sauveur: Des origènes à saint Anselme (Paris: Lethielleux, 1963) 159 (my translation).

47 Quéméneur 6.

48 Cf. *Theotokos* 271–272. On the Marian spirituality of Cluny cf. Alfredo Simón, "La Presenza della Beata Vergine nel Rinnovamento Promosso da Cluny" in Enrico Dal Covolo, S.D.B. e Aristide Serra, O.S.M., (eds.) *Storia della mariologia*, Vol. 1: *dal modello biblico al modello letterario* (Rome: Città Nuova Editrice, Marianum, 2009) 593–617.

> and bondsman [*tanquam proprium servum, tuo mancipatui trado*].[49]

In a very interesting and original piece of research, Father Mark Elvins argues on the basis of a fair amount of converging circumstantial evidence that Richard II solemnly consecrated England to Mary as "her Dowry" on the Saturday after Corpus Christi 1381. He argues that this is pictorially represented in the famous "Wilton Diptych" housed in London's National Gallery of Art.[50] If this were so, it would represent a famous pictorial consecration of a kingdom to Our Lady.

Another beautiful image of the *patrocinium* of the Virgin is that of her "protective mantle" or *Schutzmantel* as it has come to be known in German. We have already seen this in the East in the feast and icon of the *Pokrov*. Here is Jungmann's description of the Marian iconography, which would become classical in the medieval West:

> The emblem of Citeaux was the image of the Mother of God with the abbots and abbesses of the order kneeling under her mantle. Caesarius of Heisterbach (d. 1240) also knew this motif as he shows in his description of a Cistercian monk in heaven, looking about in vain for his brothers until Mary opens out her wide mantle and discloses a countless number of brothers and nuns. In the later Middle Ages especially, the motif of the protective mantle is wide-spread, commonly as an expression of protection being sought or hoped for, chiefly in connexion with the image of the Mother of God.[51]

This lovely and appealing image of the Virgin with her mantle extended over large numbers of the faithful of both sexes and every rank in society (always in minuscule of course!) was

49 Barré 147 (my translation).

50 Mark Elvins, "The Origin of the Title 'Dowry of Mary' and the Shrines of Our Lady at Westminster," a paper given to the London branch of the Ecumenical Society of the Blessed Virgin Mary on 18 May 1989.

51 Jungmann 300; cf. also *Theotokos* 93–94; Georges Gharib, "La Madonna della Misericordia: 'Sotto la tua protezione'." *Madre di Dio* 59 (maggio 1991) 13–16.

frequently rendered by late Medieval and Renaissance artists. Such depictions were also referred to as "Our Lady of Mercy" since they illustrated that one could always find God's mercy through Mary's motherly intercession.[52] It could be said that this was a pictorial way of interpreting the *Sub tuum præsidium*: "We fly to thy patronage, O Holy Mother of God." One of the most famous of these Schutzmantel or Mercy Madonnas is the wonderfully delicate and evocative *Vierge de la Miséricorde* [Virgin of Mercy] by Jean Mirailhet which is in the *Musée d'Art et d'Histoire* in Nice, France.[53]

Pope John Paul II also used this lovely image of the Virgin's protection on numerous occasions; for instance, in an Angelus address on New Year's Day of 1980,[54] in Brazil the same year,[55] in Belice, Sicily in 1982,[56] in Vienna in 1983,[57] in Liechtenstein in 1985,[58] and in supplication for the Armenians in 1987.[59] Among yet other instances,[60] he concluded an audience with pilgrims from Derry in Northern Ireland on 13 April 1989, praying: "May our Lady of Knock, Queen of Peace, spread her mantle of peace over the whole land."[61] In a letter addressed to Discalced Carmelite Nuns and dated on the Feast of St. Thérèse, 1991, he wrote:

> You [Nuns who follow the Constitutions approved respectively in both 1990 and 1991 as well as Carmelite

52 Cf. Angelo Gila, "'Maria Regina e Madre di Misericordia': Un Tema Tipico dell'Epoca Medioevale" in *Maria Madre di Misericordia: Monstra Te Esse Matrem* a cura di Piergiorgio Di Domenico e Elio Peretto (Padua: Messaggero di Sant'Antonio Editrice, 2003) 186–217.

53 This lovely image is reproduced on the cover of this book.

54 *Inseg* III/1 (1980) 10 [*ORE* 614:4].

55 *Inseg* III/2 (1980) 104 [*Brazil* 83].

56 *Inseg* V/3 (1982) 1343 [*ORE* 761:2].

57 *Inseg* VI/2 (1983) 527 [*ORE* 803:11].

58 *Inseg* VIII/2 (1985) 639 [*ORE* 905:7].

59 *Inseg* X/3 (1987) 1179 [*ORE* 1017:7].

60 Cf. *Inseg* XI/1 (1988) 757 [*ORE* 1035:10]; *Inseg* XI/3 (1988) 465; [*ORE* 1056:21]; *Inseg* XII/1 (1989) 1498 [*ORE* 1093:12].

61 *Inseg* XII/1 (1989) 807 [*ORE* 1086:11].

> Fathers and Brothers] all call upon Mary as your common Mother, whom the Order's imagery aptly depicts covering the sons and daughters of Carmel from one side to the other with her mantle.[62]

A number of times, in the course of his long pontificate, John Paul II would employ the image of Mary's mantle on New Year's Day. In his homily on 1 January 1994, he said:

> Everyone looks to her: *her divine motherhood has become the great patrimony of humanity.* Under her maternal mantle are gathered in some way too the separated peoples, those who do not know the mystery of Jesus Christ. Many, although not knowing the Son of God, know of the Virgin Mary and this already draws them closer in some way to the great mystery of the Lord's birth.[63]

In entrusting the year 1996 to the Mother of God, he used the image of Mary's protective mantle in conjunction with the ancient prayer *Sub tuum præsidium*:

> We are fast approaching the historic date of the Year 2000, an important stage in humanity's journey. May the Lord grant us to reach it renewed in spirit, ready to build a more welcoming world of solidarity. I invite you to pray for this as, together with you, I entrust 1996, which has just begun, to Mary, Mother of God and our Mother.
>
> We present our good resolutions to you, Mary. We ask you to spread the mantle of your motherly protection over us and over every day of the New Year: "O holy Mother

62 *Inseg* XIV/2 (1991) 706 [*ORE* 1211:2]. In his Letter of 1 May 1999 to Carmelite community at San Martino ai Monti in Rome on 700th Anniversary of Carmelite presence there he wrote: "May the Virgin Mary, Mother and Sister of Carmel clothe with her mantle your community, religious and parochial, in the same way she enfolds tenderly her Divine Son in the sixteenth century painting venerated in the Basilica" *Inseg* XXII/1 (1999) 859 [*Carmel in the World* XXXVII (1999) 164]. Likewise in his Message of 25 March 2001 to the Prior General of Carmelites of the Ancient Observance and the Superior General of the Discalced Carmelites on the 750th Anniversary of the Scapular of Our Lady of Mount Carmel, he wrote of Mary as spreading "the protective mantle of her mercy over her children on their pilgrimage to the holy mountain of glory" *Inseg* XXIV/1 (2001) 600 [*ORE* 1687:5].

63 *Inseg* XVII/1 (1994) 6 [*ORE* 1322:4].

> of God, despise not our petitions in our necessities, but deliver us from all dangers, O glorious and blessed Virgin!"[64]

In his Angelus address on the Solemnity of the Mother of God in the Jubilee Year 2000, he made this exhortation:

> The first day of the year is placed under the special protection of Mary. Let us begin the Year 2000 under the loving gaze of the Mother of God, who gives Christ, the Prince of Peace, to the world. May she spread the mantle of her motherhood over all of us, protect us from evil and free us from hatred and violence. May she accompany humanity on the ways of peace.[65]

In one beautiful evocative sentence in his Angelus address on 22 September 1996 in Reims, France, he prayed: "Mother most admirable, spread your mantle of tenderness over the families of this land so that they may know the happiness of loving and of transmitting life."[66] In a much more developed, but no less evocative way, he wrote to the Bishop of Leiria-Fatima, Portugal, on the occasion of the 80th anniversary of our Our Lady's final appearance at Fatima in this manner:

> What did Christ do? After invoking the mercy of heaven with the words: "Father, forgive them, for they know not what they do" (Lk. 23:34), he entrusted humanity to Mary, his Mother: "Woman, behold, your son" (Jn. 19:26). A symbolic interpretation of this Gospel event enables us to see reflected in it the final scene of the well-known and common experience of the son who, feeling misunderstood, confused and rebellious, leaves his father's house to wander into the night… And his mother's mantle protects him from the cold during his sleep, helping him to overcome his despair and loneliness. Beneath the maternal mantle, which extends from Fatima over the whole world, humanity senses anew its longing for the Father's house

64 *Inseg* XIX/1 (1996) 6 [*ORE* 1423:3].

65 *Inseg* XXIII/1 (2000) 8 [*ORE* 1624:8].

66 *Inseg* XIX/2 (1996) 431 [*ORE* 1459:4].

> and for his Bread (cf. Lk. 15:17). Dear pilgrims, as if it were possible to embrace all humanity, I ask you to say in its name and for its sake, "We fly to thy patronage, O holy Mother of God. Despise not our petitions in our necessities, but deliver us from all dangers, O glorious and blessed Virgin."[67]

Let us note in this marvelous passage how the Holy Father wove Our Lady's mantle into the parable of the prodigal son (Lk. 15:11–32) in order to accentuate her role in the reconciliation of sinners and then asked all to recite the *Sub tuum præsidum* as a means of entrusting all humanity to her.

He would use the image of Mary's mantle in his prayers of entrustment to her in many countries of the former Eastern Bloc: in Georgia,[68] Ukraine,[69] Kazakhstan,[70] Armenia,[71] and Bulgaria.[72] In a message to Hungarians celebrating the millennium of St. Stephen, he wrote:

> *Salvum fac populum tuum, Domine, et benedic hereditati tuæ!* With this invocation, which the *Te Deum* also puts on our lips, we turn to the Lord to implore his help in the new millennium now beginning. We ask for it through the intercession of the Blessed Virgin Mary, the *Magna Domina Hungarorum*, whose veneration has had so great a role in the precious heritage of King St. Stephen. He offered his crown to her as a pledge of his entrustment of the Hungarian people to her heavenly protection. How many images depicting this act are found in your churches! Following the holy king's example, may you also put your future under the mantle of the One to whom God entrusted his Only-begotten Son![73]

67 *Inseg* XX/2 (1997) 456–457 [*ORE* 1514:6].

68 *Inseg* XXII/2 (1999) 852 [*ORE* 1617:5].

69 *Inseg* XXIV/1 (2001) 1264 [*ORE* 1699:3].

70 *Inseg* XXIV/2 (2001) 391–393 [*ORE* 1711:3].

71 *Inseg* XXIV/2 (2001) 475 [*ORE* 1712:6].

72 *Inseg* XXV/1 (2002) 862 [*ORE* 1745:6].

73 *Inseg* XXIII/2 (2000) 196 [*ORE* 1656:5].

Here he gracefully made reference to the tradition of St. Stephen's entrustment of the Hungarian people to Our Lady[74]—perhaps the first such recorded act in history—while exhorting them to put their future under Our Lady's mantle.

John Paul's last reference to Our Lady's mantle seems to have occurred on 15 May 2004 in an audience given to the Little Work of Divine Providence on the vigil of the canonization of its founder, Saint Luigi Orione (1872–1940).[75] To their Act of Consecration to Our Lady, the Pope added the conclusion:

> Mary, shining star of the morning, placed by God on the horizon of humanity, gently spread your mantle over us, pilgrims on the paths of time, amidst numerous risks and snares, and come to our aid now and at the hour of our death. Amen!"[76]

From a specifically theological perspective Arnold Bostius (+1499),[77] a Flemish Carmelite, wrote about Mary's patronage and protection of his order in his major Marian work, *De Patronatu et Patrocinio Beatissimae Virginis Mariae in Dicatum sibi Carmeli Ordinem*. Although he did not use the word "consecration" to describe the Carmelite's relationship to Mary, because that meaning had not yet been appropriated to the word, he used all the equivalent Latin expressions such as *dicare, dedicare, devovere,*

74 Cf. Louis Nagyfalusy, S.J., "Le Culte de la Sainte Vierge en Hongrie, 'Regnum Marianum'," *Maria* 4:645–646, 649–650.

75 Cf. Matthew and Margaret Bunson, *John Paul II's Book of Saints* (Huntington, IN: Our Sunday Visitor Publishing Division, 2007) 99–101.

76 *OR* 17–18 maggio 2004, p. 6 [*ORE* 1844:7].

77 Cf. Nilo Geagea, O.C.D., *Maria, Madre e Decoro del Carmelo: La pietà mariana dei Carmelitani durante i primi tre secoli della loro storia* (Rome: Institutum Historicum Teresianum, 1988) 369–438; Luca Di Girolamo, "Teologia Devota: Da Jean Gerson (+ 1429) ad Arnoldo Bostio (+ 1499)," in Enrico Dal Covolo, S.D.B., e Aristide Serra, O.S.M. (eds.), *Storia della mariologia*, Vol. 1: *dal modello biblico al modello letterario* (Rome: Città Nuova Editrice, Marianum, 2009) 970–978; Luigi Gambero (ed.), *Testi Mariani del Secondo Millennio, 4: Autori medievali dell'Occidente sec. XIII-XV* (Rome: Città Nuova, 1996) 678–683; Emanuele Boaga, O.Carm., *Con Maria sulle vie di Dio: Antologia della marianità carmelitana* (Rome: Edizioni Carmelitane, 2000) 82–87.

sub qua vivere, etc.;[78] and he maintained, as the Venerable Pope Pius XII would in his Letter, *Neminem Profecto*, of 11 February 1950,[79] that the wearing of the Carmelite scapular was an explicit sign of the acceptance of Mary's patronage and protection, of the Carmelite's belonging to her.[80] All of this is magnificently synthesized in John Paul II's Message of 25 March 2001 to the Prior General of Carmelites of the Ancient Observance and the Superior General of the Discalced Carmelites on the 750th Anniversary of the scapular of Our Lady of Mount Carmel:

> This intense Marian life, which is expressed in trusting prayer, enthusiastic praise and diligent imitation, enables us to understand how the most genuine form of devotion to the Blessed Virgin, expressed by the humble sign of the Scapular, is consecration to her Immaculate Heart (cf. Pius XII, Letter *Neminem profecto latet* [11 February 1950: *AAS* 42, 1950, pp. 390–391]; Dogmatic Constitution on the Church *Lumen Gentium*, n. 67). ...
>
> The sign of the Scapular points to an effective synthesis of Marian spirituality, which nourishes the devotion of believers and makes them sensitive to the Virgin Mother's loving presence in their lives. The Scapular is essentially a "habit." Those who receive it are associated more or less closely with the Order of Carmel and dedicate themselves to the service of Our Lady for the good of the whole Church (cf. "Formula of Enrolment in the Scapular," in the *Rite of Blessing of and Enrolment in the Scapular*, approved by the Congregation for Divine Worship and the Discipline of the Sacraments, 5 January 1996). Those who wear the Scapular are thus brought into the land of Carmel, so that they may "eat its fruits and its good things" (cf. Jer. 2:7), and experience the loving and motherly presence of Mary in their daily commitment to be clothed in Jesus

78 I. Bengoechea, O.C.D., "Un precursor de la consagración a María en el siglo XV: Arnoldo Bostio (1445–1499)," *Estudios Marianos* 51 (1986) 218; cf. also Redemptus M. Valabek, O. Carm., *Mary, Mother of Carmel: Our Lady and the Saints of Carmel*, I (Rome: Institutum Carmelitanum, 1987) 74.

79 *AAS* 42 (1950) 390–391 [*OL* #452–54].

80 Bengoechea 224–25; Valabek 76.

> Christ and to manifest him in their life for the good of the Church and the whole of humanity (cf. "Formula of Enrolment in the Scapular," cit.).
>
> Therefore two truths are evoked by the sign of the Scapular: on the one hand, the constant protection of the Blessed Virgin, not only on life's journey, but also at the moment of passing into the fullness of eternal glory; on the other, the awareness that devotion to her cannot be limited to prayers and tributes in her honour on certain occasions, but must become a "habit," that is, a permanent orientation of one's own Christian conduct, woven of prayer and interior life, through frequent reception of the sacraments and the concrete practice of the spiritual and corporal works of mercy. In this way the Scapular becomes a sign of the "covenant" and reciprocal communion between Mary and the faithful: indeed it concretely translates the gift of his Mother, which Jesus gave on the Cross to John and, through him, to all of us, and the entrustment of the beloved Apostle and of us to her, who became our spiritual Mother.[81]

An interesting liturgical application of this imagery is found in the medieval ceremonial for the consecration of virgins. After the imposition of the veil, the bishop blessed the newly consecrated and exhorted them to live "without stain beneath the mantle of Holy Mary, Mother of Our Lord Jesus Christ."[82] The language of the *patrocinium* is very well attested to with regard to Mary, as even a cursory glance at the index of Father Barré's magisterial anthology of medieval Marian prayers will indicate.[83] Pope John Paul II continued to use the terminology of

81 *Inseg* XXIV/1 (2001) 600–602 [*ORE* 1687:5].

82 R. Metz, "La Consécration des Vierges dans l'église Romaine," in *Études d'historie de la Liturgie* (P.U.F., 1954) 177 quoted in Quéméneur 7.

83 Barré 330–41.

the *patrocinium* in expressions such as "commit,"[84] "commend,"[85] "place in the hands of Mary"[86] or "under the protection of the Holy Mother of God"[87] until the end of his pontificate.

The Modern Period

This heritage of the *patrocinium* of Mary would find expression in the Marian Congregations (sodalities) established by the Belgian Jesuit, Jean Leunis, in 1563 for the students of the Collegio Romano.[88] The admission to the Congregation, which had as its aim the formation of militant Christians after the ideals of St. Ignatius Loyola and was placed under the patronage of Our Lady, soon became an act of oblation to the Virgin. The text of one of these early admission ceremonies by Father Franz Coster (+ 1619) was published in the *Libellus sodalitatis* in 1586 and is most likely the very formula which he first used to receive students into the Congregation, which he had founded at Cologne in 1576. In it, the sodalist chooses Mary as "Lady, Patroness and Advocate" and begs her to receive him as her *servum perpetuum.*[89] Father Quéméneur underscores the fact that the Marian Congregations introduce yet another perspective into the subject of Marian consecration inherited from the late Middle Ages: the corporate dimension.

---

84 *Committere* continues to be the verb of choice in Latin papal texts which speak of "consecration" to Mary. Cf. *Inseg* II/1 (1979) 364 [*Talks* 165]; *Inseg* II/1 (1979) 860–61 [*ORE* 577:9]; *Inseg* II/1 (1979) 1635 [*ORE* 589:2]; *Inseg* II/2 (1979) 1093 [*ORE* 608:9]; *Inseg* IV/2 (1981) 1045 [*ORE* 715:18].

85 Cf. "commend," *Inseg* I (1978) 73 [*Talks* 136]; "raccomando," *Inseg* I (1978) 131 [*Talks* 212]; "commend," *Inseg* II/1 (1979) 1103; "commendamus," *Inseg* II/1 (1979) 860–61 [*ORE* 577:9]; "raccomandiamo," *Inseg* II/1 (1979) 1066 [*ORE* 581:10]; "encomiendo," *Inseg* II/1 (1979) 1315 [*ORE* 586:10–11]; "recommende," *Inseg* II/2 (1979) 141; "empfehle," *Inseg* II/2 (1979) 184 [*ORE* 597:6].

86 Cf. *Inseg* II/1 (1979) 1391 [*Poland* 72]; *Inseg* III/1 (1980) 237–38 [*ORE* 619:4]; *Inseg* IV/2 (1981) 576, 579 [*ORE* 711:10].

87 Cf. *Inseg* II/1 (1979) 1029 [*ORE* 581:6–7]; *Inseg* II/2 (1979) 597 [*U.S.A.* 132]; *Inseg* II/2 (1979) 1356 [*ORE* 614:7–8]; *Inseg* II/2 (1979) 1429 [*ORE* 616:5]; *Inseg* III/1 (1980) 1322 [*Africa Ap* 362]; *Inseg* III/1 (1980) 1847 [*ORE* 640:7].

88 Cf. E. Villaret, S.J., "Marie et la Compagnie de Jésus," *Maria* II:962–968; "Cons" 402.

89 Jungmann 303.

> Since the Middle Ages there was a tendency for people prompted by sentiments of piety to group together, to form confraternities and various kinds of spiritual associations. There still existed such partly temporal and partly spiritual institutions as trade guilds and professional associations. In these, consecration corresponds to an oath; it is something like the "sacrament" of initiation, the formula for entrance.[90]

In 1622 the Marian Congregation admission formulae of the Italian Jesuit, Pietro Antonio Spinelli, as well as that of Father Coster were published in the book, *Hortulus Marianus* of Father de La Croix. The two formulae are described respectively as *modus consecrandi* and *modus vovendi* to the Blessed Virgin. Jungmann comments that this is the first appearance of the word *consecrare* (to consecrate) with the meaning of putting oneself under the *patrocinium* of Mary and it is taken as being synonymous with the word *devovere* which in classical Latin meant to devote oneself to a deity.[91] In effect, the understanding from the beginning of this usage has been that, by the act of consecration to Our Lady, the sodalist places himself at the service of Christ the King through her mediation and under her patronage.[92] The use of the term "consecration" with the meaning of giving oneself completely to Mary in order to belong more perfectly to Christ, enters into the common Catholic lexicon from this period, and Pope John Paul II continued to use it in this sense throughout his pontificate.[93]

---

90 Quéméneur 8.

91 Jungmann 304.

92 Villaret 968.

93 Cf. *Inseg* II/1 (1979) 1036 [*ORE* 580:3]; *Inseg* II/1 (1979) 1412–19 [*Poland* 103–15]; *Inseg* II/1 (1979) 1470–01 [*Poland* 189]; *Inseg* II/2 (1979) 177 [*ORE* 597:2]; *Inseg* II/2 (1979) 290 [*ORE* 599:9]; *Inseg* II/2 (1979) 468–70 [*Ireland* 88–92]; *Inseg* III/1 (1980) 1068–70 [*Africa Ap* 39–42]; *Inseg* III/1 (1980) 1253 [*Africa Ap* 280–282]; *Inseg* IV/1 (1981) 128; *Inseg* IV/2 (1981) 458–59 [*ORE* 708:5]; *Inseg* IV/2 (1981) 1219 [*ORE* 718:10] (In this instance the Italian text which the Pope read clearly says "avevo consacrato" whereas the English translation gives "dedicated" instead); *Inseg* IX/2 (1986) 91–94 [*ORE* 948:5]; *Inseg* X/1 (1987) 993 [*ORE* 985:2]; *Inseg* X/1 (1987) 1111 [*ORE* 987:4]; *Inseg* X/1 (1987) 1279 [*ORE* 989:13]; *Inseg* X/3 (1987) 1176 [*ORE* 1017:6–7]; *Inseg* X/3 (1987) 1186 [ORE 1016:12]; *Inseg* XI/1 (1988) 422 [*ORE* 1028:22]; *Inseg* XI/1 (1988) 571 [*ORE* 1030:12]; *Inseg* XI/3

During virtually the same period of time that the Jesuit Marian Congregations were being born, confraternities of the Holy Slavery of Mary were germinating in the soil of Spain. In fact, the earliest of these, founded under the inspiration of Sister Agnes of St. Paul at the convent of the Franciscan Conceptionists at Alcalá de Henares, dates from 2 August 1595[94] and thus antedates the foundation of the sodality movement. The first theologian of this "Marian slavery," as it was practiced in Alcalá, was the Franciscan Melchior de Cetina, "who composed in 1618 what may be called the first 'Handbook of Spirituality' for the members of the confraternity."[95]

(1988) 1240 [*ORE* 1061:1]; *Inseg* XII/1 (1989) 102 [*ORE* 1073:1]; *Inseg* XII/1 (1989) 935 [*ORE* 1092:6]; *Inseg* XII/1 (1989) 1152 [*ORE* 1091:18]; *Inseg* XII/2 (1989) 1029 [*ORE* 1116:12]; *Inseg* XIII/1 (1990) 354 [*ORE* 1130:10]; *Inseg* XIII/1 (1990) 424 [*ORE* 1130:11]; *Inseg* XIII/2 (1990) 390 [*ORE* 1156:5]; *Inseg* XIII/2 (1990) 576 [*ORE* 1157:13]; *Inseg* XIV/1 (1991) 1218 [*ORE* 1191:5]; *Inseg* XIV/1 (1991) 1224–1225 [*ORE* 1191:8, 10]; *Inseg* XIV/2 (1991) 258 [*ORE* 1204:7]; *Inseg* XIV/2 (1991) 938 [*ORE* 1214:3]; *Inseg* XIV/2 (1991) 966 [*ORE* 1213:16]; *Inseg* XV/1 (1992) 475, 478 [*ORE* 1230:15]; *Inseg* XV/1 (1992) 479 [*ORE* 1230:15]; *Inseg* XV/1 (1992) 1272–1273 [*ORE* 1239:7–8]; *Inseg* XV/2 (1992) 141 [*ORE* 1260:4]; *Inseg* XV/2 (1992) 199–200 [*ORE* 1259:8]; *Inseg* XV/2 (1992) 309 [*ORE* 1262:2]; *Inseg* XV/2 (1992) 365 [*ORE* 1262:10]; *Inseg* XVI/2 (1993) 516 [*ORE* 1304:9]; *Inseg* XVI/2 (1993) 1088 [*ORE* 1314:9]; *Inseg* XVII/1 (1994) 544–545 [*ORE* 1332:10]; *Inseg* XVIII/1 (1995) 464 [*ORE* 1383:7]; *Inseg* XVIII/1 (1995) 1579 [*ORE* 1394:4]; *Inseg* XVIII/1 (1995) 1667 [*ORE* 1395:7]; *Inseg* XIX/1 (1996) 1294–1295 [*ORE* 1442:1]; *Inseg* XIX/2 (1996) 753 [*ORE* 1468:1]; *Inseg* XX/2 (1997) 46 [*ORE* 1500:2]; *Inseg* XX/2 (1997) 268 [*ORE* 1509:2]; *Inseg* XXI/2 (1998) 1005 [*ORE* 1569:6]; *Inseg* XXII/1 (1999) 1181 [*ORE* 1601:6]; *Inseg* XXII/1 (1999) 1440 [*ORE* 1598:11]; *Inseg* XXIII/1 (2000) 457 [*ORE* 1636:10]; *Inseg* XXIII/1 (2000) 1103, 1104 [*ORE* 1649:5]; *Inseg* XXIII/1 (2000) 1116 [*ORE* 1651:5]; *Inseg* XXIII/1 (2000) 1134–1135, 1136 [*ORE* 1652:7]; *Inseg* XXIII/2 (2000) 1055 [*ORE* 1672:3]; *Inseg* XXIV/1 (2001) 445 [*ORE* 1686:8]; *Inseg* XXIV/1 (2001) 600 [*ORE* 1687:5]; *Inseg* XXIV/1 (2001) 1128 [*ORE* 1696:2]; *Inseg* XXIV/2 (2001) 57 [*ORE* 1703:5]; *Inseg* XXIV/2 (2001) 341 [*ORE* 1713:12]; *Inseg* XXV/2 (2002) 498 [*ORE* 1765:III]; *Inseg* XXVI/2 (2003) 95–96 [*ORE* 1808:2]; *Inseg* XXVI/2 (2003) 920 [*ORE* 1829:3]; *Inseg* XXVII/2 (2004) 507 [*ORE* 1870:8]; *Inseg* XXVII/2 (2004) 698 [*ORE* 1874:2]; *Inseg* XXVIII (2005) 89–90 [*ORE* 1880:5].

94 Cf. Gaffney 146; Canal 250 and especially J. Ordoñez Marquez, "La Cofradia de la Esclavitud en las Concepcionistas de Alcalá," *Estudios Marianos* 51 (1986) 231–48.

95 Cf. Juan de los Angeles – Melchior de Cetina, *Esortazione alla devozione della Vergine Madre di Dio: Alle origini della "schiavitù mariana,"* introduzione, traduzione e note di Stefano M. Cecchin, O.F.M. (Vatican City: Pontificia Academia Mariana Internationalis, 2003); Gaffney 146; Canal 252–53; Gaspar Calvo Moralejo, O.F.M., "Fray Melchior de Cetina, O.F.M., el primer teólogo de la 'Esclavitud Mariana' (1618)," *Estudios Marianos* 51 (1986) 249–271.

As the seventeenth century progressed, the confraternities multiplied and papal approval followed. One of the great promoters and proponents of this spirituality was the Trinitarian, Simon de Rojas (1552–1624),[96] who was canonized by Pope John Paul II on 3 July 1988. Here is how the Holy Father characterized his Marian spirituality in the canonization homily:

> One aspect of our Saint, which must be emphasized, is, without a doubt, his most unique and faithful love of Our Lady which he had shown since childhood. This intense Marian experience constantly increased within him … One very typical way he had of living and broadcasting this devotion, was the "servitude" or filial surrender of himself to the Mother of God. … In fact, the new Saint is a providential model for us of Marian life, which lies within our reach. He perfectly expressed his will to belong to Mary, in one of his favorite exclamations: "Our Lady, may I be completely yours, thus I shall have nothing to fear!"[97]

The Augustinian, Bartolomé de los Rios (1580–1652),[98] extended the work of his friend, de Rojas, into the Low Countries and propagated it by means of his writings, which were known and cited by Saint Louis de Montfort.[99] In his *Hierarchia Mariana*, he provides this formula of dedication:

> I choose you today, O Holy Virgin, as my Lady, my Queen and my Empress and I recognize in myself what I truly am, your servant and slave, beseeching and begging by the majesty of your most sweet name … that you admit me into your family to serve you with the humility of a slave and with the love of a son … grant, O sovereign Virgin, that this ardent desire to serve you as my Queen and Lady of incomparable greatness until the last breath of my life may never depart from my will.[100]

96 Cf. Juan Pujana, "Simon de Rojas," *DSp* 14:877–884; Gaffney 147; Canal 253–254; *John Paul II's Book of Saints* 143–144.

97 *Inseg* XI/3 (1988) 23 [*ORE* 1049:2].

98 Cf. Quirino Fernandez, "Los Rios y Alarcon, (Bartolomé de)," *DSp* 9:1013–1018.

99 Cf. *Treatise on True Devotion* #160; Gaffney 148; Canal 255–259.

100 Quoted in Canal 259, translated by Rodolfo Vargas y Rubio.

Perhaps the single most important figure to emerge thus far in our brief consideration of the forms of Marian consecration in the spiritual journey of the Church is Cardinal Pierre de Bérulle (1575–1629).[101] Founder of the Oratory of Jesus and promoter of the Teresian reform of Carmel in France,[102] his greatest glory in terms of the history of spirituality is probably one of which he was never conscious, that of being the "founder of the French School" of spirituality. His spiritual paternity would enrich the Church through Saint John Eudes and the Venerable Jean-Jacques Olier, Saints Louis-Marie Grignion de Montfort and Jean-Baptiste de la Salle. His disciples of even the second and third generations would continue to develop his doctrine with their own refinements and emphases. The depth of thought and the ponderousness of his style rendered him somewhat inaccessible so that often his immediate followers such as Olier and Eudes presented the fruits of his contemplation in ways which were much more appealing to a wider public,[103] but there can be no doubt that he was "le chef d'école."

Of specific interest to us is that, while visiting Spain in 1604, Bérulle, who had been a member of the Marian Congregation in his days in the Jesuit College of Clermont, came into contact with the confraternities of the Slaves of the Virgin and, in particular, with that of Alcalá de Henares where he went to see the General of the Carmelites.[104] This exposure evidently had a notable influence on the development of his own spirituality, for he would eventually formulate a "vow of servitude" to the Virgin Mary because of his conviction that, in the divine design, God

---

101 Cf. A. Molien, "Bérulle," *DSp* 1:1539–1581; André Rayez, S.J., "La Dévotion Mariale chez Bérulle et ses Premiers Disciples" in *Maria* III.31–72; *Theotokos* 79–80. The French Oratory of Jesus and Editions du Cerf published 8 volumes of his *Œuvres Complètes* in a critical edition in 1995–1996.

102 Cf. Stéphane-Marie Morgain, O.C.D., *Pierre de Bérulle et les Carmèlites de France* (Paris: Éditions du Cerf, 1995).

103 Cf. Raymond Deville, P.S.S., L'école française de spiritualité, n. 11 de la "Bibliothèque d'Histoire du Christianisme," (Paris: Desclée, 1987) 29.

104 Cf. A. Molien, "Bérulle," *DSp* 1:1547.

wished to include in the vocation and predestination of Jesus Christ His divine filiation as well as the Divine Maternity, i.e., His being son of the Father and of Mary.[105] Hence Mary, the first to have made the vow of servitude to Jesus, "pure capacity for Jesus filled with Jesus,"[106] relates one perfectly to Jesus. Here are his words:

> To the perpetual honor of the Mother and the Son, I wish to be in the state and quality of servitude with regard to her who has the state and quality of the Mother of my God ... I give myself to her in the quality of a slave in honor of the gift which the eternal Word made of himself to her in the quality of Son.[107]

He formulated a similar vow to Jesus Christ in honor of the state and "form of a servant"[108] which He took upon Himself at the Incarnation,[109] a vow of which Jesus

> himself in his own person is the author and teacher, of which the Holy Virgin is the first and longest professed, and of which the apostles are the first and oldest superiors ... it is the vow and solemn profession of Christians at Baptism.[110]

The late Father Vincent Vasey, S.M., in his posthumously published paper on the Mariology of Bérulle, anticipates the question as to why the vow to Mary should precede the vow to Christ:

---

105 *Opuscule de piété*, 93, 1103 quoted in Paul Cochois, *Bérulle et l'École française, n. 31 de "Maîtres Spirituels"* (Paris: Editions du Seuil, 1963) 105. Cf. also William M. Thompson (ed.), *Bérulle and the French School: Selected Writings* (New York: Paulist Press, 1989) 14–16; 41–50; Théodore Koehler, S.M., "Servitude (saint esclavage)," *DSp* 14:738–41. This insight of Bérulle is vindicated in *Ineffabilis Deus* [*Pii IX Acta* I:599; *OL* #34]; *Munificentissimus Deus* [*AAS* 42 (1950) 768; *OL* #520], and *Lumen Gentium* #61.

106 Quoted in Cochois 105.

107 M. Rigal, *Les Mystères de Marie*, in *Coll. Les Lettres Chrétiennes* (Paris, 1961) 204, translated in *Theotokos* 80.

108 Phil. 2:7.

109 Text given in Deville 43.

110 *Narré de ce qui s'est passé sur les Élévations à Jésus et à la très sainte Vierge* 614. Quoted in Cochois 103 (my translation).

> Logically, the vow of servitude to Mary should take place first; the vow to Jesus should come after. In fact, Bérulle introduced the two vows about the same time; the first consecration or vow of service was made to Mary and then a vow of service to Jesus, to respect the due hierarchy in accord with Dionysian categories.
>
> Nothing strange—that Bérulle should consider the Virgin as his intermediary hierarch—for, he considered his own vocation as that of an hierarch with the duty of leading his subjects to a share in Mary's mystical graces and then, through the Virgin, to a participation in the mysteries of Christ, and, finally, through the mysteries of Christ to the life of the Trinity. To summarize his thought: *per Mariam ad Iesum; per Iesu mysteria ad Trinitatem.*[111]

The heritage of Cardinal Pierre de Bérulle would, in a certain sense, synthesize what had taken place before him and lay a solid foundation for his spiritual children.[112] Surely among them all, his most direct heir, who has been raised to the honors of the altar, is Saint John Eudes. A member of the Sodality at the Jesuit College in Caen from his youth, formed in the Oratory of Jesus by Bérulle and his immediate successor, Charles de Condren, Eudes was probably the greatest missioner and popularizer of the French School.[113] In his first book, *The Kingdom of Jesus*, a kind of handbook of Bérullian spirituality intended for a wide public, he offers this counsel about how a Christian should relate to Mary:

> You must see and adore her Son in her, and see and adore Him alone. It is thus that she wishes to be honored, because

111 Vincent R. Vasey, S.M., "Mary in the Doctrine of Bérulle on the Mysteries of Christ," *Marian Studies* 36 (1985) 63; cf. Cochois 107–108. The reference to "Dionysian categories" refers to the categories in the writings of Pseudo-Dionysius the Areopagite (6th century).

112 Cf. M.-Th. Poupon, O.P., *Le poème de la parfaite consécration à Marie* (Lyon: Librairie de Sacré-Cœur, 1947) 336–374.

113 Cf. *Theotokos* 201–202; L. Barbé, C.J.M., "La Vierge dans la Congrégation de Jésus et Marie," *Maria* III:163–179; Charles Lebrun, C.J.M., *The Spiritual Teaching of St. John Eudes*, trans. Basil Whelan, O.S.B. (London: Sands and Co., 1934) 260.

> of herself and by herself she is nothing, but her Son Jesus is everything in her, her being, her life, her sanctity, her glory, her power and her greatness. You should thank Our Lord for the glory He has given to Himself through His admirable Mother. You must offer yourself to Him and ask Him to give you to her, causing all your life and all your acts to be consecrated to the honor of her life and her actions. You must pray that He will make you participate in her admirable love for Him and in her other virtues. You must ask Him to employ your life in her honor, or rather to honor Himself in her, in whatever way He pleases.
>
> You must recognize and honor her first as the Mother of God, then as your own Mother and Queen. You must thank her for all the love, glory and perfect service she rendered to Her Son Jesus Christ our Lord. You must refer to her, after God, your being and your life, subjecting yourself entirely to her as her slave, imploring her to direct you in all your affairs and to assume full power over you, as over something belonging entirely to her, and to dispose of you as she pleases, for the greater glory of her Divine Son.[114]

In this carefully measured exhortation, the Norman Saint highlights the Christocentrism of Bérulle and synthesizes his vows of servitude to Jesus and Mary while retaining his emphasis on Mary's complete relativity to Christ. Also to be noted is his accent on "Jesus living in Mary," a characteristic of the French School given classic form in the well-known prayer of the Venerable Jean-Jacques Olier,[115] the founder of the Seminary

---

114 *Œuvres Complètes du Vénérable Jean Eudes*, VI (Vannes: Imprimerie Lafoyle Frères, 1905–11) 189; Saint John Eudes, *The Life and Kingdom of Jesus in Christian Souls*, trans. by a Trappist Father (New York: P. J. Kenedy & Sons, 1946) 272.

115 Cf. the analysis of this prayer by Irenée Noye, P.S.S., "O Jesus Living in Mary," trans. Roger M. Charest, S.M.M., *Queen of All Hearts* 32:5 (Jan.-Feb., 1982) 9. Pope Saint John Paul II commented briefly but appreciatively on this prayer at the close of his annual retreat with the Roman Curia on 27 February 1988; cf. *Inseg* XI/1 (1988) 502 [*ORE* 1029:2].

and Company of Saint-Sulpice.[116] Probably Eudes' most mature expression of belonging to Mary is to be found in his "Contract of Holy Matrimony with the Most Blessed Virgin Mary, the Mother of God" which he wrote and signed in his own blood at Caen on 28 April 1668.[117] While the terminology may be initially jarring to modern sensibilities, it should be noted that Bérulle himself proposed to his sons in the Oratory that they should consider their relation to Jesus and Mary as a marriage (*alliance*).[118] An analysis of the text will indicate the delicacy, Christocentrism, theological precision and creativity of this document.

Not surprisingly, during this golden era of French spirituality, France itself would be consecrated to Mary in 1638 by Louis XIII under the influence of Cardinal Richelieu.[119] Many other nations followed suit, as Father Jungmann tells us:

> At the command of King Philip IV of Spain, in 1643 the South American Spanish colonies were dedicated to Mary through a "solemn consecration." In 1664 the same thing was done for Portugal and all her colonies at the instigation of King John IV. ... Something similar happened in Austria in the following year at the order of Emperor Ferdinand III. ... At Mass on Easter day 1674 the missionary to the Indians, Jacques Marquette, S.J., solemnly consecrated the

116 Cf. *Theotokos* 272–273; Pierre Pourrat, P.S.S., "La Dévotion à Marie dans la Compagnie de Saint-Sulpice," *Maria* III:153–162. On the editing of Olier's manuscripts and the authenticity of the works attributed to him, cf. John O. Barres, *Jean-Jacques Olier's Priestly Spirituality: Mental Prayer and Virtue as the Foundation for the Direction of Souls* (Rome: Pontificia Universitas Sanctæ Crucis, Thesis ad Doctoratum in Theologia, 1999) 63–84, 225–226.

117 Saint John Eudes, *Letters and Shorter Works*, trans. Ruth Hauser (New York: P. J. Kenedy & Sons, 1948) 318–323.

118 Vasey 61.

119 Cf. Maurice Vloberg, "Le Vœu de Louis XIII," *Maria* V:519–533; René Laurentin, *Le voeu de Louis XIII: Passé ou avenir de la France 1638–1988* (Paris: O.E.I.L., 1988). In his entrustment of France to Our Lady on 14 August 1983, the Pope would make explicit reference to the earlier consecration of France to Mary by Louis XIII, cf. *Inseg* VI/2 (1983) 206 [*ORE* 798:4].

new mission on the Mississippi along with his Indians to the Immaculata.[120]

Saint Louis-Marie Grignion de Montfort

Into this French ecclesial context, characterized at its highest levels by ardent love for the Mother of God, was born Louis-Marie Grignion (1673–1716) at Montfort-la-Cane.[121] (Wishing to give no impression of self-importance, he would eventually identify himself by the name of Montfort, the town of his birth and Baptism, rather than by Grignion, his family name.) This Saint, described as "the last of the great Bérullians"[122] and the greatest proponent of Marian consecration produced by the "French School," was first educated at the Jesuit College in Rennes where he was a member of the Marian Congregation[123] and then for eight years under the influence of the Sulpicians founded by Olier.[124]

If Bérulle had already indicated the link between Baptism and his "vow of servitude to Jesus," de Montfort would associate Mary with one's Baptismal commitment as well. What he

120 Jungmann 305–06.

121 Cf. *Theotokos* 250–251. An enormous body of literature has built up on de Montfort e.g., Stefano De Fiores (gen. ed.), *Jesus Living in Mary: Handbook of the Spirituality of St. Louis Marie de Montfort* (Bay Shore, NY: Montfort Publications, 1994). The Centre International Montfortain of Rome continues publishing scholarly studies on the Saint and updating the bibliography on him.

122 Henri Bremond, *Histoire Litteraire du Sentiment Religieux en France depuis la Fin des Guerres de Religion jusqu'a Nos Jours*, Vol. IX: *La Vie Chrétienne sous l'Ancien Régime* (Paris: Librairie Bloud et Gay, 1932) 272. Cf. the excellent study by François-Marie Léthel, O.C.D., "La Maternité de Marie dans le Mystère de l'Incarnation et de notre Divinisation selon saint Louis-Marie Grignion de Montfort et le Cardinal de Bérulle," in François-Marie Léthel, O.C.D., *Théologie de l'Amour de Jésus: Écrits sur la théologie des saints* (Venasque: Éditions du Carmel, 1996) 103–138.

123 Cf. Stefano De Fiores, S.M.M., *Itinerario spirituale di S. Luigi Maria di Montfort (1673–1716) nel periodo fino al sacerdozio (5 giugno 1700)*, University of Dayton: Marian Library Studies, new series 6 (1974) 59–81.

124 Cf. De Fiores 142–65; 184–203. Another excellent study which considers the influence of the "French School" on de Montfort is Benedetta Papàsogli, *Montfort: A Prophet for Our Times*, trans. Ann Nielsen, D.W. (Rome: Edizioni Monfortane, 1991) esp. 103–13; 379–98.

proposes in his great masterpiece, *The Treatise on True Devotion to the Blessed Virgin*, is the explicit renewal of one's Baptismal promises "through the hands of Mary":

> In holy baptism we do not give ourselves to Jesus explicitly through Mary, nor do we give him the value of our good actions. After baptism we remain entirely free either to apply that value to anyone we wish or keep it for ourselves. But by this consecration we give ourselves explicitly to Jesus through Mary's hands and we include in our consecration the value of all our actions.[125]

If Saint Louis had written a special formula of consecration in conjunction with his *Treatise on True Devotion*, it was evidently lost with the first and last pages of his manuscript, which was only found in 1842.[126] The formula that he has left us in *The Love of Eternal Wisdom*, a work of his youth, clearly highlights the fact that Jesus is the goal of the act of consecration which he proposes, while Mary is its intermediary:

> Eternal and incarnate Wisdom, most lovable and adorable Jesus, true God and true man, only Son of the eternal Father and of Mary always Virgin, … I dare no longer approach the holiness of your majesty on my own. That is why I turn to the intercession and the mercy of your holy Mother, whom you yourself have given me to mediate with you. Through her I hope to obtain from you contrition and pardon for my sins, and that Wisdom whom I desire to dwell in me always. …
>
> O admirable Mother, present me to your dear Son as his slave now and for always, so that he who redeemed me through you, will now receive me through you.[127]

125 *Treatise on True Devotion* #126 [*God Alone* 329].

126 Cf. *Treatise on True Devotion* #114 [*God Alone* 324] on the Saint's prophecy about this.

127 *Love of Eternal Wisdom* #223, 226 [*God Alone* 112–113]. Another beautiful and explicitly Trinitarian form of Marian consecration is found in de Montfort's *Secret of Mary* #66–69 [*God Alone* 279–281], a work which is a kind of synthesis of the *Treatise on True Devotion* and written after the *Love of Eternal Wisdom*.

While de Montfort readily and very frequently speaks of "consecrating oneself to Mary," this must always be understood as a shorthand form of "consecrating oneself to Jesus through the hands of Mary."[128] It is precisely in these terms that Pope John Paul II presents him as a proponent of authentic Marian spirituality in *Redemptoris Mater*.[129]

Perhaps, in the final analysis, the greatest contribution of this Breton Saint to the theology of Marian consecration is precisely his insistence on Mary's mediation as willed by God. This secondary and subordinate, but nonetheless real mediation of Mary described in *Lumen Gentium* #60 and 62, and presented with such conviction by Saint Louis, is well explained by one of his spiritual sons:

> Objection has been raised against this principle of Montfort, primarily because his understanding of "mediatrix," or "through Mary" has been sadly twisted. In the eyes of this missionary, no one is more approachable, more lovable, than the tender Jesus. His chapters on the tenderness, the humanness, the simplicity of Jesus in *The Love of the Eternal Wisdom*, in his *Cantiques* on Jesus—an antiochene element in his Christology—all bear this out. When he speaks of "mediators" or going *through* Mary, he is not setting up Our Lady as a barricade which must be pierced before reaching the Lord; he is not speaking of a hurdle which must be surmounted before arriving at the goal; he is not speaking of any chronological procedure. As he explains it, it is with Mary that we arrive at Jesus more quickly, love Him more tenderly, serve Him more faithfully. In Montfort's eyes, the "through Mary" brings about a more intensely immediate union with the Eternal and Incarnate Wisdom. She does not stand in the way. She is the "mysterious milieu," the atmosphere, as Gerard Manley Hopkins wrote after reading Montfort, which

128 Cf. Reginald Garrigou-Lagrange, O.P., *The Mother of The Saviour and Our Interior Life*, trans. Bernard J. Kelley, C.S.Sp. (St. Louis: B. Herder Book Co., 1957) 256, footnote #19.

129 *Redemptoris Mater* #48.

> only enhances, intensifies this union. To withdraw from this atmosphere, this milieu which God has given to us, to try to circumvent the quickening catalyst of Mary with which God has so kindly endowed us, is to ignore the role of Mary in salvation history; it is to show disrespect for God. At least implicitly, everyone comes to Jesus through the means He takes to come to us: through Mary. Again, for Montfort, this refers to the ineradicable characteristic of all salvation history: the necessary, representative, salvific, eternal consent of Mary. Far from denying the beauty of Jesus, Mary as Mediator "of intercession" with the "Mediator of redemption" affirms the uniqueness of "the one and only mediator between God and Man, the man Jesus Christ" (I Tim. 2:5) while also affirming our own weakness and the will of God in this present order of salvation.[130]

There is a sense in which the life and work of de Montfort may be seen as bringing to its culmination the concept of Marian "servitude" or "slavery" which we have traced from the Spanish confraternities and even earlier. He himself used the term frequently in his writings[131] while maintaining that "we can call ourselves, and become, the loving slaves of our Blessed Lady in order to become more perfect slaves of Jesus."[132] Of course, the term "slavery" or "servitude" grates upon the ears of many in the highly democratized era in which we live. Pope Saint John Paul II, a committed disciple of de Montfort's Marian thought,[133]

130 J. Patrick Gaffney, S.M.M., "Saint Louis Mary Grignion de Montfort and the Marian Consecration," *Marian Studies* 35 (1984) 142–144.

131 Cf. *Treatise on True Devotion* #55–56, 75–76 [*God Alone* 305–306, 312–313]; *Love of Eternal Wisdom* #211, 219 [*God Alone* 109, 110–111]; *Secret of Mary* #34, 41, 61 [*God Alone* 271, 274, 278].

132 *Treatise on True Devotion* #75 [God Alone 312–313].

133 Cf. André Frossard, *"Be Not Afraid!": Pope John Paul II Speaks Out on his Life, his Beliefs and his Inspiring Vision for Humanity*, trans. J. R. Foster (NY: St. Martin's Press, 1984) 125–127; *Pope John Paul II, Crossing the Threshold of Hope*, edited by Vittorio Messori and trans. Jenny and Martha McPhee (London: Jonathan Cape, 1994) 212–215; ibid., *Gift and Mystery: On the 50th Anniversary of My Priestly Ordination* (Vatican City: Libreria Editrice Vaticana, 1996) 41–43; ibid.,

didn't hesitate to defend de Montfort's usage of this terminology in his interview with André Frossard:

> It is well known that the author of the treatise [*on True Devotion*] defines his devotion as a form of "slavery." The word may upset our contemporaries. Personally I do not see any difficulty in it. I think we are confronted here with the sort of paradox often to be noted in the Gospels, the words "holy slavery" signifying that we could not more fully exploit our freedom, the greatest of God's gifts to us. For freedom is measured by the love of which we are capable.[134]

He spoke similarly on 4 June 1979 in reviewing the modern history of Poland's consecration to Mary and supporting the use of the term "maternal slavery of love," which was incorporated into the great Act of Consecration made on 3 May 1966, on the occasion of the celebration of the Millennium of Christianity in Poland:

> The act speaks of "servitude." It contains a paradox similar to the words of the Gospel according to which one must lose one's life to find it (cf. Mt. 10:39). For love constitutes the fulfillment of freedom, yet at the same time "belonging," and so not being free is part of its essence. However, this "not being free" in love is not felt as slavery but rather as an affirmation and fulfillment of freedom. The act of consecration in slavery indicates therefore a unique dependence and a limitless trust. In this sense slavery (non-freedom) expresses the fullness of freedom, in

---

Memory and Identity: Personal Reflections (London: Weidenfeld & Nicholson, 2005) 165–171.

134 André Frossard, *"Be Not Afraid!"* 126. On the Gospel basis of the language of "slavery," cf. François-Marie Léthel, O.C.D., *L'Amour de Jésus en Marie: Le Traité de la vraie dévotion à la Sainte Vierge, Le Secret de Marie* (Geneva: Éditions Ad Solem, 2000) I:81–119; Roman Ginn, O.C.S.O., "Slave Talk in St. Paul and St. Louis de Montfort," *Queen of All Hearts* 39 (March-April 1989) 12–13; Donald MacDonald, "From the Slavery of Sin to the Total Consecration to Christ," *Queen of All Hearts* 40 (July-August 1989) 18–19.

> the same way as the Gospel speaks of the need to lose one's life in order to find it in its fullness.[135]

In an address of 17 December 1987 to his brother Polish Bishops from the metropolitan province of Wrocław on the occasion of their "ad limina" visit, he continued to develop some of the implications of the "maternal slavery of love" which Poland had vowed to Mary, its Queen, on 3 May 1966. Once again, he chose to underscore the paradoxical nature of the language employed:

> Here it is a question not only of verbal paradoxes, but of ontological ones as well. The most profound paradox is perhaps that of life and death, expressed, among other places, in the parable of the seed, which must die in order to produce new life. This paradox is definitely confirmed by the paschal mystery.[136]

Further, considering "maternal slavery" as the path of Saints Louis de Montfort and Maximilian Kolbe and the Polish Cardinal Primates Hlond and Wyszyński, he said that this "maternal slavery"

> must reveal itself as the path towards victory, the price of freedom. For that matter, it is difficult to imagine any being less inclined to "enslave" than a mother, than the Mother of God. And if what we are speaking of is an "enslaving" through love, then from that perspective "slavery" constitutes precisely *the revelation of the fullness of freedom.* In fact, freedom attains its true meaning, that is, its own fullness, through a true good. Love is synonymous with that attainment.[137]

He would speak again of the intrinsic necessity of this paradoxical "maternal slavery" on 23 May 1990 during the "Jasna Góra cycle" which he continued for a year at his general

135 *Inseg* II/1 (1979) 1414 [*Poland* 106]; cf. also his further remarks on his taking leave of Jasna Góra on 6 June, *Inseg* II/1 (1979) 1470–1471 [*Poland* 189].

136 *Inseg* X/3 (1987) 1436 [*ORE* 1022:11].

137 *Inseg* X/3 (1987) 1436–1437 [*ORE* 1022:11].

audiences. The reference was clearly to the program of Marian consecration of Cardinal Wyszyński:

> In such times those words were spoken by the Primate of the Millennium [Cardinal Wyszyński], and they went like this: *"We entrust ourselves to your motherly 'slavery' for the Church's freedom in today's world and in Poland."*
>
> Such words cannot be forgotten. Neither can we wipe out "the paradox": "motherly slavery" as the price of freedom of conscience, the price of freedom of religion, for the Church, the individual and society.[138]

We have already noted above how John Paul emphasized the "Marian servitude" of Saint Simon de Rojas at the time of his canonization.[139] He did so again on 16 October 1988, when he described the Capuchin Blessed Honorat Koźmiński (1829–1916)[140] in the beatification homily thus:

> He abandoned himself to Christ, Incarnate Wisdom, as his slave, according to the instructions of St. Louis Grignion de Montfort. He often repeated "*totus tuus*." He asked that Mary would be for him "a protectress, a mediatrix, a helper, a guide of his sermons, a counselor for confessions, a guarantor of chastity, a consoler, a reparatrix."[141]

In his Angelus address of 27 September 1992 after the beatification of twenty-one Servants of God, he commended the example of Blessed Nazaria Ignacia March Mesa (1889–1943),[142] "who was consecrated as a 'slave' to Mary according to the model of de Montfort."[143] In his homily at the Mass for the beatification of

138 *Inseg* XIII/1 (1990) 1385 [*ORE* 1142:4].

139 Cf. above (footnote 97) 42.

140 Cf. Andreas Resch, C.Ss.R., *I Beati di Giovanni Paolo II*, Vol. II: 1986–1990 (Vatican City: Libreria Editrice Vaticana, 2002) 161–164; *Sulle Orme dei Santi. Il Santorale Cappuccino: Santi, Beati, Venerabili, Servi di Dio* (Rome: Istituto Storico dei Cappuccini, Postulazione Generale, 2000) 255–262; *John Paul II's Book of Saints* 306–307.

141 *Inseg* XI/3 (1988) 1237 [*ORE* 1063:11].

142 Cf. Andreas Resch, C.Ss.R., *I Beati di Giovanni Paolo II*, Vol. III: 1991–1995 (Vatican City: Libreria Editrice Vaticana, 2003) 61–64.

143 *Inseg* XV/2 (1992) 199 [*ORE* 1259:8].

four Servants of God on 25 October 1998, he stressed that one of them, the Franciscan Antônio de Sant'Anna Galvão (1739–1822),[144] considered himself the "son and everlasting slave" of Mary Immaculate.[145]

Nowhere is John Paul II's discipleship of de Montfort, his teaching on the "maternal slavery of love" and his insistence on the Christological basis and orientation of this teaching more powerfully illustrated than in his magisterial Letter to the Religious of the Montfort Families on the occasion of the 160th Anniversary of the Publication of *Treatise on True Devotion*, dated 8 December 2003:

> In Montfort spirituality, the dynamism of charity is expressed in particular by the symbol of the *slavery of love to Jesus,* after the example and with the motherly help of Mary. It is a matter of full communion in the *kenosis* of Christ, communion lived with Mary, intimately present in the mysteries of the life of her Son. "There is nothing among Christians which makes us more absolutely belong to Jesus Christ and his holy Mother than the slavery of the will, according to the example of Jesus Christ himself, who took on the status of a servant for love of us—*formam servi accipiens*—and also according to the example of the holy Virgin who called herself the servant and handmaid of the Lord (Lk. 1:38). The Apostle refers to himself as 'the slave of Christ' (*servus Christi*) *as though the title were an honor.* Christians are often so called in the Holy Scriptures" (cf. *Treatise on True Devotion,* n. 72). Indeed, the Son of God, who came into the world out of obedience to the Father in the Incarnation (cf. Heb. 10:7), subsequently humbled himself by making himself obedient unto death, and death on the Cross (cf. Phil. 2:7–8). Mary responded to God's will with the total gift of herself, body and soul,

144 Cf. Andreas Resch, C.Ss.R., *I Beati di Giovanni Paolo II*, Vol. IV: 1996–2000 (Vatican City: Libreria Editrice Vaticana, 2004) 209–212. He was subsequently canonized by Benedict XVI on 11 May 2007 at Campo de Marte, São Paulo, Brazil.

145 *Inseg* XXI/2 (1998) 832–833 [*ORE* 1564:3].

> forever, from the Annunciation to the Cross and from the Cross to the Assumption. The obedience of Christ and the obedience of Mary are not, of course, symmetrical because of the *ontological difference* between the divine Person of the Son and the human person of Mary. This also explains the resulting exclusivity of the fundamental salvific efficacy of obedience to Christ, from whom his own Mother received the grace to be able to obey God totally and thus collaborate in the mission of her Son.
>
> The *slavery of love* should therefore be interpreted in light of the wonderful exchange between God and humanity in the mystery of the incarnate Word. It is a true exchange of love between God and his creature in the reciprocity of total self-giving. The "spirit [of this devotion] consists in this: that we be interiorly dependent on Mary Most Holy; that we be slaves of Mary, and through her, of Jesus" (*The Secret of Mary*, n. 44). Paradoxically, this "bond of charity," this "slavery of love," endows the human being with full freedom, with that true freedom of the children of God (cf. *Treatise on True Devotion*, n. 169). It is a question of giving oneself to Jesus without reserve, responding to the Love with which he first loved us. Those who live in this love can say with St Paul: "*It is no longer I who live, but Christ who lives in me*"(Gal. 2:20).[146]

In #15 of his Apostolic Letter *Rosarium Virginis Mariæ* of 16 October 2002, John Paul again indicated how fundamental the doctrine of Montfort was in his life and how fundamental it could be for all the children of the Church:

> The Rosary mystically transports us to Mary's side as she is busy watching over the human growth of Christ in the home of Nazareth. This enables her to train us and to mold us with the same care, until Christ is "fully formed" in us (cf. Gal. 4:19). This role of Mary, totally grounded in that of Christ and radically subordinated to it, "in no way obscures or diminishes the unique mediation of Christ, but rather shows its power." This is the luminous principle

146 *Inseg* XXVI/2 (2003) 922–923 [*ORE* 1829:4].

> expressed by the Second Vatican Council which I have so powerfully experienced in my own life and have made the basis of my episcopal motto: *Totus Tuus*. The motto is of course inspired by the teaching of Saint Louis-Marie Grignion de Montfort, who explained in the following words Mary's role in the process of our configuration to Christ: "*Our entire perfection consists in being conformed, united and consecrated to Jesus Christ.* Hence the most perfect of all devotions is undoubtedly that which conforms, unites and consecrates us most perfectly to Jesus Christ. Now, since Mary is of all creatures the one most conformed to Jesus Christ, it follows that among all devotions that which most consecrates and conforms a soul to our Lord is devotion to Mary, his Holy Mother, and that the more a soul is consecrated to her the more will it be consecrated to Jesus Christ" (*Treatise on True Devotion*, n. 120).[147]

We note here, of course, the Pope's mention of his motto, *Totus Tuus*, which became a hallmark of his pontificate, and which he cited on innumerable occasions to the very end of his life and which, he tells us, was inspired by Saint Louis-Marie Grignion de Montfort. In fact, de Montfort quoted that expression three times in his masterwork, *The Treatise on True Devotion*. The first occurs in #216:3:

> Since you have now given yourself completely to Mary, body and soul, she, who is generous to the generous, and more generous than even the kindest benefactor, will in return give herself to you in a marvellous but real manner. Indeed you may without hesitation say to her … with St. Bonaventure, *Tuus totus ego sum, et omnia mea tua sunt, o Virgo gloriosa, super omnia benedicta*: "I am all yours and all that I have is yours, O glorious Virgin, blessed above all created things."[148]

---

147 *Inseg* XXV/2 (2002) 497–498 [Vatican English edition 19–20].

148 *Treatise on True Devotion* #216:3 [*God Alone* 359]. The English edition used here does not give the original Latin, which is found in the critical French edition, *Œuvres complètes de saint Louis-Marie Grignion de Montfort* (Paris: Editions du

The second occurs in #233:

> Every year at least, on the same date, they should renew the consecration following the same exercises for three weeks. They might also renew it every month or even every day by saying this short prayer: *Tuus totus ego sum, et omnia mea tua sunt*: "I am all yours and all I have is yours, O dear Jesus, through Mary, your holy Mother."[149]

The third instance is found in the supplement on practicing this devotion at Holy Communion #266:3 & 4:

> Renew your consecration saying, *Tuus totus ego sum, et omnia mea tua sunt*: "I belong entirely to you, dear Mother, and all that I have is yours." … Beg her to lend you her heart, saying, *Accipio te in mea omnia. Præbe mihi cor tuum, o Maria*: "O Mary, I take you for my all; give me your heart."[150]

Clearly, John Paul II had internalized this little book of de Montfort and adapted these passages, especially the third, so that they became his daily prayer.[151] According to authoritative testimony, in all of his manuscripts the words *Totus tuus ego sum* at the top of the page substituted for page 1; *et omnia mea tua sunt* for page 2; *Accipio te in mea omnia* for page 3; and *Præbe mihi cor tuum, o Maria* for page 4.[152] Listing all of his written quotations of *Totus tuus* would constitute a separate study in itself.

Seuil, 1982) 633. This formula is taken from St. Bonaventure, *Psalt. Majus*, cant. Ad instar illius Moïsis, Ex. 15 (*Opera omnia*, Vivès, Parisiis 1868, t. 14, 221b).

149 *Treatise on True Devotion* #233 [*God Alone* 364; *Œuvres complètes* 644]. Again this adaptation is taken from the works of St. Bonaventure as in the footnote above.

150 *Treatise on True Devotion* #266: 3 & 4 [*God Alone* 375, 376; *Œuvres complètes* 666, 667]. The last quotation is a conflation of John 19 :27 and Proverbs 23 :26.

151 Cf. *Gift and Mystery* 42–43 where the Pope informs his readers that *Totus tuus* "is an abbreviation of a more complete form of entrustment to the Mother of God which runs like this: *Totus tuus ego sum et omnia mea Tua sunt. Accipio Te in mea omnia. Præbe mihi cor Tuum, Maria.*"

152 Cf. François-Marie Léthel, O.C.D., *La Luce di Cristo nel Cuore della Chiesa: Giovanni Paolo II e la Teologia dei Santi. Esercizi Spirituali con Benedetto XVI* (Vatican City: Libreria Editrice Vaticana, 2011) 39.

Blessed William Joseph Chaminade

While it may be true to see de Montfort's teaching as the high point of the Marian consecration championed by the "French School," it would be unfair to consider the subsequent history of this phenomenon in the life of the Church simply in terms of denouement. The unfolding of this process continued even in that difficult period after the French Revolution with holy founders such as Blessed William Joseph Chaminade (1761–1850),[153] who incorporated total consecration to Mary into the Society of Mary (Marianists), which he founded, as the object of a special perpetual religious vow.[154] The various manuscripts that Father Chaminade left behind him are testimonies to his profound Marian doctrine, but they do not contain an organized treatise and, in fact, he evidently preferred to diffuse his Marian teaching viva voce. His spiritual sons have collected and published all of their founder's Marian writings.[155] The best-known interpreter of Father Chaminade is the late Father Émile Neubert, S.M. (1878–1967), who spent his life diffusing knowledge of the profoundly Marian spirituality of the founder.[156] His most famous work, *My Ideal: Jesus Son of Mary*,[157] has been translated into the principal languages of the world and has become a classic treatise on Marian spirituality

---

153 Cf. Resch, *I Beati di Giovanni Paolo II*, IV:333–336; *Theotokos* 99–100.

154 Cf. Henri Lebon, S.M., "Chaminade (Guillaume-Joseph)," *DSp* 2:454–459; Peter A. Resch, S.M., "Filial Piety," *Mariology* 3:165.

155 Cf. J.-B. Armbruster, S.M., *G.-J. Chaminade: Ecrits Marials* Vols. 1 & 2 (Fribourg, Switzerland: Séminaire Marianiste, 1966); *William Joseph Chaminade: Marian Writings*, trans. Henry Bradley, S.M. & Joseph H. Roy, S.M. (Dayton: Marianist Resources Commission, 1980) Vols. 1 & 2; William J. Kiefer, S.M. (ed.) *Mary in Our Christ-Life* (Milwaukee: Bruce Publishing Company, 1961).

156 Cf. Jean-Louis Barré, S.M., *La Mission de la Vierge Marie d'après les Écrits d'Émile Neubert S.M. (1878–1967)* (Rome: Dissertationes ad Lauream in Pontificia Facultate Theologica "Marianum" 94, 2007); *Autobiography of Father Emile Neubert, Marianist*, trans. & ed. Thomas A. Stanley, S.M. (Dayton: North American Center for Marianist Studies, Monograph Series, no. 55, 2007); *Theotokos* 266.

157 First published in French in 1933; most recent English edition by Tan Books and Publishers, Rockford, IL, 1988.

and consecration. For Father Neubert, as for Father Chaminade, Marian consecration has an implicit link with the Sacrament of Confirmation in that giving oneself to Mary allows her to be a guide for the Christian who has received the gift of the Holy Spirit in order to be a witness of Christ to the world.[158] Father Neubert drew out Mary's role in guiding the apostolate in many of his writings, especially in the fourth part of his *My Ideal: Jesus Son of Mary, Queen of Militants*[159] and *La Mission Apostolique de Marie et la Nôtre*.[160] His little classic was greatly appreciated by such Marian apostles as Saint Maximilian-Maria Kolbe[161] and the Servant of God, Frank Duff, founder of the Legion of Mary.[162]

Another notable figure who continued the great Marian tradition of the French School was the Venerable Francis Mary Paul Libermann (1802–1852),[163] Jewish convert and "second founder" of the Holy Ghost Fathers, who characterized his fledgling institute in these terms:

> What distinguishes us from all other workers in the Lord's vineyard is a quite special consecration which we make of all our society, of each of its members, of all their works and enterprises to the most holy Heart of Mary, a heart eminently apostolic and all inflamed with desires for the glory of God and the salvation of souls.[164]

---

158 Cf. *CCC* #1285.

159 First French edition in 1944; English edition by Grail Publications, St. Meinrad, IN, 1947.

160 (Paris: Alsatia, 1956). English translation: *Mary's Apostolic Mission and Ours*, trans. Joseph Stefanelli, S.M. (New Bedford, MA: Academy of the Immaculate, 2011).

161 Cf. *Scritti di Massimiliano Kolbe*. Translated from the Polish by Cristoforo Zambelli, O.F.M. Conv., (Rome: Editrice Nazionale M.I., 1997) #631 (1163).

162 Cf. Jean-Louis Barré 15.

163 Cf. *Theotokos* 219; H. Barré, "Spiritualité Mariale du Vénérable Père Libermann," *Maria* III:379–401.

164 *Theotokos* 219; cf. Michael O'Carroll, C.S.Sp., *Veni Creator Spiritus: A Theological Encyclopedia of the Holy Spirit* (Collegeville, MN: The Liturgical Press "A Michael Glazier Book," 1990) 136–38; Paul Sigrist, "Libermann (François-Marie-Paul)," *DSp* 9:764–80.

It would take us beyond our immediate scope to detail all the modern congregations in the Church in which Marian consecration constitutes an integral part of their charism. Instead, we will simply note here the impetus for Marian consecration among the faithful which spread almost like wildfire from the courageous response of the Abbé Desgenettes to the interior words which he heard telling him to consecrate his parish to the Immaculate Heart of Mary on 3 December 1836. His moribund Parisian parish of Notre-Dame des Victoires became almost overnight a vibrant center of Christian faith and worship and, through the establishment of the Archconfraternity of the Most Holy and Immaculate Heart of Mary, a catalyst for thousands of conversions.[165] It is also fascinating to note that Saint John Mary Vianney (1786–1859), the holy Curé of Ars, had already consecrated his parish to "Mary conceived without sin" a few months earlier on 1 May 1836.[166]

In the ways of Providence, the happenings at the Church of Notre-Dame des Victoires would come to be known within nine years to Saint Anthony Mary Claret (1807–1870),[167] who already had a deep and tender filial devotion to Mary. So impressed was he with what he read in the *Annals* of the Archconfraternity that he renamed a secular institute which he had founded "Daughters of the Most Holy and Immaculate Heart of Mary."[168] Eventually, under the same inspiration, he would also

165 Jean Letourneur, "Dufriche-Desgenettes," *DSp* 3:1757–59.

166 Cf. Francis Trochu, *The Curé of Ars: St. Jean-Marie-Baptiste Vianney* trans. Dom Ernest Graf, O.S.B. (Rockford, Illinois: Tan Books and Publishers, Inc., 1977) 306, n. 4. This act was explicitly referred to in Pope Benedict XVI's Letter Proclaiming a Year for Priests of 16 June 2009 and in Pope Saint John XXIII's Encyclical, *Sacerdotii Nostri Primordia*, of 1 August 1959; cf. Frederick L. Miller, *The Grace of Ars* (San Francisco: Ignatius Press, 2010) 137, 201. Pope Saint John Paul II also made reference to this same act in his address to priests, deacons and seminarians at Ars on 6 October 1986; cf. *Inseg* IX/2 (1986) 904 [*ORE* 962:9].

167 Cf. *Theotokos* 103; Naracisse García Garcés, C.M.F., "La Dévotion a la très Sainte Vierge dans la Congrégation des Missionnaires Fils du Cœur Immaculé de Marie," *Maria* III:403–428.

168 Juan Maria Lozano, C.M.F., *Mystic and Man of Action: Saint Anthony Mary Claret*, trans. Joseph Daries, C.M.F. (Chicago: Claretian Publications, 1977) 141; cf.

found a congregation of missionaries which he would call "Sons of the Immaculate Heart of Mary" and would give the name as well to a congregation for Christian doctrine that he founded in Cuba.[169] Early in his priestly life he had written: "I entrust myself totally to Mary, as her son and priest. ... Everything I do or suffer in my ministry will be done for her."[170] Later he made the consecration to the Immaculate Heart of Mary part of the ceremony of joining his missionary congregation.[171] For him, according to Father Lozano, being a Son of the Immaculate Heart of Mary meant being an instrument of the Virgin in her struggle against Satan.[172] For him, consecration to Mary has a definitely apostolic thrust because

> the mystery of Mary Immaculate, as he sees it, is not so much a mystery of beauty as it is of power. In his view, the Immaculate Virgin is the Lady of Victories, the Strong Woman who, because she was never bitten by the serpent, has kept all her forces intact to crush his head. The Saint moves, then, within a perspective drawn from the "protoevangelium" of Genesis 3:15 and the twelfth chapter of the *Apocalypse*.[173]
>
> But just as the devil avails himself of his "seed," the wicked, so the Blessed Virgin makes use of apostles whom she has chosen and formed especially to combat him. He demonstrated this historically in his very first sermon on the Heart of Mary, showing how, throughout the history of the church, the Blessed Virgin has answered each new

---

Julio Aramendia, C.F.M., "Claret (Bienheureux Antoine-Marie)," *DSp* 2:932–37.

169 Lozano 144.

170 Lozano 141.

171 Lozano 142.

172 Lozano 140.

173 This perspective is also notable in the thought of John Paul II. Three times in the course of his Encyclical, *Redemptoris Mater*, he links Genesis 3:15 to Revelation 12, speaking of Mary as "the woman" of the *Protoevangelium* and of the Apocalypse who symbolizes and "incarnates" in herself the struggle against evil and the victory over it. Cf. #11, 24, 47 [*Inseg* X/1 (1987) 689–90; 706–07; 738]; cf. also the Prayer at the Piazza di Spagna on the Solemnity of the Immaculate Conception 1991, *Inseg* XIV/2 1991) 1344–1345 [*ORE* 1220:5].

> heresy with a special intervention of her own. The last such interventions, he remarks, were the manifestation of her Heart at the Church of Notre-Dame des Victoires, in Paris, and in the foundation of her Congregation.[174]

Saint Maximilian-Maria Kolbe

The notion of Marian consecration as equipping one to be a soldier of Christ in the battle with the powers of darkness (cf. Eph. 6:12) became ever stronger in the twentieth century. We just heard it sounded above in Saint Anthony Mary Claret, and we know it had been prophesied by Saint Louis-Marie Grignion de Montfort, that Mary would have a special role to play in the latter times [*les derniers temps*][175] and that those especially consecrated to her would have a decisive role to play in the battle waged by the enemy.[176] A striking figure who incarnates these ideals is Saint Maximilian-Maria Kolbe (1894–1941),[177] the founder of the *Militia Immaculatæ*.

The Saint would later relate that, as a young minor seminarian, he felt so impelled to enter into battle in the service of Our Lady that

> bowing his face to the floor before the altar of the Immaculata during Mass one day he promised her that he would fight for her. Although at that time he did not know how he was to do this, he thought of his "battle" as a material and bloody one. The military life and career, for which he had an obvious inclination, appeared to him to

---

174 Lozano 135.

175 *Treatise on True Devotion* #49–59 [God Alone 303–307].

176 *Treatise on True Devotion* #56–57 [*God Alone* 306]. Not inappropriately, John Paul II has been proposed as one of these. Cf. "Il Papa Giovanni Paolo II tra gli 'apostoli degli ultimi tempi'," *Spiritualità Monfortana* 6 (Rome: Centre International Montfortain, 2006) 9–19.

177 Cf. *Theotokos* 214–215; Alessandro M. Apollonio, F.I., *Mariologia Francescana: Da san Francesco d'Assisi ai Francescani dell'Immacolata* (Rome: Dissertationes ad Lauream in Pontificia Facultate Theologica "Marianum," 1997) 109–196.

> be in perfect harmony with that of a knight devoted to his Lady.[178]

On 16 October 1917, three days after the final apparition of Our Lady in Fatima and a few months before his priestly ordination, Maximilian, together with six other Conventual Franciscan colleagues, founded the *Militia Immaculatæ*. It was in direct response to Masonic demonstrations which had been held in Saint Peter's Square where banners were carried depicting Saint Michael the Archangel being crushed by Lucifer bearing slogans such as, "The devil will govern in the Vatican and the Pope will act as Swiss Guard for him."[179] By this time, Maximilian had discovered how he would engage in the battle as Our Lady's "knight."

His ideal was chivalrous, but eminently practical: he and his companions would consecrate themselves totally to Our Lady in order to be instruments in her hands for the extension of the Kingdom of the Heart of Jesus. Here is how he explained the rationale for the *Militia* and its consecration to one of his confreres a few years after its foundation, distinguishing it from the Confraternity of the Miraculous Medal headquartered in Paris:

> In regard to the confraternity from Paris, it limits itself to prayer alone, while the M.I., although it employs prayer as its main weapon, nevertheless immerses itself in action with all the means that circumstances permit … Moreover, we consecrate ourselves to the Immaculate without reserve and that constitutes the essence of the M.I.; the Parisian Association doesn't have this. All our sufferings, deeds, thoughts, words, action, life, death, eternity and all of us are always the irrevocable possession (what a delight!) of the Immaculate Queen of heaven and earth. So even when we are not thinking of it (as we like to reflect on it)

178 Antonio Ricciardi, O.F.M. Conv., *St. Maximilian Kolbe: Apostle of Our Difficult Age*, trans. Daughters of St. Paul (Boston: St. Paul Editions, 1982) 27.

179 *Scritti* #1277 (2261–2262); #1278 (2265); #1328 (2340).

> she directs every one of our actions, prearranges all the circumstances, repairs the damage from our falls and leads us lovingly toward heaven, and through us she is pleased to implant good ideas, sentiments and examples everywhere in order to save souls and lead them to the good Jesus. There is, therefore, a beautiful difference.[180]

Maximilian subsequently became familiar with de Montfort and saw the movement that he founded as a means of fulfilling his prophecy on the latter times,[181] and was also conscious of standing in the great tradition of Marian slavery. Although he did not employ the word with the frequency of de Montfort, he leaves no doubt about its implications in the following text:

> You belong to her as her own property. Let her do with you what she wishes. Do not let her feel herself bound by any restrictions following from the obligations a mother has towards her own son. Be hers, her property; let her make free use of you and dispose of you without any limits, for whatever purpose she wishes.
>
> Let her be your owner, your Lady and absolute Queen. A servant sells his labor; you, on the contrary, offer yours as a gift: your fatigue, your suffering, all that is yours. Beg her not to pay attention to your free will, but to act towards you always and in full liberty as she desires.
>
> Be her son, her servant, her slave of love, in every way and under whatever formulation yet devised or which can be devised now or in the future. In a word, be all hers.
>
> Be her soldier so that others may become ever more perfectly hers, like you yourself, and even more than you; so that all those who live and will live all over the world may work together with her in her struggle against the infernal serpent.
>
> Belong to the Immaculate so that your conscience, becoming ever purer, may be purified still more, become

180 *Scritti* #56 (379) [trans. in Anselm W. Romb, O.F.M. Conv., *The Kolbe Reader* (Libertyville, Illinois: Franciscan Marytown Press, 1987) 15] emphasis my own.

181 *Scritti* #1129 (1980) [Romb 36–39].

> immaculate as she is for Jesus, so that you too may become a mother and conqueror of hearts for her.[182]

Standing in the great tradition, which we have been sketching, Maximilian brings a note of urgency about the battle, Mary's "struggle against the infernal serpent" (cf. Gen. 3:15) and, hence, the all-consuming goal of his life was to mobilize an army, a militia completely at her disposal. This is clearly illustrated in the official Act of Consecration for the Militia Immaculatæ:

> If it pleases you, use all that I am and have without reserve, wholly to accomplish what was said of you: "She will crush your head," and, "You alone have destroyed all heresies in the whole world." Let me be a fit instrument in your immaculate and merciful hands for introducing and increasing your glory to the maximum in all the many strayed and indifferent souls, and thus help extend as far as possible the blessed kingdom of the most Sacred Heart of Jesus. For wherever you enter you obtain the grace of conversion and growth in holiness, since it is through your hands that all graces come to us from the most Sacred Heart of Jesus.[183]

In the doctrine and practice of Saint Maximilian, the practice of Marian consecration and the worship of the Eucharist were inseparable, as Father Peter Damian Fehlner rightly points out in his foreword in *For the Life of the World: Saint Maximilian and the Eucharist*:

> Since there is so intimate and unbreakable a link between consecration to the Immaculate and sharing in the sacrificial consecration of Jesus as victim on the Cross, it is only logical that our progress in perfection and our growth in holiness should be facilitated by our conscious and deliberate affirmation of the consecration to His Mother our dying Savior made of the Church and of every believer

182 *Scritti* #1334 (2361) [Romb 194] emphasis my own.

183 *Scritti* #37 (345–346); #1329 (2345–2346); #1331 (2351) [Romb 159–60] emphasis my own.

> (cf. Jn. 19:25–27) and which the present Vicar of Christ repeats wherever he visits.
>
> Love of the Word Incarnate, and therefore of the Eucharist, is not genuine if not sacrificial. Such a love had the Immaculate Virgin throughout her life, nowhere more so than at the foot of the Cross, for the conversion and salvation of souls. Hence the link between consecration to the Immaculate and participation in the mystery of the Cross—the sacrifice for the life of the world—in the struggle for souls between the Woman and her Seed on the one hand and serpent and his brood on the other.[184]

In the course of Father Domański's suggestive book, many of the interdependent dynamics of Saint Maximilian's Eucharistic and Marian spirituality are noted. While it is not possible to work out the implications here, it is fascinating to note that de Montfort's doctrine links Marian consecration to Baptism; Chaminade's doctrine links Marian consecration at least implicitly to Confirmation; and Kolbe's, in various ways, to the Eucharist. Thus, consecration to Our Lady—according to these three Marian Saints and many others—may be understood as the most profound way of living out the three Sacraments of Christian initiation. At every step in the Christian life, Mary is there to encourage, strengthen and guide with her motherly help the one who entrusts himself to her. We will continue to see how Saint John Paul II would draw out these realities.

It is particularly interesting to note how fully Saint John Paul II identified with the Marian spirituality and the Marian consecration of Saint Maximilian. In his homily on 4 June 1979 at Częstochowa preceding his entrustment of Poland on his first trip there after his election as Pope, he stated:

> Everything *through Mary*. This is the authentic interpretation of the presence of the Mother of God in the mystery of Christ and of the Church, as is proclaimed by

184 Jerzy Domański, O.F.M. Conv., *For the Life of the World: Saint Maximilian and the Eucharist* (New Bedford, MA: Academy of the Immaculate, 1993) 11–12.

> Chapter VIII of the Constitution *Lumen Gentium*. This interpretation corresponds to the tradition of the saints, such as Bernard of Clairvaux, Grignion de Montfort and Maximilian Kolbe.[185]

In his prayer at the Shrine of Our Lady of the Miraculous Medal in Paris on 31 May 1980, John Paul made a graceful reference to Maximilian's visit to that same Marian shrine before he began his mission in Japan exactly fifty years before.[186] Likewise his Prayer of Entrustment of the Church of Japan to Our Lady in the Conventual Franciscan Church of the Immaculate in Nagasaki, Japan, made very explicit references to the missionary zeal of Maximilian and his profound love of the Immaculate.[187] One of the great moments of his pontificate was the canonization of Saint Maximilian as a "martyr of charity" on 10 October 1982. In the homily on that occasion the Pope stated that "The inspiration of his [Maximilian's] whole life was *the Immaculate Virgin*, to whom he entrusted his love for Christ and his desire for martyrdom."[188] The next day, in his address to Polish pilgrims, he said: "See what the man who absolutely entrusted himself to Christ through the Immaculate is capable of!"[189]

Now let us pay particular attention to Saint John Paul's words about Saint Maximilian's consecration to the Immaculate. On 26 February 1994 he addressed these words to Conventual Franciscan student friars commemorating the 100th anniversary of Saint Maximilian's birth:

> Fr. Maximilian Mary Kolbe, born on 8 January 1894 in Zdunska Wola, Poland, was a shining figure because of *the strong love with which he consecrated his life to the Immaculate Virgin and because of the heroic gift of his life*

185 *Inseg* II/1 (1979) 1415 [*Poland* 107].

186 *Inseg* III/1 (1980) 1545 [*France* 54].

187 *Inseg* IV/1 (1981) 569–570 [*Far East* 321–322].

188 *Inseg* V/3 (1982) 755 [*ORE* 755:1].

189 *Inseg* V/3 (1982) 789 [*ORE* 756:12 alt.].

> for his brothers, that sacrifice which led him to his terrible death in the bunker of Auschwitz. He remains with us as a *prophet and a sign of the new era, the era of the civilization of love.*
>
> Even as a cleric at the Seraphicum College here in Rome, he tried to share with his fellow students the radical nature of consecration to the Immaculate Virgin, urging them to be soldiers of her who was given to us as the dawn which precedes the rising Sun that saves, Christ the Lord.[190]

On 15 June 2000, he addressed the Chapter of Franciscan Sisters of the Immaculate in this way:

> St. Maximilian Kolbe's entire life was inspired by the Immaculate. Your institute is dedicated to her and in addition to the three traditional religious vows, includes a "Marian" vow by which each religious consecrates herself totally to Mary for the coming of Christ's kingdom in the world. …
>
> Stand at the foot of the Cross with Mary, the Immaculate Virgin to whom your religious family is consecrated![191]

Just a few days later, on 19 June 2000, the Pope addressed the General Assembly of Fr. Kolbe's Missionaries of the Immaculate with another strong exhortation to live the Kolbean Marian consecration to the full:

> As I join in your thanksgiving to God for the road you have travelled so far, I hope that the General Assembly will be a favourable occasion for you to reflect ever more deeply on your spirituality of total consecration to the Immaculate, following the example of St. Maximilian Kolbe, the martyr of Auschwitz. …
>
> Your institute is distinguished by its *Marian charism* drawn from the teachings and example of St. Maximilian Kolbe, whose love for the Immaculate is well known. He sensed that the mystery of the Immaculate contains the

190 *Inseg* XVII/1 (1994) 544–545 [*ORE* 1332:10].

191 *Inseg* XXIII/1 (2000) 1103, 1104 [*ORE* 1649:5].

> profound synthesis of the misfortune of original sin, the tragic story which ensued for sinful humanity and the divine plan of salvation which culminated in the Word becoming incarnate in the Blessed Virgin's womb. Spurred by this inner certainty, Fr. Kolbe urged that the truth about the Immaculate be sown in the heart of every man and woman, so that the Blessed Virgin—as he said—would be able to establish the throne of her Son in everyone by bringing each person to a deeper knowledge and love of the Gospel. He also observed that when we consecrate ourselves to the Immaculate, we become instruments of divine mercy in her hands, as she herself was in God's hands. And he urged people to let Mary take them by the hand and lead them, walking "calmly and securely under her guidance."[192]

Finally, on 18 September 2001, the Holy Father addressed a letter to Father Eugenio Galignano, O.F.M. Conv., on the occasion of the International Kolbe Congress at the Seraphicum, in which he stated

> From his youth he [St. Maximilian] wanted to belong unreservedly to Mary, she whom God had thought of from all eternity, the Mother of the Son. The Blessed Virgin was the creature who knew better than anyone how to embrace the plan of redemption that the Most Blessed Trinity willed, in Christ, for all humanity. "How many mysteries about Jesus—wrote St. Maximilian—the Divine Spirit, living and working in you, must have revealed only and exclusively to your immaculate soul" (*SK*, 1236).
>
> He strongly believed that the person who is close to Mary is docile to the breath of the Paraclete, knows how to receive his inspiration and can adhere fully to Christ. He seems to suggest that whoever wants to know and preach the Gospel should draw close to the Immaculata with confidence, because She intimately knew the mysteries of the Son of God. …

192 *Inseg* XXIII/1 (2000) 1134–1135, 1136 [*ORE* 1652:7].

> Fr. Kolbe has left this heritage to his confreres, the Friars Minor Conventual, and, through their efforts and their witness, to the whole Christian community. The Militia of the Immaculate, founded by him and recently recognized as a public and international Association of the faithful, has made this consecration to Mary its own in a special way, so that the Gospel may continue to be preached generously to all and be a light for all humanity.[193]

It should be noted that, in each of these texts, the Pope spoke or wrote unabashedly about Marian "consecration." Even though, as we shall see, he used the term "entrustment" even more frequently to express "belonging entirely to the Mother of God," he saw absolutely no difficulty in using the terminology of "consecration," hallowed by five hundred years of use in the Church and utilized by Saint Maximilian-Marian Kolbe.

Standing also in this great spiritual tradition of Marian consecration as equipping one for active service in the Church Militant was the Servant of God Frank Duff (1889–1980).[194] In 1918, after being challenged to a rereading of de Montfort's *Treatise on True Devotion*, which he had initially considered as "wildly extravagant," Duff tells us

> the sudden realization came to me that the book was true, a complete conviction that what I had been regarding as exaggerated and unreal was fully justified. The excesses, which I thought I found in the book were really deficiencies in myself, wide gaps of knowledge and comprehension.[195]

In the wake of a discussion on that book by a Dublin conference of the Saint Vincent de Paul Society four years later on 7 September 1921, the Legion of Mary was born,[196] and Duff insisted that "the starting of the Legion was divinely held up for several years

193 *Inseg* XXIV/2 (2001) 340, 341[*ORE* 1713:12].

194 Cf. *Theotokos* 125; O'Carroll, *Veni Creator Spiritus* 73–74.

195 Robert Bradshaw, *Frank Duff: Founder of the Legion of Mary* (Bay Shore, N.Y.: Montfort Publications, 1985) 55.

196 Bradshaw 67–68.

until de Montfort had provided the soil or atmosphere in which the Legion could take life."[197] The apostolate of the Legion, which has been responsible for remarkable works of charity and evangelization since its foundation, is built on a promise addressed to the Holy Spirit in which the legionary declares himself to be the "soldier and child" of Mary and prays:

> Let thy power overshadow me, and come into my soul with fire and love, And make it one with Mary's love and Mary's will to save the world; So that I may be pure in her who was made Immaculate by Thee; So that Christ my lord may likewise grow in me through Thee; So that I with her, His Mother, may bring Him to the world and to the souls who need Him; So that they and I, the battle won, may reign with her for ever in the glory of the Blessed Trinity.[198]

In this same spirit the 1961 edition of *The Official Handbook of the Legion of Mary* devotes an entire section to "the duty of legionaries towards Mary"[199] and commends in particular the consecration of Saint Louis de Montfort.[200]

These historical considerations, far from being exhaustive or constituting a definitive study of Marian consecration in the life of the Church, nonetheless illustrate a remarkable consistency and convergence in the practice of placing one's life, one's work and the apostolate itself in the hands of Mary.[201] Apart from the pontifical acts of consecration that we will study next, the

197 Frank Duff, *The Woman of Genesis* (Dublin: Praedicanda Publications, 1976) 73; cf. also 75.

198 *The Official Handbook of the Legion of Mary* (Dublin: Concilium Legionis Mariae, 1961) 52–53.

199 128–147.

200 142–147.

201 Besides the articles on the subject in *Theotokos* and *NDM*, further helpful summaries of the history of Marian consecration may be found in J. Laurenceau, O.P., "Aperçus sur l'histoire de la consécration à Marie," *Cahiers Marials* 137 (1 avril 1983) 66–84; W. G. Most, "Marian Consecration as Service: Historical, Theological and Spiritual Reflections," *Miles Immaculatæ* 24 (1988) 443–445 and Alessandro M. Apollonio, F.I., "La consacrazione a Maria," *Immaculata Mediatrix* I:3 (2001) 49–101.

Church's cumulative wisdom on Marian consecration in the spiritual journey of the Church might be seen as summarized in two magisterial texts. The first is the laconic but nonetheless lapidary statement made in the Second Vatican Council's Decree on the Apostolate of the Laity:

> Everyone should have a genuine devotion to her [Mary] and entrust his life to her motherly care.[202]

The second is contained in Pope Saint John Paul II's Marian Year Encyclical, *Redemptoris Mater*, #48:

> Marian *spirituality*, like its corresponding *devotion*, finds a very rich source in the historical experience of individuals and of the various Christian communities present among the different peoples and nations of the world. In this regard, I would like to recall, among the many witnesses and teachers of this spirituality, the figure of Saint Louis Marie Grignion de Montfort, who proposes consecration to Christ through the hands of Mary, as an effective means for Christians to live faithfully their baptismal commitments. I am pleased to note that in our own time too new manifestations of this spirituality and devotion are not lacking.[203]

As one thoroughly formed in the tradition of this spirituality of Marian consecration, John Paul was ever deepening and developing its major lines, as we have seen here and as we will continue to see.

202 "Hanc devotissime colant omnes suamque vitam atque apostolatum eius maternae curae commendent." *AA* #4.

203 *Inseg* X/1 (1987) 739 [St. Paul edition 68].

CHAPTER TWO

The Papal Magisterium and Papal Acts of Consecration

If, as we have just seen, Pope Saint John Paul II was the heir of the great ecclesial tradition of Marian consecration, manifested in various ways in the course of the Church's millennial tradition, he might be said to be even more explicitly the successor of the legacy of papal consecration to the Hearts of Jesus and Mary.[1] In his handling of the history of "devotional" consecration, Jungmann rightly sees the necessity of reckoning with the phenomenon of consecration to the Sacred Heart of Jesus as intimately related to the consecration to Mary and her Immaculate Heart.[2] Of necessity this leads us to a brief consideration here of the meaning of the term "heart" as the object of consecration and the historical background of these pontifical acts of consecration.

It might be fairly said that the impetus for consecration to the Hearts of Jesus and Mary stems from Saint John Eudes and is expressed in his prayer, *Ave Cor Sanctissimum*, which he addressed jointly to the Hearts of Jesus and Mary as *Cor amantissimum Jesu*

1 Cf. Arthur Burton Calkins, "The Cultus of the Hearts of Jesus and Mary in the Papal Magisterium from Pius IX to Pius XII," *Acta Congressus Mariologici-Mariani Internationalis in Sanctuario Mariano Kevelaer (Germania) Anno 1987 Celebrati* II: *De Cultu Mariano Saeculis XIX et XX usque ad Concilium Vaticanum II Studia Indolis Generalioris* (Rome: Pontificia Academia Mariana Internationalis, 1991) 355–392; "The Hearts of Jesus and Mary in the Magisterium of Pope John Paul II," *Acta Congressus Mariologici-Mariani Internationalis in Civitate Onubensi (Huelva - Hispania) Anno 1992 Celebrati* IV: *De Cultu Mariano Saeculo XX a Concilio Vaticano II usque ad Nostros Dies* (Vatican City State: Pontificia Academia Mariana Internationalis, 1999) 147–167.

2 Cf. Jungmann 307–14. While Jungmann's enumeration of the principal facts is valuable, that cannot be said for his grasp of their theological import.

et Mariæ. He conceived of the two as "one heart" in terms of the text in the Acts of the Apostles 4:32 and thus prayed: To you we offer, we give, we consecrate, we immolate our heart [*Tibi cor nostrum offerimus, donamus, consecramus, immolamus*].[3] Clearly, the Saint and the subsequent ecclesial tradition understood the heart as the most apt symbol of the love of Jesus and of Mary[4] so that the heart is ultimately equivalent to the person, a theological application of the figure of speech known as synecdoche.[5]

The human heart as a natural symbol—and, indeed, there is much to be said in favor of seeing it as the preeminent symbol of the person[6]—evokes many levels of meaning; these become immeasurably enriched from the supernatural perspective. Let us listen to what Pope John Paul II refers to as "the richness of anthropological resonance ... that the word 'heart' awakens." In a remarkable homily given on 28 June 1984 at the Gemelli Polyclinic[7] and Faculty of Medicine in Rome, he said:

> This word [heart] evokes not only sentiments proper to the affective sphere, but also all those memories, thoughts, reasonings, plans, that make up man's innermost world. The heart in biblical culture, and also in a large part of other cultures, is that essential center of the personality in which man stands before God as the totality of body and soul, as I who am thinking, willing and loving, as the

3 Saint John Eudes, *The Sacred Heart of Jesus*, trans. Richard Flower, O.S.B. (New York: P. J. Kenedy & Sons, 1946) 173–74. For a discussion of the "conjoint" cultus of the Hearts of Jesus and Mary, cf. Arthur Burton Calkins, "The Union of the Hearts of Jesus and Mary in St. Francis de Sales and St. John Eudes," *Miles Immaculatæ* 25 (1989) 454–95.

4 On the heart as the natural symbol of the person and the application of this symbolism to the Hearts of Jesus and Mary, cf. Arthur Burton Calkins, "Why the Heart?" *Homiletic & Pastoral Review* 89:9 (June 1989) 18–23.

5 Cf. Louis Verheylezoon, S.J., *Devotion to the Sacred Heart: Object, Ends, Practice, Motives*. First edition, 1955 (Rockford, Illinois: Tan Books and Publishers, Inc., 1978) 29.

6 Cf. *Études Carmélitaines: Le Cœur* (Paris: Desclée de Brouwer, 1950).

7 It was in this hospital that the Pope recuperated from the attempt made on his life and underwent surgery on several other occasions.

center in which the memory of the past opens up to the planning of the future.

Certainly, the human heart that interests the anatomist, the physiologist, the cardiologist, the surgeon, etc., and their scientific contribution—I am happy to acknowledge in such a place as this—takes on great importance for the serene and harmonious development of man in the course of his earthly existence. But the significance, according to which we now refer to the heart, transcends these partial considerations to reach the sanctuary of personal self-awareness in which is summarized and, so to speak, condensed the concrete essence of man, the center in which the individual decides on himself in the face of others, the world, and God himself.

Only of man can it be properly said that *he has a heart.* It cannot be said, obviously, of a pure spirit, nor even of an animal. The *redire ad cor* ('returning to the heart') from the scattering of multiple external experiences is a possibility reserved uniquely to man.[8]

This brief consideration of the "anthropological resonance" of the word "heart" provides an appropriate preamble to considering the Sacred Heart of Jesus as a symbol. In what is perhaps the single most important passage in his monumental Encyclical Letter, *Haurietis Aquas*, the Venerable Pope Pius XII taught authoritatively about the aptness of the Heart of Jesus as a symbol and the various levels of its symbolism:

The Heart of the Incarnate Word is deservedly and rightly considered the chief sign and symbol of that threefold love with which the divine Redeemer unceasingly loves His eternal Father and all mankind.

It is a symbol of that *divine love* which He shares with the Father and the Holy Spirit but which He, the Word made flesh, alone manifests through a weak and perishable body, since "in Him dwells the fullness of the Godhead bodily" (Col. 2:9).

8 *Inseg* VII/1 (1984) 1974–1975 [*ORE* 843:9].

> It is, besides, the symbol of that *burning love which, infused into His soul*, enriches the human will of Christ and enlightens and governs its acts by the most perfect knowledge derived both from the beatific vision and that which is directly infused.
>
> And finally—and this in a more natural and direct way—it is the symbol also of *sensible love*, since the body of Jesus Christ, formed by the Holy Spirit, in the womb of the Virgin Mary, possesses full powers of feelings and perception, in fact, more so than any other human body.[9]

Saint John Paul II, standing within the great dogmatic tradition so carefully developed and consolidated by the magisterial teaching of Pius XII, presents the Heart of Jesus as a symbol in terms of his own unique anthropological insights:

> From our faith we know that at a determined time in history, "the Word became flesh and made his dwelling among us" (Jn. 1:14). From that moment *God began to love with a human heart*, a true heart capable of beating in an intense, tender and impassioned way. The Heart of Jesus has truly experienced feelings of joy before the splendor of nature, the candor of children, the glance of a pure young man; feelings of friendship toward the Apostles, Lazarus, the disciples; feelings of compassion for the sick, the poor, the many persons tried by struggle, by loneliness, by sin, feelings of anguish before the prospect of suffering and the mystery of death. There is no authentically human feeling that the Heart of Jesus did not experience …
>
> Of the infinite power that is proper to God, the Heart of Christ kept only the defenseless power of the love that forgives. And in the radical loneliness of the Cross, he accepted being pierced by the centurion's lance so that from the open wound there might pour out upon the

9 *AAS* 48 (1956) 327–328; Francis Larkin, SS.CC. (ed.), *Haurietis Aquas: The Sacred Heart Encyclical of Pope Pius XII* (Orlando, Florida: Sacred Heart Publications Center, 1974) 23–24 (emphasis mine). The statement has been deemed so important from a dogmatic perspective that it has been included in the more recent editions of Denzinger's *Enchiridion Symbolorum*, an authoritative, but unofficial collection of documents of the magisterium, cf. *D-H* #3924.

> world's ugly deeds the inexhaustible torrent of a mercy that washes, purifies and renews.
>
> In the Heart of Christ, therefore, there meet divine richness and human poverty, the power of grace and the frailty of nature, an appeal from God and a response from man. In the Heart of Christ the history of mankind has its definitive place of arrival, because "the Father has assigned all judgment to the Son" (Jn. 5:22). *Therefore, willing or not, every human heart must refer to the Heart of Christ.*[10]

The texts that we have just cited on the Heart of Jesus cannot simply be predicated of the Heart of Mary without any further qualification. This is so because the Heart of Jesus is a human symbol of a Divine Person, whereas the Heart of Mary is the symbol of a human creature. Nonetheless, in an analogous way, which keeps this distinction in mind, Mary's Immaculate Heart is also the uniquely appropriate symbol of her person. Hence the decree of the Sacred Congregation of Rites establishing the Feast of the Immaculate Heart of Mary states:

> With this devotion the Church renders the honor due to the Immaculate Heart of the Blessed Virgin Mary, since under the symbol of this heart she venerates with reverence the eminent and singular holiness of the Mother of God and especially her most ardent love for God and Jesus her Son and moreover her maternal compassion for all those redeemed by the divine Blood.[11]

If, then, the Heart of Jesus evokes the whole mystery of the God-Man, the Heart of Mary likewise calls to mind her motherhood of Christ and of the Church, as well as her altogether unique role in the work of our salvation.

10 *Inseg* VII/1 (1984) 1975–1976 [*ORE* 843:9] (final emphasis my own).

11 Decree of 4 May 1944, *AAS* 37 (1945) 50 [English translation in *ORE* 959:12].

Movements in favor of Consecration to the Hearts of Jesus and Mary

From about the time of the beatification of Saint Margaret Mary Alacoque (1647–1690) in 1864, a groundswell in favor of the consecration of the world to the Sacred Heart of Jesus and the consecration of the world to the Immaculate Heart of Mary began to gain momentum. Each initiative seems to have been an independent, even if complementary one. As far as I have been able to determine, the earliest would appear to have been that promoting the consecration of the world to the Immaculate Heart of Mary. It was in the form of a petition presented to Blessed Pope Pius IX in 1864 by Cardinal Gousset of Rheims and supported by Archbishop de la Tour-d'Auvergne of Bourges, Bishop Mermillod and other Bishops of France and Spain.[12]

Both movements surfaced in the course of the First Vatican Council (1869–70). The Archbishop of Bourges strove to win the support of all the Council Fathers for the consecration to Mary's Heart, first requested six years earlier, and for the establishment of a feast in honor of her Queenship.[13] During the same period, Père Henri Ramière, S.J. (1821–1884), the great animator of the Apostleship of Prayer,[14] who was serving as *peritus* to the Archbishop of Beauvais,

> submitted to the Bishops present in Rome a request whereby the Holy Father was asked … to consecrate the whole Church to the Sacred Heart [of Jesus]. The request was already supported by two hundred and seventy-two

12 Cf. G. Geenen, O.P., "Les Antécédents Doctrinaux et Historiques de la Consécration du Monde au Cœur Immaculé de Marie," *Maria* I:863; Gabriele Roschini, O.S.M., "La Consacrazione del Mondo al Cuore Immacolato di Maria" in *Il Cuore Immacolato di Maria, Settimana di Studi Mariani* (Rome: Edizioni Marianum, 1946) 56.

13 Geenen 863.

14 Cf. Gérald de Becker, SS.CC., *Lexique Pour la Théologie du Cœur du Christ* (Paris: Editions Téqui, 1975) 295–96; Pierre Vallin, "Ramière (Henri)," *DSp* 13:63–70.

> Bishops when the Franco-German war broke out and the Council was adjourned.[15]

Notwithstanding the volatile political situation in much of Western Europe after the constrained adjournment of the Council, the drive for the consecration to the Sacred Heart of Jesus gained momentum with the approach of the second centenary of the "great revelation" of the Lord made to Saint Margaret Mary in 1675.[16] Cardinal Desprez, the Archbishop of Toulouse, addressed a letter to all the Catholic Bishops in the world in 1874, to which a new petition was attached; and in April of 1875, Père Ramière presented the petition to Pius IX together with the names of the 534 Bishops and 23 Superiors General who subscribed to it.[17]

Consecration of the Human Race to the Sacred Heart of Jesus

In response to Père Ramière, Blessed Pius IX said, "I shall do what you want, but in my own way."[18] He then instructed the Sacred Congregation of Rites to prepare a formula of consecration that he himself approved and had published along with an invitation to Catholics throughout the world to unite in consecrating themselves to the Sacred Heart of Jesus.[19] The Holy Father invited all to choose for this special act of consecration the 16th of June 1875, the second centenary of the best known and arguably most important of the apparitions of Christ to

15 Verheylezoon 143.

16 Cf. Monseigneur François-Léon Gauthey (ed.), *Vie et Œuvres de Sainte Marguerite-Marie Alacoque* (Paris: Ancienne Librairie Poussielgue, 1920) 2:103 [Margaret Williams, R.S.C.J., *The Sacred Heart in the Life of the Church* (NY: Sheed and Ward, 1957) 116–117].

17 Arthur R. McGratty, S.J., *The Sacred Heart Yesterday and Today* (New York: Benziger Brothers, Inc., 1951) 222–224.

18 Verheylezoon 143.

19 The Latin decree and the Act of Consecration in Italian are published in *ASS* 8 (1874–1875) 402–404. An English translation of the prayer is found in *The Treasury of the Sacred Heart* (New York: D. & J. Sadlier & Co., 1879) 330–334.

Saint Margaret Mary at Paray-le-Monial.[20] The consecration was solemnly made in churches throughout the world on that date while the Pope himself made it in his private chapel,[21] but not publicly in the Vatican Basilica as the petition had asked.[22]

In 1891, during the pontificate of Leo XIII, a vast movement surfaced in Italy, led by the Cardinal Archbishops of Milan and Turin, in favor of the consecration of the dioceses of Italy to the Most Holy Heart of Mary.[23] It was at the Marian Congress of Turin in September of 1898 that this *votum* was given concrete form, and that was primarily due, it appears, to the initiative of the Pope himself in his Brief, *Mariani Coetus*, of 2 August 1898.[24] The project of the Archbishop of Turin was unanimously approved by the Congress, which petitioned the Holy Father for the consecration of Italy to the Most Holy Heart of Mary by means of a formula adopted at the Congress.[25] By a rescript of 12 December 1898, the Sacred Congregation of Rites approved the proposed formula not only for those dioceses that had requested it, but also for those that would do so in the future.[26]

Earlier in that same year, on 10 June 1898, Blessed Mary of the Divine Heart Droste zu Vischering (1863–1899),[27] a spiritual daughter of Saint John Eudes, had written to Pope Leo XIII that the Lord desired him to consecrate the entire

20 McGratty 224.

21 Verheylezoon 144.

22 McGratty 223.

23 Roschini 56.

24 Geenen 864. For the text of the brief cf. Santino Epis, "La Consacrazione dell' Italia a Maria: Un Capitolo di Storia e un Impegno Permanente," in De Fiores, Epis, Amorth, *La Consacrazione dell'Italia a Maria* (Rome: Edizioni Paoline, 1983) 67–68.

25 Epis 75–77.

26 *ASS* 31 (1898–1899) 538–540.

27 Beatified by Pope Paul VI on 1 November 1975. Cf. de Becker 116–117; Constantin Becker, "Marie du Divin Cœur," *DSp* 10:485–86; Louis Chasle, *Sister Mary of the Divine Heart*, trans. a Member of the Order (London: Burns & Oates, Ltd., 1906); Pierre Cras, "Mother Mary of the Divine Heart: A Divine Messenger," in John J. Sullivan, S.J. (ed. & translation), *Divine Masterpieces* (Paterson, N.J: St. Anthony Guild Press, 1960) 161–184.

human race to the Heart of Jesus. Although deeply touched, he did not immediately act upon the letter. It seems that his first intention was to wait to make the consecration in the Jubilee Year of 1900.[28] The nun began a second letter on the Feast of the Immaculate Conception that year which her confessor only allowed to be dispatched on the Feast of Epiphany in 1899.[29] He was even more deeply moved by this second letter. Then there was a further intervention of Divine Providence. On 1 March 1899, the Pope had to undergo major surgery for a tumor[30] which, given the fact that he was almost ninety years old and that a general anesthetic could not be administered, was most successful.

In gratitude to God, he decided to delay the consecration no longer. He had the question of the theological aspects of the proposed consecration and his authority to consecrate the unbaptized carefully studied.[31] Evidently the principal agent of the study was the Jesuit Cardinal Camillo Mazzella (1833–1900), a noted exponent of the neo-scholastic revival and Prefect of the Congregation of Rites.[32] The Abbé Chasle, commissioned by the Superior General of the Sisters of the Good Shepherd to write the first biography of Blessed Mary of the Divine Heart, benefited from consulting some of the major protagonists involved in this fascinating episode in the Church's history and shared his researches with Leo XIII himself three years after

---

28 Chasle 365–366.

29 Although she was German, she wrote the letter in French. The original text is given in Charles Lebrun, C.J.M., *Le Bienheureux Jean Eudes et le Culte Public du Cœur de Jésus*, deuxième édition (Paris: P. Lethielleux, 1918) 232–236; an English translation is supplied in McGratty 228–230.

30 Cras 182.

31 McGratty 230–231; Cras 181–182.

32 Cf. J. Flynn, "Mazzella, Camillo," *NCE* 9:523–24; on the Cardinal's role in the formulation of the theology of the consecration, cf. also Francesco Degli Esposti, *La Teologia del Sacro Cuore di Gesù da Leone XIII a Pio XII* (Rome: Casa Editrice Herder, 1967) 26–27; 47–48.

Blessed Mary's death.[33] Here is part of his account of the role of the Cardinal Prefect in this matter:

> No one could have given a more favorable testimony than Cardinal Mazzella, S.J., Prefect of the Sacred Congregation of Rites, who knew everything [regarding Mother Mary of the Divine Heart's request for the consecration of the human race to the Sacred Heart of Jesus]; he says: "This is a very touching letter, and certainly appears to have been dictated by Our Lord." At the same time it was agreed that the proofs needed to justify this proposed act should be sought elsewhere. "My Lord Cardinal," Leo XIII said, "take this letter and lay it aside; at the present moment it must not be taken into account." It was therefore resolved that the consecration of the human race to the Sacred Heart should be brought forward, as the consequence of an application of the principles of theology, and of Catholic tradition, and not as the result of any private revelation. The Cardinal left the Vatican commissioned to examine the question *in se*, that is to say, from the point of tradition only, putting aside the supernatural information of the person who had petitioned Leo XIII to take up the matter.[34]

The Cardinal's reply was positive, and on Easter Sunday, 2 April 1899, as Prefect of the Sacred Congregation of Rites, he signed a decree announcing the Pope's intention to consecrate

33 Chasle xxx-xxxi.

34 Chasle 368–369. It should be noted that Pius XII took a similar position vis-à-vis the revelations to Saint Margaret Mary Alacoque in *Haurietis Aquas*: "It must not be said that this devotion has taken its origin from some private revelation of God and has suddenly appeared in the Church; rather, it has blossomed forth of its own accord as a result of that lively faith and burning devotion of men who were endowed with heavenly gifts, and who were drawn towards the adorable Redeemer and His glorious wounds which they saw as irresistible proofs of that unbounded love. Consequently, it is clear that the revelations made to St. Margaret Mary brought nothing new into Catholic doctrine. Their importance lay in this that Christ Our Lord, exposing His Sacred Heart, wished in a quite extraordinary way to invite the minds of men to a contemplation of, and a devotion to, the mystery of God's merciful love for the human race" *AAS* 48 (1956) 340 [Larkin trans. 35–36].

the entire world to the Sacred Heart of Jesus.[35] It is fascinating to note the rather striking parallel between the successful recovery of Leo XIII and the consecration of the world to the Heart of Jesus in 1899, and the recovery of John Paul II and the consecration of the world to the Immaculate Heart of Mary on the first anniversary of the attempt on his life on 13 May 1982.

Thus it was that Pope Leo XIII issued his great Encyclical Letter on consecration to the Sacred Heart of Jesus, *Annum Sacrum*, explaining the rationale of this act and directing that a triduum[36] be held in the principal church of every town and village concluding on the 11th of June 1899, with the recitation of the Act of Consecration of the Human Race to the Sacred Heart of Jesus published along with the Encyclical.[37] Because of the significance of this act, which Leo referred to as "the greatest of my pontificate,"[38] and the Encyclical which carefully developed its rationale, it will be advantageous for us to note some of the underlying theological principles made explicit in it. They will shed considerable light on subsequent papal acts relating to Marian consecration.

The Encyclical carefully outlines the twofold basis for Christ's Kingship over all creatures: His natural right as Son of God and His acquired right as Redeemer of the human race:

> This world-wide and solemn testimony of allegiance and piety is especially appropriate to Jesus Christ, who is the Head and supreme Lord of the race. His empire extends

---

35 *ASS* 31 (1898–1899) 701–702; cf. also Chasle 370–371; Gérald de Becker, SS.CC., *Les Sacrés-Cœurs de Jésus et de Marie: Étude Doctrinale* (Rome: Etude Picpuciennes #5, 1959) 142.

36 Blessed Maria Droste zu Vischering died on 8 June 1899 at the hour of First Vespers of the Feast of the Sacred Heart of Jesus, just before the beginning of the triduum. Cf. Cras 183.

37 *ASS* 31 (1898–1899) 651–652. The prescribed Act of Consecration begins: "Most Sweet Jesus, Redeemer of the Human Race, look down upon us humbly prostrate before Thine Altar ..." and may be found in many manuals of devotion. Cf. *Enchiridion Indulgentiarum – Preces et Pia Opera* [*The Raccolta*] (NY: Benziger Brothers, Inc., 1957) #271.

38 McGratty 232.

> not only over Catholic nations and those who, having been duly washed in the waters of holy Baptism, belong of right to the Church, although erroneous opinions keep them astray, or dissent from her teaching cuts them off from her care; it comprises also all those who are deprived of the Christian faith, so that the whole human race is most truly under the power of Jesus Christ. For He who is the Only-begotten Son of God the Father, having the same substance with Him and being the brightness of His glory and the figure of His substance (Heb. 1:3) necessarily has everything in common with the Father, and therefore sovereign power over all things …
>
> But this is not all. *Christ reigns not only by natural right as the Son of God, but also by a right that He has acquired.* For He it was who snatched us "from the power of darkness" (Col. 1:13) and "gave Himself for the redemption of all" (I Tim. 2:6). Therefore not only Catholics, and those who have duly received Christian Baptism, but also all men, individually and collectively, have become to Him "a purchased people" (I Pt. 2:9).[39]

Since the sovereignty of Christ is already established over us by nature and conquest, why should there be an explicit consecration? Leo answers thus:

> To this twofold ground of His power and domination He graciously allows us, if we think fit, to add voluntary consecration [*devotio voluntaria*]. Jesus Christ, our God and our Redeemer, is rich in the fullest and perfect possession of all things: we, on the other hand, are so poor and needy that we have nothing of our own to offer Him as a gift. But yet, in His infinite goodness and love, *He in no way objects to our giving and consecrating* [*demus, addicamus*] to Him what is already His, as if it were really our own; nay, far from refusing such an offering, He positively desires it and

39 *ASS* 31 (1898–1899) 647, 648 [Carlen 2:451–452]. Italics mine. On this point cf. the excellent commentary of Degli Esposti 24. It is of notable significance that Saint Louis-Marie Grignion de Montfort had neatly summarized the bases of Christ's reign in the *Treatise on True Devotion* #38, where he stated that "Jesus is king by nature and by conquest."

> asks for it: "My son, give me thy heart." We are, therefore, able to be pleasing to Him by the good will and the affection of our soul. *For by consecrating ourselves to Him we not only declare our open and free acknowledgment and acceptance of His authority over us* [*Nam ipsi devovendo nos, non modo et agnoscimus et accipimus imperium eius aperte ac libenter*], but we also testify that if what we offer as a gift were really our own, we would still offer it with our whole heart. We also beg of Him that He would vouchsafe to receive it from us, though clearly His own.[40]

Having established the reason for making an explicit act of consecration, the Pontiff next answers the question: "Why make this consecration to the Heart of Jesus?"

> Since there is in the Sacred Heart a symbol and a sensible image of the infinite love of Jesus Christ [*Quoniamque inest in Sacro Corde symbolum atque expressa imago infinitæ Iesu Christi caritatis*] which moves us to love one another, therefore is it fit and proper that we should consecrate ourselves to His most Sacred Heart—an act which is nothing else than an offering and a binding of oneself to Jesus Christ, seeing that whatever honor, veneration and love is given to this divine Heart is really and truly given to Christ Himself [*ideo consentaneum est dicare se Cordi eius augustissimo: quod tamen nihil est aliud quam dedere atque obligare se Iesu Christo, quia quidquid honoris, obsequii, pietatis divino Cordi tribuitur, vere et proprie Christo tribuitur ipsi*].[41]

Here, in specifying the Heart of Jesus as the "symbol and sensible image of the infinite love of Jesus Christ," Leo is at once recognizing the symbolic value of the heart in this *cultus* and also declaring its equivalence with the person of Jesus Christ.[42] In other words he is defining the formal object of the consecration.

40 *ASS* 31 (1898–1899) 648–649 [Carlen 2:452–53]. Italics mine. Cf. Degli Esposti 25.

41 *ASS* 31 (1898–1899) 649 [Carlen 2:453].

42 Cf. Degli Esposti 25, 31–32.

Since he had been asked to consecrate the entire human race to the Sacred Heart of Jesus, and had the matter studied, as we have seen above,[43] he also deals with his authority to do this.

> We hold the place of Him who came to save that which was lost, and who shed His blood for the salvation of the whole human race. And so We greatly desire to bring to the true life those who sit in the shadow of death. As We have already sent messengers of Christ over the earth to instruct them, so now, in pity for their lot with all Our soul We commend them, and as far as in us lies We consecrate them to the Sacred Heart of Jesus [*Sacratissimo Cordi Iesu commendamus maiorem in modo et, quantum in Nobis est, dedicamus*].[44]

Let us note the precision of the Pope here with his careful use of language as signaled by Monsignor John F. Murphy:

> We note in the consecration of Leo XIII the use of two words, *commendamus* and *dedicamus*. These terms are not here employed as synonyms. Thus the Holy Father would commend *all*; and inasmuch as was in his power [*quantum in Nobis*] would consecrate in a less perfect manner those over whom his influence was less direct.[45]

It would seem that this distinction was based on Cardinal Mazzella's appreciation of a

> celebrated page of the *Summa* [*Theologiæ* III, q. 59, a. 4], where the angelic Doctor, in speaking of Our Lord's kingdom, distinguishes between those who submit themselves to Him, *quantum ad executionem potestatis*, that is to say, who obey His laws; or those who submit only *quantum ad potestatem*; that is to say, who without knowing Him and remaining outside His fold are yet His subjects,

43 Cf. pp. 82-84.

44 *ASS* 31 (1898–1899) 649 [Carlen 2:453].

45 John F. Murphy, *Mary's Immaculate Heart: The Meaning of the Devotion to the Immaculate Heart of Mary* (Milwaukee: The Bruce Publishing Company, 1951) 99; cf. also Roschini 67–70.

> and whether they will or not, cannot divest themselves of the strict obligation of coming back to Him.[46]

It is also of interest to note that in the official Latin text of *Annum Sacrum* and the Act of Consecration, the word *consecrare* does not occur. The words of the Act that are usually rendered into English as "behold, each one of us freely consecrates himself today to Thy Most Sacred Heart" are: *en hodie Sacratissimo Cordi tuo se quisque nostrum sponte dedicat.*[47] Only the Act itself is mentioned once in the Encyclical as *formula Consecrationis*,[48] and this designation appears as the heading of the Act as well. Although the word consecrate has become a "consecrated" term in English and many other modern languages with the meaning of "offering or binding" oneself to Jesus or His Mother, that is not always the case in Latin.[49]

It should also be noted that Saint John Paul II duly reminded the Church of this important Act of Consecration 100 years after the event in his "Message for the Centenary of the Consecration of the Human Race to the Sacred Heart of Jesus." In that Message he insisted on the validity and importance of Pope Leo's Act and how it expresses a response to the desires of Jesus' Heart that the members of His Church might unite with Him in His offering to the Father.

> The consecration of the human race to the Heart of Jesus was thus presented by Leo XIII as "the summit and crowning of all the honors which have been customarily paid to the Most Sacred Heart" (*Annum sacrum*, p. 72). Such a consecration, the encyclical explains, is owed to Christ, Redeemer of the human race, for who he is in

---

46 Chasle 369–70. This text from the *Summa* was in fact specifically cited in *Annum Sacrum*, cf. *ASS* 31 (1898–1899) 648 [Carlen 2:452].

47 *ASS* 31 (1898–1899) 651.

48 *ASS* 31 (1898–1899) 651.

49 We have seen above on p. 40 that, according to Father Jungmann, the first usage of the word *consecrare* in this context was in Spinelli's *Hortulus Marianus* of 1622. Papal Latinists have obviously and consistently opted for a more classical vocabulary.

> himself and what he has done for human beings. Since in the Sacred Heart the believer encounters the symbol and the living image of the infinite love of Christ, which in itself spurs us to love one another, he cannot fail to recognize the need to participate personally in the work of salvation. For this reason every member of the Church is invited to see consecration as the giving and binding of oneself to Jesus Christ, the King "of prodigal sons," the King of all who are waiting to be led "into the light of God and of his Kingdom" (*Formula of Consecration*). Consecration, thus understood, is to be joined to the missionary activity of the Church herself, because it answers the desire of Jesus' Heart to propagate in the world, through the members of his Body, his total gift of self for the Kingdom, and to unite the Church ever more intimately to his offering to the Father and his being for others.[50]

Pope Leo XIII's Consecration of the Human Race to the Sacred Heart of Jesus, Father Michael O'Carroll tells us, "gave a certain stimulus to the practice of consecration to the Immaculate Heart."[51] This should not be surprising, because the *cultus* of the Two Hearts had developed side by side from the time of Saint John Eudes[52] and, while maintaining the necessary distinction between "devotion" to the Sacred Heart of Jesus as an act of *latria* and that to the Immaculate Heart of Mary as an act of *hyperdulia*, the two "acts of religion" are obviously complementary and not mutually exclusive.[53] Consequently we find that at the National Marian Congress held at Lyons in 1900 the following *vota* were adopted:

1. that after the consecration of the human race to the

50 *Inseg* XXII/1 (1999) 1294 [*ORE* 1597:1].

51 *Theotokos* 108.

52 The Saint was described by Saint Pius X at the time of his beatification as "the father, doctor and apostle of the [liturgical] devotion to the Most Holy Hearts of Jesus and Mary," cf. *AAS* 1 (1909) 480. Pius XI used the same titles in the Decree of Canonization, cf. *AAS* 17 (1925) 490 [errata corrected 727].

53 This important distinction between *latria* and *hyperdulia* will be dealt with in the second part of this work.

> Sacred Heart should come the consecration of the universe to the Most Holy Virgin under the title of Queen of the universe;
>
> 2. that a feast called the feast of the universal royalty of Mary be instituted and celebrated yearly with a proper office;
>
> 3. that the Holy Father would deign to add to the Litany of Loreto the invocation, "Queen of the universe, pray for us."[54]

In that same year, following Leo's Act of Consecration, Father Alfred Dechamps launched a movement in Toulouse in favor of the consecration of individuals, families, parishes, dioceses and the whole human race to the Immaculate Heart of Mary.[55]

The impetus in favor of consecration to the Sacred Heart of Jesus continued during the pontificates of his immediate successors, Saint Pius X and Pope Benedict XV.[56] On 22 August 1906, Pius X prescribed that an annual renewal of the Consecration to the Sacred Heart of Jesus should take place each year on the Feast of the Sacred Heart according to the Leonine formula.[57] Petitions for a consecration to the Immaculate Heart of Mary, similar to that of Leo XIII to the Sacred Heart of Jesus, continued to pour into Rome, representing millions of supporters. There were those of Father Dechamps' "Marian Crusade" and those of the Archconfraternity of Notre Dame des Victoires in 1906; those of the Montfortian Father Gebhard in the name of the Archbishop of Ottawa in 1907; those of Father Le Doré, Superior General of the Eudists in 1908 and 1912; and those of Father Lintelo, a Belgian Jesuit, in 1914.[58] On one occasion in 1907, Pius X indicated that he was favorably disposed to the initiative;[59] and in 1914, on the occasion of

54 Geenen 864 (my translation).

55 Geenen 865; Roschini 56–57.

56 Degli Esposti 66.

57 *ASS* 39 (1906) 569–570.

58 Geenen 865.

59 Roschini 57; Geenen 865.

the Eucharistic Congress in Lourdes, which was also a Marian Congress, the Saint indicated that he awaited the right moment for a celebration which would be strictly Marian.[60] In 1907, the same Pontiff also approved and indulgenced Saint Louis-Marie de Montfort's Act of Consecration to Our Lady and another addressed to the Immaculate Heart of Mary for use by groups.[61]

Benedict XV would provide further stimulus that the consecration to the Sacred Heart of Jesus become ever more rooted among the faithful in his letter to Father Mateo Crawley-Boevey, SS.CC. (1875–1960),[62] *Libenter Tuas* of 27 April 1915 on the consecration of families,[63] and in his letter to the Bishops of Poland on the occasion of the consecration of their nation to the Heart of Jesus.[64] And evidently as a response to petitions addressed to him by Berthe Petit[65] to consecrate the world to the Sorrowful and Immaculate Heart of Mary, Benedict concluded his letter to the Dean of the Sacred College of Cardinals on 31 May 1915, eight days after Italy had entered World War I, with an exhortation to invoke Mary's Sorrowful and Immaculate Heart.[66]

60 Roschini 58; Geenen 866.

61 *The Raccolta* #96, 390; *Theotokos* 108. It should be recalled that the saintly pontiff died on 20 August 1914.

62 Cf. F. Larkin, "Crawley-Boevey, Mateo," *NCE* 4:16; "Intronisation" in de Becker, *Lexique du Sacré Cœur* 171–173.

63 *AAS* 7 (1915) 203–205; English trans. in Timothy Terrance O'Donnell, *Heart of the Redeemer: An Apologia for the Contemporary and Perennial Value of the Devotion to the Sacred Heart of Jesus* (Manassas, Virginia: Trinity Communications, 1989) 167–69; Degli Esposti 69–70.

64 *AAS* 13 (1921) 11.

65 Cf. I. Duffner, M.S.C., *Berthe Petit, Tertiaire Franciscaine (1870–1943) et La Dévotion au Cœur Douloureux et Immaculé de Marie* (La Seyne-sur-Mer: Bénédictines Camaldules, 1955); Louis Colin, C.Ss.R., *Berthe Petit Apôtre du Cœur Douloureux et Immaculé de Marie* (Paris: Nouvelles Éditions Latines, 1967); Édouard Glotin, S.J., *La Bible du Cœur de Jésus* (Paris: Presses de la Renaissance, 2007) 594–596; Joseph A. Pelletier, A.A., *The Immaculate Heart of Mary* (Worcester, Massachusetts: An Assumption Publication, 1976) 125–147; *The Sorrowful and Immaculate Heart of Mary: Message of Berthe Petit, Franciscan Tertiary (1870–1943)*, trans. a Nun of Kylemore Abbey (Kenosha, Wisconsin: Franciscan Marytown Press, 1974).

66 *The Sorrowful and Immaculate Heart* 33.

During the pontificate of Pius XI, there were further refinements by the magisterium on the matter of consecration to the Most Sacred Heart of Jesus. The first of these occurred in the Encyclical, *Quas Primas*, of 11 December 1925, by which he instituted the liturgical feast of Christ the King. In accord with the teaching of his predecessor Leo XIII in *Annum Sacrum*, Pius XI taught that Christ deserves the title "King" not only in a metaphorical but also in a strict sense,[67] that He is King by natural as well as by acquired right [*iure non tantum nativo sed etiam quæsito*].[68] Conscious of the theological principles already established, he noted:

> The kingship and empire of Christ have been recognized in the pious custom, practiced by many families, of dedicating themselves [*se dedicarent ac dederent*] to the Sacred Heart of Jesus; not only families have performed this act of dedication, but nations, too, and kingdoms. In fact, the whole of the human race was at the instance of Pope Leo XIII, in the Holy Year of 1900, consecrated to the Divine Heart [*consecrata est*].[69]

Finally, he concluded:

> Therefore by Our Apostolic Authority We institute the Feast of the Kingship of Our Lord Jesus Christ to be observed yearly throughout the whole world on the last Sunday of the month of October—the Sunday, that is, which immediately precedes the Feast of All Saints. We further ordain that the dedication of mankind to the Sacred Heart of Jesus [*generis humani Sacratissimo Cordi Iesu dedicatio*], which Our predecessor of saintly memory, Pope Pius X, commanded to be renewed yearly, be made annually on that day.[70]

About this mandate and its basis, Father Degli Esposti comments:

---

67 *AAS* 17 (1925) 595–596 [Carlen 3:272].

68 *AAS* 17 (1925) 599 [Carlen 3:276–273].

69 *AAS* 17 (1925) 606 [Carlen 3:276–277].

70 *AAS* 17 (1925) 607 [Carlen 3:277].

> It is commonly accepted by the commentators that Pius XI placed the last stone in the doctrine of the consecration to the Sacred Heart with the connection which he made on the dogmatic, historical, social and liturgical plane between the *cultus* to the Sacred Heart and the Kingship of Christ.[71]

The second of these refinements was presented in the course of his great Encyclical on reparation to the Sacred Heart of Jesus, *Miserentissimus Redemptor*, of 8 May 1928. The fundamental argument of the Encyclical is that the two greatest acts of worship that can be offered to the Sacred Heart of Jesus are consecration and reparation; and while the objective of the Encyclical is to present authoritative teaching on reparation, the meaning of consecration is also expounded authoritatively.

Consecration, the Pope insists, is the greatest homage that we can offer to the Lord.

> Assuredly among those things which properly pertain to the worship of the Most Sacred Heart, a special place must be given to that Consecration [*consecratio*], whereby we devote [*devovemus*] ourselves and all things that are ours to the Divine Heart of Jesus, acknowledging that we have received all things from the everlasting love of God. When Our Saviour had taught Margaret Mary, the most innocent disciple of His Heart, how much He desired that this duty of devotion [*devotionis officium*] should be rendered to him by men, moved in this not so much by His own right as by His immense charity for us; she herself, with her spiritual father, Claude de la Colombière, rendered it the first of all.[72]

It will be noted that he derives the exigency for this consecration from the revelations of Paray-le-Monial. These had already been given the maximum approbation of the Church in the Bull

71 Degli Esposti 136 (my translation).

72 *AAS* 20 (1928) 167–168 [Carlen 3:322].

Ecclesiæ Consuetudo of 13 May 1920, issued by Benedict XV for the canonization of Saint Margaret Mary Alacoque.[73]

Pius XI sees the consecration to the Sacred Heart not merely as a "pious devotion," but as an act that will have significant consequences.

> Now these things so auspiciously and happily begun as We taught in Our Encyclical Letter "Quas primas," We Ourselves, consenting to very many long-continued desires and prayers of Bishops and people, brought to completion and perfected, by God's grace, when at the close of the Jubilee Year, We instituted the Feast of Christ the King of All, to be solemnly celebrated throughout the whole Christian world. Now when We did this, not only did We set in a clear light that supreme sovereignty which Christ holds over the whole universe, over civil and domestic society, and over individual men, but at the same time *We anticipated the joys of that most auspicious day, whereon the whole world will gladly and willingly render obedience to the most sweet lordship of Christ the King*. For this reason, We decreed at the same time that this same Consecration should be renewed every year on the occasion of that appointed festal day, *so that the fruit of this same Consecration might be obtained more certainly and more abundantly, and all peoples might be joined together in Christian charity and in the reconciliation of peace, in the Heart of the King of kings and Lord of lords.*[74]

Clearly, according to Pius, consecration to the Sacred Heart, when taken seriously, will bring about the reign of Christ the King.

Two further precisions about consecration are made in the course of the development of this magisterial teaching on reparation:

73 *AAS* 12 (1920) 486–513; Degli Esposti 74.

74 *AAS* 20 (1928) 168–169 [Carlen 3:323]. Italics mine.

> The first and foremost thing in consecration is this, that the creature's love should be given in return for the love of the Creator [*Nam, … illud est in consecratione primum ac præcipuum ut amori Creatoris creaturæ amor rependatur*].[75]

In other words, consecration to the Sacred Heart of Jesus is an act of latreutic worship (an exercise of the virtue of religion) and an act of love (the theological virtue of charity).

The second precision is based explicitly on the teaching of Saint Thomas Aquinas on the virtue of religion, the moral virtue, which excels all others because it pertains to our duties towards God. In the corpus of article 8, question 81 of the *Secunda secundæ* of the *Summa Theologiæ* the Common Doctor holds that the second signification of the word holiness [*sanctitas*] denotes firmness [*firmitas*]. Pius XI says:

> To consecration, therefore, whereby we are devoted to God and are called holy to God, by that holiness and stability which, as the Angelic Doctor teaches, is proper to consecration (*ST* II-II. q. 81, a. 8 c), there must be added expiation [*Consecrationi igitur, qua Deo devovemur et sancti Deo vocamur, ea sanctitate ac firmitate quæ, ut docet Angelicus, consecrationis est propria, addenda est expiatio*].[76]

The reason, then, that Pius expects abundant fruit from this consecration is precisely because it implies a permanent, stable relationship with Jesus Christ. How could members of the Church live their consecration to Christ without rendering the Church and the world more holy?

Consecration of the World to the Immaculate Heart of Mary

It should also be noted that during the reign of Pius XI the decree permitting the *cultus* or veneration of Our Lady of Fatima was issued by the Bishop of Leiria, Portugal, on 13 October

75 *AAS* 20 (1928) 169 [Carlen 3:323].

76 *AAS* 20 (1928) 169 [Carlen 3:323].

1930, and that on 13 May 1931, the Bishops of Portugal consecrated their dioceses and their country to the Immaculate Heart of Mary. In 1934, in his letter *Ex officiosis litteris*, the Pope congratulated Portugal "on the extraordinary favors which the Blessed Virgin and Mother of God has just heaped upon the country."[77]

Thus the impetus toward consecration to the Immaculate Heart of Mary also continued to gain momentum. The French Marian Congresses of Lourdes (1930), Liesse (1934) and Boulogne-sur-Mer (1938) petitioned the Holy Father to make an official consecration of the human race to the Immaculate Heart of Mary.[78] But the incentive not only came from the ranks of theologians and signers of petitions; it also came from what may be called the "charismatic order."[79] Just as the *cultus* of the Sacred Heart of Jesus developed notably after the revelations to Saint Margaret Mary, even though as Pope John Paul II pointed out in his Letter to Peter-Hans Kolvenbach, S.J., of 5 October 1986, "the elements of this devotion belong in a permanent fashion to the spirituality of the Church throughout her history,"[80] and as the decisive spur toward the Consecration of the Human Race to the Sacred Heart came from Blessed Mary of the Divine Heart, so we should not be surprised at the interventions from the "charismatic order" in favor of the parallel and analogous consecration to the Immaculate Heart of Mary. We have already made reference to the role Berthe Petit would play in this regard until her death in 1943.[81] Another very important protagonist—virtually unknown up to now, unfortunately—was Blessed Alexandrina Maria da Costa (1904–1955), a humble Portuguese

77 *AAS* 26 (1934) 628 (my translation). Cf. also Geenen 867; Roschini 59.

78 Geenen 868; *Theotokos* 108.

79 Cf. Joseph de Sainte-Marie, O.C.D., *Reflections on the Act of Consecration at Fatima of Pope John Paul II on 13th May 1982*, trans. William Lawson, S.J. (Chulmleigh, Devon: Augustine Publishing Co., 1983) 8–9. This booklet had originally appeared in French as an article in *Marianum* 44 (1982) 88–142.

80 *Inseg* IX/2 (1986) 843 [*ORE* 960:7].

81 Cf. above (footnote 65) 92.

laywoman and Salesian cooperator, who was beatified by Saint John Paul II on 25 April 2004.[82] At the Lord's express invitation, she willingly became a victim soul so that the consecration of the world to the Immaculate Heart of Mary might be accomplished; and she specifically requested this consecration by the Pope through her spiritual director, Father Mariano Pinho, S.J.[83]

Of these "charismatic agents" promoting consecration to the Immaculate Heart of Mary, surely the one whose efforts are best known is the Servant of God Lúcia dos Santos, Sister Lúcia of the Immaculate Heart of Mary, O.C.D. (1907–2005), the last seer of Fatima to die.[84] She tells us in her memoirs that on 13 July 1917, Our Lady said she would return to ask for the consecration of Russia to her Immaculate Heart.[85] She testifies that those words of Our Lady were fulfilled on 13 June 1929, in Tuy, Spain.[86] Twice, in fact, she spoke of the "consecration of Russia to the Sacred Hearts of Jesus and Mary,"[87] while on the majority of occasions she spoke of the consecration as only to the Immaculate Heart of Mary, but she added on 18 May 1936 that the Lord wills this consecration to Mary's Heart

82 Cf. *John Paul II's Book of Saints* 175.

83 On her role in asking for the consecration of the world to the Immaculate Heart of Mary, cf. Francis Johnston, *Alexandrina: The Agony and the Glory* (Rockford, Illinois: Tan Books and Publishers, 1982) 40–41; Gabriele Amorth, *Dietro un sorriso. Alessandrina Maria da Costa* (Cinisello Balsamo: Edizioni Paoline, 1992) 55–62; Umberto M. Pasquale, S.D.B., *Messaggera di Gesù per la Consacrazione del Mondo al Cuore Immacolato* (Rome: Postulazione Casa Generalizia Salesiana, n.d.).

84 On 15 May 1991, just after his return to Rome from his second pilgrimage to Fatima, Pope John Paul II said: "During our century the Church's experience of Fatima has developed *in connection with a special entrustment to the Heart of the Mother of the Redeemer*," *Inseg* XIV/1 (1991) 1254 [*ORE* 1191:11].

85 Cf. Antonio Maria Martins, S.J., (ed. and translation), *Memórias e Cartas da Irmã Lúcia* (Porto, Portugal: Simo Guimarães, Filhos, Lda., 1973) 219, 227, 341; Louis Kondor, S.V.D., (ed.), *Fatima in Lucia's Own Words*, trans. Dominican Nuns of Perpetual Rosary (Fatima, Portugal: Postulation Centre, 1976) 104, 108, 162.

86 Martins 465; Kondor 200.

87 Letter of 29 May 1930 to Father Gonzalves, Martins 405; letter of 12 June 1930 to the same, Martins 411.

> because I want my whole Church to acknowledge that consecration as a triumph of the Immaculate Heart of Mary, so that it may extend its veneration later on, and put the devotion to this Immaculate Heart beside the devotion to My Sacred Heart.[88]

On 13 May 1938, the Bishops of Portugal consecrated their country again; this time in thanksgiving to the Immaculate Heart of Mary.[89] In June of that year, prompted by Father Mariano Pinho, S.J., Blessed Alexandrina Maria da Costa's spiritual director, they wrote to Pius XI asking him to consecrate the world to the Immaculate Heart of Mary.[90] Pope Pius XI died on 10 February 1939 and was succeeded on 2 March of that same year by his Secretary of State, Cardinal Eugenio Pacelli, who took the name of Pius XII. It was evidently at this point that the matter became somewhat complex as the Portuguese hierarchy strove to amalgamate the respective requests of Lúcia and Alexandrina. Here is the result of the late Father Joseph de Sainte-Marie's efforts to sort out the issues:

> In October 1940, they [the Bishops of Portugal] sought to combine the testimony of Sister Lúcia with that of Alexandrina, and they ordered her [Lúcia] to write herself to the Holy Father, asking him to consecrate the world to the Heart of the Blessed Virgin. But Lúcia, until then, had received from Heaven requests bearing only on the consecration of Russia, not on that of the world. When she received the order from her bishop she took to prayer, on October 22nd, asking for light on what she should do. She received from Our Lord, not from Our Lady, the following answer (remember that the war was raging at the time): "Tribulation will grow. I shall punish the nations for their crimes with war, famine, persecution of My Church, persecution, which will fall especially on him who is My

88 Martins 415. I substituted the word "veneration" for "cult" which is used in the Martins translation because of the unhappy associations of this word in the English-speaking world.

89 Geenen 867; Roschini 59.

90 Joseph de Sainte-Marie 16.

> Vicar on earth. His Holiness will obtain the shortening of these days of tribulation if he meets My wishes and makes the act of consecration to the Immaculate Heart of Mary of the entire world with special mention of Russia."[91]

The response to this cumulative impulse for consecration to the Immaculate Heart of Mary came from the Venerable Pope Pius XII on 31 October 1942 in the course of a radio broadcast to pilgrims at Fatima celebrating the Silver Jubilee of the last of the 1917 apparitions.[92] Concluding the broadcast, he prayed:

> To you and to your Immaculate Heart, We, the common father of the vast Christian family, We, the Vicar of Him to whom was given "all power in heaven and on earth," and from whom We have received the care of so many souls redeemed by His Blood; to you and to your Immaculate Heart in this tragic hour of human history, We commit, We entrust, We consecrate [*confiamos, entregamos, consagramos*; *affidiamo, rimettiamo, consacriamo*], not only the Holy Church, the mystical body of your Jesus, which suffers and bleeds in so many places and is afflicted in so many ways, but also the entire world torn by violent discord, scorched in a fire of hate, victim of its own iniquities … Finally, just as the Church and the entire human race were consecrated to the Heart of your Jesus, because by placing in Him every hope, It may be for them a token and pledge of victory and salvation; so, henceforth, may they be perpetually consecrated to you, to your Immaculate Heart [*assim desde hoje Vos sejam perpetuamente consagrados também a Vós e ao vosso Coração Imaculado*; *così parimenti da oggi siano essi in perpetuo consacrati anche a Voi, al vostro Cuore Immacolato*], O Our Mother and Queen of the

91 Joseph de Sainte-Marie 17. Martins published two letters of Lúcia to Pope Pius XII carrying out the orders of the Portuguese hierarchy: that of 24 October 1940 (which was not sent), 431–433; and that of 2 December 1940 (which was sent), 437–439.

92 He himself had been consecrated a bishop on 13 May 1917, the day of the first of the six apparitions of Our Lady to the three little shepherds of Fatima. John Paul II called attention to this fact in his homily at Fatima on 13 May 1982, cf. *Inseg* V/2 (1982) 1574 [*Portugal* 81].

> world, in order that your love and protection may hasten the triumph of the Kingdom of God.[93]

The Act of Consecration, originally made in Portuguese, was renewed in Italian in Saint Peter's Basilica on the Feast of the Immaculate Conception, 1942.[94] It was referred to many times by Saint John Paul II, especially in his own major Consecrations to the Immaculate Heart of Mary of 13 May 1982 and 25 March 1984.[95] Such a significant text requires a careful analysis.

1. The Pope was careful to indicate the equivalence of the Immaculate Heart of Mary with her person by saying twice: "To you and to your Immaculate Heart." In this he was not only following the common teaching of theologians, but he was also consciously following the line taken by Leo XIII in *Annum Sacrum*, where his predecessor had said that consecration to the Sacred Heart of Jesus is "an act which is nothing else than an offering and a binding of oneself to Jesus Christ."[96]

With the publication of the Mass of the Immaculate Heart of Mary mandated by Pius XII for the entire Latin Rite on 4 May 1944 as a memorial of this Consecration, the formal object of the *cultus* was further clarified by the Decree of the Sacred Congregation of Rites which stated that the Church, under the symbol of the Immaculate Heart of Mary,

> venerates with reverence the eminent and singular holiness of the Mother of God and especially her most ardent love

93 *AAS* 34 (1942) 318–319, 324–325; *OL* #374, 380 [alt.]. Cf. *AAS* 34 (1942) 313–25 for the text of the radio message and the Act of Consecration in both Portuguese and Italian.

94 Geenen 869. Père Laurenceau comments on the slight differences between the Portuguese text of 31 October and the Italian text used on this occasion, cf. Laurenceau 76.

95 8 December 1981, *Inseg* IV/2 (1981) 869, 873 [*ORE* 714:2, 12]; 13 May 1982, *Inseg* V/2 (1982) 1574–1575, 1586 [*Portugal* 81; *ORE* 735:5]; 19 May 1982, *Inseg* V/2 (1982) 1759 [*Portugal* 200]; 25 March 1984, *Inseg* VII/1 (1984) 775; *ORE* 828:9; 31 December 1984, *Inseg* VII/2 (1984) 1684; *ORE* 869:4; 22 September 1986, *Inseg* IX/2 (1986) 699; 16 October 1988, *Inseg* XI/3 (1988) 1240 [*ORE* 1061:1].

96 *ASS* 31 (1898–1899) 649 [Carlen 2:453].

for God and Jesus, her Son, and moreover her maternal compassion for all those redeemed by the divine Blood.[97]

2. Likewise following the precedent set by Leo XIII, Pius XII referred to himself as "the common father of the vast Christian family" and "the Vicar of Him to whom was given 'all power in heaven and on earth,'" thus supplying the rationale for his consecration of the whole human race as well as the Church. On this basis, he prayed for separated Christians, "the peoples separated by error or discord,"[98] and he also explicitly included those without Christian faith: "Extend your protection to unbelievers and to them who still stand in the shadow of death. Grant them peace. May the Sun of truth dawn in their lives."[99] By using the words *confiamos, entregamos, consagramos* in Portuguese and *affidiamo, rimettiamo, consacriamo* in Italian he seemed to signal the groups whom he had in mind: unbelievers, separated Christians and Roman Catholics with the verbs becoming stronger as his immediate authority reached its maximum.[100]

3. It is clear that the analogy with Leo's earlier Consecration to the Sacred Heart of Jesus is quite deliberate. Pius XII found no conflict between the two acts, but rather saw them as complementary and evidently intended in the Divine plan. This is made manifest in the conclusion of the prayer of consecration itself, in the establishment of the Feast of the Immaculate Heart of Mary,[101] in any number of references[102] which link his Act of Consecration and Leo's together, and most explicitly in the conclusion of Pius' monumental Sacred Heart Encyclical, *Haurietis Aquas*:

97 *AAS* 37 (1945) 50 [*ORE* 959:12]. Cf. above 79.

98 *AAS* 34 (1942) 318, 325 [*OL* #378].

99 *AAS* 34 (1942) 318, 324 [*OL* #377].

100 The English translation appears a bit less nuanced here.

101 *AAS* 37 (1945) 51.

102 Cf. The letter *Ex officiosis litteris* to the Bishop of Autun of 15 February 1948, *AAS* 40 (1948) 107 [*OL* #443]; the Encyclical, *Auspicia quædam*, of 1 May 1948, *AAS* 40 (1948) 171 [*OL* #451].

> That graces for the Christian family and for the whole human race may flow more abundantly from devotion to the Sacred Heart, let the faithful strive to join it closely with devotion to the Immaculate Heart of the Mother of God. By the will of God, the Most Blessed Virgin was inseparably joined with Christ in accomplishing the work of man's redemption so that our salvation flows from the love of Jesus Christ and His suffering, intimately united with the love and sorrows of His Mother [*ex Iesu Christi caritate eiusque cruciatibus cum amore doloribusque ipsius Matris intime consociatis sit nostra salus profecta*]. It is, then, highly fitting that after due homage has been paid to the Most Sacred Heart of Jesus, Christian people who have obtained divine life from Christ through Mary, manifest similar piety and the love of their grateful souls for the most loving heart of our heavenly Mother.
>
> The memorable act of consecration [*consecrationis ritus*] by which We Ourselves, in the most wise and loving dispositions of Divine Providence, solemnly dedicated [*dicavimus ac devovimus*] the Church and the whole world to the Immaculate Heart of the Blessed Virgin Mary, is in perfect accord with devotion to the Sacred Heart.[103]

4. In this Consecration Pius XII, mindful of the request of Sister Lúcia, made implicit allusion to Russia with these words:

> To the peoples separated by error or discord, and especially to those who profess special devotion to you and among whom there was once not a home where your venerated icon was not honored (today perhaps hidden and awaiting better days), grant peace and lead them back to the one fold of Christ under the one and true Shepherd.[104]

But on 7 July 1952, in his Apostolic Letter, *Sacro Vergente Anno*, Pius made his reference more explicit:

> Just as not many years ago We consecrated the entire world to the Immaculate Heart of the Virgin Mother of God, in

103 *AAS* 48 (1956) 352 [*OL* #778].

104 *AAS* 34 (1942) 318, 325 [*OL* #378].

> a most special way, so now We dedicate and consecrate all the peoples of Russia to that same Immaculate Heart.[105]

One stone remained to be placed in the doctrinal structure of the consecration to the Immaculate Heart of Mary, however, in order to establish the basis of that act beyond any shadow of a doubt. Leo XIII had grounded the Consecration to the Sacred Heart of Jesus on the Kingship of Christ by nature and by acquired right,[106] and Pius XI had further corroborated this *theologoumenon* in his Encyclical, *Quas Primas*.[107] It was really a matter of making explicit what was already implicit in the 1942 Consecration itself, since the act had begun with the words "Queen of the most holy Rosary."[108]

This final stone was supplied in another radio address to Fatima on the occasion of the coronation of the statue of Our Lady in the Cova da Iría on 13 May 1946. In that notable allocution Pius XII said:

> She [Mary] is mysteriously related in the order of the hypostatic union with the most Blessed Trinity, with Him Who alone, by essence, is Infinite Majesty, King of kings and Lord of lords, being firstborn Daughter of the Father, pure Mother of the Word, beloved Spouse of the Holy Spirit. She is the Mother of the Divine King to Whom from the maternal womb the Lord God gave the throne of David and enduring royalty in the House of Jacob, Who proclaimed that all power had been given to Him in heaven and on earth. *He, the Son of God, decrees for His heavenly Mother the glory, the majesty, the power of His own kingdom.* Associated as Mother and Helper with the King of Martyrs in the ineffable work of the redemption of mankind, she is forever most powerfully associated in the distribution of graces and divine redemption.

---

105 *AAS* 44 (1952) 511 [*OL* #576].

106 Cf. above 86.

107 Cf. above 93.

108 *AAS* 34 (1942) 317, 324 [*OL* #373].

> Jesus is King of the eternal ages by nature and by conquest. *Through Him, with Him, and under Him, Mary is Queen by grace, by divine relationship, by conquest, by singular election. Her kingdom is as vast as that of her divine Son from Whose dominion nothing is excluded.*[109]

With a wonderful clarity and conciseness Pius XII lays out the reasons for Mary's Queenship: it is totally subservient to the Kingship of Christ, derived from it and at the same time united to it. Father William G. Most comments:

> We should not think of her dominion as something as it were separate from that of her Son: no, in royal rule as in all else, she forms a sort of unitary principle with Him. Just as her offering melted together with His on Calvary, so as to form the one great price of Redemption, so her Queenship and His Kingship are one authority, inseparable.
>
> We can easily see then, that we can, with theological exactness, say much the same of consecration to her as Pope Leo XIII said of consecration to Christ the King. We recognize by our consecration that she, as Queen of the Universe with Him, already has fullest rights to our service.[110]

On 11 October 1954, toward the conclusion of the first Marian Year in the Church's life, the Venerable Pius XII issued his Encyclical Letter, *Ad Cæli Reginam*, on the Queenship of Mary. In that document he not only reaffirmed what he had said in the 1946 radio broadcast on Mary's Queenship, but he

109 *AAS* 38 (1946) 266 [Brother Stanley G. Mathews, S.M., (ed.), *Queen of the Universe: An Anthology on the Assumption and Queenship of Mary* (Saint Meinrad, Indiana: Grail Publications, 1957) 233–34]. Italics mine. Interestingly, Saint Louis-Marie Grignion de Montfort had employed virtually the same terminology in #38 of his *Treatise on True Devotion*, where he wrote, "Mary is Queen of heaven and earth by grace as Jesus is king by nature and conquest."

110 William G. Most, *Vatican II – Marian Council* (Athlone, Ireland: St. Paul Publications, 1972) 136. Cf. also his commentary on the text of Pius XII's radio message in *Mary in Our Life: Our Lady in Doctrine and Devotion* (New York: P. J. Kenedy & Sons, 1955) 51–55.

also explicitly underscored the role of analogy[111] in arriving at a correct understanding of Mary's Queenship:

> We may certainly conclude that just as Christ, the new Adam, must be called King, not only because He is the Son of God, but also because He is our Redeemer; so, by a certain kind of analogy [*quodam analogiæ modo*], the most Blessed Virgin is Queen, not only because she is the Mother of God, but also because, as the new Eve, she was associated with the new Adam.
>
> And so it is that Jesus Christ, alone, God and man, is King in the full, proper, and absolute sense of the term. Yet Mary also, although in a restricted way and only by analogy [*quamvis temperato modo et analogiæ ratione*], shares in the royal dignity as the Mother of Christ who is God, as His associate in the labors of the Divine redemption, and in His struggle against His enemies and in the victory He won over them all. From this association with Christ the King she obtains a splendor and eminence surpassing the excellence of all created things.[112]

Finally, in that same Marian Year Encyclical which commemorated the 100th anniversary of the proclamation of the Dogma of the Immaculate Conception by Blessed Pius IX and declared the Queenship of Mary in a solemn manner, the Pope mandated the annual renewal of the Consecration to the Immaculate Heart of Mary on the newly established Feast of her Queenship.[113] In this way, he confirmed that consecration to Mary is related to her Queenship, just as Pius XI had linked consecration to the Sacred Heart with the Kingship of Christ in *Quas Primas*.[114] Now the correlation was not only theologically, but also liturgically established.

---

111 The theological understanding of analogy and its specific application to the question of Marian consecration will be studied in detail in the second part of this work.

112 *AAS* 46 (1954) 635 [Mathews 245].

113 *AAS* 46 (1954) 638 [*OL* #714].

114 Cf. Firmin M. Schmidt, O.F.M. Cap., "Our Lady's Queenship in the Light of *Quas Primas*," *Marian Studies* 4 (1953) 118–133 and above 52.

It remains to be noted that the theology and devotion to the Hearts of Jesus and Mary reached a remarkable culmination during the pontificate of Pius XII. No doubt his crowning magisterial achievement in this field was his great Sacred Heart Encyclical, *Haurietis Aquas*. It was a brilliant summary of all that had preceded it, continuing the work of Leo XIII, Pius XI and even his own, while presenting the biblical, patristic and theological foundations of the *cultus* with great precision "so that the faithful, better instructed, could practice it with greater fervor."[115] In the course of this extremely rich document the Pope mentions that

> this devotion is an act of religion of high order; it demands of us a complete and unreserved determination to devote and consecrate ourselves to the love of the divine Redeemer [*quatenus plenam et absolutissimam se devovendi et consecrandi voluntatem a nobis postulet Divini Redemptoris amori*], Whose wounded Heart is its living token and symbol.[116]

In effect, he says that consecration is the only really appropriate response to the love of Christ and he concludes the document by exhorting the faithful to unite devotion to the Immaculate Heart of Mary to this devotion.[117] He sees the consecration to her Heart as a divinely intended complement to the consecration to His Heart.[118] His teaching on Marian consecration as well is so remarkably thorough that the American Montfort Fathers were

115 Degli Esposti 240 (my translation). Cf. also the excellent overview of the Encyclical in Mario Luigi Cardinal Ciappi, O.P., *The Heart of Christ the Centre of the Mystery of Salvation*, trans. Leslie Wearne and Andrew Wade (Rome: Cuore di Cristo Publishers, 1983) 87–94.

116 *AAS* 48 (1956) 311 [Larkin 9].

117 Cf. above 103.

118 Cf. his Letter to the chaplain of the Grand Retour, 2 July 1948. *Le Grand Retour* 16:1 (août-septembre 1948) quoted in Hubert M. Pocock, S.M.M. (ed.), *Pius XII on Consecration to Mary* (Bay Shore, N. Y.: Montfort Publications, 1956).

able to compile a sizeable anthology of the Venerable Pius XII's teaching on consecration to Mary.[119]

After the great momentum for Marian consecration that peaked in the pontificate of Pius XII, the initiatives of his two immediate successors are seen as less dramatic, but both build on the foundation laid by Pius. So close to the era of Pius, Pope Saint John XXIII did not have to overstress his legacy. In his first Encyclical, *Ad Petri Cathedram*, Pope John alluded approvingly to his predecessor's Act of Consecration to the Immaculate Heart of Mary;[120] and again, a few months later in a radio message broadcast to the Italian National Eucharistic Congress in Catania, Sicily, he spoke of the good results to be sought from the consecration of Italy to the Immaculate Heart of Mary, carried out by the bishops of Italy earlier that same day, 13 September 1959.[121]

At the conclusion of the third session of the Second Vatican Council on 21 November 1964, Blessed Pope Paul VI alluded to the consecration performed by his predecessor, the Venerable Pope Pius XII, and announced that he had decided to send a special mission to Fatima to present the Golden Rose, the sign of special papal favor.

> The world to which this Ecumenical Council intends to devote great and loving consideration and care … Our predecessor, Pius XII, not without heavenly inspiration, solemnly dedicated to the Immaculate Heart of the Virgin Mary. We have decided that it is only right for Us to commemorate [*commemorari*] this very holy act of devotion in a special way here today. And so with this in mind, We have decided to send a special mission in the near future to bring the Golden Rose to the church at Fatima … In this way We commit [*committimus*] the human race,

119 Cf. Pocock cited in previous footnote. Pages 51–55 contain a helpful appendix on the Consecrations to the Sacred Heart of Jesus and the Immaculate Heart of Mary according to Pius XII.

120 *AAS* 51 (1959) 518 [*TPS* 5:374].

121 *AAS* 51 (1959) 712–73 [*TPS* 6:94].

> its difficulties and anxieties, its just aspirations and ardent hopes, to the protection of our heavenly Mother.
>
> O Virgin Mother of God, most august Mother of the Church, We commend [*commendamus*] the whole Church and the Ecumenical Council to you ... We commend [*commendamus*] the whole human race to your Immaculate Heart, O Virgin Mother of God.[122]

This renewal of the consecration made by the Venerable Pius XII, together with the proclamation of Mary as "Mother of the Church," which immediately preceded it, needs to be assessed in the light of the complex situation which had built up to a *crescendo* during the last week of the Council's third session.[123] Father Wiltgen, acknowledged as an impartial historian of the Council, says of these initiatives of Paul VI that they were to be

> considered a partial reply to 510 heads of dioceses, archdioceses and patriarchates from seventy-six countries who had petitioned Pope Paul to consecrate the entire world during the Council to the Immaculate Heart of Mary, as requested by Our Lady of Fatima. The signatures of these prelates had been delivered to the Holy Father on February 3, 1964, by Archbishop Sigaud of Diamantina, Brazil. But the bishops of Germany and France, as well as Cardinal Bea, were known to be opposed to such a consecration, and it did not take place.[124]

Given the cross-currents in the Council at the time, these actions of Blessed Paul VI are seen to have been quite bold.[125]

---

122 *AAS* 56 (1964) 1017–1018 [*TPS* 10:140–141]. Léon Vandergheynst in his study *Le Pape et le Consécration du Monde a Marie* (Bruxelles: La Pensée Catholique; Paris: Office General de Livre, 1968) argues forcefully that this act was a "consecration" in the strict sense.

123 Cf. Ralph M. Wiltgen, S.V.D., *The Rhine Flows into the Tiber: A History of Vatican II* (Rockford, Ill.: Tan Books and Publishers, Inc. 1985) 234–243.

124 Wiltgen, 241. On the distinction between the request for the consecration of Russia to the Immaculate Heart of Mary and the consecration of the whole world, cf. Joseph de Sainte-Marie, O.C.D. 16–18.

125 Cf. Arthur Burton Calkins, "Mary and the Church in the Papal Magisterium Before and After the Second Vatican Council," in *Mary at the Foot of the Cross – IX: Mary: Spouse of the Holy Spirit, Coredemptrix and Mother of the Church. Acts*

Even if this reaffirmation was not all that certain of the Council Fathers wished, the Pope clearly expressed his will on this matter. Another factor that is almost never alluded to by commentators is that the Council Fathers did go on record in favor of Marian consecration in the Decree on the Apostolate of the Laity. We have already made reference to this above,[126] but it is worth noting again because it is a text that uses one of the classic terms for consecration, *commendare*, and yet its import has thus far been virtually ignored:

> Perfect model of this apostolic spiritual life is the Blessed Virgin Mary, Queen of Apostles. While on earth her life was like that of any other, filled with labors and the cares of the home; always, however, she remained intimately united to her Son and cooperated in an entirely unique way in the Savior's work. And now, assumed into heaven, "her motherly love keeps her attentive to her Son's brothers, still on pilgrimage amid the dangers and difficulties of life, until they arrive at the happiness of the fatherland." Everyone should have a genuine devotion to her and entrust his life to her motherly care. [*Hanc devotissime colant omnes suamque vitam atque apostolatum eius maternae curæ commendent.*][127]

Further, although Marian consecration is not explicitly referred to in the following text, given the powerful magisterial endorsement we have already seen for it, it must be recognized as included:

> The Sacred Synod … admonishes all the Church's children generously to foster the cult toward the Most Blessed Virgin, particularly the liturgical cult. Moreover, they should esteem highly practices and pious exercises

of the Ninth International Symposium on Marian Coredemption (New Bedford, MA: Academy of the Immaculate, 2010) 35–38.

126 Cf. above (chapter 1, footnote 202) 73.

127 *AA* #4; Sacrosanctum Oecumenicum Concilium Vaticanum II: Constitutiones, Decreta, Declarationes (Vatican City: Typis Polyglottis Vaticanis, 1974) 468; Flan 771–772.

> toward her, which have in the course of centuries been commended by the Magisterium.[128]

Father Most argues convincingly that "the greatest of these recommended practices is Marian consecration."[129]

On 22 May 1966, Blessed Paul VI addressed a radio message to those assembled for the dedication of the national votive church erected on Mount Grisa near Trieste in commemoration of the consecration of Italy to the Immaculate Heart of Mary, and he used the occasion to comment on the significance of this national act.[130] Even more significantly, on 13 May 1967, he issued his Apostolic Exhortation, *Signum Magnum*, to coincide with the fiftieth anniversary of the first apparition of Mary to the children of Fatima and his own pilgrimage to that shrine. Recalling the great Act of Consecration of the Venerable Pius XII in 1942 and his own reaffirmation of it in 1964, he went on to make this appeal.

> So now We urge all members of the Church to consecrate [*consecrent*] themselves once again to the Immaculate Heart of Mary, to translate this pious act into concrete action in their daily lives. In this way they will comply ever more closely with God's will and as imitators of their heavenly Queen, they will truly be recognized as her offspring.[131]

In other significant documents and allocutions of the pontificate of Paul VI as well, references to entrustment to Mary are not wanting. Thus, in the Apostolic Letter, *Apostolorum Limina*, of 23 May 1974, he entrusted the Holy Year to Mary;[132] and in his Apostolic Exhortation, *Paterna Cum Benevolentia*, of 8 December 1974, he entrusted to Mary's intercession the reconciliation which he so ardently desired as the fruit of the

128 *LG* #67 (Unger 17).

129 Most, *Vatican II* 160; cf. also 52 and 134–137.

130 Cf. *Insegnamenti di Paolo VI*, IV (1966) 255–257.

131 *AAS* 59 (1967) 475 [*TPS* 12:286].

132 *AAS* 66 (1974) 307 [*TPS* 19:161].

Holy Year observance.[133] We find him making the same kinds of statements in his semi-annual addresses to his collaborators in the central government of the Church.[134] Perhaps the most heartfelt and poignant of these acts of entrustment came on the Solemnity of the Immaculate Conception in 1975:

> Listen, O Mary, to our filial voice, echoing the sentiments of the whole Church on this tenth anniversary of the Second Vatican Council, and at the happy conclusion of this Holy Year, and we earnestly implore your special heavenly assistance in this critical hour for the spiritual and civil destiny of the world.
>
> To you, spiritual Mother of the Mystical Body of Christ, which is the Church, we entrust the deliberate Christian commitment which we assumed with holy Baptism, and we confirm it in the spirit of renewal, which has marked the sacred Jubilee that we have just celebrated, and which must mark our witness as living members of the Catholic Church in the years to come.
>
> To you, the Mother of the Church, we therefore entrust our commitment to reconciliation, which has likewise been strengthened during the Holy Year: reconciliation with God, reconciliation with all men our brethren, the longed-for complete reconciliation with all those who believe in our one Teacher and Redeemer, your Son Jesus Christ, ever increasing reconciliation through justice, liberty, cooperation among the different social groups, and finally reconciliation between the peoples and nations in a watchful and sincere spirit of security, collaboration and peace.[135]

Significantly, but not surprisingly, the appositeness of this very act of entrustment was singled out by the then Cardinal Wojtyła at the end of the retreat which he preached to Pope

133 *AAS* 67 (1975) 23 [*TPS* 19:332].

134 Cf. Address of 22 June 1974, *Insegnamenti di Paolo VI* 12 (1974) 738–739 [*TPS* 19:126]; Address of 22 December 1976, *AAS* 69 (1977) 46 [*TPS* 22:21].

135 The Italian text may be found in *Marianum* 38 (1976) 397–398; the English text is in *ORE* 403:12 and Paul VI, *Mary – God's Mother and Ours* (Boston: St. Paul Editions, 1979) 218–19.

Paul VI and his co-workers just three months later. Here are his words:

> Both holy scripture, so rich in metaphor as we have just found, and the experience of the faithful see the Mother of God as the one who in a very special way is united with the Church at the most difficult moments in her history, when the attacks on her become most threatening. And this is in full accord with the vision of the woman revealed in Genesis and Revelation. Precisely in periods when Christ, and therefore his Church, Pope, bishops, priests, religious and all the faithful become the sign which provokes the most implacable and premeditated contradiction, Mary appears particularly close to the Church, because the Church is always in a way her Christ, first the Christ-child and then the crucified and risen Christ.
>
> If in such periods, such times in history, *there arises a particular need to entrust oneself to Mary*—as the Holy Father did on 8th December 1975, the 10th anniversary of the end of the Council—that need flows directly from the integral logic of the faith, from rediscovery of the whole divine economy and from understanding of its mysteries.
>
> The Father in heaven demonstrated the greatest trust in mankind by giving mankind his Son (cf. Jn. 3:16). The human creature to whom he first entrusted him was Mary, the woman of the *proto-evangelium* (cf. Gen. 3:15), then Mary of Nazareth and Bethlehem. *And until the end of time she will remain the one to whom God entrusts the whole of his mystery of salvation.*[136]

136 Karol Wojtyła, *Sign of Contradiction* (New York: Crossroad-Seabury, 1979) 205. Italics mine. Perhaps one of the most striking instances of the notion of God's "entrusting" of himself to Mary in his papal magisterium occurs in *Redemptoris Mater* #39: "For it must be recognized that before anyone else it was God himself, the Eternal Father, who *entrusted himself to the Virgin of Nazareth*, giving her his own Son in the mystery of the Incarnation." [*Etenim oportet agnoscere Deum ipsum, æternum Patrem, imprimis se credidisse Virgini Nazarethaæe, dando ei suum Filium in Incarnationis mysterio*.] *Inseg* X/1 (1987) 726 [St. Paul edition 55]. In the Latin text the verb *credere* is used in the sense of entrusting or committing something to someone.

CHAPTER THREE

The Polish Context

Having considered at least some of the high points of the history of Marian consecration in the spiritual journey of the Church and the authoritative acts of the papal magisterium fostering this deliberate relationship of entrusting oneself entirely into the hands of Mary, we will now consider yet another set of circumstances which provide further context for understanding Saint John Paul II's "program of consecration and entrustment to Mary."

National Marian Piety

The deep Marian piety of his native Poland and its inherent exigency to express itself in consecration to the Mother of God surely penetrated Karol Wojtyła to his very core.[1] This can be seen in his very first papal utterance from the central loggia of St. Peter's Basilica on the evening of Monday, 16 October 1978. I cite it, because I am convinced that such spontaneous remarks at such a significant moment in his life and in the life of the Church cannot and should not be undervalued:

> I was afraid to accept this nomination, but I did it in the spirit of obedience to our Lord Jesus Christ and of total confidence in His Mother, the most holy Madonna … And so I present myself to you all to confess our common faith, our hope, our confidence in the Mother of Christ and of the Church…[2]

1 Cf. Edward D. O'Connor, C.S.C., "The Roots of Pope John Paul II's Devotion to Mary," *Marian Studies* 39 (1988) 83–85.

2 *Inseg* I (1978) 3 [*Talks* 48–49]. In effect this first public statement quite evidently follows very closely what he tells us of his response to the canonical question

We will discover that this theme of "confidence in the Mother of Christ and of the Church" figures profoundly in his theology of entrustment [*affidamento*].

In introducing an Italian translation of the Marian homilies of the former Cardinal Wojtyła, the Servant of God Cardinal Stefan Wyszyński, the late Primate of Poland, said, "We are profoundly convinced that the election of this 'Polish Pope' to the Apostolic See is due above all to the work of the Madonna, Our Lady of Jasna Góra; before her our own Polish Pope, at that time Cardinal Wojtyła, Archbishop of Krakow, loved often to kneel in fervent prayer."[3] Indeed, Jasna Góra, the Bright Mountain, for well over 600 years the privileged sanctuary of Mary's special presence in the life of the Polish nation through her miraculous icon of Częstochowa, has been the very heart not only of Polish Marian devotion, but also of Polish Catholicism, culture and national identity. Its rich history is well recorded and carefully reflected upon in Fr. Marian Załęcki's *Theology of a Marian Shrine, Częstochowa*.[4] Together with another Marian shrine closer to his native Wadowice and his episcopal see of Krakow, Kalwaria Zebrzydowska,[5] it figures prominently in

put to him in the conclave after his election as Pope in *Redemptor Hominis* #2, *Inseg* II/1 (1979) 552, 611 [*Messages* 501].

3 *Omelie* 5.

4 University of Dayton: *Marian Library Studies*, new series 8 (1976). (Henceforth cited as Załęcki.)

5 Cf. the Pope's moving description of this shrine to André Frossard as "a sanctuary which is so dear to me and which I visited so often in my youth, and later as priest and bishop. I can tell you that, in the manner of devotion shown by the people to whom I belong, I found there what I had discovered in the treatise [of Saint Louis de Montfort *on True Devotion to the Blessed Virgin*]," Frossard 127. His address there on 7 June 1979 is a testimony to his deep attachment to this Marian holy place, cf. *Inseg* II/1 (1979) 1476–1479 [*Poland* 197–201]. Finally, he made reference to this Marian shrine in his *Gift and Mystery: On the 50th Anniversary of My Priestly Ordination* (Nairobi, Kenya: Paulines Publications Africa, 1996) 43. Cf. also George Weigel, *Witness to Hope: The Biography of Pope John Paul II* (NY: Harper Collins Publishers, 1999) 25–26, 313–314.

all the stages of the life of Karol Wojtyła up to the time of his election as Pope and, indeed, throughout his pontificate.[6]

National Consecrations

Above, I spoke of the exigency of Poland's unique relationship with the Mother of God to express itself in consecration. In fact, on his first return to Poland as Pope, the Holy Father himself enumerated these great acts of dedication in Polish history during his pilgrimage to Jasna Góra, the Bright Mountain of Częstochowa.[7] The first and, indeed, the archetype of these acts was constituted by the famous vows of Jan Kazimierz [John Casimir], King of Poland, which he made in 1656. Here is Dr. Williams' account of the circumstances that led up to it:

> Near the outset of the Swedish Flood [*Potop*], 1655–1660, during which almost all of the Commonwealth was invaded by the Lutheran king Charles X Vasa (1654–60) of Sweden, Jasna Góra was, along with Lwow, one of the few strongholds to turn back the Protestant foe. Early in the war, King John II Casimir Vasa, had had to escape by way of Cracow into exile in Silesia, which was at that time under the crown of Bohemia. Because of the valor of the peasants, who fought the Protestants after their lords and marshals had surrendered, John Casimir, quickened by the miraculous defense of Jasna Góra under the protection of the Virgin, returned to the stricken Commonwealth by way of the Carpathians and entered Lwow [Lviv], which was still in the hands of a palatine and a captain loyal to the Polish Crown. In the Catholic Cathedral of Lwow in 1656, in the presence of his own Queen, John Casimir committed himself in a kind of heavenly nuptial covenant

---

6 Cf. George Huntston Williams, *The Mind of John Paul II: Origins of His Thought and Action* (New York: The Seabury Press, 1981) 38–42; he visited Jasna Góra as Pope in 1979, 1983, 1987 and 1991. After the first visit he prepared each time by yearlong cycles of prayers to Our Lady in Polish at the end of his Wednesday general audiences.

7 The entire homily and act of consecration of 4 June 1979 is a moving testimony to the Pope's and his nation's Marian devotion; cf. *Inseg* II/1 (1979) 1410–1419 [*Poland* 99–115].

to the Virgin of Częstochowa, declaring her Queen of Poland.[8]

He further promised to seek permission from the Holy See to celebrate an annual feast of Mary, Queen of Poland.[9] This was eventually conceded for the third of May. An interesting link between John Paul II and the vows of Jan Kazimierz was forged when, on his second trip to Poland, he crowned the image of the Mother of God before which the famous vows of 1 April 1656 were made.[10]

But there are many others as well. He referred, quite deliberately, to these vows in his discourse to the Polish Bishops of the Wrocław region during their "ad limina" visit on 17 December 1987.[11] On receiving Lech Wałęsa on 5 February 1991, on his first state visit to the Vatican as President of the Third Republic of Poland, he referred to Poland as a "bulwark of Christianity" in terms of its strategic geographical position, and said:

> Against this background we are not surprised at the prophetic gesture of King John Casimir who, when entrusting our nation and its people to the patronage of Our Lady, proclaimed her the Queen of Poland. His example and intuition of faith have had specific results in our times.[12]

Further in that same year, he quoted the beginning of Jan Kazimierz' vow formula in his Jasna Góra cycle prayer of 1 May,[13] referred devoutly to the icon before which the vows

---

8 Williams 39. Not only was this an instance of putting himself and his kingdom under the *patrocinium* of Mary, but it even antecedes the "Contract of Holy Matrimony with the Most Blessed Virgin Mary, Mother of God" made in the same spirit by Saint John Eudes twelve years later; cf. above (chapter one, footnote 117) 47.

9 Cf. Załęcki 127–28 for the text of the vows in Latin and English.

10 *Inseg* VI/1 (1983) 1582 [*ORE* 791:6–7].

11 *Inseg* X/3 (1987) 1439 [*ORE* 1022:11].

12 *Inseg* XIV/1 (1991) 292 [*ORE* 1177:3].

13 *Inseg* XIV/1 (1991) 1089 [*ORE* 1189:3].

were made in his visit to the pro-cathedral of Lubaczów on 2 June,[14] and commented at length on this action of the Polish King the next day at a Mass in the sports stadium of the same city.[15] On 26 August 1993, a special "Prayer of the Church in Poland Entrusting her Mission to Mary in the New Historical Situation" was recited at Jasna Góra with the Primate, Bishops and President present. It was also recited at Castel Gandolfo in the Pope's presence; and in his introduction, the Holy Father made specific reference to the vows of Jan Kazimierz on 1 April 1656.[16] At the end of his homily in Lviv on 26 June 2001 for the beatification of Archbishop Józef Bilczewski[17] and Zygmunt Gorazdowski,[18] he expressed his joy at bowing before the image that was a reminder of the vows made by Jan Kazimierz in 1656:

> Dear Brothers and Sisters, I entrust you to the protection of Mary, the loving Mother of God, who for centuries you have venerated in the image which it will be my joy to crown today. I am happy to be able to bow before this image which recalls the vows of King Jan Casimir. [19]

Maria Winowska, in her article "Le Culte Marial en Pologne," makes the point that while Poland cannot claim a monopoly on Mary's Queenship, and France, for instance, had been consecrated to her 18 years earlier, nonetheless there are unique features in the consecration of Poland and Mary's queenly reign in that country. She singles out three characteristics of that reign in Poland. It is (1) social, (2) apostolic and (3) missionary in nature.[20] With regard to the first characteristic, the very text

14 *Inseg* XIV/1 (1991) 1433 [*ORE* 1194:8].

15 *Inseg* XIV/1 (1991) 1435–1437 [*ORE* 1194:9].

16 *ORE* 1305:2. I could find no reference to these remarks in the *Insegnamenti*.

17 Cf. *John Paul II's Book of Saints* 328–329.

18 Cf. *John Paul II's Book of Saints* 550–551.

19 *Inseg* XXIV/1 (2001) 1325 [*ORE* 1700:4, 7].

20 *Maria* 4:690. (Henceforth cited as Winowska.) Father Jan Pach also attaches great significance to the social dimension of Marian consecration in Poland vis-à-vis the tradition in France. Cf. Jan Pach, O.S.P.P.E., *Maria nell'Insegnamento del Cardinal Stefan Wyszyński*: Dissertationes ad Lauream in Pontificia Facultate Theologica "Marianum," #49 (Roma, 1989) 94, 256.

of Jan Kazimierz' vows is expiatory in nature; he recognizes that he and his nobles had abused the peasants.

> As I clearly see, too, with stricken heart, because of the cries and anguish of the peasants, that thy Son, equitable judge, lashed my kingdom during the past seven years with plagues, wars and other disasters, then I do vow that on the restoration of peace, I will, with all the other estates, utilize every means to avert further misfortunes, and I will strive that all people of my kingdom shall be freed from all unjust burdens and oppression. May this be so, O most merciful Lady and Queen. Obtain the grace of thy Son, that I succeed in executing these vows.[21]

About this social aspect Williams remarks, "Although his promise was frustrated by the magnates and the gentry after the Treaty of Oliwa of 1660, the peasants and their priests still regarded the Queen of Heaven as their ultimate recourse."[22]

Concerning the apostolic and missionary characteristics of Poland's fealty to Mary, Winowska says, "Hemmed in between schism, heresy and Islam, Poland has had to defend its territory over the centuries in order to defend its faith."[23] Even during the partition of the country between Russia, Prussia and Austria,[24] the great principle of unity was "the Queen of Poland," especially in her shrine on the Bright Mountain. Rallying around their Queen, Poles retained both their faith and their national identity against overwhelming odds, even to the point of sending missionaries to evangelize in other countries. Even prior to the dissolution of the Communist ascendancy, the exceptional strength of the Church in Poland was unique in the countries of the Eastern Bloc and of the world. How could its vitality be explained? In his homily at Jasna Góra on 4 June 1979, John Paul II put it thus:

---

21 Załęcki 127–28.

22 Williams 39.

23 Winowska 694 (my translation).

24 Cf. Williams 22–23.

> During the great novena [of years before the celebration of the millennium of Christianity in Poland in 1966], the Cardinal Primate [Wyszyński] expressed himself as follows with regard to the significance of the shrine of Częstochowa for the life of the Church: "What has happened at Jasna Góra? We are still unable to give an adequate answer. Something has happened that is beyond our powers of imagining ... Jasna Góra has shown itself an inward bond in Polish life, a force that touches the depths of our hearts and holds the entire nation in the humble yet strong attitude of fidelity to God, to the Church and to her Hierarchy ... For many of us it was a great surprise to see the power of the Queen of Poland display itself so magnificently."
>
> It is no wonder then that I too should come here today. I have, in fact, taken with me from Poland to the chair of St. Peter in Rome this "holy habit" of the heart, which has been built up by the faith of so many generations, has been tested by the Christian experience of so many centuries, and is deeply rooted in my soul.[25]

Jan Kazimierz was not the initiator of this fealty of the Polish people to Mary, but he did give it concrete expression. Says Winowska: "In deciding to consecrate his kingdom to Mary officially, King Jan Kazimierz was only obeying a passionate desire of his people. It could be said without exaggeration that in those years of liberation, Mary was more the Queen of Poland than he was its king."[26]

When, after 123 years of subjugation by other governments, Poland became independent and launched its Second Republic (1918–1939), it was only natural that the Polish bishops would rededicate their country to its Queen. This was done at Jasna Góra on 27 July 1920 (just two months after the birth of Karol Wojtyła) in these words:

---

25 *Inseg* II/1 (1979) 1411 [*Poland* 101].

26 Winowska 691 (my translation).

> Most Holy Virgin Mary! Behold, we Polish bishops, in the name of all our dioceses, on behalf of all faithful sons and daughters of Poland, we pay you our deepest respect and our humble homage. Once again, we choose you for our queen, our sovereign, and we flee to your powerful protection … weed out from our hearts the seeds of discord; cleanse our souls from sins and from the national vices that we may praise and serve God and you in the purity of our hearts, queen of the Polish crown! We dedicate and consecrate ourselves to you today. Therefore, defend us, watch over us as your property.[27]

This act of the Polish bishops "on behalf of all faithful sons and daughters of Poland" was to launch a phenomenon of public corporate Marian consecration most probably unique in the annals of any nation in any century. Poland's "day in the sun" as an independent and sovereign nation was short-lived, only twenty-one years. And yet as the smoke of World War II cleared away and Poland burrowed out from under the devastation and carnage of the holocaust,[28] its bishops regrouped again at Jasna Góra on 8 September 1946 under the Primate of Poland, Cardinal August Hlond, together with 700,000 of the faithful, to re-consecrate the nation to Mary, this time particularly to her Immaculate Heart.

> Immaculate Virgin, most pure Mother of God! As King Jan Kazimierz once, after the Swedish invasion, elected Thee patroness and queen of the nation and commended to thy special care and defense the republic, so do we the children of the Polish nation at this historic moment stand before thy throne with tributes of love, worship, and thankfulness. To thee and to thy Immaculate Heart[29] we dedicate ourselves in the entire nation and the resurrected republic … To thy Son and our Redeemer we pledge to preserve faith in his teachings and his law, to defend his

27 Polish text and English translation given in Załęcki 133.

28 Cf. Polish understanding of this term in Williams 23.

29 The repetition of the phraseology of Pius XII's Act of Consecration of 31 October 1942 is obviously deliberate.

> gospel and his Church and to work for his Kingdom on earth. Our Lady and Queen! To thee we flee for protection. Surround with thy maternal care the Polish family and guard its holiness ... Unite the nation in harmony and brotherly love. Give to this Polish land, soaked with blood and tears, peaceful and praiseworthy existence in truth, justice and freedom. Be the Polish republic's queen, guide, light and patroness.
>
> Powerful aid of the faithful! Enfold the Pope and the Holy Church with thy protecting cloak; be their shield in days of oppression. Give to the Church freedom and effective action. Obtain for her leaders apostolic and holy zeal. Withhold the flood of atheism. Show to those who have strayed from the Church the way to the unity of Christ's sheepflock. Lead them to the truth with the tenderness of thy Immaculate Heart ...
>
> Mother of God and our Mother, accept our offering and our vows. Gather all of us to thy Immaculate Heart and unite us forever with Christ and his holy kingdom.[30]

This act is significant also in that it was influenced by the message of Fatima[31] and followed in the wake of the great consecratory prayer of the Venerable Pius XII on 31 October 1942 by less than four years. It was duly noted by that Pontiff not only once but twice in his letters to the Polish Episcopate: *Flagranti semper animi*[32] of 18 January 1948 and *Cum iam lustri abeat*[33] of 1 September 1951. Also of moment is the fact that this collegial act of the Polish bishops preceded Karol Wojtyła's ordination to the priesthood by less than two months.

30 The entire text in Polish and English is given by Załęcki 134.

31 Załęcki 133.

32 *AAS* 40 (1948) 324–328 [*OL* #442].

33 *AAS* 43 (1951) 775–778 [*OL* #541–546].

Correlation with the Thought of the Servant of God Cardinal Stefan Wyszyński

A further note might be added here about Cardinal Hlond. Polish by birth, but educated in Turin as a Salesian of Saint John Bosco and then later in Rome, he was named Primate of Poland by Pius XI whom he had first met when he was superior of a Salesian house in Vienna.[34] He had inherited the deep Marian piety of his native Poland and that of Don Bosco. Having suffered with Poland through the Second World War, and having been arrested by the Gestapo, he maintained a boundless confidence in the Mother of God until the end of his life. The spiritual testament that he left read: "Keep working under the protection of Our Blessed Mother. Victory, when it comes, will be the victory of the Most Blessed Virgin. *Nil desperandum!*"[35] Evidently he spoke virtually the same words on his deathbed.[36] John Paul II has quoted them on several occasions: shortly after his elevation to the Cardinalate on 30 October 1967,[37] and as pope on 10 May 1979 to Frank Duff,[38] on 19 June 1983 during his second papal visit to Poland,[39] and on 17 December 1987 to the Bishops of the Province of Wrocław on their "ad limina" visit.[40]

34 Cf. B. Stasiewski, "Hlond, Augustyn," *NCE* 7:41; Robin Anderson, *Between Two Wars: The Story of Pope Pius XI* (Chicago: Franciscan Herald Press, 1977) 28.

35 Andrzej Micewski, *Cardinal Wyszyński: A Biography*, trans. William R. Brand and Katarzyna Mroczkowska-Brand (New York: Harcourt Brace Jovanovich, Publishers, 1984) 42.

36 These words are sometimes quoted in two different ways: "The victory, *when* it comes, will come through Mary," and, "The victory, *if* it comes, will come through Mary."

37 *Omelie* 127.

38 Bradshaw 233.

39 *Inseg* VI/1 (1983) 1600 [*ORE* 791:10].

40 *Inseg* X/3 (1987) 1436 [*ORE* 1022:11]. On this occasion the quote of Cardinal Hlond is given: "Victory, if it comes, will be victory through Mary." Cardinal Wyszyński supplies the citation in Italian with the conjunction *se* (if) as well. Cf. *Omelie* 5.

Cardinal Hlond was succeeded as Primate of Poland by Stefan Wyszyński, whom John Paul referred to on the occasion of his funeral as "the Primate of the Millennium,"[41] which means, opines one of his biographers, "not only that he created the program in celebration of the Millennium, but also that he was one of the greatest Polish church figures of ten centuries."[42] Created Cardinal by Pope Pius XII in 1953, he was unable to attend the consistory in Rome for the conferral of the red hat (which he would only receive on 14 May 1957) and, in fact, was arrested by Polish authorities on 25 September 1953 and sent into "forced isolation" until 28 September 1956.[43] Providentially, it was during this difficult period in Wyszyński's life that his "program of entrustment" to Mary was conceived.[44] Here are some of the pertinent facts as supplied by Andrzej Micewski, a biographer of the Cardinal:

> Maria Okońska and Janina Michalska obtained permits and visited Komańcza [where Wyszyński was being detained at the time] on March 25, 1956, which was the Feast of the Annunciation as well as the anniversary of Stefan Wyszyński's consecration as bishop. On that day, the Primate disclosed his Marian program, telling the two women that on December 8, 1953, while imprisoned in Stoczek, after deep reflection, *he had made his act of submission to the Blessed Virgin for the freedom of the Church and Poland.*[45]
>
> The Primate's main idea was to defend the faith of the nation against militant atheism by means of the power

41 *Inseg* IV/1 (1981) 1219 [*ORE* 687:8].

42 Micewski 455.

43 Cf. "Biography of Card. Stefan Wyszyński: 1901–1981," *ORE* 687:2, 12. (Henceforth cited as Biography.)

44 Cf. Pach 71.

45 So significant does John Paul II consider this personal act of Wyszyński of 8 December 1953 that, in crowning a famous image of Our Lady and the Divine Child from Stoczek Warminski during his second visit to Poland, he mentioned this place as the site where Stefan Wyszyński composed and made this consecration which would have such a powerful impact on the subsequent history of the nation. Cf. *Inseg* VI/1 (1983) 1583 [*ORE* 791:7].

> of the Virgin Mary. *Having dedicated himself personally in submission to her motherhood for the sake of the Church and the nation, he had slowly been forming the idea that the tormented homeland ought to dedicate itself in submission to Mary, as a national community, for the freedom of its own Church and of the Church throughout the world.*[46]

Hence, in the course of his confinement an expansive plan of pastoral action was conceived which would embrace not only the Church in Poland, but the Church Universal and which would eventually issue in four collective acts of consecration to Mary. The first of these acts would be in commemoration of the three hundredth anniversary of the vows of King Jan Kazimierz in 1656. The year 1956 was proclaimed a special "Marian Year" for Poland, and its culminating point was the celebration that took place at Jasna Góra on 26 August 1956, the Feast of Our Lady of Częstochowa. It featured an updated renewal of the king's vows that the Primate himself composed. He would later say about this particular inspiration:

> The thought of renewing the Vows of Kazimierz on their three hundredth anniversary sprang up in my spirit there in Prudnik, not far from Głogówek, where three hundred years ago the king and the Primate thought about how to free the nation from its twin subjugations: to foreign power and to social misery. When, later in my imprisonment, I followed almost the same track, from Prudnik to the southeast [to Komańcza], to the mountains, I went with the thought: There must be new Vows of Renewal! And it was precisely there that they sprang up, in the southeast, among the mountains. They were written and transferred from there to Jasna Góra.[47]

The circumstances surrounding the renewal of these vows were undoubtedly even more poignant than those that had prevailed ten years earlier because of the absence of the Cardinal Primate, Stefan Wyszyński. One of the sobering focal points of

46 Micewski 154. Italics mine.

47 Micewski 156.

the ceremony that day on the Virgin's Bright Mountain was the empty episcopal chair surmounted by his coat of arms. Part of the deeply moving text reads:

> We, Polish bishops and *the royal priesthood, the people acquired by the redeeming Blood of thy Son*, are again coming to thy throne, O Mary, mediatrix of all graces, mother of mercy and of all consolation ... We stand before thee with hearts filled with gratitude that in the time of glory and in the days of frightening disaster thou wert for us the ever assisting Virgin. We stand before thee also with contrite and guilty hearts because we have not yet fulfilled the promises made by our fathers. Look upon us with the eyes of thy mercy and listen to the voices of millions dedicated to thee, as the people of God.
>
> Queen of Poland! Today, we renew the vows of our ancestors and recognize thee anew as our patroness and queen of our Polish nation. To your special protection and defense we commit ourselves and our possessions as well. We appeal humbly to thy aid and mercy in the struggle to remain faithful to God, to the Holy Cross, to the Gospel, to the Holy Church and its shepherds, to our fatherland, the vanguard of Christendom, consecrated to thy Immaculate Heart and to the Sacred Heart of thy Son. Remember us, O Virgin Mother, before the throne of God; be mindful of the people dedicated to you, who still want to be thy kingdom under the care of the best Father of all nations on the earth.
>
> Queen of Poland! We promise thee to do what lies in our power that Poland may in truth be the kingdom of thy Son and thine, subjected to thee entirely in its social and national life ...
>
> In the fulfillment of these vows we see the living "votum" of the nation, which pleases thee more than those of granite and bronze. May this total dedication impel us to a worthy preparation of our great anniversary of a thousand years of Christianity. On the eve of Poland's 1000th anniversary of baptism we recall that thou wert the first who sang the hymn of liberation from sin; that thou

> wert the first who stood in defense of the little ones and showed to the world the Sun of Justice, Christ our God. We want to remember that thou art the Mother of our way, truth and life, that in thy holy face we easily recognize thy Son to whom thou wilt surely lead us.
>
> O Queen of Poland! Accept our promises, strengthen them in our hearts and bring them before the throne of the Almighty God. Into thy hands we entrust our past and future, our national and social life, the Church of thy Son and all that we love in God. Therefore, lead us throughout this Polish land to the gates of the heavenly country and through the door of the new life in Jesus, the Blessed Fruit of thy womb.[48]

The act itself had been led by Bishop Michał Klepacz of Łódź, who functioned as head of the Council of Bishops. Approximately one million of the faithful stood before the monastery of Jasna Góra, "repeating loudly and full of emotion after each of the verses read by the bishop: 'Queen of Poland, we promise!'"[49] It had been decided that the Primate would pronounce the vows ten minutes before they were recited at Jasna Góra, but later it was discovered that both recitations took place virtually simultaneously.[50]

As Fr. Marian Załęcki, O.S.P., pointed out, this renewal of the "vows of the nation," also called "the vow of Jasna Góra," in effect inaugurated the "Great Novena" (1957–1966) in preparation for the solemn celebration of the Millennium of Christianity in Poland.[51] The pastoral plan for this "Great Novena" was to be an important phase of the "program of entrustment" drawn up by Cardinal Wyszyński during his imprisonment and presented to Bishops Klepacz and Choromański three days after the renewal of the Vows of Jan Kazimierz.[52] The official inauguration of

48 The entire text in Polish and English is given in Załęcki 139–44.

49 Micewski 158–59.

50 Micewski 157–58.

51 Załęcki 145; Pach 75–82.

52 Micewski 156; Biography 2.

this ambitious program of the "renewal of Polish society in the Catholic spirit" took place on 3 May 1957 and was to reach its apex exactly nine years later at Jasna Góra on 3 May 1966 with the solemn proclamation of the "Act of complete servitude to the Mother of God for the freedom of the Church in Poland and in the whole world."[53] One of the features of this nine-year period would be the peregrination of a copy of the famous icon of Our Lady of Częstochowa, blessed by Pope Pius XII, to all the dioceses and parishes of Poland.[54]

On 1 March 1961, the Cardinal gave an address to the priests of the capital in the Warsaw Major Seminary Chapel in which he revealed some of his rationale for this program of the "Great Novena" by speaking of a "fortunate Divine atavism":

> My dearest Brothers! In the tragic disturbance of the human catastrophe in the garden, God Himself revealed the delicate hand of a Maiden. Prophetic dreams and visions longed for her. *Ecce Virgo concipiet et pariet* … There will be Emmanuel! … There will be "God with us"! … And they believed! Esther entreated the king, as the mother of the sons of Zebedee entreated Christ, as Mary entreated at Cana, and later prayed for the disciples of Jesus beneath the Cross, on Calvary. There must be someone of a delicate, motherly soul, for it is necessary to give birth … birth! …
>
> At the moment set by God, God the Heavenly Father Himself gave his Word Everlasting, His Son begotten before all ages—to a Woman. Why did He not give Him to the Sanhedrin, or the Synagogue? Why did He not give Him to Zion, to the temple? After all, generations prayed there. He gave Him to Mary, a maid from Nazareth!
>
> A sort of Divine atavism is repeated here, the giving of everything to a Woman. Even on Calvary God did the same! His Apostles, the Church born from the side of

53 Biography 2, 12. It should be noted that there are two explicitly national Marian feasts celebrated in Poland with Jasna Góra as focal point: the Feast of Mary, Queen of Poland (3 May), which hearkens back to the vows of Jan Kazimierz, and the Feast of Our Lady of Częstochowa (26 August).

54 Micewski 174–75.

> Christ on the Cross, He gave again to a Woman. He gave Her the Apostle, and in him—all of humanity. "Behold your Son"! Let us call this a happy, Divine atavism. From Eden to Calvary![55]

Convinced that this "atavism" is a fundamental dimension of God's providential plan, Cardinal Wyszyński carried this same conviction about the necessity of consecration to Mary with him to the Second Vatican Council. On the Council floor he spoke of the tradition of "Marian slavery" or the "slavery of love" taught by Saint Louis-Marie Grignion de Montfort and how this had been lived in Poland from times past. He proposed that all the Bishops, united with the Pope, should consecrate the Church to Mary in the Council Hall; and then, on returning home, that they should repeat the act in all the dioceses of the world; and finally, that it should be performed in every parish.[56] Ultimately, the rationale behind such an act was detailed in a *Memoriale* submitted in the name of the Polish hierarchy. It would be a profession of faith in the unique intercession of Mary as Mother of God and a means of beseeching her for (1) the freedom to practice the faith and live according to Christian principles; (2) the unity of all Christians as "one flock under one shepherd"; and (3) peace among all the nations on earth.[57] The proposal was not accepted by the Council Fathers as such, but, as we have

55 "Oddanie Się Matce Boga Zywego," trans. Rev. Seraphim Michalenko, M.I.C., typescript 7–8.

56 Salient passages from the Latin text of this intervention are provided in Karol Wojtyła, "Znaczenie Kardynała Stefana Wyszyńskiego dla Współczesnego Kościoła," *Zesztyty Nauke* KUL 3 (1971) 34. Interestingly he used the word *committerent* for his proposal and then spoke of its repetition in the dioceses and parishes of the world as an *actus consecrationis*. One wonders if it was due to this speech of Cardinal Wyszyński and the influence of the Polish hierarchy that the already cited text of *Apostolicam Actuositatem* #4 recommended entrustment to Mary.

57 *Cf. Acta Synodalia Sacrosancti Concilii Oecumenici Vaticani II*, Vol. III, Periodus IIIa, Pars I, 444; Wojtyła, "Znaczenie" 34. The complete text of the *Memoriale* was published in *Marianum* 28 (1966) 41–51.

seen above, Pope Paul VI did entrust the Church to Mary in the presence of the Council Fathers on 21 November 1964.[58]

This "act of servitude" would be deeply engraved on the consciousness of Karol Wojtyła. As Archbishop of Krakow he entered wholeheartedly into the spirit of the "Great Novena." He led a renewal of the consecration of the priests of the Archdiocese of Krakow to Our Lady at Jasna Góra on 23 April 1963, a year after this had been done by his predecessor, Archbishop Eugeniusz Baziak.[59] He consecrated the entire Archdiocese of Krakow to Our Lady in the Royal Metropolitan Cathedral of the Wawel on 5 September 1965, before the concluding session of the Second Vatican Council.[60] He wrote a brief analysis of the solemn national "act" in advance of the event for the benefit of his clergy[61] and addressed the faithful of the Archdiocese during the "Great Novena"[62] and even after its official conclusion,[63] reflecting on the significance of renewing the vows of Baptism in the hands of Mary.[64]

He preached one of the principal homilies at Jasna Góra on that occasion, one which already shows some of the main contours of his own "program of entrustment."[65] Later, he

58 Cf. above (chapter 2, footnote 122) 109.

59 Cf. the homily he delivered on that occasion in Karol Wojtyła, *Il Buon Pastore: Scritti, Discorsi e Lettere Pastorali*, trad. Elzbieta Cywiak e Renzo Panzone (Rome: Edizioni Logos, 1978) 31–41.

60 The text of this act is also to be found in *Il Buon Pastore* 109–111.

61 "Tysiacleci chrztu a oddanie Matce Boskiej," *Notificationes e Curia Metropolitana Cracoviensi* 1965: 189–195.

62 Cf. letters of 10 July 1963 and 21 August 1965 (*Il Buon Pastore* 49–52; 81–85) and his discourse of August 1965 (*Il Buon Pastore* 93–102).

63 Cf. his homily preceding the leave-taking of the copy of the national "pilgrim" icon of Częstochowa from the Cathedral of the Wawel on 8 May 1966 (Karol Wojtyła, *Chiamati all'Amore: Itinerari di Santità* [Rome: Edizioni Logos, 1980] 61–64), the text of an "act of consecration" dating from a few days after the great "act of servitude" at Jasna Góra (*Chiamati all'Amore* 67–70) and his pastoral letter of 25 January 1967 (*Il Buon Pastore* 137–142).

64 Cf. his pastoral letter of 14 February 1966 (*Il Buon Pastore* 122) and his act of consecration of May 1966 made a short time after the "act of servitude" made at Jasna Góra (*Chiamati all'Amore* 70).

65 *Omelie* 71–81.

wrote commentaries on it[66] and frequently referred to it in his preaching.[67] As Archbishop of Krakow, his was the third signature on the document after that of the Primate and the once-imprisoned Archbishop of Poznań.

While the text of this "act of servitude" for such a solemn moment in the life of a nation is of necessity rather lengthy, nevertheless because of its importance as a landmark and point of reference in the Pope's spirituality and theology, it deserves to be presented substantially.

> Our Father, who art in heaven, Father of Our Lord Jesus Christ, whom you gave to the world by the power of the Holy Spirit, through Mary your servant, the virgin Mother of God and mother of the Church! Father of all God's children, of all nations and races, and from whom all fatherhood comes in heaven and on earth! We beseech you today, through Our Lord Jesus Christ, Mediator between heaven and earth, through the intercession of the mother of Christ and our mother, and through the intercession of all the holy patrons of Poland! …
>
> Today, after completing our examination of conscience throughout the nine year novena, which prepared us for the celebration of the Millennium, and after renewing our baptismal vows, in this jubilee year, called the *Te Deum of the Polish nation*, we cry unto you with grateful hearts: 'Blessed be the Holy Trinity and undivided Unity. Let us give glory to God because He has shown mercy to us.' …
>
> Today, we want to lay the foundation for the preservation of the gift of faith for the future generations of Poland for at least another thousand years. We will accomplish this through the reliable hands of our Blessed Mother, whose protection and aid we experienced throughout the ages. Full of gratitude to the Mother of Christ, whom your Son gave to his Holy Church, we recall

66 "Komentarz teologiczno-diszpasterski do aktu dokonanego na Jansnej Gorze dnia 3 maja 1966 R," *Ateneum Kapłanskie* 79 (1972) 5–21; "Oddanie Bogurodzicy w swietle nauki Soboru," *Przewodnnik Katolicki* n. 26 (1972) 228.

67 Cf. *Omelie* 32, 58–59, 127–128.

her comforting presence in the Church's history and in our native land. She was the one who persevered at the foot of the Cross of Christ on Calvary. With gratitude in our hearts we recall her maternal protection in years gone by and we are confident that thanks to her alone the faith in Poland was preserved. Therefore, Father, we are eager to place our beloved native land in the hands of Mary for another thousand years. Virgin Mother, mother of the Church, queen of Poland and our Lady of Częstochowa, you are given to us, as our strength in the defense of the Polish nation! …

On this day, with hopeful hearts we place under your eternal and maternal yoke of love, all the baptized children of God of the Polish nation, and all that Poland stands for, for freedom of the Church in the entire world and in our native land, for the spread of Christ's kingdom on earth.

Therefore, we place all our people in Poland and outside, in a slavery of love for the intention of the Church. From this day on, our beloved mother and queen of Poland, look upon us Poles, your nation, as on your possession, as an instrument in your hands for the good of the Church, to which we are most grateful for the light of faith, for the power of the Cross, for the spiritual unity of love and peace …

Having offered ourselves for the intention of the Church, which is the living Christ in our times, we believe, that through you, we are placing ourselves in slavery towards Christ himself and his salvific work on earth. O blessed and glorious Virgin, we trust that by this act of deep faith and confidence we will obtain freedom for the Church, and your protection for our native land for another thousand years of faith. Please accept our confidence and strengthen it in our hearts and place it at the throne of the Triune God. Amen.[68]

We have already noted the emergence of the terminology of "Marian servitude" or "slavery" at the end of the 16th century in Spain and the defense of this terminology given by Pope John

68 The entire text in Polish and in English is given in Załęcki 153–157.

Paul II.[69] Here is how the then Cardinal Archbishop of Krakow contextualized this conception the day of this act of consecration:

> From the height of the cross He who was our Redeemer, He who made us sons of God, entrusts the disciple to the Mother. One could say that from the height of the cross he consigned him to the "slavery" of Mary. This peculiar link which unites the disciples of Christ and the apostles to the Mother of the Son of God was called from the 17th century "the holy slavery." But in His entrustment of the disciple to the Mother one finds a great directive of the history of the whole Church, of all Christianity. Not only was the first disciple, John, entrusted to her, but all the disciples are entrusted to "her holy slavery," all the apostles and all who have received Baptism.[70]

Wojtyła showed his awareness of the historical provenance of the concept of "holy slavery" in the 17th century. For now it is sufficient to note Fr. Załęcki's comment on the link between the 1966 "act of servitude" and Grignion de Montfort:

> The consecration bears a great resemblance with the consecration used by St. Louis de Montfort. His idea of the personal consecration into slavery to Mary found its full expression in the "collective" consecration of Poland. To be a slave of Christ through Mary makes a man truly free. Mary does not hold anything for herself but perfects and offers it to Christ. Then it is obvious that the "personal" consecration of St. Louis de Montfort was imitated in the Polish "collective" consecration to express the desire of Christian freedom as a suffering people—servant of the Lord. Filled with a deep gratitude to the Mother of Christ for her special and most blessed presence in the Christian history of Poland, the bishops headed by the Primate Stefan Cardinal Wyszyński consecrated their people and land into the slavery of Mary to ensure the freedom

69 Cf. above (chapter 1, footnotes 94–100) 41-42, (footnotes 131–146) 51-56.

70 *Omelie* 79 (my translation).

and success of the Church in the second millennium of Poland's history.[71]

In a homily at Jasna Góra for the Feast of Our Lady of Częstochowa in 1977, Cardinal Wojtyła said about being "slaves of Mary": "We are not ashamed of this because this means the fullness of our liberty and our dignity."[72]

There were yet two more national acts of consecration of the Polish nation after the great "act of servitude" of the Millennium in which the Pope, as Archbishop of Krakow, played a part. On 5 September 1971, the Polish episcopate made an "act of consecration to Holy Mary, Mother of the Church" at Jasna Góra. It will be recalled that the title "Mother of the Church" was proclaimed by Pope Paul VI on 21 November 1964 at the conclusion of the third session of the Council.[73]

There was contestation within the Council about this title for a variety of reasons including fear of ecumenical offense, and it had been dropped from the chapter on Mary in the schema on the Church without ever having been put to a vote, by the action of the Theological Commission;[74] but, on the other hand, there was some strong support for it which, in effect, was vindicated by the action of Blessed Paul VI and subsequent history. Not surprisingly, some of the strongest support came from Cardinal Wyszyński and the Bishops of Poland.[75] Further, the same year as the consecration to Mary, Mother of the Church, a special Mass formulary for the *Festum Beatae Mariae Virginis Matris Ecclesiæ* to be celebrated on Pentecost Monday was approved by the Holy See for use in Poland on 11 October 1971.[76] And again that

71 Załęcki 292.

72 *Omelie* 58 (my translation).

73 Cf. *AAS* 56 (1964) 1014–18; *TPS* 10:137–40.

74 Cf. Wiltgen 240–41; *Theotokos* 251–53; Gerard Philips, "La Vierge au IIe Concile du Vatican et L'Avenir de la Mariologie," *Maria* 8:63.

75 Wiltgen 154, 240.

76 Cf. Ignazio M. Calabuig Adan, O.S.M., "Tre Messe in onore della Beata Vergine *Madre della Chiesa*," *Marianum* 36 (1974) 70–78.

same year, Cardinal Wojtyła would write an article in praise of the Primate of Poland noting "the role that Polish millennial devotion (966–1966), centered in Jasna Góra, played in that proclamation" of the title of "Mary, Mother of the Church."[77]

Here are salient excerpts of the text:

> We come to you, O Mother, for help. We desire to commit to you the Church of Christ and the entire world. We feel ourselves to be a small, living part of the Church of your Son. It is our Church, therefore, we have a right to offer it to you. At the same time we are a small living part of the human family, which is our family, hence we can also offer it to you.
>
> The Second Vatican Council called us to responsibility for the Church and the moral face of the world. But above all, you yourself sensitized our hearts to the sorrows of all peoples and of the universal Church. You yourself inspired us to dedicate the whole nation to you, both those living in the homeland and those beyond its borders, with the Millennial Act of Jasna Góra, to the slavery of your maternal love for the freedom of the Church in Poland and in the world. In the spirit of that act we feel ourselves urged by you with an obligation to urgency for supernatural help for the Church and the world.
>
> We do this in most intimate union with the intentions of the Holy Father Pope Paul VI who, proclaiming you Mother of the Church, in the presence of all the Fathers of the Council, entrusted the whole Church of Christ and the human family to your maternal heart.[78]

Here, as well as in the consecration of 1966, we may note what might be called the "vicarious" dimension of the act. It is performed not just for Poland, but on behalf of the entire Church. Cardinal Wojtyła had already alluded to this in commenting on the millennial act of consecration:

---

77 Williams 175, 375; Karol Wojtyła, "Znaczenie" 33–35.

78 *"O Matce i Krolowej Polakow" – Refleksje, modlitwy, piesni* (Jasna Góra, Rzym: Paulini, 1982) 263–66. English translation by Dr. John Grondelski and Fr. Ignatius Kuziemski.

> And so, thanks to the connection in time which occurred between the preparation for the millennium of Baptism and the subsequent sessions of Vatican Council II, there took form as though a fuller expression of our millennium. The Church in Poland entered anew into the consciousness of the universal Church and at the same time, it gained anew the consciousness of its own deep bond with the whole Christian *Universitas*. … And Cardinal Stefan Wyszyński, bringing as it were to conclusion the idea of this gift which the Church in Poland, part of the Christian *Universitas*, desired to offer "to other parts and to the whole Church" carried out on the 3rd of May 1966 at Jasna Góra the Millennial Act of handing over to the maternal slavery of Mary: "[…] that the whole and individual parts experience growth."[79]

Bringing this concept of Poland's self-consecration to Mary as its gift to the universal Church to a high point of culmination, the Polish episcopate took the bold initiative on 7 June 1976 whereby, acting vicariously, they consecrated mankind to Mary.[80] Here is the Pope's own description:

> On June 7, 1976, they consecrated to you *all of humanity*, all the nations and peoples of the modern world, and their brothers and sisters who are close to them by faith, by language and by the destinies they share in history, extending this consecration to the furthest limits of love as is demanded by your heart, the heart of a Mother who embraces each and every person, always and everywhere.[81]

In his own "Act of Consecration to the Mother of God" made on his first return to Poland as Pope on 4 June 1979, he summed up all of these previous acts by the Polish episcopal body and ratified them:

79 Wojtyła, "Znaczenie" 32–33. English translation by Father Seraphim Michalenko, M.I.C.

80 The text used on this occasion was that of the Act of Consecration that Pope Paul VI had made on 8 December 1975. Cf. above (chapter 2, footnote 135) 112.

81 *Inseg* II/1 (1979) 1417 [*Poland* 111].

> By the inscrutable designs of divine Providence I am today present here at Jasna Góra, in my earthly homeland, Poland, and I wish first of all to confirm the acts of consecration and of trust that at various times—"in many and various ways"—were pronounced by the Cardinal Primate and the Polish Episcopate. In a very special way I wish to confirm and renew the act of consecration pronounced at Jasna Góra on May 3, 1966, on the occasion of the millennium of Poland. With this act the Polish bishops wished, by giving themselves to you, Mother of God, "in your maternal slavery of love," to serve the great cause of *the freedom of the Church* not only in their own homeland but in the whole world …
>
> Today I come to Jasna Góra as its first pilgrim Pope, and I wish to renew the entire heritage of trust, of consecration and of hope that has been accumulated here with such magnanimity by my Brothers in the Episcopate and my fellow-countrymen.[82]

Thus did Saint John Paul pay tribute to the collective episcopal consecrations to Mary, Queen of Poland, which set such a remarkable precedent and unparalleled example in 20th century Catholicism and which contributed so much to his own perspective and theology. Cardinal Stefan Wyszyński, for his part, considered the Pope's act of 4 June 1979 as an "official recognition of the Polish Marian path" which he himself had been so instrumental in charting and as a stage of the systematic preparation of Catholic opinion for a future act of consecration of the Church and the world to Our Lady.[83]

The influence of the "Primate of the Millennium" on Pope John Paul II's program of Marian consecration and entrustment can hardly be underestimated. We might say that Wojtyła inherited a double portion of his spirit (cf. II Kgs. 2:9–12). Before the assembled episcopate of Poland on 19 June 1983, John Paul said:

82 *Inseg* II/1 (1979) 1417 [*Poland* 111].

83 Pach 87–88.

> My first steps during my pilgrimage this year in the homeland were directed to the Warsaw Cathedral, to the tomb of Cardinal Stefan Wyszyński of holy memory, the Primate of the Millennium. I celebrated the first Holy Mass for him, recommending to God his immortal soul and also giving thanks for the service he rendered to the Church in Poland for over thirty years as Bishop and as Primate.
>
> It is indeed difficult to express the importance of this service, not only with regard to the Church in Poland, but also with regard to the universal Church. …
>
> In this meeting of the Polish Episcopal Conference I wish to render homage one more time, after his death, to the memory of the great Primate, to whom the Church, Poland, and all of us—I in particular—owe so much.[84]

The Pope, on his first return to Poland, had already acknowledged the stature of the Primate while he was still living:

> The Cardinal Primate has become a … keystone … The keystone is that which forms the arch, which reflects the strength of the foundations of the building. The Cardinal Primate *shows the strength of the foundation of the Church, which is Jesus Christ.* This is what his strength consists of. The Cardinal Primate has been teaching for over thirty years that *he owes his strength to Mary,* the Mother of Christ. We all know well that it is possible, thanks to Mary, to make the strength of the foundation that is Christ shine out, and effectively to become a keystone of the Church.[85]

Recuperating in the Gemelli Polyclinic from the attempt on his life, he would repeat the same words in his letter to the Polish nation on the occasion of the death of the "Primate of the Millennium."[86]

---

84 *Inseg* VI/1 (1983) 1585–86 [*ORE* 791:7].

85 *Inseg* II/1 (1979) 1376 [*Poland* 50–51].

86 *Inseg* IV/1 (1981) 1218 [*ORE* 687:8].

CHAPTER FOUR

Marian Consecration in Recent Theological Reflection

Now it remains for us to consider some representative contemporary theological reflection on this phenomenon of Marian consecration that we have been tracing in the spiritual journey of the Church.

The Postconciliar Context

The first thing to be noted is that after the cresting of what might be described as the "Marian Era" which flourished under the Venerable Pius XII, the impetus for consecration to Our Lady declined in much of the Catholic Church along with other Marian devotions. Consequently, theologians wrote little in the conciliar and immediate postconciliar period about the foundations of this practice. Two notable exceptions were the publication of essays produced on the occasion of the fourth centenary of the Jesuit Marian Congregations in 1963[1] and the papers produced for a study week on this topic, which was promoted by the Italian *Collegamento Mariano Nazionale* in 1968 in the light of the Second Vatican Council.[2]

We have already noted that this was not the case in Poland during that same period where the Marian theology of chapter 8 of *Lumen Gentium*, commented upon at length by Cardinal

1 *Quatrième Centenaire des Congrégations Mariales. Documents du Congrès Européen* Rome 8–2 September 1963. Italian trans. *La consacrazione nella Congregazione Mariana* (Rome: Edizioni Stella Matutina, 1963).

2 *Teologia e Pastorale della Consacrazione a Maria* (Padua: Edizioni Messaggero, 1969).

Wojtyła,[3] blended harmoniously with Cardinal Primate Wyszyński's ambitious "program of Marian entrustment."[4] Within the first eleven years following the Second Vatican Council, Poland's Bishops consecrated the nation three times to the Madonna on her Bright Mountain of Częstochowa. With the accession of Karol Wojtyła to the papacy, this tradition, dormant in many areas of the Western Church in the immediate postconciliar period, was brought to the fore in a striking way.

John Paul's "program of entrustment" was soon noted by theologians and faithful and became a stimulus for pastoral practice and theological reflection.[5] Hence, not surprisingly, the bulk of more recent theological deliberation on this subject was occasioned by the praxis and magisterium of John Paul II. Before taking note of these developments, however, it would be apposite to take into consideration those that developed in the immediate wake of Vatican II.

A good illustration of the application of the Council's orientations to the theology of Marian consecration may be found in the French Montfort journal, *Cahiers Marials* #86, of 15 January 1973. Its first article by the Sulpician exegete, Henri Cazelles, was devoted to a study of the consecration of Christ and the consecration of man.[6] It sought to ground the practice of Marian consecration, particularly as recommended by Saint Louis-Marie Grignion de Montfort, on a solid biblical and Christological foundation. In it Père Cazelles reviewed the

---

3 Besides the documentation already cited, Cardinal Wojtyła produced a commentary on all the documents of the Council in which this chapter featured prominently: *Sources of Renewal: The Implementation of Vatican II*, trans. P. S. Falla (San Francisco: Harper & Row Publishers, 1980) 100–111.

4 Cf. above (chapter 3, footnotes 41–85) 125-139.

5 Appropriately one of the first collections of essays to be published on Marian consecration in his pontificate took his motto as its title: *Totus Tuus: attualità e significato della consacrazione a Maria* (Rome: Santuario Madonna del Divino Amore, 1978). It, too, was sponsored by the Italian *Collegamento Mariano Nazionale*.

6 H. Cazelles, P.S.S., "Consécration du Christ et consécration de l'homme," *Cahiers Marials* 86 (15 janvier 1973) 5–13.

difference between the sacred and the profane, God's calling of his people to holiness (cf. Lev. 19:2), the holiness and consecration of Christ as Priest by the Holy Spirit and His own self-consecration (cf. Jn. 17:19), the consecration of the Christian in Baptism and the renewal of one's Baptismal commitment "through the hands of Mary" as proposed by de Montfort.

The second article by Canadian Montfort Father J.-P. Michaud attempted to describe Marian consecration from the perspective of being at the service of the mystery of God's dwelling among men.[7] It considered Mary at the time of the Annunciation as giving herself freely to this mystery by her response, "Be it done to me according to your word" (Lk. 1:38); the consecration of her virginity to God; her service to the revelation of Christ at Cana (Jn. 2:1–11); her collaboration in the great price of our salvation on Calvary and her acceptance of spiritual motherhood on our behalf (Jn. 19:25–27); her presence in the Cenacle as Mother (Acts 1:14); and her continued service of intercession on behalf of her children even in glory (*Lumen Gentium* #62). The thrust of the presentation was to indicate that as Mary, by virtue of her consecration, "devoted herself totally [*totaliter devovit*] to the Person and work of her Son" (*Lumen Gentium* #56), so the Christian who follows her example must do no less.

A further article by the editor, Father Alphonse Bossard, expatiated at length on the nature of the total gift (consecration) to Christ through Mary according to Montfort.[8] In it he underscored Montfort's insistence on this consecration as the perfect renewal of the promises of Baptism and the Christocentrism of de Montfort's vision.

This brief synopsis may serve to underscore the point that, especially since the Second Vatican Council, there has been a

7 J.-P. Michaud, S.M.M., "Au service du Mystère de Dieu avec les Hommes," *Cahiers Marials* 86 (15 janvier 1973) 15–22.

8 A. Bossard, S.M.M., "Le don total au Christ par Marie selon Montfort," *Cahiers Marials* 86 (15 janvier 1973) 29–48.

strong motivation to illustrate the Trinitarian, Christological, ecclesial, biblical, liturgical and anthropological dimensions of the practice of Marian consecration.[9] These, in turn, were seen as providing possible bases for ecumenical dialogue by demonstrating that the entrusting of oneself, of groups and of the entire Church to the Mother of God is not an unhealthy accretion, but an organic element in the development of the Catholic tradition.[10] Particularly since the Council, theologians have been concerned above all to show that the "total gift of oneself [to Mary] for life and for eternity"[11] has a thoroughly Christological perspective in that it flows from the will of Christ and is ultimately oriented to Him. Theological research in this area, then, as in all other areas of Mariology and Marian spirituality, aims at illuminating the fact that "in the Virgin Mary everything is relative to Christ and dependent upon Him."[12]

We have already noted that the word "consecration" as a description of the giving of oneself to Mary—while its first use dates at least from Saint John of Damascus[13] and it has held a certain "pride of place" for the past three hundred fifty years[14]—is surely not the only term used to delineate the relationship of "belonging" to Mary. Nonetheless, it has provided a helpful point of departure for analyzing the theological content of this

9 These are listed among the characteristics of genuine Marian devotion outlined by Paul VI in his Apostolic Exhortation, *Marialis Cultus*, #25–37, *AAS* 66 (1974) 135–49 [Paul VI, *Mary - God's Mother and Ours* 122–138].

10 Cf. Congregation for Catholic Education, *The Virgin Mary in Intellectual and Spiritual Formation* (25 March 1988) #14, *Marianum* 50 (1988) 40–41 [*ORE* 1043:20].

11 This is the description of Marian consecration made by the Venerable Pius XII in his allocution to representatives of the Marian Congregations on 21 January 1945 that has since become a classic definition. Cf. Domenico Bertetto, S.D.B., *Il Magistero Mariano di Pio XII* (Rome: Edizioni Paoline, 1956) #136; *OL* #389.

12 *Marialis Cultus* #25, *AAS* 66 (1974) 135 [Paul VI, *Mary - God's Mother and Ours* 122–123].

13 Cf. above (chapter 1, footnote 42) 28.

14 Cf. above (chapter 1, footnote 91) 40; F. M. Franzi, "Per un orientamento sul tema della 'consacrazione a Maria,'" in *Teologia e Pastorale della Consacrazione a Maria* 8.

consistent phenomenon in the life of the Church. Père Henri Cazelles, whose study on the consecration of Christ we have already noted, undertook a further biblical investigation ten years later on the Holy Spirit as the agent in the consecration of Christ, Mary and the Church.[15] Such essays have had the merit of highlighting the primary initiative of God in consecrating, the mission of the Christ as the "consecrated" of the Father, Mary as the consecrated creature *par excellence* and Baptism as the fundamental Christian consecration.

The Meaning of "Entrustment" vis-à-vis "Consecration"

Pope Saint John Paul II's own "program of Marian consecration and entrustment," launched from the first months of his pontificate, also introduced a further consideration into the contemporary theological discussion of Marian consecration. After detailing some of his most important and solemn acts of consecration to Our Lady, Father Stefano De Fiores, S.M.M., an influential Italian Mariologist (1933–2012), pointed out:

> Regarding the expressive language of these acts, Pope Wojtyła is not bound by a stereotyped formula, but has recourse to various terms, which take into account the pastoral context: to entrust, to consecrate, to dedicate, to offer, to commend, to serve [*affidare, consacrare, dedicare, offrire, raccomandare, servire*] ... His preference is for the binomial: *affidare-consacrare*, with the noticeable pre-eminence of the first verb. Thus, from 7 June 1981, the neologism entrustment [*affidamento*] enters into the texts, arousing interest and some theological interpretations.[16]

One of the principal considerations of theologians, then, in the course of his pontificate was the discussion of the meaning

15 H. Cazelles, P.S.S., "L'Esprit qui consacre le Christ, Marie, l'Eglise," *Cahiers Marials* 133 (15 juin 1982) 131–45.

16 Stefano De Fiores, S.M.M., *Maria nella Teologia Contemporanea* (Rome: Centro di Cultura Mariana "Mater Ecclesiae," 1987 [2a ed.]), 331 (my translation).

of entrustment [*affidamento*] and whether this word is an exact synonym for consecration, or in what sense it differs. First, it may be helpful to point out that the word does not express a new concept in the context of acts of offering to Our Lady, even if John Paul II made much more extensive use of it than popes before him. It should be pointed out that the Venerable Pius XII used the words *affidiamo* and *consacriamo* in his Consecration of the world to the Immaculate Heart of Mary on 31 October 1942,[17] and Blessed Paul VI chose the word *affidiamo* together with synonyms like *confidiamo* and *consegniamo* to describe the entrustment of our Christian commitment to Our Lady in his prayer on the Solemnity of the Immaculate Conception in 1975.[18] Further, the history of Marian consecration illustrates that the Latin equivalents of this term such as *committere* and *commendare* are well attested in the tradition and find their context especially in the Medieval *patrocinium*.[19]

Nevertheless, it is quite legitimate to inquire about the nuances conveyed by the words entrust/entrustment (*affidare/affidamento*) and whether these signal a shift in direction or a further precision in the meaning of the "gift of oneself to Mary." Bishop Francesco Franzi (1910–1996), Auxiliary Bishop of Novara, one of the first to note the papal preference for this term, underscores its appropriateness in the first instance vis-à-vis the very theologically weighty word consecration.

> It is known that not a few objections have been made to "consecration to Mary." The term "consecration" summons to mind a religious content so profound that it seems to correspond uniquely to the relationship, which we have with God. It refers us instinctively, in fact, to the ontological state of consecration accomplished in us by Baptism which truly "grafts" us into Christ and makes us "his," participants in Him …

17 Cf. above (chapter 2, footnote 93) 100, (footnote 100) 102.

18 Cf. above (chapter 2, footnote 135) 112.

19 Cf. above (chapter 1, footnotes 44–51) 29-31.

> It is clear that we cannot use the term "consecration" in a univocal sense—when we speak of our relationship with Mary whether in our "being" or in our "moral conduct." True, we have bonds with her—those which we express by affirming that Mary is mother to us and that we are her children—but certainly these are not identical to those which bind us to Christ … [20]
>
> In comparison the term "entrustment" seems more suitable. It is simpler; it refers to normal relationships among men and does not immediately express a religious content, which reminds us of God. Given today's mentality, suspicious of unduly enlarging the area of the "religious," it can prove to be more welcome.
>
> We must beware, however, of the risk of impoverishing the significance of "entrustment" by not paying sufficient attention to that particular category of relations with Mary to which the term refers and is meant to confirm, constituting an act of faith in such relations and a coherent commitment of life.
>
> Thus it is very important to consider with care the significance which such "entrustment" acquires in the discourse of the Holy Father [particularly of the morning of 7 June 1981].[21]

After analyzing the text of the John Paul's "consecration" of Pentecost 1981, which became the paradigm of the "acts of consecration" of 13 May 1982 and 25 March 1984, Bishop Franzi makes a number of helpful theological precisions and then draws this conclusion:

> Those who speak of "entrustment to Our Lady" and those who speak of "consecration to Our Lady," in substance wish to express the same reality, a relationship which one acknowledges having with the Holy Virgin and which he wishes to reaffirm.

---

20 The Bishop was obviously referring to the necessity of invoking the principle of analogy, which will be treated in part two of this work.

21 Mons. Francesco Maria Franzi, "'Consacrazione' o 'affidamento'?" *Miles Immaculatae* 17 (1981) 218–19 (my translation).

> I perceive that the Holy Father himself uses the one and the other term indiscriminately, almost as if they were two synonyms, without any difference of content between the two expressions ... [22]
>
> When we speak of "entrustment to Mary" and of "consecration to her," in substance we intend to recognize who Mary is for us; what she does for us; who we are for her; what we, consequently, ought to do toward her.[23]

Ultimately, then, he sees the two terms as equivalent and proposes that it is a matter of pastoral sensitivity as to which word, "consecration" or "entrustment," is more appropriate on a particular occasion.[24]

Father Stefano De Fiores also saw the word entrustment as bringing enrichment to the discussion of this topic in that it implies a special confidence in Mary. Interestingly the root "trust" is clearly present in the English word "entrust" even as the root "fid" (from "fiducia") is equally apparent in the Italian word "affidamento." Hence, he says of the word entrustment that

> It includes an attitude of interior trust, which expresses itself in a corresponding act. In order to make an act of entrustment it is then necessary to have trust [the Italian word also implies confidence, reliance, even assurance] in the person to whom one entrusts himself or hands something over, even his own life.[25]

---

22 This would seem to be verified especially in the Consecration of Ireland to Mary where five times the Holy Father repeated the phrase, "We entrust and consecrate to you"; cf. *Inseg* II/2 (1979) 469 [*Ireland* 89–90], and in the letter to the Bishops of the Church dated 8 December 1983 in which he presented the text of "the Act of Consecration and Entrustment" which he asked them to make on 24 or 25 March 1984 in union with him; cf. *Inseq* VII/1 (1984) 417 [*ORE* 823:2]. In his consecration of Brazil to Our Lady on 19 October 1991 he prayed: "O Virgin of the Cliff, we come before your beautiful image ... to consecrate our lives to you and entrust to you the new evangelization," cf. *Inseg* XIV/2 (1991) 938 [*ORE* 1214:3], using the word "consecrate" for persons while retaining "entrust" for projects.

23 Franzi 225–26 (my translation).

24 Franzi 227–28.

25 De Fiores, *Maria nella teologia contemporanea* 335 (my translation).

Later, De Fiores would become more opposed to the use of the term "consecration" and more insistent on the use of the term "entrustment,"[26] as we shall see subsequently.

There are others who took an even more decisive position at an earlier stage. Canon René Laurentin (1917-2017), for instance, stated that the word consecration is not suitable to express our relationship with Mary. He forthrightly stated that:

> In the strict sense of the word there is no consecration except to God. But in current language we speak of "to consecrate oneself" [sic] to a project, to one's affairs, to one's family. This has a meaning that is quite banal: not to neglect, to attend to.
>
> No doubt, one can use this banal sense to say: "I consecrate myself to Mary." Unfortunately this language obscures what is essential. We say: "I consecrate myself," while forgetting that it is God who consecrates, according to the proper sense of the word.
>
> The consecration is made to Mary, or to her Heart, while to a certain extent implicitly forgetting God whom we just guess at, as in a mist. Its priority, its gratuitousness becomes hazy or disappears. What is essential becomes marginal.[27]

Because he believes that the analogical use of the term consecration confuses the theological task unnecessarily[28] and constitutes "a scandal for the ecumenical dialogue,"[29] Laurentin

26 Cf. his articles on *affidamento* and *consacrazione* in his *Maria, Nuovissimo Dizionario* Vol. 1 (Bologna: Edizioni Dehoniane, 2006).

27 René Laurentin, "Consecration and Entrustment: A Commitment to the Hearts of Jesus and of Mary – its Meaning for Our Personal Lives and the Life of Our People," trans. Sisters Edita Telan, M.I.C. and Rachel de Mars, M.I.C. in *The Alliance of the Hearts of Jesus and Mary: The International Theological/Pastoral Conference, Manila, Philippines, 30 November – 3 December 1987, Texts and Documents* (Manila: Bahay Maria, 1988) 242.

28 Cf. Laurentin, "Consecration" 238–40; also his *A Year of Grace with Mary: Rediscovering her Presence and her Role in our Consecration*, trans. Msgr. Michael J. Wrenn (Dublin: Veritas, 1987) 126–31.

29 Laurentin, "Consecration" 239.

prefers rather to speak of Mary's role in our consecration to God[30] and concludes that

> If we can only, in this proper sense, be consecrated to God, it is worth entrusting ourselves to Mary for that purpose. Whoever is entrusted to this very loving mother, beloved of God, is not lost and those who have done so have never been disappointed.[31]

In saying this Laurentin obviously preferred to distance himself from the tradition represented by Saint Louis-Marie Grignion de Montfort,[32] who held that the consecration to God [Christ] through Mary also includes a consecration to Mary:

> It follows that we consecrate ourselves at one and the same time to Mary and to Jesus. We give ourselves to Mary because Jesus chose her as the perfect means to unite himself to us and unite us to him. We give ourselves to Jesus because he is our last end.[33]

On the other side of the consecration/entrustment issue is the position espoused by the late Père Joseph de Sainte-Marie, O.C.D. (+ 1985). After a lengthy excursus on the complementarity of the terms "consecration" and "sanctification,"[34] and with the understanding that sanctification is the final end of consecration,[35] he defines consecration to Mary as the covenant

---

30 Laurentin, *A Year of Grace* 11, 131–34.

31 Laurentin, *A Year of Grace* 134.

32 Strangely, at one point in his Manila presentation on the question of consecration, he compares Saint Maximilian Kolbe with Saint Louis de Montfort and says of the latter that he "was no less intensely apostolic and missionary, not without a megalomania similar to that of Kolbe, when he built, with a shovel and a wheelbarrow, the mountain of Pontchâteau to the glory of the Cross," Laurentin 249. This is a very regrettable comment on two great saints and teachers of Marian consecration. With regard to the Pontchâteau affair, cf. Benedetta Papàsogli, *Montfort: A Prophet for Our Times* (Rome: Edizioni Monfortane, 1991) 345–360.

33 *Treatise on True Devotion* #125; cf. also Alphonse Bossard, S.M.M., "Se consacrer à Marie," *Cahiers Marials* 137 (1 avril 1983) 100–01.

34 Joseph de Sainte-Marie, *Teologia e Spiritualità della Consacrazione a Maria* III-2 – III-59.

35 Joseph de Sainte-Marie, *Teologia* III-7.

we make with her in order to permit her to exercise fully in us her maternal function—consecrating, sanctifying and enlivening us.[36] Again he says that

> To consecrate oneself to Mary, as we have said, is to make a covenant with her, which allows us to live more deeply that which we made with Christ in our Baptism. We see clearly now the two complementary dimensions, or better, the double movement:
>
> is to give oneself to Mary in order to receive from her, through her, with her and in her the life of Christ;
>
> and to receive from Mary the life of Christ in order to give her the glory which Christ himself wishes through her, or rather which he wishes to receive through himself in her.[37]

Hence, from Père Joseph de Sainte-Marie's perspective, the act performed by Pope John Paul II on 13 May 1982 in Fatima "was an act of 'affidamento,' of entrusting, not a consecration properly so called,"[38] because

> To consecrate humanity or a particular people to God is to entrust it to Him; but it is to do something more—it is to undertake at the same time to sanctify that humanity and to start it at once on the road to conversion and sanctification.[39]

While Laurentin argued that the word consecration says too much, Joseph de Sainte-Marie argued that the word entrustment doesn't say enough.

Another factor that may be well considered at this point is John Paul's own intention in his use of the cognate terms "entrust" and "entrustment" and their meaning in his own mother tongue. The late Father Jerzy Domanski, O.F.M. Conv., an expert on the writings of Saint Maximilian-Maria Kolbe, pointed out that in

36 Joseph de Sainte-Marie, *Teologia* III-58 – III-59.

37 Joseph de Sainte-Marie, *Teologia* V-11 – V-12 (my translation).

38 Joseph de Sainte-Marie, *Reflections* 19.

39 Joseph de Sainte-Marie, *Reflections* 29.

the writings of Saint Maximilian one meets the interchangeable use of two terms: consecration (in Polish: *poswiecenie)* and self-giving/abandonment[40] (in Polish: *oddanie*).[41] The late Father George Kosicki, C.S.B. (1928–2014), had considered at some length the meaning of the Polish word most frequently used by John Paul II, translated into Italian as "affidare" and into English as "entrust." The word is *zawierzać*, the same word employed in Cardinal Wyszyński's various consecrations of Poland.[42]

Let us allow Father Kosicki to share some of his discoveries about this word:

> I continued to wonder about the word "entrust" until I met a priest from Poland, a colleague of the present Pope while at the University of Lublin where Karol Wojtyła taught as Bishop of Krakow. I asked him about the word "entrust" and its Polish meaning, mentioning that I was disappointed that he didn't use the word "consecrate" to Mary in his *Letter to all Priests* [of 8 April 1979[43]]. His response was very clear and reassuring. He pointed out that the Polish word "zawierzać" (translated as "entrust") is a strong word and is used for what we call in English "consecration" to Mary. He went on to say that the Polish word, which is the equivalent root word to the English "consecration" (viz. "*konsekracia*"), is usually reserved for the consecration at Mass. He went further to point out that the word "entrust" was a special word for John Paul II because of the way he has used it in his Polish writings. He added that the motto of John Paul, "Totus Tuus," (I am) all yours (Mary), means, "I consecrate myself to you,

40 This second term suggests all the richness of meaning associated with the French word *abandon* as used by the writers of the seventeenth century French School, especially by Jean-Pierre de Caussade, S.J. Cf. J. Neville Ward, "Abandon" in Gordon S. Wakefield (ed.), *The Westminster Dictionary of Christian Spirituality* (Philadelphia: The Westminster Press, 1983) 1–2; P. Pourrat, "Abandon," *DSp* 1:1–49.

41 Cited in Franzi 227.

42 Cf. George W. Kosicki, C.S.B., *Born of Mary* (Stockbridge, Massachusetts: Marian Press, 1985) 64.

43 *Inseg* II/1 (1979) 860–61; *ORE* 577:9.

Mary," and is what Pope John Paul has in mind when he uses "zawierzać" (translated into English as "entrust"). In short the Polish "to entrust" means "to consecrate."[44]

Let us consider the word that would best describe our relationship to Mary. Recently, a priest pointed out to me that for him the word "entrust" was a strong word because it was a general word and it can be used in a variety of ways in applying the word to Mary. The word "consecrate," however, is so strong a word that when it is applied to Mary it needs to be nuanced. It is something like the word "homage" where a distinction has to be made between *cultus latriæ* (worship of God) and *cultus hyperduliæ* (the homage we pay to Mary). This priest went on to point out that in translating a word from another language, the strong word usually becomes a weaker one. This seems to be the case with the word "entrust" when used as a translation for the Polish word used by John Paul II. The word "entrust," however, has the strength of describing what the Father did in his relationship to Mary (entrusting the Word to her) and what Jesus did in his own relationship to Mary and further what he did in his relationship to us on the Cross (Jn. 19:25–27). On the other hand we cannot dismiss the word "consecration" in regard to Mary after Vatican II. In choosing a proper word for this relationship the main point must be kept before us, namely, the reality that Mary is our mother and that, even more, she is charged with the role of preparing us, the Bride, the disciples, and this by way of the Cross. This is the role of Mary in spiritual warfare. Our part in this warfare means more than just a relationship with her as mother; it also means a relationship with her as queen-mother, standing with her at the Cross of Jesus. It seems that the word "entrust" could be used on two levels: first of all a confiding of our lives to Mary as mother and then, secondly, a confiding of our lives to Mary as queen, our leader in this spiritual warfare. The word "consecrate," however, is a word that makes clear this second aspect of

44 Kosicki 66–67.

> our relationship to Mary as our leader in spiritual warfare, leading us to the Cross and so on to the Cenacle to be fully Church.[45]

I believe that I have now sufficiently illustrated the principal issues involved in the contemporary discussion of "consecration or entrustment" in order to justify my own usage of both words in the title of this work and in describing Pope John Paul II's program as one of "consecration and entrustment" to Mary. I believe that each word can be justified and offer shades of meaning not conveyed by the other. In the next chapter we will consider further the philosophical and theological concept of analogy and its validity.

The Recovery of the Biblical Concept of Welcoming/ Receiving Mary

Another helpful insight of Stefano De Fiores regarding the question of the Christian's relationship to Mary revolves around the seemingly simple statement made in John 19:27: "And from that hour the disciple took her to his own home." The rich biblical theme of receiving/welcoming Mary provides a scriptural way of describing further this relationship of the disciple with Mary.

> To receive (*lambanein*) in the Johannine vocabulary is the verb of faith: it indicates a spiritual attitude, "it implies an availability and participation by the subject" and an interior disposition of openness. When it is concerned with the person of Jesus, as in John 1:12, "it is practically synonymous with *pistéuein*" (to believe)—says I. de la Potterie—concluding that "to receive Jesus and to receive his Mother" are, definitively, two equivalent attitudes.[46]
>
> If I must express a preference, this would be for the biblical expression put in evidence in our time in the exegesis

45 Kosicki 74–75.

46 De Fiores, *Maria nel Teologia Contemporanea* 327 (my translation). It might be noted that the word translated here as "receive" has the sense of "to receive graciously" or "to welcome." Cf. I. de la Potterie, S.J. "La parole de Jésus 'Voici ta Mère' et l'accueil de Disciple (Jn. 19, 27b)," *Marianum* 36 (1974) 33–35.

> of John 19:27: the welcome of Mary on the part of the disciple whom Jesus loved. To welcome Mary with all the richness of spiritual attitudes which the Johannine term allows, is a realistic and simple proposal, which has the advantage of being biblical and therefore potentially also ecumenical. To receive Mary signifies being open to her and her maternal mission, bringing her into one's own spiritual inwardness where Christ is already welcomed as also his other gifts in faith: it is an expression which evokes all Christian and Marian spirituality (although at different levels) of the New Testament. From the cultural point of view the welcome of the other is a categorical imperative if one wishes to construct a society, which is truly a communion.[47]

Bishop Franzi presented the matter in this way:

> How shall we describe this gesture of the apostle? Is he "entrusted" to Mary? Is he "consecrated" to her?
>
> It seems to us, in fact, that neither the one expression nor the other succeeds in saying all.
>
> The Gospel is simpler and more profound: it states the fact: "he received her"—that is the response to a reality in that case joyously known: "she is your mother."[48]

Here, the Bishop's remark is a good reminder that no one word, neither "entrustment" nor "consecration," nor even "welcome," can exhaust the richness of the disciple's relationship with Mary. The concept of "welcoming Mary into one's life," as Saint John Paul II put it on a number of significant occasions, will nonetheless bring out yet further dimensions in the Christian's relationship with Mary.

47 De Fiores, *Maria nel Teologia Contemporanea* 328 (my translation).

48 Franzi 226 (my translation).

Traditional Elements of the Theology of Marian Consecration largely absent from the Postconciliar Discussion

Finally, it might be noted that two themes traditionally related to the question of Marian consecration seem to be largely absent from contemporary discussion. The first is that of Our Lady's Queenship. It might be noted that this emphasis is at least implicitly present in the prayers of Saints Ildephonsus of Toledo and John of Damascus, who address Mary as "Lady" or "My Lady,"[49] and in the whole tradition of "Marian slavery."[50] Furthermore, the papal magisterium of the Venerable Pope Pius XII solemnly proposed Our Lady's Queenship as the doctrinal basis for the public acts of consecration to the Immaculate Heart of Mary and mandated the annual renewal of the consecration of the world to the Immaculate Heart every year on the Feast of the Queenship that he instituted.[51] I am aware of only two modern authors who have continued to treat of the theological link between Mary's Queenship and consecration to her: the late Father William G. Most (1914–1999)[52] and the late Monsignor Brunero Gherardini (1925–2017).[53]

The second theme is that of Mary's mediation. The two principal and most consistent proponents of Marian consecration

49 Cf. above (chapter 1, footnotes 35–43) 26-29. Interestingly the Venerable Pius XII cites both of these early witnesses of Marian consecration as attesting to Mary's queenship in his Encyclical, *Ad Cæli Reginam*, *AAS* 46 (1954) 629–30; *OL* #690.

50 Cf. above (chapter 1, footnotes 94–100) 41-42, especially the prayer of Bartolomé de los Rios (footnote 100) 42.

51 Cf. above (chapter 2, footnotes 109–113) 104-106.

52 Cf. the helpful bibliography on this topic and the treatment of the relationship between Mary's Queenship and consecration to her in William G. Most, "Marian Consecration as Service: Historical, Theological and Spiritual Reflections," *Miles Immaculatæ* 24 (1988) 441–451.

53 Cf. Brunero Gherardini, *Sta La Regina alla Tua Destra: Saggio storico-teologico sulla Regalità di Maria* (Rome: Edizioni Vivere In, 2002) 170–190. In this book, which is probably the most erudite and thorough study yet written on Our Lady's Queenship, Gherardini clearly favors the concept of "consecration" as much stronger and more deliberate than "entrustment."

among the canonized Saints of the Church are surely Louis-Marie Grignion de Montfort and Maximilian-Maria Kolbe. Both of them insist in their writings and formulae of consecration on this principle of Mary's maternal mediation as justifying the "total gift of oneself" to Mary.[54] So did the eminent Thomistic scholar, Père Reginald Garrigou-Lagrange, O.P.[55] The matter was summarized succinctly by Pius XII in an address to a Marian Congress in India at the conclusion of the Marian Year of 1954:

> But let not those without the Household of the Faith mistake for a moment the meaning, the source and the scope of your age-old devotion to Mary. Every flower your children lay at her feet, every song you sing to her matchless beauty, every appeal to her power and compassion must be known for what it is, first and finally: the expression and reflexion of your personal dedication, after her example, to the living Christ; to the Divine Child Whom she deserved, albeit through no merit of her own, to bear at Bethlehem; to the Divine Teacher, Who deigned to be taught human wisdom at her holy home in Nazareth; to the Divine Victim and Victor over sin and death, Whose redemptive Sacrifice she saw completed on Calvary. To Jesus, then, through Mary, leads the spiritual path of that authentic Marian devotion you proudly and publicly profess once more today, at the close of her historic Centenary. If you have entrusted to her maternal care and vigilance the most delicate and urgent of your family and social problems—witness the ardent resolution of your successive Marian Congresses—the light and strength you seek is not hers

54 With regard to Saint Louis de Montfort, cf. *Love of Eternal Wisdom* #207, 223; *Treatise on True Devotion* #24, 25, 28, 55 86, 142; *Secret of Mary* #35–37; Patrick Gaffney, S.M.M., *Mary's Spiritual Maternity according to St. Louis de Montfort* (BayShore, NY: Montfort Publications, 1976) 30–34; Idem, "Mary," in *Jesus Living in Mary: Handbook of the Spirituality of St Louis Marie de Montfort* (Bay Shore, NY: Montfort Publications, 1994) 710–712. With regard to Saint Maximilian Maria Kolbe, cf. the entry under *mediazione* in the analytical index of *Scritti di Massimiliano Kolbe* (Rome: ENMI Editrice Nazionale M.I., 1997) 2559.

55 Reginald Garrigou-Lagrange, O.P., *The Mother of the Saviour and Our Interior Life*, trans. Bernard J. Kelly, C.S.Sp. (St. Louis: B. Herder Book Company, 1957) 270–276; *The Three Ages of the Interior Life* II trans. Sister Timothea Doyle, O.P. (St. Louis: B. Herder Book Company, 1948) 265–271.

> to give, but only to procure from the Sacred Heart of her Son and Savior. She is the crystal-pure Channel, not the Fountain, of that superabundant divine grace you beg through her Immaculate Heart for home and Church and country.[56]

The theme of Mary's mediatory role in our salvation was not entirely absent in Father De Fiores' earlier discussion of the problematic of consecration/entrustment to Mary when he cited contemporary authors,[57] although he gave it scant attention elsewhere in his study of contemporary Mariology when he considered it in an ecumenical context and eventually opted for the concept of "presence" as a more auspicious route to be pursued in dialogue.[58] As we shall see in the next chapter, he—along with a number of others in the leadership of the Pontifical International Marian Academy and allied institutions such as the Pontifical Faculty of Theology at the Marianum in Rome—had effectively sought to minimize any discussion of Marian mediation as it had been previously understood.

Happily, Father Alfredo Marranzini, S.J., in his analysis of the theological significance of the Pope's Act of Consecration and Entrustment of 25 March 1984, touched upon both of these themes as he attempted to sum up the nature of this act. His definition would seem to provide an appropriate conclusion to our consideration of contemporary theological reflection on the phenomenon of Marian consecration in the spiritual journey of the Church.

56 *AAS* 46 (1954) 726–727.

57 Cf. De Fiores, *Maria nella Teologia Contemporanea*, quoting K. Rahner 320; quoting J. Alfaro 322.

58 De Fiores, *Maria nella Teologia Contemporanea* 248–50. Cf. also his "Linee di Sviluppo della Riflessione Teologica sul Ruolo Storico di Maria," in *Il Ruolo di Maria nell'oggi della Chiesa e del Mondo* (Rome: Edizioni Marianum, 1979) 205–18, especially 208 where he considers the same proposal. In his treatment of the history of Marian consecration, naturally he adverts to the principle of necessity, "Cons" 404–405, 408.

This [consecration] is an act of love directed to a creature who was chosen by God in a unique manner for a mission which no one can leave out of consideration, and who has reciprocated such predilection by carrying out her duties in the most unconditional manner. Such an act of love, proximately oriented to a being who, notwithstanding her sublime holiness and her rank as Queen beside her Son, remains entirely in the human sphere, has as its only end the thrice "holy" Lord of whose glory the earth is full (cf. Is. 6:3). The acceptance of the mediation of a creature does not constitute an obstacle to an immediate offering to God and his exclusive adoration, but facilitates it and makes it concrete and in the final analysis is willed by God Himself and corresponds to our human makeup.[59]

59 Alfredo Marranzini, S.J., "L'Atto di Affidamento e Consacrazione a Maria," *Civiltà Cattolica* 135 (1984) 28 (my translation); ibid., "Consacrazione a Maria in Prospettiva Teologico-Antropologica," in *Madonna: Rivista di Cultura Mariana* 27 (agosto 1979) 72–73.

PART TWO

THE THOUGHT OF POPE JOHN PAUL II

CHAPTER FIVE

The Theological Problem of Marian Consecration and the Principles of its Resolution

When one speaks of consecration "to Mary" or "to her Immaculate Heart," one immediately raises a theological question: How is it possible to legitimate the application to Mary of a term, which, in its elementary sense, applies only to God? Let us begin with a traditional Catholic definition of the term "consecration":

> In the strict sense, consecration signifies the total dedication of a person or thing to God and His service, and its consequent separation from ordinary human use. By the act of consecration a state or stable condition is inaugurated: what is consecrated thereafter belongs exclusively to God. In common Christian usage the term is applied to the conversion of bread and wine into the Body and Blood of Christ, to elevation to the episcopate, to the solemn blessing of churches, altars, sacred vessels, and cemeteries. But the idea of consecration is realized also in Baptism, which may indeed be called the fundamental consecration of the Christian life. Through it the baptized person, by a title distinct from that of creation, belongs and is consecrated to God. Confirmation also, and the Sacrament of Orders, involving the Christian more fully in the service of God, can be considered consecrations, or at least as enlargements of the consecration of Baptism.
>
> In addition to this type of consecration, there is another that exists when an individual not only belongs to God, but also sees the relationship and is freely determined

by his own choice to accept it, to live in accord with the responsibilities it imposes, and perhaps also to undertake good works or practices that are not obligatory by reason of his baptismal commitment. Thus, from the 4th century, the vow of virginity, accompanied by the liturgical blessing, was called a consecration. Later, the vows of religion were recognized as having a similar character. Similarly, any engagement undertaken by an individual to accept his already existing baptismal obligations, or to enlarge the scope of his service to God, can be considered a kind of consecration, although the idea is less perfectly realized in a determination not stabilized by vow and unratified by the authority of the Church.[1]

Given this definition, which represents classical Catholic theology reaffirmed by the usage of the Second Vatican Council,[2] how can "consecration to Mary" escape the charge of idolatry or, at the very least, of being a misnomer? This is precisely the *status quaestionis*, which must inevitably be addressed at the beginning of any such study.[3] Because this question has been posed explicitly since the dawning of the golden age of

1 N. Lohkamp, "Consecration, Personal," *NCE* 4 (New York: McGraw-Hill Book Company, 1967) 209; cf. also Joseph de Finance, S.J., "Consécration," *DSp* 2:1576–1579.

2 Cf. *LG* #28 speaks of bishops as sharers in the consecration and mission of Jesus. *CD* #15 says that bishops have been consecrated as true priests of the New Testament. *PC* #5 speaks of the special consecration of religious as a fuller expression of their baptismal consecration. *AA* #3 refers to the fact that all the laity by virtue of Baptism and Confirmation are consecrated in order to offer spiritual sacrifices and bear witness to Christ throughout the world. *AG* #18 speaks of the deeper consecration made to God by religious as signifying the intimate nature of the Christian vocation. *AG* #39 states that priests should be aware that their very lives are consecrated to the service of the missions. *PO* #2 describes bishops as sharers of the consecration and mission of Christ. *PO* #7 speaks of the unity of the consecration and mission of priests and bishops. *PO* #12 says that priests who have already received the consecration of Baptism are consecrated to God in a new way through Ordination so that they may become living instruments of Christ the Eternal Priest.

3 Cf. Alphonse Bossard, S.M.M., "Se Consacrer à Marie," *Cahiers Marials* 137 (1 avril 1983) 97–98; Stefano De Fiores, S.M.M., *Maria Presenza viva nel popolo di Dio* (Rome: Edizioni Monfortane, 1980) 365–67; "Cons" 395; Alfredo Marranzini, S.J., "L'Atto di Affidamento e Consacrazione a Maria," *Civiltà Cattolica* 135:2 (1984) 17, 19.

French spirituality inaugurated by Cardinal Pierre de Bérulle, which brought it into prominence, the same author cited above provides us further data that leads in the direction of a solution.

> Strictly speaking, one can consecrate himself only to God, for only God has the right to man's total dedication and service. Consecration to Christ, to the Sacred Heart, is legitimate because of the Hypostatic Union. But "consecration" to the Blessed Virgin, or even to St. Joseph or to other saints, is not unknown to Christian piety. In the case of St. Joseph or the other saints, this is to be understood as consecration in a broad sense of the term, and it signifies no more than an act of special homage to one's heavenly protector. The case of the Blessed Virgin, however, is not the same. The importance of her role in Christian spirituality is such that formulas of dedication to her appear to have more profound meaning. Her position in the economy of salvation is inseparable from that of her Son. Her desires and wants are His, and she is in a unique position to unite Christians fully, quickly, and effectively to Christ, so that dedication to her is in fact dedication to Christ. French spirituality has made much of consecration to Mary. Cardinal Bérulle encouraged the vow of servitude to Jesus and Mary. St. John Eudes propagated the devotion of consecration not only to the Sacred Heart, but to the heart of Mary as well. But the practice achieved its strongest expression in the *Traité de la vraie dévotion à la Sainte Vierge* of St. Louis Marie Grignion de Montfort. The act of personal consecration according to de Montfort, is an act of complete and total consecration. It consists in giving oneself entirely to Mary in order to belong wholly to Jesus through her.[4]

In effect, the author of this article points to a resolution of this problem along two complementary lines. First, and admittedly only very implicitly, he evokes the principle of analogy. Second, and quite explicitly, he points to the unique role of Mary in the

4 Lohkamp; cf. also de Finance 1579–1582.

mystery of Christ and the economy of our salvation, specifically her mediation.

5.1. The Principle of Analogy

I say that he evokes the principle of analogy implicitly because he says, "Strictly speaking, one can consecrate himself only to God." The late Father Stefano De Fiores frequently adverted to the principle of analogy in dealing with the subject of Marian consecration in his earlier writings. Here are two excerpts from his article on consecration in the *Nuovo Dizionario di Mariologia*:

> The only way to be able to apply a term to God and to a creature is to have recourse to analogy, which is based precisely on the likeness in the difference. The analogical use of consecration referred to Mary maintains a sense of "total and perpetual gift" which is required in order to bring this usage in line with the light of revelation and theology ... The gift to her is analogous to that which is made to God since it maintains the significance of the total and perpetual gift, but on the different level proper to a creature.[5]

Analogy, in the classical sense in which this term is used by St. Thomas Aquinas and his followers, denotes "a kind of predication midway between univocation and equivocation."[6] Here is the Angelic Doctor's own description of what he meant by analogous predication:

---

5 "Cons" 409, 412 (my translation); cf. also the section on the analogical use of "consecration" with regard to Mary in his *Maria nella Teologia Contemporanea* 323–325. In his article "Consacrazione" in *Maria: Nuovissimo Dizionario* I, he recognized the historical use of the term "consecration" in its analogical sense (383–386), but indicated his clear preference for alternative language, particularly for the word entrustment (387–389). This is further substantiated in his article "Affidamento" in Volume I of the same *Maria: Nuovissimo Dizionario* (1–20).

6 G. P. Klubertanz, "Analogy," *New Catholic Encyclopedia* 1 (New York: McGraw-Hill Book Company, 1967) 463.

> It is evident that terms which are used in this way [i.e. analogically] are intermediate between univocal and equivocal terms. In the case of univocity one term is predicated of different things according to a meaning [*ratio*] that is absolutely one and the same; for example, the term *animal*, predicated of a horse or of an ox, signifies a living sensory substance. In the case of equivocity the same term is predicated of various things according to totally different meanings, as is evident from the term *dog*, predicated both of a constellation and of a certain species of animal. But in those things which are spoken of in the way mentioned previously [i.e.] analogically, the same term is predicated of various things according to a meaning that is partly the same and partly different: different as regards the different modes of relation, but the same as regards that to which there is a relation. [*In his vero quae praedicto modo dicuntur, idem nomen de diversis praedicatur secundum rationem partim eamdem, partim diversam. Diversam quidem quantum ad diversos modos relationis. Eamdem vero quantum ad id ad quod fit relatio.*][7]

Even more precisely, when one speaks of "consecration to God" and "consecration to Mary," one is effectively speaking in the first place of what the disciples of St. Thomas call the "analogy of attribution." Gardeil says that

> In the analogy of attribution there is always a primary (or principal) analogate (or analogue), in which alone the idea, the formality, signified by the analogous term is intrinsically realized. The other (secondary) analogates have this formality predicated of them by mere extrinsic denomination.[8]

Following this paradigm, then, "consecration to God" is the primary analogate, whereas "consecration to Mary" is a secondary analogate. In other words, the term "consecration" signifies

7 *In XI Metaph.* lect. 3, no. 2197 quoted in H. D. Gardeil, O.P., *Introduction to the Philosophy of St. Thomas Aquinas IV: Metaphysics*, trans. John A. Otto (St. Louis: B. Herder Book Co., 1967) 50–51.

8 Gardeil 53.

something that is common to both analogates, the recognition of our dependence on them, but since God is our Creator and Mary is a creature, that dependence cannot be exactly the same.[9]

But it can be held as well that such usage of the term "consecration to Mary" is also an instance of the "analogy of proportionality" which Gardeil explains in this way:

> It will be remembered that in the analogy of attribution the (secondary) analogates are unified by being referred to a single term, the primary analogue. This marks a basic contrast with the analogy now under consideration, that of proportionality; for here the analogates are unified on a different basis, namely by reason of the proportion they have to each other. Example: in the order of knowledge we say there is an analogy between seeing (bodily vision) and understanding (intellectual vision) because seeing is to the eye as understanding is to the soul.[10]

Theologians have long recognized that there exists an analogy, a certain "likeness in difference" between Jesus and Mary, a certain symmetry and complementarity, though not identity, between them.[11]

This concept of the analogy between Jesus and Mary is explicitly cited in the papal magisterium itself. It is beautifully illustrated by the Venerable Pius XII in his Encyclical, *Ad Cæli Reginam* of 11 October 1954:

---

9 Cf. J. Bittremieux, "Consecratio Mundi Immaculato Cordi B. Mariae Virginis," *Ephemerides Theologicae Lovanienses* 20 (1943) 102; Gabriele Roschini, O.S.M., "La Consacrazione del Mondo al Cuore Immacolato di Maria" in *Il Cuore Immacolato di Maria, Settimana di Studi Mariani* (Rome: Edizioni Marianum, 1946) 60.

10 Gardeil 54.

11 On the principle of analogy as it pertains to Mariology, cf. José M. Bover, S.J., "El Principio Mariologico de Analogia," *ASC* XI:1–13; Gabriele M. Roschini, O.S.M., *Dizionario di Mariologia* (Roma: Editrice Studium, 1961) 30–31; Roschini, *Maria Santissima nella Storia della Salvezza* I: *Introduzione Generale* (Isola del Liri: Tipografia Editrice M. Pisani, 1969) 171–177; Brunero Gherardini, *La Madre: Maria in una sintesi storico-teologica* (Frigento: Casa Mariana Editrice, seconda edizione riveduta e aggiornata, 2007) 284–286; Emile Neubert, S.M., *Mary in Doctrine* (Milwaukee: Bruce Publishing Company, 1954) 5–8.

From these considerations, the proof develops on these lines: If Mary, in taking an active part in the work of salvation, was, by God's design, associated with Jesus Christ, the source of salvation itself, in a manner comparable to that in which Eve was associated with Adam, the source of death, so that it may be stated that the work of our salvation was accomplished by a kind of 'recapitulation,' in which a virgin was instrumental in the salvation of the human race, just as a virgin had been closely associated with its death; if, moreover, it can likewise be stated that this glorious Lady had been chosen Mother of Christ 'in order that she might become a partner [*consors*] in the redemption of the human race'; and if, in truth, 'it was she who, free of the stain of actual and original sin and ever most closely bound to her Son, on Golgotha offered that Son to the Eternal Father together with the complete sacrifice of her maternal rights and maternal love, like a new Eve, for all the sons of Adam, stained as they were by his lamentable fall,'[12] then it may be legitimately concluded that as Christ, the new Adam, must be called a king not merely because he is Son of God, but also because he is our Redeemer, so analogously [*ita quodam analogiæ modo*], the Most Blessed Virgin is queen not only because she is Mother of God, but also because, as the new Eve, she was associated with the new Adam.

Certainly, in the full and strict meaning of the term, only Jesus Christ, the God-Man, is King; but Mary, too, as Mother of the divine Christ, as his associate in the redemption [*socia in divini Redemptoris opera*], in his struggle with his enemies and his final victory over them, has a share, though in a limited and analogous way [*quamvis temperato modo et analogiæ ratione*], in his royal dignity.[13]

12 He is citing here his Encyclical Letter, *Mystici Corporis*, of 29 June 1943: *AAS* 35 (1943) 247 [*OL* #383].

13 *D-H* #3915–3916. *AAS* 46 (1954) 634–635. I have used here the English translation in the recently published Latin-English bilingual edition.

Mary, then, shares in the royal dignity of Jesus; as he is King so she is Queen, "though in a limited and analogous way." John Paul II in his general audience address of 23 July 1997 adverted to this teaching of Pius XII on the Queenship of Mary as well:

> My venerable Predecessor Pius XII, in his Encyclical *Ad Coeli Reginam* to which the text of the Constitution *Lumen Gentium* refers, indicates as the basis for Mary's Queenship in addition to her motherhood, her co-operation in the work of the Redemption. The Encyclical recalls the liturgical text: 'There was St Mary, Queen of heaven and Sovereign of the world, sorrowing near the Cross of our Lord Jesus Christ' (*AAS* 46 [1954] 634). It then establishes an analogy between Mary and Christ [*Essa stablisce poi un'analogia tra Maria e Cristo*], which helps us understand the significance of the Blessed Virgin's royal status. Christ is King not only because he is Son of God, but also because he is the Redeemer; Mary is Queen not only because she is Mother of God, but also because, associated as the new Eve with the new Adam, she cooperated in the work of the redemption of the human race (*AAS* 46 [1954] 635).
>
> In Mark's Gospel, we read that on the day of the Ascension the Lord Jesus 'was taken up into heaven, and sat down at the right hand of God' (16:19). In biblical language 'to sit at the right hand of God' means sharing his sovereign power. Sitting 'at the right hand of the Father,' he establishes his kingdom, God's kingdom. Taken up into heaven, Mary is associated with the power of her Son and is dedicated to the extension of the Kingdom, sharing in the diffusion of divine grace in the world.
>
> In looking at the analogy between Christ's Ascension and Mary's Assumption, we can conclude that Mary, in dependence on Christ, is the Queen who possesses and exercises over the universe a sovereignty granted to her by her Son [*Guardando all'analogia fra l'Ascensione di Cristo e l'Assunzione di Maria, possiamo concludere che, in dipendenza da Cristo, Maria è la regina che possiede ed*

> *esercita sull'universo una sovranità donatale dallo stesso suo Figlio*].[14]

We can also say, then, that the consecration to the Immaculate Heart of Mary bears a proportionate relationship to the consecration to the Sacred Heart of Jesus because it is rooted in the latter.[15] It is interesting to note that Père Bossard, basing himself on the teaching of de Montfort, says that the consecration to Christ through Mary also implies a consecration to Mary. In that sense, Mary is the means or proximate end that leads to Christ who is the final end of the consecration.[16] This, in effect, is what the Venerable Pope Pius XII understood and taught regarding his consecration of the world to the Immaculate Heart of Mary.[17] In the words of Father Firmin Schmidt, O.F.M. Cap.:

> It is especially worthy of note that an obvious parallel is established between the consecration to the Sacred Heart by Leo XIII and this consecration by Pius XII to the Immaculate Heart. Consecration, by its very nature, is an expression of reverent submission and an acknowledgment of the dominion of him to whom the consecration is made. In the consecration to the Sacred Heart there is the recognition of Our Lord's supreme dominion. In the consecration to the Immaculate Heart there is also a true dominion recognized in Our Blessed Mother. However, Mary's dominion is subordinate to that of Christ and dependent upon Him. Pope Pius XII himself in subsequent documents confirmed the significant parallel between the two consecrations.[18]

As we have already seen, in his great Encyclical on the Queenship of Mary, *Ad Cæli Reginam*, Pius XII specifically taught

14 *Inseg* XX/2 (1997) 56 [*ORE* 1502:7].

15 Cf. Bittremieux 102; Roschini 60.

16 Cf. above 150.

17 Cf. above 103; 106.

18 Firmin M. Schmidt, O.F.M. Cap., "The Universal Queenship of Mary," *Mariology* 2:510.

that Mary's Queenship, one of the fundamental dogmatic bases of consecration to her, is analogous to the Kingship of Christ. "Mary," he said, "has a share, though in a limited and analogous way [*quamvis temperato modo et analogiæ ratione*], in his royal dignity." Hence it might be said, in effect, that the magisterium of the Church recognizes an "analogy of attribution" between the consecration to the Sacred Heart of Jesus and to that of the Immaculate Heart of Mary and, even more explicitly, an "analogy of proportionality." Monsignor John F. Murphy summed up the issue fairly succinctly, even while writing before the issuance of *Ad Cæli Reginam*:

> In the devotion to the Sacred Heart, we consecrate ourselves to our Lord inasmuch as the redemption of Christ and the shedding of His blood gave Him a claim to all men. Analogously, a consecration can also be made to Mary because of her share in this Redemption and the all-embracing claims of her Motherhood.
>
> We say "analogously," for though the term "consecration" is used in reference to both Christ and to Mary, when used in reference to Mary and her Immaculate Heart, it has a partly identical and a partly different meaning. The difference arises because of the divergence in the sovereignty or dominion of Jesus and Mary upon which the consecration is based. The analogy, however, is not simply made metaphorically, but is an analogy of proper proportionality and, further, an analogy of attribution, for our dependence of Mary, the reason for our act, is essentially a dependence on God.[19]

In his earlier writing Father De Fiores clearly summarized the classical position:

> It has become an acquired datum for all that "consecration" in the strict sense and according to biblical usage implies an act of *latria* (adoration) and is reserved to God. Nevertheless it is possible to speak of consecration to Mary

19 Murphy, *Mary's Immaculate Heart* 98.

> not merely in a metaphorical sense, but in a proper sense, even if analogical, secondary, derivative and instrumental.[20]

Closely related to the principle of analogy in terms of seeing our relationship to Mary in proportion to our relationship to God is the traditional distinction made in Catholic theology about cultus.[21] Here is a classical presentation of that doctrine:

> Ordinarily understood, cult implies three acts: intellectual recognition of another's excellence, voluntary submission, and an act expressing this recognition and submission. If this cult is offered to a person whose excellence is uncreated, it is called *latria*; if to a person whose excellence is created, it is called *dulia*. If, however, this created excellence is altogether and entirely singular, as in the case of the Blessed Mother, the cult offered is called *hyperdulia* …
>
> Participating in the virtue of religion, moreover, is the virtue of supernatural dulia and consequently that of hyperdulia. Accordingly, the devotion we manifest towards Our Lady, though immediately elicited by hyperdulia, does not for that reason fail to participate in the nature of that devotion which is the act of the virtue of religion. The devotion one has to God's saints does not terminate in them, but reaches even to God in the servants of God …
>
> Now the privileges of the Blessed Mother upon which hyperdulia is founded differ in degree and *nature* from those of the saints which cause us to venerate them. Mary shares more than the ordinary grace of adoptive filiation. To her is attributed the plenitude of grace, and over and above this great gift is added the specifically distinct privilege of special affinity to God, the grace of Divine Motherhood. Mary, as the Mother of God, enjoys therefore a special relationship not only with the Second

20 *Maria nella Teologia Contemporanea* 323 (my translation). Cf. also his article "Consacrazione" in *Maria: Nuovissimo Dizionario* I:383–386. Cf. also de Finance *DSp* 2:1579 whom he seems to follow closely on this point.

21 Ordinarily I prefer to use this word in its Latin form in order to avoid the connotations of the word "cult" in present English usage. Further, the Latin term embraces a broader range. It may refer to the worship rendered to God as well as to the highest degree of veneration rendered to Mary and to the veneration we render to the angels and the saints.

> Person of the Blessed Trinity, but mediately, through Him, with the other Persons of the Godhead. All other creatures, even St. Joseph, no matter how closely associated with Christ, pertain to the Hypostatic Union only extrinsically; the Blessed Mother, however, intrinsically.[22]

It ought to be noted that these distinctions are deeply rooted in the practice of the Church and the theology of the medieval schoolmen, especially Saint Thomas Aquinas who discusses *hyperdulia* in his *Summa Theologiae*.[23] For him the homage and worship which we owe God comes under the cardinal or moral virtue of justice of which the virtue of religion is a specific part.[24] This is to be distinguished from the infused theological virtues, such as faith, hope and charity, which have God as their object, whereas the virtue of religion has as its object the honor, reverence and worship which are owed to God as a matter of justice. Saint Thomas further distinguishes between the proper and immediate acts which this virtue elicits, which are acts of *cultus* in the strict sense, and those acts which are directed to our neighbor but are ultimately motivated by the desire to honor God.[25] Hence, when Monsignor Murphy speaks of *dulia* and *hyperdulia* as participating in the virtue of religion, he is following this well-established terminology.

While by no means repudiating the traditional teaching on *hyperdulia*, the term was evidently not used in the Second Vatican Council's treatment of Our Lady because of its pastoral orientation, but the reality was surely confirmed.

> This cult of Mary, as it has always existed in the Church, though it is altogether singular, differs essentially from the cult of adoration, which is shown to the Incarnate Word

---

22 John F. Murphy, "Origin and Nature of Marian Cult," Juniper Carol, O.F.M., ed., *Mariology* 3:10–11; cf. also A. Buono, "Hyperdulia," *Dictionary of Mary* (New York: Catholic Book Publishing Co., 1985) 129–130.

23 Cf. *ST* II-II, q. 103, a. 4; III, q. 25, a. 5.

24 *ST* II-II, q. 81, a. 4.

25 *ST* II-II, q. 81, a. 1, ad 1.

> equally with the Father and the Holy Spirit, and which the Marian cult promotes in a special way.[26]

Again, in his great *magna charta* of Marian devotion, *Marialis Cultus*, Blessed Paul VI underscores the reality of *hyperdulia* without using the term.

> The development, desired by us, of devotion to the Blessed Virgin Mary is an indication of the Church's genuine piety. This devotion fits—as we have indicated above—into the only worship that is rightly called "Christian," because it takes its origin and effectiveness from Christ, finds its complete expression in Christ, and leads through Christ in the Spirit to the Father. In the sphere of worship this devotion necessarily reflects God's redemptive plan, in which a special form of veneration is appropriate to the singular place which Mary occupies in that plan. Indeed every authentic development of Christian worship is necessarily followed by a fitting increase of veneration for the Mother of the Lord. Moreover, the history of piety shows how "the various forms of devotion towards the Mother of God that the Church has approved within the limits of wholesome and orthodox doctrine" have developed in harmonious subordination to the worship of Christ, and have gravitated towards this worship as to their natural and necessary point of reference.[27]

Before continuing the thread of our exposition of the *status quæstionis* following the lines suggested in Father Lohkamp's article cited above, I would like to discuss briefly the question of the nature of Marian consecration as an act of the virtue of religion in order to establish a further point of reference in our inquiry into the "program of consecration and entrustment" to Mary of Pope Saint John Paul II. I present first the conclusion of a rigorous study of Marian consecration according to the canons

26 LG #66 (*Unger* 16). In *Redemptoris Mater* #42 John Paul II adds a further gloss to this assertion of the Council: "This cult is altogether special; it bears in itself and *expresses* the profound *link* which exists *between the Mother of Christ and the Church*" (*Inseg* X/1 (1987) 731; St. Paul Editions, 60).

27 *AAS* 66 (1974) 134 [Paul VI, *Mary – God's Mother and Ours* 97].

of classic Thomistic theology. This study was done by Father Juan Ramon Urquia Barroso, S.M., and presented to the Faculty of Theology of the University of Fribourg in 1958. Father Urquia draws a conclusion, which we are now in a position to comprehend more readily, given the exposition of terms already presented.

> Marian consecration, we say, is an elicit act of Religion. It is what is deduced in projecting over the previous positive results the light of Moral Theology, such as St. Thomas and his best commentators expound it. Thus we emphasize the essential religious value of certain acts of cult which are performed in honor of Mary. Not all of them are elicit acts of hyperdulia. There are some, such as prayer and sacrifice, whose intrinsic religious nature can not be justified either by the implicit religious character of hyperdulia, or by the governance of religion, or even less by attributing a strictly religious but relative value to them. The same thing occurs with Marian consecration. It is not an act of hyperdulia, but of religion. From religion it receives its essential content. Only God can require of man an act such as implies an absolute submission. Strictly speaking, we do not consecrate ourselves to Mary as the object *cui*, but to God through her mediation. Such a consecration renders religious cult to God as Supreme Being, and a cult of hyperdulia to Mary as Mediatrix at the same time. By this we do not impoverish Marian consecration. On the contrary, it is precisely as an act of religion that it acquires its full value, that which has been given to it throughout history, and which with greater or less clarity we really express in saying that we consecrate ourselves to Mary, and through her to God, or that we consecrate ourselves to God through Mary.[28]

Quite deliberately, Father Urquia rejects the principle of analogy as a solution to the theological question of Marian

28 Juan Ramon Urquia Barroso, S.M., *The Theological Content of Consecration to Mary*, trans. Robert Wood, S.M. (Dayton: Marianist Resources Commission, n.d.) 102–103.

consecration. He is not willing to recognize that Marian consecration could be addressed immediately to God (as an act of *latria*) as well as also being addressed mediately to Mary (as an act of *hyperdulia*). He will not allow that Mary could be the object *cui*, the person to whom the consecration is made, even if not the final object of the consecration. His argument seems somewhat confusing since, in the final analysis, he does admit that Marian consecration renders "a cult of hyperdulia to Mary as Mediatrix at the same time."

It would seem that the crux of Urquia's problem is that he refuses to recognize what Monsignor Murphy points out, i.e., that *hyperdulia* participates in the virtue of religion. A more balanced solution of the question, which makes implicit use of the principle of analogy, still seems to be that offered by Saint Louis-Marie Grignion de Montfort:

> It follows that we consecrate ourselves at one and the same time to Mary and to Jesus. We give ourselves to Mary because Jesus chose her as the perfect means to unite himself to us and unite us to him. We give ourselves to Jesus because he is our last end.[29]

I submit that this is also the sense in which it has been used by the magisterium. The consecration made by the Venerable Pius XII on 31 October 1942 really was addressed to Mary, as have been the subsequent Pontifical acts, and he readily adverted to the fact that this consecration was complementary (analogical) to that made to the Sacred Heart of Jesus and that it was addressed to Mary as the object *cui*:

> Finally, just as the Church and the entire human race were consecrated to the Heart of your Jesus, because by placing in Him every hope, It may be for them a token and pledge of victory and salvation; so, henceforth, may they be perpetually consecrated to you, to your Immaculate Heart

29 *Treatise on True Devotion* #125; cf. also Francesco M. Franzi, "Per un orientamento sul tema della 'consacrazione a Maria,'" in *Teologia e Pastorale della Consacrazione a Maria* 8.

> [*così parimenti da oggi siano essi in perpetuo consacrati anche a Voi, al vostro Cuore Immacolato*], O Our Mother and Queen of the world, in order that your love and protection may hasten the triumph of the Kingdom of God.[30]

To what extent do the Marian consecrations made by Pope Saint John Paul II verify the conclusions we have reached? Surely he uses the language of analogy while favoring the term "entrust" by using it much more frequently than "consecrate."[31] Granted that he does not explicitly call our attention to the fact that he is making use of the principle of analogy in the examples which we are about to cite, he does advert to that principle in a number of his more theological addresses and documents.[32] His most illuminating statements on this subject for our purposes would seem to be in his Apostolic Letter *Mulieris Dignitatem* issued on the occasion of the closing of the Marian Year:

> *God speaks in human language*, using human concepts and images. If this manner of expressing himself is characterized by a certain anthropomorphism, the reason is that man is "like" God: created in his image and likeness. But then, *God too* is in some measure "like man," and precisely because of this likeness, he can be humanly known. At the same time, the language of the Bible is sufficiently precise to indicate the limits of the "likeness," the limits of the "analogy." For biblical Revelation says that, while man's "likeness" to God is true, the *"non-likeness"* which separates the whole of creation from the Creator is *still more essentially true.* Although man is created in God's likeness, God does not

30 *AAS* 34 (1942) 318–19, 325 [*OL* #380 (alt.)]. Pius was quite explicit about the analogy between the Kingship of Christ and the Queenship of Mary, which provide solid doctrinal bases for the respective consecrations as we have noted above (chapter 2, footnotes 67–68 and 101–118) 93, 102-107.

31 Cf. De Fiores, "Consacrazione," in *Maria: Nuovissimo Dizionario* I:377.

32 Cf. his Encyclical, *Dominum et Vivificantem*, #64, *Inseg* IX/1 (1986) 1543 [*ORE* 940:14]; his address to entrepreneurs in Buenos Aires of 11 April 1987, *Inseg* X/1 (1987) 1250 [*ORE* 988:13]; his homily for the First Sunday of Lent, 21 February 1988, *Inseg* XI/1 (1988) 492–93 [*ORE* 1030:10]; his address to the first group of the Bishops of India on the "ad limina" visit, 6 April 1989 [*Inseg* XII/1 (1989) 749; *ORE* 1085:3].

> cease to be for him the one "who dwells in unapproachable light" (I Tim. 6:16): he is the "Different One," by essence the "totally Other."[33]
>
> If God's love for the human person, for the Chosen People of Israel, is presented by the Prophets as the love of the bridegroom for the bride, such an analogy expresses the "spousal" quality and the divine and non-human character of God's love: "For your Maker is your husband … the God of the whole earth he is called" (Is. 54:5). The same can also be said of the spousal love of Christ the Redeemer: "For God so loved the world that he gave his only Son" (Jn. 3:16). It is a matter, therefore, of God's love expressed by means of the Redemption accomplished by Christ. According to Saint Paul's Letter, this love is "like" the spousal love of human spouses, but naturally it is not "the same." For the analogy implies a likeness, while at the same time leaving ample room for non-likeness.[34]

Here, then, follow some examples of John Paul's analogous use of the term entrustment (and other cognate forms) on the levels of both *latria* and *hyperdulia*:

> I am going to the Basilica of Notre-Dame, the Mother of the Churches of this diocese, and one of the most venerable religious buildings of this nation. There I wish to entrust to the Lord and to the Blessed Virgin my wishes for the whole of the French people.[35]
>
> God bless Brazil! I entrust it to Christ and to his Mother: Mary "Aparecida."[36]

33 *Inseg* XI/3 (1988) 258–59, 330 [*ORE* 1058:4].

34 *Inseg* XI/3 (1988) 301, 366 [*ORE* 1058:11]. In this case the Latin word rendered into English as "analogy" is *comparatio* while the Italian translation renders the word *analogia*, but in any case the text still serves admirably as a depiction of the classic scholastic concept of analogy, likeness in difference.

35 *Inseg* III/1 (1980) 1522 [*France* 26].

36 *Inseg* III/2 (1980) 270 [*Brazil* 390].

> Praying I entrust to Christ and his Mother all that has been accomplished in the last few months and is being accomplished.[37]

> Entrust yourselves to him [Christ] in your daily prayer, entrust yourselves to Mary, the Mother of Sorrows.[38]

> And now, Lord, I beseech You for my brothers and sisters, the Catholics of the Congo. I entrust them to You, since You have permitted me to visit them in their country … I entrust them also to Your holy Mother, the Blessed Virgin Mary, Mother of the Church and our Mother. May she take them under her motherly protection and watch over them in their difficulties! May she teach them to stand at the foot of Your cross and to gather around her while waiting for Your coming, at the end of time![39]

Here are representative instances of the linking of *hyperdulia* and *dulia*:

> May God preserve you, Turin! And you, always keep his Law! May God reward you, Turin, for this hospitality that you have given today to this Pope John Paul II who came to you as a pilgrim! This is my wish, which I entrust to the Great Mother of God, to the intercession of your Saints, to your goodwill![40]

> I entrust these sentiments to the prayer that we now raise to Our Lady, and to the intercession of the Martyr Paul Miki and his heroic companions who met death proclaiming the blessed names of Jesus and Mary.[41]

> I am happy to entrust this prayer to the intercession of the Blessed Virgin, "Salus Populi Romani," who has so often, in the course of the centuries, borne witness to her motherly care for this city. And I entrust it also to the intercession of the Holy Apostles Peter and Paul, whose blood bathed this Rome of ours, drawing from it that

37 *Inseg* III/2 (1980) 1792, 1794 [*ORE* 668:18].

38 *Inseg* IV/1 (1981) 910 [*ORE* 679:7].

39 *Inseg* III/1 (1980) 1147 [*Africa Ap* 148].

40 *Inseg* III/1 (1980) 918 [*ORE* 630:11].

41 *Inseg* III/2 (1980) 1103 [*ORE* 658:2].

> germination of Christian faith, which no event, however adverse, was ever subsequently able to suffocate.[42]
>
> Finally, I entrust you to the intercession of all the holy martyrs of Nagasaki, and especially to the protection of Mary, Queen of Martyrs and Mother of the Church.[43]
>
> I entrust these wishes to Saints Benedict, Cyril and Methodius, the Patron Saints of Europe; I entrust these wishes to the Blessed Virgin, the Queen of Peace; finally I entrust these wishes of mine to the Blessed Virgin of Jasna Góra, the Mother of Poland.[44]
>
> In all your efforts I commend you to the Blessed Virgin Mary and to Saint Joseph, to whom the Cathedrals of Trivandrum are dedicated.[45]
>
> To him [Saint Joseph], and to the Virgin Mary, I wish to entrust all of you today, along with your fellow workers—your brothers and sisters—throughout Italy and the world.[46]

Lastly, here are illustrations of the analogous application of entrustment on the level of *latria, hyperdulia* and *dulia* simultaneously:

> To the Holy Family of Nazareth I entrust every family, and I cordially impart to you, Venerable Brothers and beloved sons and daughters, especially to every home, my Apostolic Blessing.[47]
>
> To this Holy Family of Nazareth, unparalleled model of every familial community, human and Christian, I entrust the sacred pledge which you have assumed before God, the Church and society, as well as your intentions, your ideals and your plans.[48]

42 *Inseg* IV/1 (1981) 120 [*ORE* 671:7].

43 *Inseg* IV/1 (1981) 559 [*Far East* 308].

44 *Inseg* IV/1 (1981) 806 [*ORE* 678:2].

45 *Inseg* IX/1 (1986) 393.

46 *Inseg* XI/2 (1988) 1095 [*ORE* 1040:8].

47 *Inseg* III/2 (1980) 391, 394 [*ORE* 646:19].

48 *Inseg* IV/1 (1981) 35 (my translation).

> I entrust each family to Him [Christ the Lord], to Mary, and to Joseph. To their hands and their hearts I offer this Exhortation: May it be they who present it to you, venerable Brothers and beloved sons and daughters, and may it be they who open your hearts to the light that the Gospel sheds on every family.[49]

While, then, it may be readily admitted that the Holy Father speaks of entrustment (and its cognate forms) to God, to Mary and to the Saints analogously, even though in each of these cases the meaning is proportionately different, would he hold that Marian consecration (or entrustment) is in the first instance an act of religion (hence *latria*) and secondarily an act of *hyperdulia*? The following illustrations should point in the direction of a reply:

> Once more I entrust you to Christ *through the hands and the heart of the Mother of God.*[50]
>
> Therefore in particularly difficult days my thought turns to Divine Providence and, *through the intercession of the Queen of Poland, the Mother of Christ,* entrusts to it this beloved nation of mine, my homeland.[51]
>
> I entrust your concerns and your hopes—*through the hands of the Blessed Virgin*, venerated with such love and confidence by the Rumanian ecclesiastical community—to the Almighty and Merciful Lord.[52]
>
> And *through the motherly intercession of the Virgin of the Angels*, I entrust all of you to the goodness of God.[53]
>
> I entrust you to Jesus, the Good Shepherd, through the mediation of his Mother, who is also our Mother.[54]

---

49 *Inseg* IV/2 (1981) 1045, 1130 [*ORE* 715:18].

50 *Inseg* I (1978) 57 [*Talks* 118] (emphasis mine).

51 *Inseg* IV/2 (1981) 1279, 1280–81 [*ORE* 717:14] (emphasis mine).

52 *Inseg* V/1 (1982) 52 [*ORE* 724:12] (emphasis mine).

53 *Inseg* V/1 (1982) 854 [*ORE* 728:10] (emphasis mine).

54 *Inseg* XI/2 (1988) 1224 [*ORE* 1041:5].

> Our Lady of Peace, once again we entrust to you the Church of this diocese, of all the dioceses of this country. Through your mediation we consecrate them to your Son.[55]

> Let us commend the souls of our loved ones to the Blessed Virgin, whom we invoke as "Queen of Saints." Through her, whose image is often found on Christian tombs, let us entrust to God's mercy all the souls who are waiting to be received into the eternal dwellings.[56]

These examples clearly demonstrate a Christocentric, and ultimately theocentric, perspective on the Pope's part. But is this always the case, especially in the explicitly Marian consecrations? First, let us listen to the Pope's description of what he was about to do at Fatima on 13 May 1982 in the homily that preceded the act of consecration.

> Consecrating the world to the Immaculate Heart of Mary means drawing near, *through the Mother's intercession*, to the very Fountain of life that sprang from Golgotha ... It means consecrating this world to the pierced heart of the Savior, bringing it back to the very source of its redemption ...
>
> *Consecrating ourselves to Mary means accepting her help to offer ourselves and the whole of mankind to Him* who is holy, infinitely holy; it means accepting her help—by having recourse to her motherly heart, which beneath the cross was opened to love for every human being, for the whole world—in order to offer the world, the individual human being, mankind as a whole, and all the nations to Him who is infinitely holy ...
>
> My heart is oppressed when I see the sin of the world and the whole range of menaces gathering like a dark cloud over mankind, but it also rejoices with hope as I once more do what has been done by my Predecessors, when they consecrated the world to the heart of the Mother, when they consecrated especially to that heart

55 *Inseg* XIII/2 (1990) 576 [*ORE* 1157:13].

56 *Inseg* XIV/2 (1991) 1051 [*ORE* 1215:1].

> those peoples which particularly need to be consecrated. Doing this means consecrating the world to Him who is infinite holiness.[57]

Next, let us listen to his greeting to English-speaking pilgrims at his first general audience in Rome after his return from Fatima.

> Last week I myself went on pilgrimage to Portugal, especially to Fatima, in order to give thanks that the mercy of God and the protection of the Mother of Christ had saved my life last year.
>
> The message of Fatima is a call to conversion and penance, the first and most basic call of the Gospel. Today it is more urgent than ever, when evil is threatening us through errors based on denial of God. The message of Fatima puts us on our guard. It also invites us to approach anew the Fountain of Mercy by an act of consecration. Mary wishes us to draw near to it: each one of us, each nation, and the whole world.[58]

In this context it would be difficult not to see the above reference to "approaching anew the Fountain of Mercy by an act of consecration" as a specific reference to what, in fact, he did at Fatima, particularly since he used the same terminology in the homily he delivered there. Moreover, in his annual visit to the Gesù on New Year's Eve of 1984, he referred to the consecration of 25 March of that year in this way:

> This Act of Consecration was a drawing nearer of the world, *through the Mother of Christ and Our Mother*, to the source of life, poured out on Golgotha: it was a bringing back of the world to the same fount of Redemption, and at the same time, a recourse to the Madonna's help in order to offer men and peoples to him who is infinitely holy.[59]

57 *Inseg* V/2 (1982) 1573–76, 1582–84 [*Portugal* 79–83] (emphases mine).

58 *Inseg* V/2 (1982) 1763.

59 *Inseg* VII/2 (1984) 1684 [*ORE* 869:4 trans. slightly altered] (emphasis mine).

Consistently, then, and hardly surprisingly, we see that the Holy Father's own testimony corroborates the great theological tradition which we have already delineated in broad strokes, i.e., that Marian consecration is in the first instance an act of religion directed to God [*latria*] without ceasing at the same time to be also an act of *hyperdulia*. The last cited quotation says this quite succinctly.

5.2. The Principle of Mary's Maternal Mediation

We are now ready to consider the other theological principle underlying Marian consecration already alluded to in Father Lohkamp's treatment of "personal consecration." He says:

> [Mary's] position in the economy of salvation is inseparable from that of her Son. *Her desires and wants are His, and she is in a unique position to unite Christians fully, quickly, and effectively to Christ, so that dedication to her is in fact dedication to Christ.* ... The act of personal consecration according to De Montfort, is an act of complete and total consecration, *It consists in giving oneself entirely to Mary in order to belong wholly to Jesus through her.*[60]

In effect, he is simply recapitulating the fundamental thrust of Marian consecration throughout the ages and at the same time reaffirming the teaching on Mary which is detailed in the eighth chapter of *Lumen Gentium*, the Second Vatican Council's Dogmatic Constitution on the Church. While the entire eighth chapter (#52–69) touches upon Mary's role in our redemption, the following passages seem particularly pertinent to our consideration of Marian consecration:

> This Sacred Synod, which is engaged in expounding the doctrine about the Church, in which the divine Redeemer works out our salvation, intends diligently to explain both the role of the Blessed Virgin in the mystery of the Incarnate Word and of the Mystical Body [*munus Beatæ Virginis in mysterio Incarnati Verbi et Corporis Mystici*], and

60 Lohkamp, 209 (my emphasis).

> the duties of the redeemed people toward God's Mother, that is, the Mother of Christ and the Mother of all people, especially of the believers.[61]
>
> To that heavenly messenger she gave the reply: "Behold the handmaid of the Lord, be it done to me according to thy word" (Lk. 1:38). In that way Mary, a daughter of Adam, by giving consent to the divine word, became the Mother of Jesus. And as she embraces God's salvific will with all her heart and unhampered by any sin, she devoted herself totally as the Lord's handmaid to the person and work of her Son. Thus, in virtue of the grace of God Almighty, *she put herself, under him and together with him, in the service of the mystery of redemption.* [*Semetipsam ut Domini ancillam personae et operi Filii sui totaliter devovit, sub Ipso et cum Ipso, omnipotentis Dei gratia, mysterio redemptionis inserviens.*] Rightly therefore the Holy Fathers believe that Mary was used by God not merely passively, but that she cooperated by a free faith and obedience in human salvation. Really, as St. Irenaeus said, she, being "obedient became the cause of salvation both for herself and for the whole human race."[62]

If the above texts underscore the unique, unparalleled role of Mary in our salvation (in the language of *Lumen Gentium*: "in the mystery of Christ and of the Church"), then the ensuing passage does so in a way that bears very directly on the issue of Marian consecration:

> This motherhood of Mary in the economy of grace, moreover, perdures unceasingly, beginning with the consent she trustingly gave at the annunciation, which she upheld unwaveringly under the cross, even to the perpetual fulfillment of all the elect. To wit, when she had been taken into heaven, she did not lay aside this saving role; rather, she continues by her manifold intercession to win for us the gifts of eternal salvation … No creature, really, can ever be put in a class with the Incarnate Word

61 *LG* #54 (*Unger* 7).

62 *LG* #56 (*Unger* 9; emphasis mine).

> and Redeemer. Nevertheless, just as Christ's priesthood is shared in, by various ways, both by the ministers and by the believing people, and just as the one goodness of God is in reality poured out upon creatures in diverse ways, in the same manner, the unique mediation of the Redeemer does not exclude, in fact it calls forth, from the one fountainhead, a varied cooperation shared among the creatures. The Church does not hesitate to profess such a subordinate role of Mary. She has experience of it constantly and commends it to the hearts of the faithful, with a view that, supported by her motherly protection, they may cling more intimately to the Mediator and Savior. [*Tale autem munus subordinatum Mariae Ecclesia profiteri non dubitat, iugiter experitur et fidelium cordi commendat, ut hoc materno fulti praesidio Mediatori ac Salvatori intimius adhaereant.*][63]

The conciliar teaching on the presence of Mary in the mystery of Christ and the Church was readily assimilated by the Archbishop of Krakow and given expression in his *vademecum* on the documents of the Second Vatican Council. Here is how he presented it to the clergy, religious and faithful of his archdiocese:

> In our present study, which is concerned with the enrichment of faith in the ways pointed out by Vatican II, we must first underline the solution chosen by the Council with its decision not to promulgate a separate document concerning Our Lady but to include what would have been the content of such a document in the Dogmatic Constitution on the Church. This in a sense confirms that *the mind of the Church is permeated in a special way by the mystery of the Mother of God, which is fully present in the mystery of Christ the Incarnate Word and hence in that of the Mystical Body of Christ.*[64]

63 *LG* #62 (*Unger* 13).

64 Karol Wojtyła, *Sources of Renewal: The Implementation of Vatican II*, trans. P. S. Falla (San Francisco: Harper & Row Publishers, 1980) 100–01 (emphasis mine).

> As will be seen, the whole attitude of the ancient and modern Church to the Mother of God is based not only on the exceptional honour due to her divine maternity but also on her awareness of the redemption and her own participation in the work of Christ: she 'cooperated in the work of man's salvation,' as the Constitution says. This active cooperation on Mary's part is expressed above all in her obedience. By being thus obedient she did not merely submit passively to the salvific action of the Most Holy Trinity, but with all her life and behaviour embraced it and shared in it: so that *our consciousness of redemption must always see the 'maternal act' as united to not only the 'act of Christ' but also 'under and with him,'* as the Council declares.[65]

Very significantly, already in the immediate postconciliar period Cardinal Wojtyła was giving positive attention to the mediatorial role of Mary at a time when there was a widespread preoccupation with explaining that Mary's mediation does not compete with that of Christ or with debunking the caricature of Mary's mediation as a shield of mercy against the wrath of her Son.[66] It is also interesting to note the consistency of Wojtyła's thought. He already uses the term "maternal mediation," which will be one of the great highlights of his Marian Year Encyclical, *Redemptoris Mater*:

> Mary's divine maternity is a unique fact in the history of our salvation, closely linked with the incarnation of the Word to which it belongs. But her spiritual maternity in the order of grace goes far beyond that fact, extending as

65 *Sources of Renewal* 105 (emphasis mine).

66 Cf. Eamon R. Carroll, O.Carm., *Understanding the Mother of Jesus* (Wilmington, Delaware: Michael Glazier, Inc. 1979) 81–82, 92–96; Frederick M. Jelly, O.P., "The mystery of Mary's mediation," *Homiletic and Pastoral Review* 80:8 (May 1980) 11–20; Anthony J. Tambasco, *What are they saying about Mary?* (New York: Paulist Press, 1984) 46–48. The brief treatment of this matter by Dr. Tambasco seems notably flawed by his unwillingness to take a clear position with regard to the reparative value of the redemption and, consequently, with regard to Mary's unique collaborative role in it. For a resume of the whole question, cf. Roschini, *Maria Santissima nella Storia della Salvezza* II: *Il Dogma Mariano, Parte* I 111–252; Gherardini 287–324.

> widely as her Son's work of redemption 'until the eternal fulfillment of all the elect' (*LG* 62). *The Mother of God fulfills her universal maternity as a mediatrix in the economy of grace.* The Church professes its faith in that maternal mediation of divine grace, while clearly distinguishing it from the mediation of the Redeemer himself ...
>
> Thus the mediation of the Mother of God is subordinate to the unique mediation of Christ, which alone constitutes the foundation and source of the supernatural economy of grace and salvation. *Nevertheless Mary's mediation, as an expression of her spiritual maternity in the order of grace, is universal in its range and is specially efficacious.*[67]

Not only was the conciliar teaching on Mary's insertion into the mystery of Christ and her maternal mediation deeply appreciated and consistently preached by our Holy Father as Archbishop of Krakow,[68] but also it became a keystone of his papal service as Bishop of Rome. Here is a portion of his treatment of this theme in his first Encyclical Letter, *Redemptor Hominis.*

> The aim of any service in the Church, whether the service is apostolic, pastoral, priestly or episcopal, is to keep up this dynamic link between the mystery of the Redemption and every man.
>
> If we are aware of this task, then we seem to understand better what it means to say that the Church is a mother and also what it means to say that the Church always, and particularly at our time, has need of a Mother. We owe a debt of special gratitude to the Fathers of the Second Vatican Council, who expressed this truth in the Constitution *Lumen Gentium* with the rich Mariological doctrine contained in it ...
>
> We who form today's generation of disciples of Christ all wish to unite ourselves with her [Mary] in a special way. We do so with all our attachment to our ancient tradition and also with full respect and love for the members of all the Christian Communities.

67 *Sources of Renewal* 107–08 (emphases mine).

68 e.g. *Omelie* passim.

We do so at the urging of the deep need of faith, hope and charity. For if we feel a special need, in this difficult and responsible phase of the history of the Church and of mankind, to turn to Christ, who is Lord of the Church and Lord of man's history on account of the mystery of the Redemption, we believe that nobody else can bring us as Mary can into the divine and human dimension of this mystery. Nobody has been brought into it by God himself as Mary has. It is in this that the exceptional character of the grace of the divine Motherhood consists. Not only is the dignity of this Motherhood unique and unrepeatable in the history of the human race, but Mary's participation, due to this Maternity, in God's plan for man's salvation through the mystery of the Redemption is also unique in profundity and range of action. [*Nemo ut Maria eo introductus est ab ipso Deo. In hoc quippe singularis indoles gratiæ maternitatis divinæ consistit. Non solum est unica minimeque iterabilis huius maternitatis dignitas in humani generis historia, sed unica etiam—quod attinet ad eius profunditatem et ad amplitudinem eius actionis—participatio est, qua Maria, propter eandem maternitatem, consilio divino de salute humana communicavit per mysterium Redemptionis*] …

The special characteristic of the motherly love that the Mother of God inserts in the mystery of the Redemption and the life of the Church finds expression in its exceptional closeness to man and all that happens to him. It is in this that the mystery of the Mother consists. The Church, which looks to her with altogether special love and hope, wishes to make this mystery her own in an ever deeper manner. For in this the Church also recognizes the way for her daily life, which is each person.

The Father's eternal love, which has been manifested in the history of mankind through the Son whom the Father gave, "that whoever believes in him should not perish but have eternal life," comes close to each of us through this Mother and thus takes on tokens that are of more easy understanding and access by each person. Consequently,

> Mary must be on all the ways for the Church's daily life. Through her maternal presence the Church acquires certainty that she is truly living the life of her Master and Lord and that she is living the mystery of the Redemption in all its life-giving profundity and fullness. [*Æternus Patris amor, qui in historia humani generis per Filium est manifestatus, quem Pater dedit, "ut omnis qui credit in eum non pereat, sed habeat vitam æternam," nobis offertur per hanc Matrem atque hoc modo signa accipit ad intellegendum accommodatiora et faciliora ciuque homini. Ita fit, ut Maria in omnibus viis contidianæ vitæ Ecclesiæ versetur oporteat. Eo quod ut Mater præsens adest, Ecclesia certum habet se reapse vitam vivere Magistri sui et Domini, se e mysterio vivere Redemptionis cum tota eius vivificatoria plenitudine.*][69]

While the Pope does not speak explicitly here of Mary's relationship to the Sacraments and to the Eucharist, he lays a solid foundation for understanding it which I would summarize in the following points. (1) In accord with the great tradition, he emphasizes the uniqueness of Our Lady's divine maternity and her participation in the mystery of the redemption. (2) He declares that the eternal love of the Father, manifested through the Son, comes close to us through the Mother. He presents it as axiomatic that "no one can bring us into the divine and human mystery of the redemption as Mary can" precisely because "nobody has been brought into it by God himself as Mary has." Although he would draw out the nature of this maternal mediation and its mode of operation at much greater length in the third part of his Marian Encyclical, *Redemptoris Mater* (#38–47), and in many other places,[70] the foundation already appears here: "Mary's participation ... in God's plan for man's salvation ... is ... unique in profundity and range of action." (3) Thus,

69 *Redemptor Hominis* #22 *Inseg* II/1 (1979) 607–608;658–659 [U.S.C.C. Edition 97, 98; *Messages* 558–561].

70 For an excellent introduction to Marian mediation in John Paul II, cf. Manfred Hauke, "La Mediazione materna di Maria secondo papa Giovanni Paolo II," *Maria Corredentrice: Storia e Teologia* VII (Frigento: Casa Mariana Editrice, 2005) 35–91.

he concludes that Mary must be on all the ways of the Church's daily life.

In #9 of his next Encyclical, *Dives in Misericordia*, of 30 November 1980, the Pope presented Mary as the Mother of Mercy, underscoring that she was uniquely called to bring people close to the mystery of mercy:

> Mary is also the one who obtained mercy in a particular and exceptional way, as no other person has. At the same time, still in an exceptional way, she made possible with the sacrifice of her heart her own sharing in revealing God's mercy. This sacrifice is intimately linked with the cross of her Son, at the foot of which she was to stand on Calvary. Her sacrifice is a unique sharing in the revelation of mercy, that is, a sharing in the absolute fidelity of God to His own love, to the covenant that He willed from eternity and that He entered into in time with man, with the people, with humanity; it is a sharing in that revelation that was definitively fulfilled through the cross. No one has experienced, to the same degree as the Mother of the crucified One, the mystery of the cross, the overwhelming encounter of divine transcendent justice with love: that "kiss" given by mercy to justice. No one has received into his heart, as much as Mary did, that mystery, that truly divine dimension of the redemption effected on Calvary by means of the death of the Son, together with the sacrifice of her maternal heart, together with her definitive "fiat." [*Maria insuper est, quæ singulari prorsus extraordinarioque pacto—sicut alius nemo—misericordiam cognovit et eodem tempore item eximio perquam modo consecuta est cordis sui sacrificio, ut propria evenire posset participatio sua ipsius revelationis divinæ misericordiæ. Quod sacrificium proxime cohæret cum eius Filii cruce, sub qua etiam ille in Calvariæ loco adstitit. Ipsius proinde sacrificium hoc peculiaris omnino communicatio est in patefacienda misericordia; nempe communicatio est absolutæ Dei fidelitatis erga proprium amorem ad fœdus, quod inde ab ævo sempiterno voluit quodque in tempore pepigit cum homine, cum populo,*

cum genere humano; participatio est revelationis illius, quæ semel est in æternum per crucem transacta. Similis Mariæ, Crucifixi Matris, nemo mysterium crucis est expertus, hoc est iustitiæ transcendentis divinæ cum amore consternantem congressionem: "osculum" illud iustitiæ impertitum a misericordia. Similis Mariæ hoc mysterium animo nemo suscepit: eam rationem vere divinam redemptionis, quæ per Filii mortem in Calvariæ monte acta est una cum materni cordis eius sacrificio et cum decretoria ipsius "fiat."]

Mary, then, is the one who has the deepest knowledge of the mystery of God's mercy. She knows its price, she knows how great it is [*Ergo Maria ea quidem est quæ divinæ misericordiæ interius percipit mysterium; cuius præterea novit pretium intellegitque ipsum quam sit magnificum*]. In this sense, we call her the Mother of mercy: Our Lady of mercy, or Mother of divine mercy; in each one of these titles there is a deep theological meaning, for they express the special preparation of her soul, of her whole personality, so that she was able to perceive, through the complex events, first of Israel, then of every individual and of the whole of humanity, that mercy of which "from generation to generation" people become sharers according to the eternal design of the most Holy Trinity.

The above titles which we attribute to the Mother of God speak of her principally, however, as the Mother of the crucified and risen One; as the One who, having obtained mercy in an exceptional way, in an equally exceptional way "merits" that mercy throughout her earthly life and, particularly, at the foot of the cross of her Son; and finally as the one who, through her hidden and at the same time incomparable sharing in the messianic mission of her Son, was called in a special way to bring close to people that love which He had come to reveal. [*de illa nempe, quæ more extraordinario misericordiam experta "meretur" æquabili modo talem misericordiam progrediente omni sua vita terrestri ac præsertim infra Filii crucem; ac de ea tandem, quæ absconditam incomparabilemque simul per communionem messianici Filii sui muneris destinata peculiari*

> *ratione est ad hominibus illum apportandum amorem, quem ipse revelatum venerat.*][71]

With a few bold strokes the Pope sketches once again the mystery of Mary and her unique role in the work of our redemption. (1) He begins by stating that she "obtained mercy in a particular and exceptional way, as no other person has," thus alluding to the preservative redemption of her Immaculate Conception. (2) Then he states that "the sacrifice of her heart" … "is a unique sharing in the revelation of mercy," thus alluding to her intimate union with Jesus in the offering of His perfect sacrifice on Calvary.[72] (3) "No one," he insists, "has experienced, to the same degree as the Mother of the crucified One, the mystery of the cross," hence "she knows its price."[73] (4) "Having obtained mercy in an exceptional way, in an equally exceptional way" the Mother of mercy "'merits' [*"meretur"*] that mercy throughout her earthly life and, particularly, at the foot of the cross of her Son."[74] (5) Thus, Mary "was called in a special way" to bring to people that love which Jesus "had come to reveal."[75]

---

71 *Inseg* III/2 (1980) 1510–1511 [St. Paul Edition 30–31].

72 Cf. Arthur Burton Calkins, "The Heart of Mary as Coredemptrix in the Magisterium of Pope John Paul II" in *S. Tommaso Teologo: Ricerche in occasione dei due centenari accademici* (Città del Vaticano: Libreria Editrice Vaticana "Studi Tomistici" #59, 1995) 320–335.

73 On Our Lady's knowledge of the price [*pretium*] of the redemption, cf. St. Bonaventure, *Collationes de septem donis Spiritus Sancti*, 6 in *Doctoris seraphici S. Bonaventuræ … Opera Omnia*, vol 5, ed PP. Collegii a S. Bonaventura (Ad Claras Aquas [Quaracchi]: Ex Typographia Collegii S. Bonaventuræ, 1891) p. 486.

74 Cf. St. Pius X's Encyclical, *Ad Diem Illum*, of 2 February 1904, in which he speaks of how Mary merited [*"promeruit"*] to become the reparatrix of the lost world and how she merits [*promeret*] *de congruo* what Christ merits *de condigno* [*AAS* 36 (1903–1904) 453–454; *Our Lady: Papal Teachings*, trans. Daughters of St. Paul (Boston: St. Paul Editions, 1961) hereafter cited as *OL* #233–234]. For a discussion of this terminology cf. Juniper B. Carol, O.F.M., "Our Lady's Coredemption," in Juniper B. Carol, O.F.M. (ed.), *Mariology*, 2 (Milwaukee: Bruce, 1957) 383, 409–411.

75 This seems to parallel without the use of more technical language St. Pius X's conclusion about Mary as *princeps largiendarum gratiarum ministra* in *Ad Diem Illum* [*ASS* 36 (1903–1904) 454; *OL* #234].

In this highly significant excerpt of *Redemptor Hominis*, one sees how fully John Paul II had appropriated the eighth chapter of *Lumen Gentium* on the presence of Mary in the mystery of Christ and the Church and at the same time made it uniquely his own. Already in this text one can clearly see the foundation of the teaching he will develop on Mary's maternal mediation in *Redemptoris Mater*: no one else can conduct us as Mary can into the mystery of the redemption.

By his vigorous insistence on the conciliar teaching on Mary's role in the mystery of Christ and the Church, which is "a mystery best described dynamically as her maternal mediation,"[76] he was effectively providing a necessary theological foundation for his "program of consecration and entrustment." The most developed presentation of his teaching on Mary's mediation is to be found in *Redemptoris Mater* #38–41. Although a very significant body of papal doctrine had already evolved on this issue,[77] the climate

---

76 Peter D. Fehlner, O.F.M. Conv., "Mulieris Dignitatem," *Miles Immaculatæ* 25 (1989) 9.

77 Benedict XIV, Apostolic Constitution *Gloriosae Dominæ* of 27 September 1748 [*OL* #4]; Pius VII, Apostolic Constitution *Quod Divino Afflata Spiritu* of 24 January 1806 [*OL* #14]; Blessed Pius IX, Encyclical Letter *Ubi Primum* of 2 February 1849 [*OL* #23]; Apostolic Constitution *Ineffabilis Deus* of 8 December 1854 [*OL* #64]; Leo XIII, Encyclical Letter *Supremi Apostolatus* of 1 September 1883, *ASS* 16 (1889) 113 [*OL* #81]; Encyclical Letter *Octobri Mense* of 22 September 1891, *ASS* 24 (1891–1892) 195–96 [*OL* #113–14]; Encyclical Letter *Jucunda Semper* of 8 September 1894 *ASS* 27 (1894–1895) 178–80, 182–84 [*OL* #149–52, 155–56, 161, 163]; Encyclical Letter *Adiutricem Populi* of 5 September 1895, *ASS* 28 (1895–1896) 130–31, [*OL* #169–72]; Encyclical Letter *Fidentem Piumque* of 20 September 1896, *ASS* 29 (1896–1897) 206 [*OL* #194]; Letter to the Archbishop of Turin *Mariani Coetus* of 2 August 1898 [*OL* #209]; Saint Pius X, Encyclical Letter *Ad Diem Illum* of 2 February 1904, *ASS* 36 (1903–1904) 450–51 [*OL* #222, 224, 226–28, 233–35]; Letter *Summa Deus Hominum* of 27 November 1907 [*OL* #253]; Benedict XV, Allocution to the Consistory of 24 December 1915 [*OL* #261]; Letter *Il 27 Aprile 1915* to Cardinal Pietro Gasparri of 5 May 1917, *AAS* 9 (1917) 266, [*OL* #263]; Letter *Inter Sodalicia* of 22 May 1918, *AAS* 10 (1918) 182 [*OL* #267–68]; Allocution *Il Nous serait difficile* of 6 April 1919 [*OL* #271–72]; Pius XI, Encyclical Letter *Miserentissimus Redemptor* of 8 May 1928, *AAS* 20 (1928) 178 [*OL* #287]; Encyclical Letter *Caritate Christi Compulsi* of 3 May 1932, *AAS* 24 (1932) 192 [*Carlen* 3:482]; Homily given at reading of Decree "de tuto" for the canonization of St. Jeanne Antide Thouret of 15 August 1933 [*OL* #323, 325]; Encyclical Letter *Ingravescentibus Malis* of 29 September 1937, *AAS* 29 (1937) 375, 380 [OL #338, 343]; Venerable Pius XII, Letter to Cardinal Luigi Maglione, *Superiore Anno* of

at the Second Vatican Council was not auspicious for its full assimilation.[78] What John Paul has managed to do is to re-present the teaching on Marian mediation, completely in the context of the Council's presentation of Mary in the mystery of Christ and the Church and in terms of his own unique mode of thought and style of exposition.

At the press conference on the day of the release of *Redemptoris Mater*, 25 March 1987, Cardinal Joseph Ratzinger, then Prefect of the Congregation for the Doctrine of the Faith, said of the Pope's treatment of the issue of Our Lady's mediation:

---

15 April 1940, *AAS* 32 (1940) 145 [*OL* #356–57]; Decree "de tuto" of 11 January 1942 for the canonization of St. Louis Marie Grignion de Montfort *AAS* 34 (1942) 44 [Michael O'Carroll, C.S.Sp., *Mediatress of All Graces* (Westminster, Maryland: Newman Press, 1958) 161]; Encyclical Letter *Mystici Corporis* of 29 June 1943, *AAS* 35 (1943) 247–48 [*OL* #384]; Radio Message *Bendito Seja O Senhor* of 13 May 1946, *AAS* 38 (1946) 264 [*OL* #407]; Apostolic Letter *Per Christi Matrem* of 15 May 1947, *AAS* 40 (1948) 536 [*OL* #428]; Allocution on the canonization of St. Louis Marie Grignion de Montfort of 21 July 1947, *AAS* 39 (1947) 410–13 [*OL* #431–32]; Encyclical Letter *Mediator Dei* of 20 November 1947, *AAS* 39 (1947) 582–583 [*OL* #440]; Letter *Ex Officiosis Litteris* of 15 February 1948, *AAS* 40 (1948) 107–08 [*OL* #444]; Exhortation to priests *Menti Nostræ* of 23 November 1950, *AAS* 42 (1950) 701 [*OL* #465, 466]; Encyclical Letter *Doctor Mellifluus* of 25 May 1953, *AAS* 45 (1953) 382 [*OL* #578]; Radio Message to Italian Catholic Action of 8 December 1953, *AAS* 45 (1953) 850–51 [*OL* #624–25]; Encyclical Letter *Sacra Virginitas* of 25 March 1954, *AAS* 46 (1954) 189 [*OL* #641]; Encyclical Letter *Ad Cæli Reginam* of 11 October 1954, *AAS* 46 (1954) 636–37 [*OL* #709]; Radio Message to National Marian Congress of India of 8 December 1954, *AAS* 46 (1954) 727 [*OL* #760]; Letter *Gloriosam Reginam* of 8 December 1955, *AAS* 48 (1956) 75 [*OL* #770]; Encyclical Letter *Haurietis Aquas* of 15 May 1956, *AAS* 48 (1956) 352 [*OL* #778]; Apostolic Constitution *Sedes Sapientiæ* of 31 May 1956, AAS 48 (1956) 354 [*OL* #779]; Saint John XXIII, Allocution at St. Mary Major of 15 February 1959, *AAS* 51 (1959) 136 [*OL* #851]; Blessed Paul VI, address at Lombard Seminary of 8 December 1966 [Domenico Bertetto, S.D.B., *La Madonna nella Parola di Paolo VI* (Roma: LAS, 1980) 408]; Letter *Gloriosa Dicta* of 15 April 1967, *AAS* 59 (1967) 484; Apostolic Exhortation *Signum Magnum* of 13 May 1967, *AAS* 59 (1967) 465–75 [St. Paul Editions, N.C.W.C. trans. 4, 7, 8]; Homily at Beatification of St. Maximilian Kolbe of 17 October 1971, *Insegnamenti di Paolo VI* IX (1971) 907–909 [*TPS* 16 (1971) 240–41]; Letter *È con sentimenti* of 13 May 1975 to Cardinal Suenens, *AAS* 67 (1975) 358 [*Mary – God's Mother and Ours* 194–95].

78 Cf. *Theotokos* 242–45; Michael O'Carroll, C.S.Sp., "Still Mediatress of All Graces?" *Miles Immaculatæ* 24 (1988) 121–25; Thomas Mary Sennott, O.S.B., "Mary, Mediatrix of All Graces, Vatican II and Ecumenism," *Miles Immaculatæ* 24 (1988) 151–54; William G. Most, "Marian Consecration as Service: Historical, Theological and Spiritual Reflections," *Miles Immaculatæ* 24 (1988) 453, n. 52.

> Without doubt this is the point on which theological and ecumenical discussion will be concentrated. The Second Vatican Council also had already made use of the title "Mediatrix" (*LG* 62) and spoke of the extent of Mary's mediation (*LG* 60 and 62). However, until the present time this subject had never been dealt with so extensively in a document of the Magisterium. As regards its content, the encyclical does not go beyond what was already said by the Council, whose terminology it follows. However, it examines more deeply the Council's statements and gives them a new weight for theology and religious piety.[79]

Here I simply wish to allow the Pope to present his own teaching on Mary's "maternal mediation":

> In effect, Mary's mediation *is intimately linked with her motherhood.* It possesses a specifically maternal character, which distinguishes it from the mediation of the other creatures who in various and always subordinate ways share in the one mediation of Christ, although her own mediation is also a shared mediation. In fact, while it is true that 'no creature could ever be classed with the Incarnate Word and Redeemer,' at the same time 'the unique mediation of the Redeemer does not exclude but rather gives rise among creatures to *a manifold cooperation* which is but a sharing in this unique source.'[80]
>
> Mary *entered, in a way all her own, into the one mediation* 'between God and men' *which is the mediation of the man Christ Jesus.* If she was the first to experience within herself the supernatural consequences of this one mediation—in the Annunciation she had been greeted as 'full of grace'—then we must say that through this fullness of grace and supernatural life she was especially predisposed to cooperation with Christ, the one Mediator of human salvation. *And such cooperation* is *precisely this mediation subordinated* to the mediation of Christ.[81]

---

79 *ORE* 981:21.

80 *Inseg* X/1 (1987) 724–725 [St. Paul edition 54].

81 *Inseg* X/1 (1987) 727 [St. Paul edition 56].

> Mary, who from the beginning had given herself without reserve to the person and work of her Son, could not but pour out upon the Church, from the very beginning, her maternal self-giving. After her Son's departure, her motherhood remains in the Church as maternal mediation: interceding for all her children, the Mother cooperates in the saving work of her Son, the Redeemer of the world. In fact the Council teaches that the 'motherhood of Mary in the order of grace ... *will last without interruption* until the eternal fulfillment of all the elect' (*Lumen Gentium* #62). With the redeeming death of her Son, the maternal mediation of the handmaid of the Lord took on a universal dimension, for the work of redemption embraces the whole of humanity.[82]

The excerpts which we have presented, especially the above selections of *Redemptoris Mater*, provide strong evidence of the Pope's thorough grasp of Mary's mediation, subordinate and secondary to that of Christ, completely derivative from it and totally dependent upon it and at the same time "special and extraordinary" [*Quod munus est et peculiare et extraordinarium*].[83] Since her capacity for being a mediatrix is proportionally analogous to her being [*agere sequitur esse*], Mary's is the highest form of all modes of creaturely mediation. This, in turn, is proportionally analogous to the honor that we owe her [*hyperdulia*] which supercedes that owed to all the saints and angels. All of this, then, provides the context of the proposal, which John Paul II makes toward the end of his Marian Year Encyclical:

> I would like to recall, among the many witnesses and teachers of this [Marian] spirituality, the figure of Saint Louis-Marie Grignion de Montfort, who proposes *consecration to Christ through the hands of Mary*, as an effective means for Christians to live faithfully their baptismal commitments. I am pleased to note that in our

---

82 *Inseg* X/1 (1987) 727–728 [St. Paul edition 57].

83 *Inseg* X/1 (1987) 725, 727 [St. Paul edition 54, 56].

> own time too new manifestations of this spirituality and devotion are not lacking.[84]

Without a clear grasp of the authentic doctrine of Marian mediation, it is impossible to build a solid foundation for the practice of Marian consecration.[85] This John Paul has no doubt perceived since his reading of de Montfort as a young man. An excellent illustration of his thorough grasp and application of this principle may be found in his prayer of entrusting Zaire to Our Lady on the hundredth anniversary of its initial consecration and evangelization:

> Permit me, O Mother of Christ and Mother of the Church, permit me, Pope John Paul II, who has the privilege of taking part in this jubilee, to recall and at the same time renew this missionary consecration, which took place in this land at the beginning of its evangelization.
>
> *To consecrate itself to Christ through you! To consecrate itself to you for Christ!*[86]

---

84 *Inseg* X/1 (1987) 739 [St. Paul edition 68] (emphasis mine).

85 Since the first edition of this book, many studies have been written on Mary's maternal mediation. Cf. Arthur Burton Calkins, "Mary 'Minister of Grace' in the Magisterium and in the Contemporary Roman Liturgy," in *Mary at the Foot of the Cross* – IV: *Mater Viventium (Gen. 3:20). Acts of the Fourth International Symposium on Marian Coredemption* (New Bedford, MA: Academy of the Immaculate, 2004) 29–70; Manfred Hauke, *Mary, Mediatress of Grace*. Supplement to *Mary at the Foot of the Cross* – IV (New Bedford, MA: Academy of the Immaculate, 2004); Manfred Hauke, *Maria, "Mediatrice di Tutte le Grazie": La Mediazione Universale di Maria nell'Opera Teologica e Pastorale de Cardinale Mercier* (Lugano: Europress FTL, 2005); Arthur Burton Calkins, "Mary, Mediatrix of All Graces, in the Papal Magisterium of Pope John Paul II," in *Mary at the Foot of the Cross* – VII: *Coredemptrix, Therefore Mediatrix of All Graces. Acts of the Seventh International Symposium on Marian Coredemption* (New Bedford, MA: Academy of the Immaculate, 2008) 17–63, as well as all of the articles in this volume; Lázaro Ilzo Daniel, *La Mediazione Materna di Maria in Cristo negli Insegnamenti di Giovanni Paolo II* (Lugano: Europress FTL, 2011); Gloria Falcão Dodd, *The Virgin Mary, Mediatrix of All Grace: History and Theology of the Movement for a Dogmatic Definition from 1896 to 1964* (New Bedford, MA: Academy of the Immaculate, 2012).

86 *Inseg* III/1 (1980) 1069 [*Africa Ap* 41] (emphasis mine)

CHAPTER SIX

The Christ-centered Character of the Act of Consecration

In his "Annual Survey of Recent Mariology" for 1984, the late Father Eamon R. Carroll, O. Carm. (1921–2008), noted that "the deeply Christological character of the 'act of entrusting'" of 25 March 1984 had gone largely unnoticed.[1] He took up this theme again in a talk presented on 7 September 1985 to a conference of the Western Region of the Mariological Society of America at St. Mary's Cathedral in San Francisco. Speaking about that "act of entrusting of the world to the Blessed Virgin" near the end of the Extraordinary Holy Year of the Redemption, he said:

> What was missed was the intensely Christ-centered character of the "act of entrusting," that it was basically an association with the consecration that Jesus made of himself to the Father's will and to his redemptive mission, that, after the example of our Lady and with her assistance, we too are to enter into the consecration Jesus made of himself, just as in the Eucharist (Prayer Three) we beg the Father to send upon us the Spirit of his Son to make us an "everlasting gift," that is a permanent victim together with Christ …
>
> Any genuine Christian consecration can only be a sharing in the consecration of Christ, a participation in his self-consecration: "For these I consecrate myself, so that they may be consecrated in truth" (Jn. 17:19). Any consecration we make can only be a response to the consecratory action of God, to his gift in Christ Jesus. The

1 *Marian Studies* 35 (1984): 167–168.

> Savior shares his own self-consecration in various ways, he communicates his holiness to us by many gifts, for example, the sacraments of baptism and the Eucharist, his holy word, his Spirit and his Mother.[2]

Rightly Father Carroll emphasizes the Christocentrism of the 1984 act of entrusting. Of course, the same may be said for the 1982 act at Fatima which was substantially the same text, as the Holy Father himself told the Bishops of the world in his letter to them dated 8 December 1983.[3]

What he underscored in both of these references was the Holy Father's reference to John 17:19. This occurs in both the 1982[4] and 1984[5] acts of consecration/entrustment and in the homily given at the Mass in Fatima, which preceded the act of consecration.[6] This surely was one of John Paul II's major contributions to the theology of Marian consecration, as well as an irrefutable proof that he envisions consecration/entrustment to Mary as first and foremost an act of *latria* with a solid Christological foundation. Let us examine his use of the Johannine text in its immediate context in each instance. First, let us listen to his homily of 13 May 1982 in Fatima:

> *Consecrating ourselves to Mary means accepting her help to offer ourselves and the whole of mankind to Him who is holy, infinitely holy;* it means accepting her help—by having recourse to her motherly heart, which beneath the cross was opened to love for every human being, for the whole world—*in order to offer the world, the individual human being, mankind as a whole, and all the nations to Him who is infinitely holy.* God's holiness showed itself

2 "Mary: The Woman Come of Age," *Marian Studies* 36 (1985): 151, 153–54. Several other authors also readily recognized the Christological emphasis in the text of the Pope's consecration. Cf. Alfredo Marranzini, S.J., "L'Atto di Affidamento e Consacrazione a Maria," *Civiltà Cattolica* 135 (1984) 12–29.

3 Cf. *Inseg* VII/1 (1984) 417 [*ORE* 823:2]. Cf. also above, 10-11.

4 *Inseg* V/2 (1982) 1587, 1591 [*ORE* 735:12].

5 *Inseg* VII/1 (1984) 775–776 [*ORE* 828:9].

6 *Inseg* V/2 (1982) 1574, 1583 [*Portugal* 80].

in the redemption of man, of the world, of the whole of mankind, and of the nations: a redemption brought about through the sacrifice of the cross. *"For their sake I consecrate myself," Jesus had said (Jn. 17:19).*

By the power of the redemption the world and man have been consecrated to Him who is infinitely holy. They have been offered and entrusted to Love itself, merciful Love.

The Mother of Christ calls us, invites us to join with the Church of the living God in the consecration of the world, in this act of confiding by which the world, mankind as a whole, the nations, and each individual person are presented to the Eternal Father with the power of the redemption won by Christ. They are offered in the Heart of the Redeemer which was pierced on the cross.[7]

Next, we listen to the words of that Act of Consecration which he made that same day:

> "For God so loved the world that he gave his only Son, that whoever believes in him should not perish but have eternal life" (Jn. 3:16).
>
> *It was precisely by reason of this love that the Son of God consecrated himself for all mankind: "And for their sake I consecrate myself, that they also may be consecrated in truth" (Jn. 17:19).*
>
> By reason of that consecration the disciples of all ages are called to spend themselves for the salvation of the world, and to supplement Christ's afflictions for the sake of his body, that is the Church (cf. 2 Cor. 12:15; Col. 1:24).
>
> Before you, Mother of Christ, before your Immaculate Heart, *I today, together with the whole Church unite myself with our Redeemer in this his consecration for the world and for people*, which only in his divine Heart has the power to obtain pardon and to secure reparation.
>
> *The power of this consecration lasts for all time and embraces all individuals, peoples and nations. It overcomes every evil that the spirit of darkness is able to awaken*, and

7 *Inseg* V/2 (1982) 1574, 1583 [*Portugal* 80–81] (emphases mine).

> has in fact awakened in our times, in the heart of man and in his history.
>
> *The Church, the Mystical Body of Christ, unites herself, through the service of Peter's successor, to this consecration by our Redeemer …*
>
> *Hail to you, who are wholly united to the redeeming consecration of your Son!*
>
> Mother of the Church! Enlighten the People of God along the paths of faith, of hope and love! *Help us to live with the whole truth of the consecration of Christ for the entire human family of the modern world.*
>
> In entrusting to you, O Mother, the world, all individuals and peoples, *we also entrust to you the consecration itself, for the world's sake, placing it in your motherly Heart.*[8]

Finally, here is the parallel excerpt from his Act of Consecration of 25 March 1984:

> Behold, as we stand before you, Mother of Christ, before your Immaculate Heart, *we desire, together with the whole Church, to unite ourselves with the consecration which, for love of us, your Son made of himself to the Father: "For their sake," he said, "I consecrate myself that they also may be consecrated in the truth" (Jn. 17:19). We wish to unite ourselves with our Redeemer in this his consecration for the world and for the human race*, which, in his divine Heart, has the power to obtain pardon and to secure reparation.
>
> *The power of this consecration lasts for all time and embraces all individuals, peoples and nations. It overcomes every evil that the spirit of darkness is able to awaken*, and has in fact awakened in our times, in the heart of man and in his history …
>
> *Hail to you, who are wholly united to the redeeming consecration of your Son!*
>
> Mother of the Church! Enlighten the People of God along the paths of faith, hope and love! Enlighten especially the peoples whose consecration and entrustment by us you

8 *Inseg* V/2 (1982) 1587–89, 1591–92 [*ORE* 735:12] (emphases mine).

are awaiting. *Help us to live in the truth of the consecration of Christ for the entire human family of the modern world.*

In entrusting to you, O Mother, the world, all individuals and peoples, we also entrust to you this very consecration of the world, placing it in your motherly Heart.[9]

It will be readily noted that what the Pope stresses in each of these passages is the self-consecration of Christ as stated in John 17:19 and the Church's desire to be united with that consecration. The specifically Marian dimension is introduced by invoking the help of Mary who is "wholly united to the redeeming consecration of her Son"[10] for the Church to live this consecration and by entrusting the consecration itself to her.

The Consecration of Christ

Let us consider a few of the implications of this "self-consecration of Christ" as expressed in John 17:19. Perhaps the first point to be noted is that it presupposes Jesus' prior consecration by the Father as a priest upon his entry into the world (Jn. 10:36).[11] This is a datum of the tradition that is found deeply embedded in the New Testament, particularly in the Letter to the Hebrews (2:17; 5:5–6; 6:20); it is attested to by the representatives of the sub-Apostolic and Patristic tradition[12] and by one of the canons of Saint Cyril of Alexandria against Nestorius.[13] By taking on a human nature, the Son of God

9 *Inseg* VII/1 (1984) 775–776 [*ORE* 828:9–10] (emphases mine).

10 Cf. *LG* #56 [*Flan*]: "Committing herself whole-heartedly and impeded by no sin to God's saving will, she devoted herself totally, as a handmaid of the Lord, to the person and work of her Son, under and with him serving the mystery of redemption, by the grace of Almighty God."

11 Cf. André Feuillet, P.S.S., *The Priesthood of Christ and His Ministers,* trans. Matthew J. O'Connell (Garden City, N. Y.: Doubleday & Co., Inc., 1975), 37, 39, 96–97, 121, especially 125, 213. On the question of Jesus' consecration by the Father (Jn. 10:36) and his self-consecration (Jn. 17:19) in terms of the biblical evidence, this study is *facile princeps*.

12 Cf. M. E. McIver, "Priesthood of Christ," *NCE* 11:774–775.

13 *D-H* #261; Saint Cyril also touched on this theme in his preaching; cf. *PG* 74, 505–08, 544–45.

became the perfect mediator, the perfect priest, because in His two natures He could represent God to man and man to God.[14]

This is a theme frequently alluded to by John Paul II. Speaking in Bolivia to priests, brothers and seminarians he said:

> In this Marian Year, I invite all, priests, religious and seminarians, to meditate on the priesthood of Christ, whose anointing by the Holy Spirit took place in Mary's womb, when the Word became flesh.[15]

In his Holy Thursday Letter to Priests of 1989 he said simply, "As man, Christ is priest";[16] and again a few weeks later, he declared to the Plenary Assembly of the Congregation for the Evangelization of Peoples:

> By the Sacrament of Orders, priests participate in the "consecration" of Christ the Priest, which took place at the moment of the Incarnation of the Word in Mary's womb, and they become living instruments to continue his wonderful work.[17]

The French Sulpician exegete, Father André Feuillet (1909–1998), carefully discussed this prior consecration of Christ by virtue of His Incarnation from a scriptural perspective.

> The consecration that Christ received from his Father (Jn. 10:36) has been explained in two ways. Some have connected it with the consecration of Jeremiah before his birth (Jer. 1:5; Sir. 49:7). In both instances God sets someone apart, even before his coming into this world, because God intends to speak to men through this individual; thus, after speaking to us through the prophets, God now speaks to us through his Son (Heb. 1:1–2). But, as we noted in Chapter 1, other commentators prefer to think of priests and to say that Jesus was consecrated a

14 The priesthood of Christ is discussed in six articles by Saint Thomas Aquinas in *ST* III, q. 22.

15 *Inseg* XI/2 (1988) 1312 [*ORE* 1043:11].

16 *Inseg* XII/1 (1989) 543 [*ORE* 1081:6].

17 *Inseg* XII/1 (1989) 812 [*ORE* 1087:4].

> priest. As in Hebrews 5:5, so in John, Jesus receives the high priestly dignity from his Father. And, in point of fact, in New Testament times people thought of priests when they spoke of consecrated individuals.
>
> These two interpretations are by no means exclusive of each other since Jesus was conscious of being the Servant of God who resembled both prophets and priests. Nonetheless, the priestly perspective is certainly to the fore in John 10:36, for there is an evident connection between the consecration meant here and the consecration in 17:19. In short, if the Father consecrates Christ, it is that Christ may then consecrate himself and offer himself as a victim ...
>
> To say that the Son of God was consecrated a priest at the moment of his being sent into the world amounts to saying that he is a *priest in his very being as the incarnate Son of God.* The two concepts of priest and mediator are closely connected. A mediator acts as intermediary between two or more parties with which he has something in common. A priest is "consecrated" for the purpose of acting as intermediary between the holy God and men. By the very fact that divinity and manhood are united in him, the incarnate Son of God is already the perfect priestly mediator and infinitely superior to all other priests.[18]

This interpretation is verified by a number of authors, although not always put in such sharp relief as by Feuillet here.[19]

If John 10:36 may be understood as a reference to Jesus' priestly consecration by virtue of the Incarnation, then

18 Feuillet 97–98 (emphasis by the author). Joseph Ratzinger/Pope Benedict XVI takes this same position on the exegesis of John 10:36 in his *Jesus of Nazareth* Part Two: *Holy Week – From the Entrance into Jerusalem to the Resurrection* trans. Vatican Secretariat of State (San Francisco: Ignatius Press, 2011) 87.

19 Cf. Raymond Brown, S.S., *The Gospel According to John I–XII*, Anchor Bible 29 (Garden City, N. Y.: Doubleday & Co., Inc., 1966) 411; Brown, *The Gospel According to John XIII–XXI*, Anchor Bible 29a (Garden City, N. Y.: Doubleday & Co., Inc., 1970) 765–67; Ignace de la Potterie, S.J., *La Verité dans Saint Jean* 2, Analecta Biblica 74 (Rome: Pontificia Instituto Biblica, 1977) 763–67; Jean Galot, S.J., *Theology of the Priesthood*, trans. Roger Balducelli, O.S.F.S. (San Francisco: Ignatius Press, 1984), 203.

> The second consecration of Jesus of which the fourth gospel speaks—"For their sake I consecrate myself" (17:19)—corresponds to this atoning death … In consecrating himself as a victim, Jesus expresses his full acceptance of the Father's plan of salvation; he brings to fulfillment the intention behind the consecration effected by the Father in the incarnation. The sacrificial interpretation of John 17:19 is proposed by a large number of the Fathers, and we can make our own the comment of St. John Chrysostom which Bultmann[20] quotes approvingly: "What does he mean, 'I consecrate myself'? He means, 'I offer sacrifice.'"[21]

This understanding of Jesus as consecrated by the Father as priest in order to consecrate Himself as victim is implicit in the doctrine of the priesthood of Christ.[22] It is considered by St. Thomas as a separate article in his treatment of this question in the *Summa Theologiae*[23] and was held as a fundamental principle of priestly spirituality by the members of *L'École Française*.[24] Pope John Paul II faithfully passed on this datum of the tradition. Here he did so in the context of an Advent homily:

> The mystery of the Incarnation represents the beginning of the new sacrifice: *of the perfect sacrifice*. He who is conceived in the womb of the Virgin through the work of

20 Rudolf Karl Bultmann (1884–1976) was a German Lutheran theologian and professor of New Testament at the University of Marburg. He was one of the major figures of early 20th century biblical studies and a promoter of "demythologizing" the Gospels, but in this matter he sensed the right interpretation.

21 Feuillet 44; cf. also de la Potterie 761–75 for further discussion of Patristic interpretation.

22 Cf. Marranzini, "Consacrazione a Maria" 52, and Joseph de Sainte-Marie, *Teologia e Spiritualità della Consacrazione a Maria* III-41 (the latter explicitly cites both John 10:36 and 17:19).

23 *ST* III, q. 22, a. 2.

24 Cf. Cardinal Pierre de Bérulle, *La Vie de Jésus* (Paris, 1629) 188–94; Pierre Pourrat, P.S.S., *Christian Spirituality* 3, trans. W. A. Mitchell (Westminster, MD: Newman Press, 1953) 372–3; Jean Gautier, P.S.S., *Some Schools of Catholic Spirituality*, trans. Kathryn Sullivan, R.S.C.J. (Tournai: Desclée Company, 1959) 338–39; Eugene A. Walsh, S.S., *The Priesthood in the Writings of the French School: Bérulle, De Condren, Olier* (Washington, D. C.: The Catholic University of America Press, 1949).

> the Holy Spirit, he who is born that night in Bethlehem, is the eternal priest. He already brings and fulfills the sacrifice in his Incarnation. And it is that *sacrifice which "is pleasing to God."*
>
> God is pleased by that sacrifice in which the whole interior truth of man is expressed: the sacrifice *of the will and the heart.* The Son of God assumes human nature, a human body, precisely in order to initiate that sacrifice in human history.
>
> He will definitively fulfill it through his "obedience unto death" (cf. Phil. 2:8). Still, *the beginning of this obedience* is already to be found in the womb of the Virgin Mary. *Already on that night in Bethlehem:* "Lo, I have come … to do thy will, O God."[25]

He chose to underscore this reality of Christ's priest-victimhood again in his Holy Thursday Letter to Priests of 1987:

> On this extraordinary day, I wish—the same as every year—to be with you all, as also with your bishops, since we all feel a deep need to renew in ourselves the awareness of the grace of this sacrament which unites us closely to Christ, Priest and Victim …
>
> In fact, if he was a priest from the beginning of his existence, nevertheless he "became" in a full way the unique priest of the new and eternal Covenant through the redemptive sacrifice which had its beginning in Gethsemane.[26]

A further conclusion drawn by Father Feuillet as to the meaning of this text in the larger context of the high-priestly prayer of Jesus (Jn. 17) is that

> The connection which Christ makes between his own consecration as victim and the consecration of the apostles as priests ("I have consecrated myself so that they too may be consecrated in truth") shows clearly that, like all the other blessings of the new covenant, the priesthood of the

25 *Inseg* VIII/2 (1985) 1587 [*ORE* 919:9, 11].

26 *Inseg* X/1 (1987) 1306, 1312 [*ORE* 983:21, 22].

> apostles is the fruit of Christ's self-giving on the cross as an expiatory victim that men may have eternal life.[27]

Father Feuillet was not the first to offer this interpretation of the text, even if he does so with a highly developed exegetical argument. Jacques-Bénigne Bossuet, the renowned "eagle of Meaux," had already given classic expression to this concept when he said of Christ:

> He was holy, then, and consecrated to God, not only in his capacity as pontiff, but also as victim … It is for this that he sanctifies himself, offers himself, consecrates himself as property dedicated and holy to the Lord. But he also adds in speaking to his apostles: "I sanctify myself for them," so that participating by their ministry in the grace of his priesthood, they might enter at the same time into the state of victimhood, and not having at all on their own the holiness which was required to be messengers and ministers of Jesus Christ, they might find this in him.[28]

Another confirmation of this understanding of John 17:19 comes from the successor of Pope Saint John Paul II, Pope Benedict XVI, who at the Chrism Mass of Holy Thursday, 9 April 2009, preached thus to his brother priests:

---

27 Feuillet 126. On this point Galot concurs drawing the further application that the consecration of Jesus by the Father (Jn. 10:36) is an analogue for the priesthood of the faithful, while his self-consecration (Jn. 17:19) is an analogue for the hierarchical priesthood as well as specifically undertaken to effect that priestly consecration; cf. Galot 121–25. Ferdinand Prat, S.J., in his *Jesus Christ: His Life, His Teaching, and His Work* 2, trans. John J. Heenan, S.J., (Milwaukee: Bruce Publishing Co., 1950) 302–303, and F. X. Durwell, C.SS.R., in his *The Resurrection: A Biblical Study*, trans. Rosemary Sheed (New York: Sheed and Ward, 1960) 236, 307, also link this text with either apostleship or the ministerial priesthood. This application of John 17:19 to the hierarchical priesthood by Feuillet has been contested by Jean Delorme, "Sacerdoce du Christ et Ministère (A propos de Jean 17): Sémantique et théologie biblique," *Recherches de Science Religieuse* 62 (1974) 199–219. This, in turn, elicited in response the article by Henri Cazelles, "Note sur le ministère apostolique de consécration," *Bulletin de Saint-Sulpice 1* (1975): 302–307. Delorme again responded with "Sacrifice, sacerdoce, consécration," *Recherches de Science Religieuse* 63 (1975) 343–366.

28 Quoted in M.-J. Lagrange, O.P., *L'Évangile selon Saint Jean* (Paris: Gabalda & Cie., 1936) 448 (my translation).

> When Jesus says: "I consecrate myself," he makes himself both priest and victim. Bultmann was right to translate the phrase: "I consecrate myself" by "I sacrifice myself." Do we now see what happens when Jesus says: "I consecrate myself for them"? This is the priestly act by which Jesus—the Man Jesus, who is one with the Son of God—gives himself over to the Father for us. It is the expression of the fact that he is both priest and victim. I consecrate myself—I sacrifice myself: this unfathomable word, which gives us a glimpse deep into the heart of Jesus Christ, should be the object of constantly renewed reflection. It contains the whole mystery of our redemption. It also contains the origins of the priesthood in the Church, of our priesthood.[29]

In point of fact, John Paul II several times made this specifically hierarchical priestly application in the citation of this text[30] and also applied it to those who live the consecrated religious life;[31] but more frequently he applied it in a broader sense to all members of the Body of Christ who share in the common priesthood of all believers as described in *Lumen Gentium* #10 and *Presbyterorum Ordinis* #2.[32] Perhaps he said this most strongly in his Letter to All Consecrated Persons on the Occasion of the Marian Year:

> Every vocation of a baptized person reflects some aspect of that "consecration in the truth" which Christ accomplished by his Death and Resurrection and made part of his Paschal

29 *Insegnamenti di Benedetto XVI* V/1 (2009) 579–580 [*ORE* 2090:4, 8]. He continues to develop this understanding of John 17:19 in *Jesus of Nazareth* Part Two 87–90.

30 *Inseg* II/2 (1979) 642 [*U.S.A.* 192]; *Inseg* III/1 (1980) 112 [*ORE* 618:10]; *Inseg* III/1 (1980) 1762 [*ORE* 640:19]; *Inseg* XII/1 (1989) 139 [*ORE* 1076:10]; *Inseg* XII/1 (1989) 536 [*ORE* 1081:3]; *Inseg* XII/1 (1989) 1373 [*ORE* 1096:6]; *ORE* 1136:11.

31 *Inseg* IX/1 (1986) 780 [*ORE* 931:11]; *Inseg* IX/1 (1986) 1659 [*ORE* 941:6]; *Inseg* XI/3 (1988) 714–715 [*ORE* 1056:10].

32 *Inseg* II/2 (1979) 493 [*Ireland* 117]; *Inseg* III/2 (1980) 738, 741 [*ORE* 652:3]; *Inseg* VIII/1 (1985) 390–397 [*ORE* 880:6–7]; *Inseg* VIII/1 (1985) 1515 [*ORE* 892:10]; *Inseg* IX/2 (1986) 106 [*ORE* 924:4]; *Inseg* XI/2 (1988) 1928 [*ORE* 1046:4]; *Inseg* XII/1 (1989) 1588 [*ORE* 1094:14]; [*ORE* 1211:11].

> Mystery: "*For their sake I consecrate myself*, that they also may be consecrated in truth" (Jn 17:19).[33]

Such was clearly his intention in his use of the text in the acts of consecration/entrustment in 1982 and 1984. In fact, in the earlier act made at Fatima, he immediately follows the quotation of John 17:19 with this clarification:

> By reason of that consecration the disciples of all ages are called to spend themselves for the salvation of the world, and to supplement Christ's afflictions for the sake of his body, that is the Church (cf. 2 Cor. 12:15; Col. 1:24).[34]

Clearly, then, by this apposition he wished to underscore Christ's self-consecration to victimhood as a paradigm for all believers, an invitation to become "co-victims" with Him in order to supplement His afflictions for the sake of His Body, the Church (Col. 1:24).[35]

Mary "wholly united to the redeeming consecration of her Son"

It is in this light that Mary reappears in the acts of both 1982 and 1984. "Hail to you, who are wholly united to the redeeming consecration of your Son!"[36] She, by God's inscrutable design, was the first to share in Christ's sufferings as a co-victim and the one to be most fully united with that consecration consummated

33 *Inseg* XI/2 (1988) 1594, 1606–1607 [*ORE* 1043:2].

34 *Inseg* V/2 (1982) 1587, 1591 [*ORE* 735:12].

35 This very understanding of the text of John 17:19 was presented by Bernard Leeming, S.J., in his essay, "Consecration to the Sacred Heart," Augustinus Bea, S.J., Hugo Rahner, S.J., Henri Rondet, S.J., et Friedr. Schwendimann, S.J., eds. *Cor Jesu: Commentationes in Litteras Encyclicas Pii PP. XII "Haurietis Aquas"* I: *Pars Theologica* (Roma: Casa Editrice Herder, 1959) 640–652.

It is also interesting to note the development of what René Laurentin calls "La Perspective Victimale" in the spiritual and Marian theology of the 19th and 20th centuries. This perspective provides further elaboration of this implied theme of "co-victimhood" with Christ as realized in Mary and in the Christian. Cf. René Laurentin, *Marie, l'Eglise et Le Sacerdoce I: Essai sur le Développement d'une Idée Religieuse* (Paris: P. Lethielleux "Nouvelles Editions Latines," 1952) 422–467.

36 *Inseg* V/2 (1982) 1588, 1592 [*ORE* 735:12]; *Inseg* VII/1 (1984) 776.

on the Cross. She is described in *Lumen Gentium* #56 as the one who "devoted herself totally as the Lord's handmaid to the person and work of her Son" [*semetipsam ut Domini ancillam personae et operi Filii sui totaliter devovit*].[37] Further, the Council Fathers declare that

> That association of the Mother with her Son in the work of salvation is manifested from the time of Christ's virginal conception up to his death ... So too the Blessed Virgin advanced in the pilgrimage of faith, and kept up her union with her Son faithfully till the cross, where she was standing, not without divine design (cf. Jn. 19:25). There she sorrowed grievously together with her Only Son and united herself with motherly heart to his sacrifice, giving loving consent to the Immolation of the Victim born of her. [*Ita etiam B. Virgo in peregrinatione fidei processit, suamque unionem cum Filio fideliter sustinuit usque ad crucem, ubi non sine divino consilio stetit (cf. Io. 19:25), vehementer cum Unigenito suo condoluit et sacrificio Eius se materno animo sociavit, victimae de se genitae immolationi amanter consentiens.*][38]

While it evidently remained in the providence of God for this recognition of Mary as "wholly united to the redeeming consecration of her Son" to be highlighted by John Paul II, it is clear that the groundwork had already been laid in the documents of the Second Vatican Council and not just in chapter eight of *Lumen Gentium*.[39] Perhaps these texts are the most explicit:

> Perfect model of this apostolic spiritual life is the Blessed Virgin Mary, Queen of Apostles.[40]

> They [priests] always find a wonderful example of such docility in the Blessed Virgin Mary who under the

37 *Unger* 9.

38 *LG* #57, 58 [*Unger* 9, 10].

39 Cf. *LG* #46; *PC* #25.

40 *AA* #4 [*Flan* 771].

guidance of the Holy Spirit made a total dedication of herself for the mystery of the redemption of men.[41]

Without doubt Jesus is the pre-eminent One consecrated by God (Jn. 10:36) and consecrating Himself for our redemption (Jn. 17:19), but analogously and subordinately[42] Mary is consecrated "under him and together with him, in the service of the mystery of redemption."[43] She "was predestined as God's Mother from all eternity together with the Incarnation of the Divine Word."[44] As Jesus' consecration began in Mary's womb at the moment of the Incarnation, so Mary's began at the first moment of her existence.[45] As His consecration was consummated on the Cross, so was hers beneath it and in the most total cooperation with His.[46]

At the very beginning of this chapter, I cited the testimony of Father Lohkamp on consecration. There he stated that Baptism "may be called the fundamental consecration of Christian life."[47] This assertion is absolutely basic in the Christian tradition because Baptism identifies one with the consecration of Christ (cf. Rom. 6:3) and, hence, it is simply confirmed by the Second Vatican Council.[48] Hence also, John Paul II could simply state categorically, "Baptism is the first and fundamental consecration

---

41 *PO* #18 [*Flan* 896–97].

42 Cf. *LG* #62.

43 *LG* #56 [*Unger* 9].

44 *LG* #61. This doctrine that "God by one and the same decree [*uno eodemque decreto*], had established both the origin of Mary and the Incarnation of Divine Wisdom" was first declared by Blessed Pius IX in *Ineffabilis Deus*, *Pii IX Acta* I:599 [*OL* #34]. It was reiterated by the Servant of God Pius XII in *Munificentissimus Deus*, *AAS* 42 (1950) 768 [*OL* #520] and alluded to by Blessed Paul VI in *Marialis Cultus*, *AAS* 66 (1974) 136 [*Mary – God's Mother and Ours* 23]. In *Redemptoris Mater* Saint John Paul II says: "In the mystery of Christ she is *present* even 'before the creation of the world,' as the one whom the Father 'has chosen' as *Mother* of his Son in the Incarnation," *Inseg* X/1 (1987) 687 [St. Paul edition, 14].

45 *D-H* #2800, 2803 *LG* #53, 56.

46 *LG* #58.

47 Lohkamp 209.

48 Cf. *LG* #10; *PC* #5; *PO* #12.

of the human person."[49] The Church further singles out two kinds of consecration, which build on the fundamental consecration of Baptism. The first is the religious life under the vows of poverty, chastity, and obedience.

> They [religious] have dedicated their whole lives to his servitude. *This constitutes a special consecration, which is deeply rooted in their baptismal consecration and is a fuller expression of it.*[50]
>
> Right from the planting of the Church the religious life should be carefully fostered, because not only does it provide valuable and absolutely necessary help for missionary activity, but *through the deeper consecration made to God in the Church* it clearly shows and signifies the intimate nature of the Christian vocation.[51]

The other kind of consecration is accomplished in the Sacrament of Holy Orders and given for special ministerial services in the Church.

> *Like all Christians they* [priests] *have already received in the consecration of baptism the sign and gift of their great calling and grace.* So they are enabled and obliged even in the midst of human weakness to seek perfection, according to the Lord's word: "You, therefore, must be perfect, as your heavenly Father is perfect" (Mt. 5:48).
>
> But priests are bound by a special reason to acquire this perfection. *They are consecrated to God in a new way in their ordination* and are made the living instruments of Christ the eternal priest, and so are enabled to accomplish throughout all time that wonderful work of his which with supernatural efficacy restored the whole human race.[52]

With obviously no desire to derogate from the "fundamental consecration of Baptism" or the unique ministerial consecration of Holy Orders, Pope John Paul II used the term "consecrated

49 *Inseg* VII/2 (1984) 1576 [*ORE* 865:18].

50 *PC* #5 [*Flan* 614] (emphasis mine).

51 *AG* #18 [*Flan* 834] (emphasis mine).

52 *PO* #12 [*Flan* 885] (emphases mine].

life" most frequently of the vowed religious life. And to religious men and women, therefore, he very frequently proposed Mary as the model of consecrated life,[53] the one most "wholly united to the redeeming consecration of her Son." Perhaps in none of his very numerous addresses to religious did he limn in Mary as model of consecrated souls more compellingly than in his Apostolic Exhortation, *Redemptionis Donum*, of which this section forms the conclusion.

> On the feast of the Annunciation in this Holy Year of the Redemption, I place the present exhortation *in the heart of the immaculate Virgin*. Among all persons consecrated unreservedly to God, she is the first. She—the Virgin of Nazareth—is also the one *most fully consecrated to God*, consecrated in the most perfect way. Her spousal love reached its height in the divine Motherhood through the power of the Holy Spirit. She, who as Mother carries Christ in her arms, at the same time *fulfills* in the most perfect way *His call*. "Follow me." And she follows Him—she, the Mother—as her Teacher of chastity, poverty and obedience.
>
> How *poor* she was on Bethlehem night and how poor on Calvary! How *obedient* she was at the moment of the Annunciation, and then—at the foot of the cross—*obedient* even to the point of assenting to the death of her Son, who became obedient "unto death!" How *dedicated* she was in all her earthly life to the cause of the kingdom of heaven *through most chaste love*.
>
> If the entire Church finds in Mary her *first model*, all the more reason do you find her so—you as consecrated individuals and communities within the Church! On the day that calls to mind the inauguration of the Jubilee of the Redemption, which took place last year, I address myself to you with this present message, to invite you to

53 Cf. Domenico Bertetto, S.D.B., *Maria nel Magistero di Giovanni Paolo II: Primo Anno di Pontificato, 16 ottobre 1978 – 21 ottobre 1979* (Rome: Libreria Ateneo Salesiano, 1980) 56, 179; *Secondo Anno* (1981) 159–60; *Terzo Anno* (1983) 163–65; *Quarto Anno* (1984) 272–74; *Quinto Anno* (1986) 129, 198, 217; *Sesto Anno* (1986) 181, 239.

> renew *your religious consecration according to the model of the consecration of the very Mother of God.*[54]

Likewise, in his Letter to All Consecrated Persons on the Occasion of the Marian Year, he exhorted those who live the vowed life:

> Through an increased resolve on your part to live your consecration to the full, taking Mary the Mother of Jesus and of the Church as the sublime model of perfect consecration to God, your evangelical witness will grow in effectiveness and lead to a greater fruitfulness of *pastoral work for vocations.*[55]

On 7 October 1979, speaking to women religious at the National Shrine of the Immaculate Conception in Washington, he put it succinctly:

> This is the woman of history and destiny who inspires us today, the woman who speaks to us of femininity, human dignity, and love, and *who is the greatest expression of total consecration to Jesus Christ.*[56]

In his Apostolic Letter, *Mulieris Dignitatem*, he asserted Mary's primacy as the perfect creaturely model of consecration in the context of "union with God," which, of course, is completely equivalent to "union with Jesus and his redeeming consecration":

> The dignity of every human being and the vocation corresponding to that dignity find their definitive measure in *union with God.* Mary, the woman of the Bible, is the most complete expression of this dignity and vocation. For no human being, male or female, created in the image and likeness of God, can *in any* way attain fulfillment apart from this image and likeness.[57]

54 *Inseg* VII/1 (1984) 816, 842 [*ORE* 828:16] (emphasis in original).

55 *Inseg* XI/2 (1988) 1601, 1612 [*ORE* 1043:3].

56 *Inseg* II/2 (1979) 676 [*U.S.A.* 242] (emphasis mine).

57 *Inseg* XI/3 (1988) 252, 324 [*ORE* 1058:2].

Mary's Spiritual Maternity willed by Christ

Thus far, it is sufficiently clear that what one might call the "nucleus" of the acts of consecration/entrustment, which the Pope made in 1982 and 1984 is Christocentric. Why then does he go on to consecrate and entrust to Mary? This is a question to which the Holy Father was tireless in responding, and the response virtually always has reference to the words of the dying Christ to His Mother with reference to the disciple whom He loved: "Woman, behold, your son!" (Jn. 19:26). In these words he finds a confirmation of Mary's spiritual maternity, which began "with the consent she trustingly gave at the Annunciation."[58]

Theologically, a distinction is frequently made with regard to the beginning of Mary's spiritual maternity and its "promulgation." Father Otto Semmelroth, S.J., puts it this way:

> When Mary conceived the God-man, she became ontologically the Mother of the Mystical Christ. This element had to receive the addition of moral completion at Christ's sacrifice on the Cross.[59]

Father Wenceslaus Sebastian, O.F.M., differentiates these two "moments" analogously with the redemption wrought by Christ:

> The Incarnation may be considered as the Redemption in potency or "in actu primo," and the sacrifice on Calvary, as the Redemption in act, or in "actu secondo." Mary's co-operation in the production of the supernatural life follows a similar pattern. At the Incarnation, in virtue of her Divine Maternity, she conceives us to the supernatural life, whereas on Calvary she begets us …
>
> The act of Divine Motherhood is related to Christ as the Man-God and to Christ as Head of the Mystical Body. By engendering the Man-God she became the Mother of God; by begetting the Head of the Mystical Body she became the Spiritual Mother of mankind, receiving from

58 *LG* #62.

59 Otto Semmelroth, S.J., *Mary, Archetype of the Church*, trans. Maria von Eroes and John Devlin (New York: Sheed and Ward, 1963) 132.

> the grace of Headship her fullness of grace to be transmitted to men. Yet, her Spiritual Motherhood and her plenitude of grace at the Incarnation are such only *in actu primo*. They are not realized completely and effectively *in actu secundo* until Mary has co-operated with her divine Son in the Redemption … That is why theologians commonly say that she conceived us at Nazareth and bore us on Calvary.[60]

While it is true that virtually all of the popes since Benedict XIV have cited the pericope of John 19:25–27 in support of Mary's spiritual maternity,[61] one of the clearest statements of its inception was made by Pope Saint Pius X in his Encyclical, *Ad Diem Illum*:

> For is not Mary the Mother of Christ? She is, therefore, our Mother also. Indeed everyone must believe that Jesus, the Word made Flesh, is also the Saviour of the human race. Now, as the God-Man He acquired a body composed like that of other men, but as the Saviour of our race He had a kind of spiritual and mystical Body, which is the society of those who believe in Christ. "We, the many, are one body in Christ" (*Romans* 12:5). But the Virgin conceived the Eternal Son not only that He might be made man by taking His human nature from her, but also that by means of the nature assumed from her He might be the Saviour of men. For this reason the angel said to the shepherds, "Today in the town of David a Saviour has been born to you, Who is Christ the Lord" (*Luke* 2:11). So in one and the same bosom of His most chaste Mother, Christ took to Himself human flesh and at the same time united to Himself the spiritual body built up of those "who are to

60 Wenceslaus Sebastian, O.F.M., "Mary's Spiritual Maternity," *Mariology* 2:331, 335–36. Eschewing the distinction between Mary's spiritual maternity *in actu primo* and *in actu secundo* as an unnecessary "hardening of formulas," Père Salgado prefers, following the lead of Pius XII, to speak of Mary's "double title to motherhood in the supernatural order": her divine maternity and her association with the sacrifice of Calvary; cf. Jean-Marie Salgado, O.M.I., "La Visitation de la Sainte Vierge Marie: Exercice de sa Maternité Spirituelle," *Divinitas* 16 (1972) 448–49; *La Maternité Spirituelle de la Très Sainte Vierge Marie* (Vatican City: Libreria Editrice Vaticana "Studi Tomistici" #36, 1990) 192–195.

61 Cf. Salgado, *La Maternité Spirituelle* 154–159.

> believe in Him" (*John* 17:20). Consequently Mary, bearing in her womb the Saviour, may be said to have borne also all those whose life was contained in the life of the Saviour. All of us, therefore, who are united with Christ and are, as the Apostle says, "Members of His body, made from His flesh and from His bones" (*Ephesians* 5:30), have come forth from the womb of Mary as a body united to its head. Hence, in a spiritual and mystical sense, we are called children of Mary, and she is the Mother of us all.[62]

Even though John Paul's primary emphasis, following his predecessors, is on the "promulgation" or "revelation"[63] of Mary's spiritual maternity on Calvary, he nonetheless acknowledges that this "service" of Mary to the Church began from the first moment of the conception of Christ. Here is how he put it in Ephesus on 30 November 1979:

> Uttering her "fiat," Mary does not just become Mother of the historical Christ; her gesture sets her as Mother of the total Christ, as "Mother of the Church." "From the moment of the 'fiat'—St. Anselm remarks—Mary began to bear us all in her womb." That is why "the birth of the Head is also the birth of the Body," St. Leo the Great proclaims. On his part, St. Ephrem has a very beautiful expression on this subject: Mary, he says, is "the ground in which the Church was sown."
>
> In fact, from the moment when the Virgin becomes Mother of the Incarnate Word, the Church is constituted secretly, but perfectly in its germ, in its essence as the Mystical Body: there are present, in fact, the Redeemer and the first of the redeemed. Henceforth incorporation into Christ will involve a filial relationship not only with the heavenly Father, but also with Mary, the earthly Mother of the Son of God.[64]

In Fatima on 12 May 1991, he expressed this same truth thus:

62 Quoted in Sebastian 350 [also in *OL* #229–230].

63 Cf. Clément Dillenschneider, C.Ss.R., *La Mariologie de S. Alphonse de Liguori: Sources et Synthèse Doctrinale* (Fribourg: Studia Friburgensia, 1934) 159.

64 *Inseg* II/2 (1979) 1289 [*Turkey* 76–77].

> Since she [Mary] gave birth to Christ, the Head of the Mystical Body, she also had to have given birth to all the members of that one Body. Therefore, "Mary embraces each and every one *in* the Church, and embraces each and every one *through* the Church" (*Redemptoris Mater*, 47).[65]

It remains true, however, that his almost constant point of reference for Mary's spiritual maternity, as well as the basis for his program of entrustment, is Calvary. Let us listen to a catechesis on this point given in a general audience on 11 May 1983.

> "Jesus said to his mother, 'Woman, there is your son.' In turn he said to the disciple, 'There is your mother'" (Jn. 19:26, 27).
>
> In this Holy year, we turn more ardently to Mary, because a very special sign of mankind's reconciliation with God was *the role entrusted to her on Calvary to be the mother of all the redeemed.*
>
> The circumstances under which this motherhood of Mary's was proclaimed show the importance that the Redeemer attributed to it. At the very moment when he was completing his sacrifice, Jesus spoke those basic words to his mother: "Woman, there is your son;" and to the disciple: "There is your mother" (Jn. 19:26–27). And the Evangelist notes that after saying these words Jesus realized that everything was now finished. *The gift of his mother was the final gift that he was giving mankind as the fruit of his sacrifice.*
>
> It is a question then of a gesture intended to crown his redemptive work. *Asking Mary to treat the beloved disciple as her son, Jesus invites her to accept the sacrifice of his death and, as the price of this acceptance, he invites her to take on a new motherhood. As the Saviour of all mankind, he wants to give Mary's motherhood the greatest range. He therefore chooses John as the symbol of all the disciples whom he loves, and he makes it understood that the gift of his mother is the sign of a special intention of love, with which he embraces all who want to follow him as disciples, that is, all Christians and all*

65 *Inseg* XIV/1 (1991) 1217-1218 [*ORE* 1191:5].

men. Besides giving this motherhood an individual form, Jesus manifests the intention to make Mary not merely the mother of his disciples taken as a whole, but of each one of them in particular, as though each were her only son who is taking the place of her Only Son.

This universal motherhood in the spiritual order was the final consequence of Mary's cooperation in the work of her divine Son, a cooperation begun in the fearful joy of the Annunciation and carried through right to the boundless sorrow of Calvary. This is what the Second Vatican Council stressed when it showed the role that Mary was destined to fulfill in the Church. [Here he cites *Lumen Gentium*, #61 & 62.] … Mary's mediation constitutes a singular sharing in the unique mediation of Christ, which does not become in the least overshadowed, but rather endures as the central fact in the whole work of salvation.

Devotion to Our Lady therefore is not opposed to devotion to her Son. Rather it can be said that by asking the beloved disciple to treat Mary as his mother Jesus founded Marian devotion.[66] John was quick to carry out the will of his Master: from that hour onward the disciple took her into his care, showing her filial affection that corresponded to her motherly affection, *thus beginning a relationship of spiritual intimacy that contributed to deepening his relationship with his Master, whose unmistakable traces he found on his mother's face…*

The words addressed by the crucified Christ to his mother and to the beloved disciple brought a new dimension to man's religious condition. The presence of a mother in the life of grace is a source of comfort and joy. On Mary's motherly face Christians recognize a most particular expression of the merciful love of God, who with the mediation of a maternal presence has us better understand the Father's own care and goodness. Mary appears as the one who attracts sinners and reveals to them, with her sympathy and her indulgence, the divine offer of reconciliation…

66 Père Salgado noted that this simple, but striking affirmation had never been made by the magisterium before John Paul II. Cf. *La Maternité Spirituelle* 169.

> It is to this perfect mother that the Church has recourse in all its difficulties: *it entrusts to her its plans, because in praying to her and loving her it can respond to the wish expressed by the Saviour on the cross, and it is certain it will not be disappointed in its prayers.*[67]

Let us note immediately this very significant sentence: "Asking Mary to treat the beloved disciple as her son, Jesus invites her to accept the sacrifice of his death and, as the price of this acceptance, he invites her to take on a new motherhood." The price of Mary's acceptance of the sacrifice of Jesus is her new motherhood. Let us observe here that the Pope is not speaking of a passive acceptance or resignation to Jesus' death on the part of Mary, but rather of her active willing of the immolation of her Son just as the Father and Jesus Himself willed it. Speaking of her "acceptance of the sacrifice of Jesus" effectively means speaking of her immolation of herself in union with the sacrifice of Jesus. Then John Paul went on to draw the conclusion that "This universal motherhood in the spiritual order was the final consequence of Mary's cooperation in the work of her divine Son." This accords beautifully with *Lumen Gentium* #58, which speaks about how Mary

> in keeping with the divine plan, enduring with her only begotten Son the intensity of his suffering, associated herself with his sacrifice in her mother's heart, and lovingly consenting to the immolation of this victim which was born of her. Finally, she was given by the same Christ Jesus dying on the cross as a mother to his disciple, with these words: "Woman, behold thy son" (Jn. 19:26–27).[68]

Effectively, both texts speak of Mary's active collaboration in the work of redemption, from which flow her mediation and spiritual maternity.

Here again we also notice that John Paul invokes the great Marian treatise of the Second Vatican Council explicitly by citing

---

67 *Inseg* VI/1 (1983) 1200–02 [*ORE* 784:1] (emphases mine).

68 *LG* #58 [Flan}

#61 and 62 of *Lumen Gentium* on Mary's spiritual maternity and mediation, which is to be "understood in such wise that it does not derogate from the dignity and efficacy of Christ, the one Mediator, nor does it add anything."[69] We notice his emphasis on the fact that this maternal role is *entrusted* to Mary by Christ, that it is "the final gift that he was giving mankind as the fruit of his sacrifice." Delicately he underscores the fact that the beloved disciple's new relationship with Mary "contributed to deepening his relationship with his Master."

Among many frequent references to Mary's spiritual maternity in homilies and addresses,[70] he devoted sections #20–24 and 44–45 of *Redemptoris Mater* to this topic. In the Encyclical he developed the concept that the Gospel brings a radically "new dimension" to every relationship, hence also to motherhood and, therefore, to the motherhood of Mary:

> He [Jesus] announced the Kingdom: the "Kingdom of God" and "his Father's business," which add a new dimension and meaning to everything human, and therefore to every human bond, insofar as these things related to the goals and tasks assigned to every human being. Within this new dimension, also a bond such as that of "brotherhood" means something different from "brotherhood according to the flesh" deriving from a common origin from the same set of parents. *"Motherhood,"* too, *in the dimension of the Kingdom of God and in the radius of the fatherhood of God himself, takes on another meaning.*[71]

He went on to illustrate this "new dimension of Mary's motherhood" (and also her "maternal mediation") by the incident of the wedding at Cana (Jn. 2:1–11):

69 *LG* #62 [*Unger* 13].

70 Cf. *Inseg* V/2 (1982) 1800 [*ORE* 736:14]; *Inseg* V/2 (1982) 2201 [*Argentina* 23]; *Inseg* V/3 (1982) 118; *Inseg* VI/1 (1983) 966; *Inseg* VII/1 (1984) 851; *Inseg* VIII/2 (1985) 262 [*ORE* 901:2]; *Inseg* X/3 (1987) 859–60; *Inseg* X/3 (1987) 859–60 [*ORE* 1025:14]; *Inseg* XI/1 (1988) 975; 1038:11; 1201:1; 1205:3; 1206:9; 1207:4.

71 *Inseg* X/1 (1987) 701 [St. Paul edition 28].

> In John's text . . . the description of the Cana event outlines what is actually manifested as a new kind of motherhood according to the spirit and not just according to the flesh, that is to say *Mary's solicitude for human beings*, her coming to them in the wide variety of their wants and needs. At Cana in Galilee there is shown only one concrete aspect of human need, apparently a small one of little importance ("They have no wine"). But it has a symbolic value: this coming to the aid of human needs means, at the same time, bringing those needs within the radius of Christ's messianic mission and salvific power. Thus there is a mediation: Mary places herself between her Son and mankind in the reality of their wants, needs and sufferings. *She puts herself "in the middle,"* that is to say *she acts as a mediatrix not as an outsider, but in her position as mother.* She knows that as such she can point out to her Son the needs of mankind, and in fact, she "has the right" to do so. Her mediation is thus in the nature of intercession: Mary "intercedes" for mankind. And that is not all. As a mother she also *wishes the messianic power of her Son to be manifested*, that salvific power of his which is meant to help man in his misfortunes, to free him from the evil which in various forms and degrees weighs heavily upon his life.[72]

Finally, of course, he made his commentary on the classic text of John 19:25–27, and, although having commented on this famous theme hundreds of times, he presented a new theological synthesis:

> One can say that if Mary's motherhood of the human race had already been outlined, now it is clearly stated and established. It *emerges* from the definitive accomplishment of *the Redeemer's Paschal Mystery*. The Mother of Christ, who stands at the very center of this mystery—a mystery which embraces each individual and all humanity—is given as mother to every single individual and all mankind. The man at the foot of the Cross is John, "the disciple whom he loved." But it is not he alone. Following tradition,

72 *Inseg* X/1 (1987) 704 [St. Paul edition 30–31].

> the Council does not hesitate to call Mary *"the Mother of Christ and mother of mankind"*: since she "belongs to the offspring of Adam she is one with all human beings … Indeed she is 'clearly the mother of the members of Christ … since she cooperated out of love so that there might be born in the Church the faithful.'"
>
> And so this "new motherhood of Mary," generated by faith, is *the fruit of the "new" love* which came to definitive maturity in her at the foot of the Cross, through her sharing in the redemptive love of her Son.[73]

One might be inclined to think that having offered such a remarkable synthesis on Our Lady's spiritual maternity, which is at once completely consistent with the tradition and at the same time extraordinarily rich and fresh, one should not have expected any further notable insights from John Paul II on this topic, but this would be to commit a serious error. Here is the conclusion he drew on Mary's motherhood of the Church in a general audience of 23 November 1988, which Père Salgado describes as the most beautiful catechesis on the text of John 19:25–27 that he has come across in pontifical documents[74]:

> Mary's presence beside the Cross indicates her commitment of total sharing in her Son's redemptive sacrifice. Mary had willed to participate to the very depth in the sufferings of Jesus because she did not reject the sword foretold to her by Simeon (cf. Lk. 2:35); instead, she accepted, with Christ, the mysterious plan of the Father. She was the first to partake in that sacrifice, and she would forever remain the perfect model of all those who would agree to associate themselves unreservedly with the redemptive offering. …
>
> "When Jesus saw his mother, and the disciple whom he loved standing near, he said to his mother, 'Woman, behold, your son!'" (Jn. 19:26). It is an act of tenderness and filial love. Jesus does not want his mother to remain alone. In place of himself he leaves to her as a son the disciple whom Mary knows as the beloved one. Thus

73 *Inseg* X/1 (1987) 706 [St. Paul edition 33].

74 Salgado, *La Maternité Spirituelle* 171.

Jesus entrusts to Mary a new motherhood, asking her to treat John as her son. But the solemnity of that act of entrustment ("Woman, behold, your son!"), its situation at the very heart of the drama of the Cross, the sobriety and pithiness of the words which could be described as proper to an almost sacramental formula, suggest that over and above family relationships, the fact should be considered in the perspective of the work of salvation, where the woman-Mary was engaged with the Son of man in the mission of redemption. At the conclusion of this work, Jesus asks Mary to accept definitively the offering, which he makes of himself as the victim of expiation, by now considering John as her son. It is at the price of her maternal sacrifice that she receives that new motherhood.

However, that filial gesture, full of messianic meaning, goes far beyond the person of the beloved disciple, designated as the son of Mary. Jesus wishes to give Mary the mission of accepting all his followers of every age as her own sons and daughters. Jesus's gesture has therefore a symbolic value.

It is not merely a gesture of a family nature, as of a son making provision for his mother, but it is a gesture of the world's Redeemer who assigns to Mary, as "woman," a role of new motherhood in relation to all those who are called to membership in the Church. In that moment, therefore, Mary is constituted—one might almost say "consecrated"—Mother of the Church by her Son on the Cross. …

In this gift made to John and, through him, to Christ's followers and to all mankind, there is as it were a completion of the gift which Jesus made of himself to humanity by his death on the Cross. Mary is as it were "entirely one" with him, not only because they are mother and son "according to the flesh," but because in God's eternal plan they are contemplated, predestined and situated together at the center of the history of salvation. Thus Jesus thinks that he should involve his mother not only in his own oblation to the Father, but also in the gift of himself to humanity.

> Mary, on her part, is in perfect harmony with her Son in this act of oblation and of giving, as a prolongation of her *"fiat"* at the Annunciation. …
>
> Jesus, who had experienced and appreciated Mary's maternal love in his own life, wished that his disciples also in their turn should enjoy this maternal love as an element of their relationship with him in the whole development of their spiritual life. It is a question of regarding Mary as Mother and of treating her as Mother, allowing her to form us to true docility to God, to true union with Christ, to real charity in regard to our neighbor.
>
> It can be said that this aspect also of the relationship with Mary is included in the message of the Cross.[75]

This is a text of truly remarkable richness and density even in the abbreviated form in which I have cited it. Again, let us note how the Pope speaks of the new motherhood that Mary receives "at the price of her maternal sacrifice." Furthermore, we see a beautiful description of this price: "Mary was engaged with the Son of man in the mission of redemption." And even more: "Mary is … 'entirely one' with him … because in God's eternal plan they are contemplated, predestined and situated together at the center of the history of salvation." This constitutes a very strong affirmation of the doctrine solemnly taught by Blessed Pius IX in his Apostolic Constitution, *Ineffabilis Deus*, namely that "God, by one and the same decree, had established the origin of Mary along with the Incarnation of Divine Wisdom."[76] Therefore, as the Pope explains, "Jesus thinks that he should involve his mother not only in his own oblation to the Father, but also in the gift of himself to humanity. Mary, on her part, is in perfect harmony with her Son in this act of oblation and of giving, as a prolongation of her *"fiat"* at the Annunciation."

75 *Inseg GP* XI/4 (1988) 1634–1637 [*ORE* 1066:1, 16 alt.]. In the fourth paragraph from the bottom I have changed "membership of the Church" to "membership in the Church." Père Salgado lists nine fundamental points, which the Pope made in this catechesis in his book *La Maternité Spirituelle*, 171–173.

76 Cf. above (footnote 44) 214.

Thus, once again we can clearly see Mary's spiritual motherhood as the fruit of her association with the work of redemption.

To one outside the immediate "household of the faith," this highly developed interpretation of John 19:25–27 can seem to be *eisegesis* rather than *exegesis*. Thus, even a student of the Pope's thought as sympathetic as George Huntston Williams of Harvard can say:

> In what always seems an uncharacteristically and unnecessarily harsh statement of Jesus to his mother (Jn. 19:26), "Woman, behold your son!" Pope John Paul has obviously for a long time found the inference that Jesus sanctioned a universalization of her [Mary's] maternal role: "In these words I always found the place for every human being and the place for myself."[77]

It ought to be noted that Williams is surely not trying to be polemical here and that he is willing to put the best construction on the Pope's understanding of what he himself has come to see as "an uncharacteristically and unnecessarily harsh statement of Jesus to his mother." This is an illustration of the difference between reading a given text within the Catholic tradition and outside of it, an illustration of why the Fathers of the Extraordinary Synod of 1985 found it necessary to state even for the benefit of Catholic scholars that

> the exegesis of the original meaning of Sacred Scripture, most highly recommended by the Council (cf. *DV* #12), cannot be separated from the living tradition of the Church (cf. *DV* #9) *nor from the authentic interpretation of the Magisterium of the Church* (cf. *DV* #10).[78]

---

77 Williams 284. The reference is from the Act of Consecration to the Mother of God made at Jasna Góra on 4 June 1979, *Inseg* II/1 (1979) 1417 [*Poland* 110–111].

78 Final Report (*Relatio Finalis*) II. B. a. 1. *L'Osservatore Romano* (daily Italian edition) of 10 December 1985, supplemento, II; *The Extraordinary Synod - 1985* (Boston: St. Paul edition, 1986) 49. The italicized section translates "*neque ab authentica interpretatione magisterii Ecclesiæ*," which has been inexplicably omitted in both the English and Italian translations. Cf. Msgr. John F. McCarthy, "An Assessment of the Recent Extraordinary Synod," *The Wanderer* 119.11 (13 March 1986) 3. The reference to *DV* no. 9 is also missing in the English text.

One such scholar, Canon John McHugh, had already noted in the preface to his book, *The Mother of Jesus in the New Testament*, ten years earlier "that differences concerning Marian doctrine are to a large extent a consequence of much deeper differences [between Catholics and Protestants] concerning the relationship of Scripture and tradition."[79]

The perspective of Professor Williams is represented even more sharply in the treatment of John 19:25–27 by the scholars of the ecumenical task force of the American Lutheran-Catholic dialogue. They concede by way of footnote that Roman Catholics would make a distinction between Church teaching on Mary's spiritual motherhood and the teaching of Scripture. "They may accept the spiritual motherhood of Mary without claiming that it is taught by the Scriptures."[80] One could possibly understand how Lutheran scholars might come to such a conclusion without a thorough knowledge of the Catholic tradition; it is more difficult to grasp how Catholic scholars on the task force could have concurred.

The consensus of the ecumenical task force is certainly out of harmony with the above quoted statement of the Extraordinary Synod and the careful discussion on Scripture and Tradition in Canon McHugh's book.[81] Catholic scholars willingly grant that the earliest exegesis of John 19:25–27 did not explicitly find therein the doctrine of Mary's spiritual maternity which in the Patristic era was based much more on the understanding of Mary

79 John McHugh, *The Mother of Jesus in the New Testament* (Garden City, N. Y.: Doubleday & Co., Inc., 1975) xiii.

80 Raymond E. Brown et al., eds., *Mary in the New Testament* (Philadelphia: Fortress Press; New York: Paulist Press, 1978) 215; cf. entire section, 206–218. Cf. the extreme Protestant position which assumes that "death ends all human relationships," that "there is no husband and wife in heaven ... no mother and son either" and that, therefore, "there is no authoritative teaching anywhere to show that she [Mary] stands today in any relation towards God in heaven and man on earth different from that in which any other departed saint stands." in William J. Bridcut, "Our Lord's Relationship with His Mother," *One in Christ* 22 (1986) 368–370.

81 McHugh xxiii–xlviii.

as the New Eve.[82] They do hold, however, that this is an instance of the development of doctrine and a subsequent discovery of the implications contained in this passage from the beginning.[83] They see it neither as a superimposition of an element alien to the original datum nor a denial of the nucleus of that original datum, but an organic development, a deeper awareness of ramifications in the text itself, which were gradually brought to light over a period of time under the guidance of the Holy Spirit.[84] Father Domenico Bertetto, S.D.B., did not hesitate to conclude in his presentation to the Mariological Congress of Santo Domingo that the "testament of the Lord," i.e., the willing

82 Cf. *Theotokos* 139–41; Salgado, *La Maternité Spirituelle* 57–123. On p. 128 of this remarkably well researched book Père Salgado pointed out that the first author in the whole Church to base Mary's spiritual maternity on John 19:25–27 as far as we presently know was George of Nicomedia (+860); cf. also *Theotokos* 154–155.

83 Cf. *Theotokos* 253–56, 373–75; Théodore Koehler, S.M., "Les principales interpretations traditionelles de Jn. 19, 25–27 pendant les douze premiers siècles," *Etudes Mariales* 16 (1959) 119–55 and "Mary's Spiritual Maternity after the Second Vatican Council," *Marian Studies* 23 (1972) 39–68; the following contributions to the Mariological Congress held in Santo Domingo in 1965: André Feuillet, P.S.S., "De muliere parturiente et de maternitate spirituali Mariae secundum evangelium sancti Johannis (16, 21; 19, 25–27)," *MSS* 111–22; Alphonsus Mercado, O.F.M., "De Verbis Jesu ad Matrem et Discipulum (Io. 19, 26–27a) iuxta genus ioanneum. Adnotationes," *MSS* 123–37; Pastor Gutierrez Osorio, S.I., "'Ecce Mater tua' (Jn. 19, 25–27): Maternitas spiritualis Mariae in luce exegeseos SS. Patrum et scriptorum posteriorum," *MSS*, 151–60; Henri Barré, C.S.Sp., "Exegèse de Jean 19, 25–27 et développement doctrinal," *MSS* 161–71; Pierre-Reginald Masson, O.P., "'Ecce mater tua' (Jn. 19, 25–27) selon l'interpretation des théologiens," *MSS* 201–23; Jean-Marie Salgado, O.M.I., "La Maternité Spirituelle de la très Sainte Vierge Marie: Bilan Actuel," *Divinitas* 16 (1972) 17–102 and "Mise à Jour d'un Bilan: La Maternité Spirituelle de la Sainte Vierge Marie dans l'Ecriture Sainte," *Divus Thomas (Piacenza)* 87 (1984) 289–323; Aristide Serra, O.S.M., *Maria a Cana e presso la croce* (Rome: Centro di Cultura Mariana "Mater Ecclesiæ," 1985) 81–121 and *Maria secondo il Vangelo* (Brescia: Editrice Queriniana, 1988) 149–72; Giuseppe Segalla, Luigi Gambero, Théodore Koehler, *Maria ai piedi della Croce* (Casale Monferrato: Edizioni Piemme, 1989); Stefano M. Manelli, F.I., *All Generations Shall Call Me Blessed: Biblical Mariology* Revised and Enlarged Second Edition, reprint, trans. Peter Damian Fehlner, F.I. (New Bedford, MA: Academy of the Immaculate, 2005) 371–390.

84 Cf. *DV* 8.

of the gift of His Mother to the Church, is established by the ordinary magisterium of the Church.[85]

It is interesting to note that in the course of the Lenten retreat preached to Blessed Pope Paul VI and the Roman Curia in 1976, Cardinal Karol Wojtyła used the very same term employed by Father Bertetto:

> And even from the cross Jesus once again firmly asserted his mother's role in the mystery of redemption and of the Church, saying to John: "Behold your mother" and to the Mother, "Behold your son" (Jn. 19, 26–27). *These words belong in his testament.*[86]

All of the modern Popes from Leo XIII onwards have repeatedly taught that the beloved disciple represented all the faithful and indeed the whole human race.[87] Here is a representative text from the Venerable Pius XII, which exemplifies the ordinary magisterium of the modern papacy on Mary's spiritual motherhood:

> Jesus Himself from His Cross on high ratified by means of a symbolic and efficacious gift the spiritual motherhood of Mary toward men when He pronounced the memorable words: "Woman, behold thy son." *He thus entrusted all Christians, in the person of the beloved disciple, to the most Blessed Virgin.*[88]

Of this patrimony of growth in insight and appreciation of the *testamentum Domini*, John Paul II surely made his own

---

85 Domenico Bertetto, S.D.B., "Beata Virgo Maria et Testamentum Domini in Cruce," *MSS* 197, cf. entire study 181–199. On what constitutes the "ordinary magisterium," cf. *LG* #25.

86 *Sign of Contradiction* 71 (emphasis mine). He had also spoken of the gift of Mary's spiritual maternity as "the testament of Christ" in his homily of 3 May 1968 at Jasna Góra [*Omelie* 23, 27] and has done so as Pope many times, e.g., at Fatima: *Inseg* V/2 (1982) 1567, 1578 [*Portugal* 72]; at Luján in Argentina: *Inseg* V/2 (1982) 2201, 2205 [*Argentina* 23]; and in *Redemptoris Mater* #45: *Inseg* X/1 (1987) 734–35 [St. Paul edition 64].

87 Bonaventura Duda, O.F.M., "'Ecce mater tua' (Jo. 19, 26–27) in documentis Romanorum Pontificum," *MSS* 235–289.

88 *AAS* 46 (1954) 208–209 [*OL* #648].

significant contribution[89] and continued to do so until the end of his long pontificate of over 26 years. This is yet another factor which enters into the rationale of his "program of consecration and entrustment" to Mary and manifests its solid basis from the perspective of Scripture and Tradition.

89 Father Koehler in *Maria ai piedi della Croce* 77–78 briefly called attention to the contribution which John Paul II had made in expounding this text and notes that his treatment of John 19:25–27 in *Redemptoris Mater* is the most developed that any Pope had yet made.

CHAPTER SEVEN

Entrustment to Mary

If from the pontificate of Benedict XIV, whose text on Mary's spiritual maternity was incorporated almost verbatim into *Lumen Gentium* #53,[1] John 19:25–27 has been reckoned as one of the primary factors in establishing the doctrine of Mary's spiritual maternity, then it would seem as if Pope Saint John Paul II was continuing the process of mining the hidden riches of this text—and consequently the development of doctrine—in finding in it the theological justification of, indeed the mandate for, entrustment/consecration to Mary. In fact, he cited and offered commentaries on this text more than all of his predecessors and successors combined. He found in it the basis for Mary's *kenosis*,[2] Marian coredemption,[3] Mary's spiritual maternity,[4] her motherhood of the Church[5] and Marian devotion.[6] Here is a very interesting passage from a homily he preached on 2 July 1979, during the first year of his pontificate, in which he rehearses some of the major elements to be derived

1 *Theotokos* 374.

2 Cf. *Redemptoris Mater* #18.

3 Cf. Arthur Burton Calkins, "Pope John Paul II's Teaching on Marian Coredemption," in Mark I. Miravalle, S.T.D., (ed.), *Mary Coredemptrix, Mediatrix, Advocate, Theological Foundations II: Papal, Pneumatological, Ecumenical* (Santa Barbara, CA: Queenship Publishing Company, 1997) 134–144; "Pope John Paul II's Ordinary Magisterium on Marian Coredemption: Consistent Teaching and More Recent Perspectives," in *Mary at the Foot of the Cross – II: Acts of the Second International Symposium on Marian Coredemption* (New Bedford, MA: Academy of the Immaculate, 2002) 21–27.

4 Cf. above (chapter 6) 221-226.

5 Cf. *Redemptor Hominis* #22; *Redemptoris Mater* #47.

6 Cf. his audiences of 11 May 1983, 23 November 1988, 23 April 1997, 7 May 1997.

from the text and points to the first intuition of its bearing on Mary's spiritual maternity in Patristic exegesis:

> There is, in the first place, before our eyes the scene vividly described by the evangelist John: we are on Mount Calvary, there is a cross, and Jesus is nailed to it; and there is, close by, the mother of Jesus, surrounded by some women; there is also the beloved disciple, John himself; The Dying Man speaks, breathing with difficulty in the death agony: "Woman, behold, your son!" The intention is evident: Jesus wants to entrust his mother to the care of his beloved disciple.
>
> Is this all? The ancient Fathers of the Church caught sight of a deeper theological meaning behind this episode, which is apparently so simple. *Already Origen identifies the apostle John with every Christian* and, after him, the reference to this text becomes more and more frequent, to justify Mary's universal motherhood.
>
> It is a conviction that has a precise foundation in revelation: how can we fail to think, in fact, on reading this passage, of Jesus' mysterious words during the wedding at Cana (cf. Jn. 2:4) when, to Mary's request, he replies calling her "woman"—as now—and postponing the beginning of his collaboration with her in favour of men to the moment of the Passion, his "hour," as he is accustomed to call it? (cf. Jn. 7:30; 8:20; 12:27; 13:1; Mk. 14:35, 41; Mt. 26:45; Lk. 22:53.)
>
> *Mary is fully conscious of the mission which has been entrusted to her;* we find her at the beginning of the life of the Church, together with the disciples who are preparing for the imminent event of Pentecost, as the first lesson of the Mass reminds us. In this narration by Luke, her name stands out among those of the other women: the early community, gathered "in the Upper Room" in prayer, presses around her, "the mother of Jesus," as if seeking protection and comfort before the risks of a future overhung by threatening shadows …
>
> Now let us continue the celebration of Mass. In this liturgical assembly of ours, the experience of the Upper

> Room lives again mystically. Mary is with us. *We invoke her, we entrust ourselves to her.* May she help us in the resolution, which we renew here, to wish to imitate her generously.[7]

The text of Origen (c. 185–254) to which the Pope refers is this:

> The Gospels are the first fruits of all Scripture and the Gospel of John is the first of the Gospels. No one can understand the meaning of this Gospel if he has not reclined on the breast of Jesus, if he has not received from Jesus, Mary to be his Mother also … In fact, every man who has become perfect no longer lives, but Christ lives in him and, because Christ lives in him, it is said of him to Mary: Behold your son Christ.[8]

Many commentators deny that it is possible to deduce Mary's spiritual maternity as a solid conclusion from this very evocative text. The underlying logic of Origen, they argue, runs like this: in order to understand the fourth gospel well, each one ought to aspire to such perfection that he becomes in effect "another Christ" about whom Christ Himself could say to Mary, "Behold your son," namely, behold Jesus whom you bore, behold another Christ.[9] On the other hand, Father F. M. Braun, O.P., holds that

> It appears clear that Origen was at least admitting a certain maternity in Mary towards John and those like him … As inexact as the passage remains, it contains a first indication of the spiritual maternity of Mary.[10]

Father Jean-Marie Salgado, O.M.I., whose magisterial work, *La Maternité Spirituelle de la Très Sainte Vierge Marie*, takes

---

7 *Inseg* II/2 (1979) 12–13, 14 [*ORE* 592:11] (emphases mine).

8 Greek text in Cipriano Vagaggini, O.S.B., *Maria nelle Opere di Origene* (Rome: Pont. Institutum Orientalium Studiorum "Orientalia Christiana Analecta" #31, 1962) 177; Latin text in *PG* 14, 31 A-B. This translation partially adapted from versions given in *Theotokos* 254, 275.

9 Bertetto, "Beata Virgo Maria et testamentum Domini in cruce," *MSS* 186; Theodore Koehler, S.M., "Maternité Spirituelle, Maternité Mystique," *Maria* 6:582; cf. also Gutierrez, *MSS* 156; *Theotokos* 254.

10 F. M. Braun, O.P., *Mother of God's People*, trans. John Clarke, O.C.D. (New York: Alba House, 1967) 99–100.

account of all the major treatments on Mary's spiritual maternity until 1990, also maintains that, far from excluding Origen's principal idea of identification with Christ, the doctrine of Mary's universal spiritual maternity is implicitly required by such identification. He further holds that an unprejudiced reading of this text is sufficient to establish the conclusion that perfect and total identification with Christ, according to Origen, requires the acceptance of Mary's spiritual motherhood.[11] Following this same line of reasoning, I would argue that Origen, consciously or not, was also laying the groundwork for the theology of entrustment or consecration to Mary.

While the Pope does not enter directly into the scholarly controversy about what Origen intended, nor does he declare that Origen definitively established the link between John 19:26–27 and Mary's spiritual maternity (even if he seems to imply it). What he does point to is that Origen identifies the apostle John with every Christian and that subsequently this text is referred to more and more frequently as an indication of Mary's universal motherhood. In this sense, he, too, like Origen, is being evocative, suggesting that already Origen grasped a "spiritual sense"[12] in this text by his extraordinary intuition,[13] even if he did not develop it further. Interestingly, the Holy Father cites Origen again on this topic in the same evocative way in *Redemptoris Mater*.[14]

The above cited homily was preached on John 19:25–27 and Acts 1:12–14. In it John Paul also stated that

> Mary is fully conscious of the mission which has been entrusted to her: we find her at the beginning of the life of

11 Jean-Marie Salgado, O.M.I., "La maternité spirituelle de la Sainte Vierge chez les Pères durant les quatre premiers siècles," *Divinitas* 30 (1986) 58–61; *La Maternité Spirituelle* 63–65.

12 Gutierrez, *MSS* 152.

13 Duda, *MSS* 289.

14 *Inseg* X/1 (1987) 706, n. 147 [St. Paul edition 76, n. 47].

> the Church, together with the disciples who are preparing for the imminent event of Pentecost.[15]

In fact, just two months prior to that significant statement about Mary's consciousness of her mission, he had spoken of her as the one "to whose loving patronage God himself willed to entrust, through her obedient 'Yes', the fate of the whole of mankind."[16]

Christ entrusted to Mary every human being ("descending" entrustment)

Without fear of exaggeration, we may speak of a "theology of entrustment" to Mary in the mind of John Paul II, which was frequently expressed in his preaching. Here the word is particularly appropriate because it is, in fact, often used to describe what Jesus did from the Cross: He entrusted John to Mary and Mary to John.[17] "Notice, finally," said the late Father Lucien Deiss, C.S.Sp. (1921–2007),

> that it is not Mary who is first entrusted to John, but John who is first entrusted to Mary. The accent is placed on the solicitude with which Mary is to surround the disciple, a solicitude to which the disciple is to respond with the tenderness of a son.[18]

Already in a homily at Jasna Góra on the Feast of Our Lady, Queen of Poland in 1968, Cardinal Wojtyła had spoken

---

15 *Inseg* II/2 (1979) 13 [*ORE* 592:11].

16 *Inseg* II/1 (1979) 1054 [*ORE* 582:3].

17 In *Redemptoris Mater* #45 the Pope says "Ut Redemptor Mariam Ioanni committit, ita simul Ioannem concredit Mariæ" [*Inseg* X/1 (1987) 735]. The English translation has "The Redeemer entrusts Mary to John because he entrusts John to Mary" [St. Paul edition 64], but, in fact, the Latin text suggests no such causal link; it merely asserts that "As the Redeemer entrusts Mary to John, he thus at the same time entrusts John to Mary." The Italian text is equally neutral, having "Il Redentore affida Maria a Giovanni in quanto affida Giovanni a Maria" [*Inseg* X/1 (1987) 795].

18 Lucien Deiss, C.S.Sp., *Mary, Daughter of Sion*, trans. Barbara T. Blair (Collegeville, Minnesota: The Liturgical Press, 1972) 195. Don Giuseppe Segalla argues in the same vein in *Maria ai piedi della Croce* 17–18.

similarly, both in terms of the act of "entrusting" by Christ and of the "mission" of Mary.

> From the height of the cross *the Son of God entrusted to the mother a great mission*: to express the love of the Father, to express His own love linked to His martyrdom and to His death on the cross, linked to His resurrection.[19]

Countless numbers of times[20] John Paul emphasized that in John, the beloved disciple, "every man [or woman] discovers that he [or she] is a child of the one who gave the world the Son of God."[21] Here is a particularly beautiful instance of this "theology of entrustment" which was spoken to youth at Jasna Góra in 1983, with reference to John 19:26:

> We believe that, in that one man [John], Christ entrusted to her [Mary] every human being, and at the same time awoke in her heart a love which is a maternal reflection of his own redemptive love.
>
> We believe that we are loved by this love, surrounded by it, that is, by the love of God, which was revealed in the Redemption by means of the Cross, and finally by the love of the Mother, who stood beneath the Cross and who from the Heart of her Son accepted into her heart every human being.[22]

The poetic and delicate, even mystical, references to the Hearts of Jesus and Mary will be seen subsequently to be a further dimension of the Pope's thought on Marian consecration.

In a prayer for vocations in Bologna less than a month before his pilgrimage to Fatima in 1982, he coupled the notion of the "mission" entrusted to Mary from the Cross with what he

19 *Omelie* 24 (trans. and emphasis mine).

20 One has only to look up the references to John 19:25–27 given in the volumes of the *Insegnamenti* to discover the frequency with which John Paul referred to the action of Christ as "entrustment."

21 *Inseg* XII/1 (1989) 552 [*ORE* 1081:1]. The words in brackets do not appear in the original Italian text.

22 *Inseg* VI/1 (1983) 1563 [*ORE* 791:3].

would request at the great Portuguese shrine: that Mary unite our consecration to Jesus' and hers.

> We entrust our life to you, to you who welcomed the Word of God with absolute fidelity and *dedicated yourself to his plan of salvation and grace*, acceding to the action of the Holy Spirit with total docility; *to you who had from your Son the mission of receiving and caring for the disciple whom he loved (cf. Jn. 19:26); to you, each and every one of us repeats, "Totus tuus ego sum" (I am all yours), that you may take our consecration and unite it to that of Jesus and yours, as an offering to God the Father for the life of the world.*[23]

It will be recalled that in the Solemn Acts of Consecration of 1982 and 1984, after citing the text about Christ's self-consecration (Jn. 17:19) and our desire to unite ourselves to it, the Pope entrusted to Mary the world and "the [very] consecration itself, for the world's sake, placing it in your motherly Heart."[24] Notice, too, that the concepts expressed in the prayer said in Bologna are closely allied to that description of Mary in the Fatima consecration as "wholly united to the redeeming consecration of your Son."

Arguably the most authoritative, and possibly the most comprehensive, exposition of his "theology of entrustment" occurred in #45 of *Redemptoris Mater*:

> The Redeemer entrusts his mother to the disciple, and at the same time he gives her to him as his mother. Mary's motherhood, which becomes man's inheritance, is a gift: *a gift which Christ himself makes* personally to every individual. As the Redeemer entrusts Mary to John, he thus at the same time entrusts John to Mary. At the foot of the Cross there begins that special *entrusting of humanity to the Mother of Christ*, which in the history of the Church has been practiced and expressed in different

23 *Inseg* V/1 (1982) 1217 [*ORE* 731:6].

24 Cf. above 205. This entrusting of our union with the consecration of Christ is also a feature of his Letter to the Bishop of Leiria of 16 April 1983, *Inseg* VI/1 (1983) 967.

> ways. [*Iuxta Crucem ille actus incipit peculiaris, quo homo Matri Christi committitur, quique postea in Ecclesiæ historia variis modis exercebatur.*] The same Apostle and Evangelist, after reporting the words addressed by Jesus on the Cross to his Mother and to himself, adds: "And from that hour the disciple took her to his own home" (Jn. 19:27). This statement certainly means that the role of son was attributed to the disciple and that he assumed responsibility for the Mother of his beloved Master. And since Mary was given as a mother to him personally, the statement indicates, even though indirectly, everything expressed by the intimate relationship of a child with its mother. And all of this can be included in the word "entrusting." [*Totum hoc contineri potest verbo "commendationis."*] Such entrusting is *the response* to a person's love, and in particular *to the love of a mother.*[25]

In the strictest sense, of course, it is not man who initiates the act of consecration or entrusting, but God. In commenting on the Fatima consecration Father Eamon Carroll said:

> The pope's words make clear that consecration, as an act of religion, is properly directed to God alone, and that consecration is not simply a human act of religion, not something we do, or can do, independently of God's call, of the divine initiative. In the Bible, man never consecrates himself, for he is incapable of so doing. God calls the human being; the election and vocation come from God.[26]

I would argue that consecration is not **primarily** "something that we do," but that it is something that we respond to, as in the promises made before Baptism. Father Carroll's statement found support in Father Stefano De Fiores' article on consecration in the *Nuovo Dizionario di Mariologia*:

> It is God who predestines, calls, justifies and glorifies (Rom. 8:30). In particular sanctification or consecration (*hagiazein*) is a divine act, which renders Christians "holy,"

25 *Inseg* X/1 (1987) 735 [St. Paul edition 64 (alt)].

26 Carroll, *Marian Studies* 36 (1985) 153.

> or rather sanctified (I Cor. 1:2; Rom. 15:16). This passive sense is expressed by Paul with an affirmation which is at base Trinitarian: "You were washed, you were sanctified, you were justified in the name of the Lord Jesus Christ and in the Spirit of our God" (1 Cor. 6:11; cf. 2 Tim. 2:13; Eph. 2:1–6). Christians are not consecrated by themselves, but in virtue of Baptism administered "in the name of the Father and of the Son and of the Holy Spirit" (Mt. 28:19).[27]
>
> First as a commitment or ideal to actualize, consecration is a call, a grace, an action of God which touches and transforms human existence in its deepest reality.[28]
>
> Every Christian is consecrated by God and to God insofar as he is a member of the Church, the people of God who belong to him and who ought to live for him. In fact "Christ loved the church and gave himself up for her, that he might sanctify her (= consecrate her) having cleansed her by the washing of water with the word" (Eph. 5:25–26). The title of spouse and virgin attributed to the church indicates that she ought to respond to the love of Christ with the yes of faith and consecration to him of her entire life.[29]

The late Father Domenico Bertetto, S.D.B. (1914–1988), attempted a further clarification of God's initiative in consecrating by distinguishing between "descending" and "ascending" consecration:

> Consecration is above all *descending*, or rather the action of God, who communicates his perfections, his authority, his holiness, his powers to his creatures …
>
> The consecration *descending* from God implies also on that account a consecration *ascending* from the creature, conscious and free, who recognizes his belonging to God and therefore commits himself to be God's, entrusted to God, put at the service of God, according to the

27 "Cons" 396 (my translation, R.S.V.).

28 "Cons" 408 (my translation).

29 "Cons" 411–12 (my translation, R.S.V.).

> requirement of the consecration received, under the efficacious influence of the Spirit.
>
> Every ascending consecration, which John Paul II likes to call *entrustment* in order to distinguish it from descending consecration, sets out from the recognition of the relations which link the consecrated person to the One to whom he is consecrated.[30]

While one may find Bertetto's distinction helpful in emphasizing God's initiative in the "descending" consecration and ours in the "ascending" one, his contention that Pope John Paul II made such a real distinction between consecration and entrustment is simply contrary to the facts. In both the major acts of 1982 and 1984 he uses the terms synonymously in the body of the text and as a title of the latter in the cover letter sent to the Bishops of the world.[31] But of even greater significance is the fact—which we have seen the Pope emphasizing here—that **in the first instance it is Christ Himself who entrusts us to Mary**. In John Paul's exegesis of John 19:25–27 he repeats over and over again that it is Christ who, by entrusting John to Mary, has entrusted us all to her.

The theme of entrusting to Mary, particularly as a response to her motherly love, which we have seen referred to in *Redemptoris Mater* #45[32] is a fascinating one. The Pope further stated that

> the figure of Mary of Nazareth sheds light on *womanhood as such* by the very fact that God, in the sublime event of the Incarnation of his Son, entrusted himself to the ministry, the free and active ministry of a woman.[33]

30 Domenico Bertetto, S.D.B., "Consacrazione e affidamento: Senso ed esigenze dell'affidamento a Maria," Bertetto ed., *L'Affidamento a Maria* (Roma: Libreria Ateneo Salesiano, 1984) 75–76 (my translation). This thesis was also espoused by other members of the Salesian family including its Rector Major, Egidio Viganò (1920–1985); cf. De Fiores, *Maria nella Teologia Contemporanea* 331–333.

31 *Inseg* VII/1 (1984) 417 [*ORE* 823:2]. Cf. also our discussion above 145-154.

32 Cf. above 241.

33 St. Paul edition 65. Curiously, the Latin text is more sober and does not speak of God's entrusting himself to Mary: "Hic solum animadvertere placet Mariam

In this regard I would like to present some of the reflections of Dr. Joyce A. Little of the University of Saint Thomas, in Houston, which were presented at the Annual Convention of the Mariological Society of America in June of 1988, which had *Redemptoris Mater* as its theme.

Dr. Little asks, "Why does the Pope identify 'entrusting' as that which defines the importance not only of Mary, but of women in general?"[34] And again,

> Why is it that entrusting does not, at least in its most basic form refer to the relationship which exists between a father and a child, or, more specifically, between the Eternal Father in heaven and his children here on earth? To put it another way, what is the difference between fatherhood and motherhood which requires that we identify "entrusting" more with the love of a mother than with the love of a father? The answer, I believe, lies in the difference between that distancing which is implied by fatherhood, as contrasted with the immediacy which is associated with motherhood.[35]

She goes on, then, to justify this identification of distance with fatherhood by citing first Father Walter J. Ong, S.J. (1912–2003), who says that "Masculinity stands in the human psyche for a kind of otherness, difference" and that, therefore, God

---

Nazarethanam lucem effundere in mulierem ut talem eo ipso quod Deus, in praecelso eventu Incarnationis Filii, ministerio libero et actuoso mulieris est usus" [*Inseg* X/1 (1987) 736–37]. However, the Italian translation, which may well represent the Pope's thought more accurately here, is: "Qui desidero solo rilevare che la figura di Maria di Nazareth proietta luce sulla *donna in quanto tale* per il fatto stesso che Dio, nel sublime evento dell'incarnazione del Figlio, si è affidato al ministero, libero e attivo, di una donna" [*Inseg* X/1 (1987) 796]. I retain the Vatican English translation here as well, because it conforms sufficiently to other statements of the Pope on the matter of God's entrusting of himself to Mary, cf. *Inseg* III/1 (1980) 414 [*ORE* 623:8], and his "entrusting to women" in a special way, cf. *Mulieris Dignitatem* #30–31, *Inseg* XI/3 (1988) 311–316, 374–376 [ORE 1058:13] and *Christifideles Laici* #51, *Inseg* XI/4 (1988) 2056–2060, 2154–2157 [ORE 1075:17].

34 Joyce A. Little, "*Redemptoris Mater*: The Significance of Mary for Women," *Marian Studies* 39 (1988) 140.

35 Little 141–142.

> is likened to the masculine not because he has a masculine physical constitution, but because he is a source of existence that is other, different, separated (*kadosh*, the Hebrew word translated *sanctus, hagios*, "holy," means at root "separated") from all his creation, even from human beings, though they are "made in his image and likeness" … The male reproductive cell becomes effectively reproductive when it is totally detached from the male's body and joins the cell that, in the higher forms of life, remains attached to the female. Fathers are essentially distant from offspring physically. They can even be dead and buried when the child is being formed and is born.[36]

With regard to identifying immediacy with motherhood, she cites the psychiatrist Karl Stern (1906–1975), who said that "Woman, in her being, is deeply committed to *bios*, to nature itself. The words for *mother* and *matter*, for *mater* and *materia* are etymologically related."[37]

Dr. Little proceeds, then, to theologize about these distinctions between the role of a father and a mother in a way that very interestingly links "entrusting" to mothers and to Mary.

> Motherhood lies at the center of the New Covenant, because the Father entrusts his Son to a mother. But, in point of fact and as noted earlier, God entrusts every child of his making to a mother. Each of us, by our very creation, is forced, as it were, to trust the mother to whom God has entrusted us. As Stern has observed, the paradox of being human resides in the fact that, while we are the summit of God's creation,[38] each one of us must, in order to enter this life, pass through a period of "utter helplessness and dependence." We must trust our mothers for the simple reason that we are given, literally, no alternatives. For that reason alone, as Stern points out, "faith grows out of the

36 Walter J. Ong, S.J., *Fighting for Life* (Ithaca, N. Y./London: Cornell University Press, 1981) 175–176.

37 Karl Stern, *The Flight From Woman* (New York: Farrar, Strauss and Giroux, 1965) 23.

38 I do find this a rather puzzling statement.

> relation of child and mother."[39] Father, whether divine or human, lies off in the distance, beyond mother.
>
> If our relationship with God the Father does not supply the most basic instance of "entrusting," it is because we are material beings who must first be "entrusted" to a mother before there is any possibility of our coming to know our father, whether human or divine. And, for the same reason, of course, our relationship with Christ also cannot supply the most basic instance of "entrusting," inasmuch as we must also necessarily trust our mothers before we are in a position to entrust ourselves to Christ. We must, in other words, be born of flesh and blood before we can be born of water and the Spirit. No one can enter into the New Covenant by way of baptism who has not first entered into the world by way of a woman.[40]

Inter alia, she draws this very obvious conclusion, which is nonetheless hardly sufficiently appreciated, with regard to its applications on the divine or human levels:

> Mothers are therefore the first, and generally, the most influential guide children are given in this world. *Children are entrusted to mothers, in order that mothers might enable children to entrust themselves to others, initially their fathers, and, of course, ultimately their Eternal Father.* And, since not all people or things are trustworthy, children also depend on their mothers to inform them of and protect them from anyone or anything which might harm them. The child is entrusted to his mother in order that he might know, beyond her, what can and cannot be trusted.[41]

I have taken note of and referred to the arguments of Dr. Little at some length because I believe that they illustrate and provide further anthropological context for the thought of John Paul II.

39 Stern 188–89.

40 Little 144–145.

41 Little 146 (emphasis mine).

In his Apostolic Letter, *Mulieris Dignitatem*, on the Dignity and Vocation of Women on the occasion of the Marian Year John Paul wrote:

> The moral and spiritual strength of a woman is joined to her awareness that *God entrusts the human being to her in a special way.* Of course, God entrusts every human being to each and every other human being. But this entrusting concerns women in a special way—precisely by reason of their femininity—and this in a particular way determines their vocation.
>
> The moral force of women, which draws strength from this awareness and this entrusting, expresses itself in a great number of figures of the Old Testament, of the time of Christ, and of later ages right up to our own day.
>
> *A woman is strong because of her awareness of this entrusting,* strong because of the fact that God "entrusts the human being to her," always and in every way, even in the situations of social discrimination in which she may find herself. This awareness and this fundamental vocation speak to women of the dignity which they receive from God himself, and this makes them "strong" and strengthens their vocations.[42]

Evidently assuming as a foundation what he had already asserted in *Redemptoris Mater* and *Mulieris Dignitatem*, the Pope simply stated in his Post-Synodal Apostolic Exhortation, *Christifideles Laici*, that "two great tasks entrusted to women merit the attention of everyone": "the task of *bringing full dignity to conjugal life and to motherhood* " and "the task of *assuring the moral dimension of culture.*"[43] Again in Vicenza on the Feast of Our Lady's Nativity in 1991, he spoke thus:

> Mothers who are listening to me, how great is the task which God entrusts to you! How important is your role in

42 *Inseg* XI/3 (1988) 313, 375–376 [*ORE* 1058:13].

43 *Inseg* XI/4 (1988) 2058–59, 2156 [*ORE* 1075:17].

> the education of your children, the fruit of your family's love.[44]

Undoubtedly the theme of "entrusting to women," even if the Pope did not speak on it with great frequency, is an important point of reference for him and a further basis for this theology of "entrustment to Mary."

We have noted above Father Stefano De Fiores' comment that entrustment "includes an attitude of interior trust ... In order to make an act of entrustment it is necessary to have trust in the person to whom one entrusts himself."[45] Dr. Little's last lines, quoted above, also recognize the link between "entrusting" and "trust."[46] Let us hear her further on this topic.

> Mothers, it might therefore be said, stand for the realm of trust, first, in the sense that the survival of children depends primarily on the trustworthiness of mothers, and second, in the sense that mothers, more than any other person in our lives, are expected to be able to distinguish, beyond themselves, what can be trusted from what cannot. Indeed, in a larger sense, the female per se would seem to stand for the realm of trust.[47]

It is in this sense, she points out, that Mary has a crucial role to play in our lives. She assures us that her Son is worthy of all trust and that we will not be misled in entrusting ourselves totally to Him.

> Mary is our most reliable guide to Christ, the person in the best position to attest to the truth of Christ, precisely because she is his mother. She knows him as no one else among us possibly can. And because God was able to entrust his only Son to her, her Son has been able to entrust us to her guidance. When Mary counsels every one of us to "Do whatever he tells you," she is assuring us

44 *Inseg* XIV/2 (1991) 514 [*ORE* 1207:1].

45 Cf. above (chapter 4, footnote 25) 148.

46 Cf. above (chapter 4) 148.

47 Little 146–147.

> that we can entrust ourselves to him. By so doing, she is inviting every one of us to do what is, in the created order, the supremely female thing, namely to surrender ourselves to another …
>
> If Christ is the truth, then Mary is the trust. And the truth, because personal and material, cannot be efficacious in our world unless we entrust ourselves to him. For that reason, Christ requires the female mediation of his mother, for only a mother can offer us the assurance we require that we not only can believe what he says, but can also safely entrust ourselves to the Person he is.[48]

Hardly surprisingly, we find this dimension of trust in Mary was a frequent motif in the Marian teaching of John Paul II. Perhaps what might be described as his two principal catecheses on this subject were both appropriately given in the chapel of the Roman Major Seminary whose sanctuary features a beautiful depiction of Our Lady under the title of *La Madonna della Fiducia* (Our Lady of Confidence or Trust). The first of these was given on 16 February 1980.

> Mary's joy was … joy for the trust that God had shown in her by entrusting himself to her in the person of his Only Son. Bearing in her womb the Word incarnate, and giving him to the world, *she became the extraordinary depositary of God's trust in man*, so that Mary is rightly honoured as the Mother of divine confidence …
>
> Dear seminarians and dear youths, to respond to such divine trust, that is, to the grace of vocation, it is necessary above all to have confidence; the grace of the Lord is greater than our weakness, it is greater than our unworthiness, precisely as St. John expresses: "By this we shall … reassure our hearts before him whenever our hearts condemn us; for God is greater than our hearts" (I Jn. 3:19–20). We must have invincible confidence, so as always to deserve the trust of the Lord; and *Mary who is mother of God's trust in us, will thus become, at the same time, mother of our trust in him.*

48 Little 148–149.

> The pious invocation "Mater mea, fiducia mea," so dear to all those who have been formed in this Seminary, contains the deepest and fullest sense of our relationship with Mary, who is praised and venerated precisely by means of such regard of confidence, esteem and hope. In fact, "the Father's eternal love, which has been manifested in the history of mankind through the Son … comes to each of us through this Mother and thus takes on tokens that are of more easy understanding and access by each person. Consequently, Mary must be on all the ways for the Church's daily life" (*Redemptor Hominis* # 22).[49]

The second was given on 12 February 1983 and was a kind of homiletic response to a musical setting of the Gospel passage on the wedding feast of Cana (Jn. 2:1–11), which had just been performed in the Pope's presence for the feast of Our Lady of Confidence.

> What were the newly-weds feeling in their hearts at the moment that the wine ran out, as they approached the Mother of Jesus? Confidence, precisely. They had confidence in her. They had a spontaneous confidence, a confidence that said: "She can help us." Why? Maybe they did not think it, maybe they did not know it, but they felt it: "She can help us because she is the Mother, and being a mother she can understand us, she can understand our difficulties and this is the first step to helping: understanding the difficulties. And then, after having understood our difficulties, she will be able to help us."
>
> They were not thinking about *how* she could help them, but they were convinced that she *would* help them. So in the Gospel about Cana in Galilee, one discovers human confidence and at the same time the Mother of Confidence, because Mary did not disappoint the newly-weds, but rather did what they wanted: she helped them …
>
> If we have confidence in the Mother of Christ as the newly-weds at Cana did, we can entrust our worries to her, as they did. We can also entrust to her our decisions,

49 *Inseg* III/1 (1980) 414–416 [*ORE* 623:8–9] (emphasis mine).

> the interior torments which sometimes afflict us; *we can entrust all this to her, to Our Lady of Confidence, that is, to the Mother of our trust: I place my trust in you, I wish to dedicate myself to Christ, but I entrust myself to you, just as the newly-weds did.* They did not go directly to Christ to ask for a miracle, they went to Mary; they entrusted their worries, their difficulties to Mary. *In so doing, they naturally wanted to arrive at Christ*, they wanted to provoke Christ—if one can say so—and his messianic power. And thus we too, in our vocation which is a path, a spiritual walk toward Christ, *in order to be Christ's, to be an alter Christus, we too must find this Mother of our trust and we must entrust ourselves to her in order to entrust ourselves to Christ, to dedicate ourselves to Christ, to give ourselves to Christ. We must entrust ourselves to her because there is but a single course, and if we turn to her we turn to Christ*, just as the newly-weds turned to her and arrived at Christ. Thus is Mary united to her Son.[50]

On many occasions, as well, the Pope also gave clear indications that entrustment to Mary implies trust in her motherly concern for her children, that it is an act of trust, even of "abandonment"[51] to her. Here are some instances. In his first major Act of Entrustment outside of Rome, that of Mexico and Latin America, made at Guadalupe on 27 January 1979 he prayed:

> We offer and entrust to you everybody and everything for which we have pastoral responsibility, *confident that you will be with us and will help us* to carry out what your Son has told us to do (cf. Jn. 2:5). *We bring you this unlimited trust; with this trust I, John Paul II, with all my Brothers in the Episcopate of Mexico and Latin America, wish to bind you still more strongly to our ministry, to the Church and to the life of our nations.* We wish to place in your hands the

50 *Inseg* VI/1 (1983) 409–11 [*ORE* 775:10–11 (alt.)] (emphases mine).

51 Cf. above (chapter 4, footnote 42) 152.

> whole of our future, the future of evangelization in Latin America.[52]

Again, that same year at Jasna Góra, he spoke of the 1966 "act of servitude" to the Mother of God in these terms:

> Love constitutes the fulfillment of freedom, yet at the same time 'belonging,' and so not being free is part of its essence. However, this 'not being free' in love is not felt as slavery but rather as an affirmation and fulfillment of freedom. The act of consecration in slavery indicates therefore a unique dependence and a limitless trust.[53]

And then, just before renewing this consecration himself, he added:

> Consent that I should bring here, as I did already in the Basilica of St. Mary Major in Rome and later in the shrine of Guadalupe in Mexico, the mysteries of the hearts, the sorrow and suffering, and finally *the hope and expectation of this final period of the twentieth century of the Christian era.*
>
> Consent that I should *entrust* all this to Mary.
>
> Consent that I should *entrust* it to her in a new and solemn way.
>
> I am a man of great trust.
>
> I learnt to be so here.[54]

Again he prefaced the entrustment of Ireland to Mary on 30 September 1979 with these words: "I pronounce, at the close of this homily, the following words of trust and consecration."[55] Likewise, on the occasion of the centenary of the evangelization of Zaire and of its consecration to Mary by the first missionaries, he prayed:

> I entrust to you … the whole nation, which is living its own independent life today. I do so in the *same spirit of*

52 *Inseg* II/1 (1979) 165 [*Messages* 238] (emphases mine).

53 *Inseg* I/1 (1979) 1414 [*Poland* 106].

54 *Inseg* I/1 (1979) 1416 [*Poland* 109].

55 *Inseg* II/2 (1979) 468 [*Ireland* 88].

> *faith* and with the same *trust* as the first missionaries, and I do so at the same time *with all the greater joy* since *the act of consecration and abandonment* that I make now, is made with me at the same time by all the *pastors* of this Church and also by the whole *People of God*: this People of God that wishes to assume and continue with its pastors, in love and apostolic courage, the work of the construction of the Body of Christ and the approach of the kingdom of God on this earth.
>
> Accept, O Mother, *this act of trust* of ours.[56]

Again, on the occasion of the consecration of Brazil, he prayed:

> I wish to entrust to you particularly this people and this Church, this whole great and hospitable Brazil, all your sons and daughters, with all their problems and their worries, their activities and their joys. I wish to do so as Successor of Peter and Pastor of the universal Church, *entering into this heritage of veneration and love, dedication and trust*, which for centuries has been part of the Church of Brazil and of all those who form it.[57]

And, perhaps most significantly, he prayed in the course of his Act of Entrustment of the world to Mary at Fatima on 13 May 1982: "Accept our humble trust—and our act of entrusting!"[58] It should be fairly clear, then, after reviewing these representative texts that, in the mind of John Paul II, entrusting to Mary necessarily implies trust in her and is predicated upon such confidence.[59]

What Dr. Little has articulated in terms of anthropology, John Paul has fleshed out in the exercise of his teaching office: **we entrust ourselves to Mary because we trust her as a mother**

56 *Inseg* III/1 (1980) 1069–1070 [*Africa* Ap 41–42] (emphases mine).

57 *Inseg* III/2 (1980) 106; *Brazil* 185 (emphasis mine).

58 *Inseg* V/2 (1982) 1587 [*ORE* 735:12].

59 That this relationship between trust in Mary and entrustment to her has been a consistent theme in the teaching of Karol Wojtyła may be observed in a sermon he gave on 31 December 1966 [*The Word Made Flesh: The Meaning of the Christmas Season*, trans. Leslie Wearne (San Francisco: Harper & Row Publishers, 1985) 81–82], and in *Sources of Renewal* 422.

in order to entrust ourselves ever more completely to Christ. In an address to the male religious of Guatemala on 7 March 1983, he said, "I entrust you to her, to preserve and increase your fidelity to Christ and to the Church."[60] In a prayer before the statue of Our Lady of Fatima which had been brought into Saint Peter's Basilica after the Act of Entrustment on 25 March 1984, he said:

> Today we have wanted to entrust the fate of the world, of individuals, of peoples, to your Immaculate Heart in order to arrive at the very centre of the mystery of the Redemption.[61]

He puts it with great clarity in *Redemptoris Mater* that entrustment to Mary is not only willed by Christ but also has Him as its final end; He is both its *terminus a quo* and its *terminus ad quem*:

> This filial relationship, this self-entrusting of a child to its mother, not only has its *beginning in Christ* but can also be said to be *definitively directed towards him.* Mary can be said to continue to say to each individual the words which she spoke at Cana in Galilee: "Do whatever he tells you." For he, Christ, is the one Mediator between God and mankind; he is "the way, and the truth, and the life" (Jn. 14:6); it is he whom the Father has given to the world, so that man "should not perish but have eternal life" (Jn. 3:16). The Virgin of Nazareth became the first "witness" of this saving love of the Father, and she also wishes *to remain* its *humble handmaid always and everywhere.* For every Christian, for every human being, Mary is the one who first "believed," and *precisely with her faith as Spouse and Mother she wishes to act upon all those who entrust themselves to her as her children. And it is well known that the more her children persevere and progress in this attitude, the nearer Mary leads them to the "unsearchable riches of Christ"* (Eph. 3:8).[62]

60 *Inseg* VI/1 (1983) 637 [*ORE* 779:12].

61 *Inseg* VII/1 (1984) 779 [*ORE* 828:10].

62 *Inseg* X/1 (1987) 736 [St. Paul edition 65] (final emphasis mine).

This, indeed, is a beautifully rich yet concise statement on the rationale of Marian entrustment.

Our considerations about the divine initiative in consecration/entrustment, about what Father Bertetto called "descending" consecration and the appropriateness of the word "entrust" to express the disciple's relationship to Mary, all serve to reinforce this fundamental insight: **the principal Christological foundation of Marian consecration is that it is the express will of Christ as stated in John 19:26–27. Jesus Himself entrusts us to Mary.** The primary Marian entrustment, then, is a "descending" one; it comes from Him, but it is meant by Him to be complemented by an "ascending" one on our part.

This, as we have already seen, is a fundamental perspective of John Paul II. Let us listen to how he relates the "descending" to the "ascending" entrustment in his words outside the Cathedral of Turin on 13 April 1980.

> Our hearts do not forget that she was standing by the cross of Jesus (cf. Jn. 19:25): *stabat Mater dolorosa.* Nor can we forget that, from the Cross, *Jesus looked at his mother and John,* the disciple whom he loved, and, as to a special witness, indicated to the disciple Mary, as Mother, *and entrusted the disciple to his Mother*: "Behold, your mother!" "Woman, behold your son!" (Jn. 19:27, 26) We believe that in this one man, precisely in John, Jesus indicated Mary as Mother of every man—*He entrusted everyone to her, as if every man were her child, her son or her daughter.*
>
> *From this fact is derived the particular necessity that we—obedient to these words of Christ's testament—should entrust ourselves and everything that belongs to us, to Mary.*
>
> Letting myself be guided by this faith and at the same time by this hope, today I wish to renew what is part of Christ's paschal testament and entrust to the Mother of God this city and this Church which welcomes me as a pilgrim today …

> O Mother, may this prayer and this abandonment, which we renew once more, tell you everything about us.[63]

Again, in an even more emphatic way, he underscored the necessity of the "ascending" entrustment on our part in his Angelus address of 3 January 1988.

> What, then, should be our attitude towards her whom Jesus himself gave us as our mother? Our attitude cannot be other than that of the Apostle John, of whom it was said, "From that moment the disciple took her to his own house" (Jn. 19:27). To accept Mary in our lives, entrusting ourselves totally to her: this is what Our Lady expects of each of us. Entrustment is the only response adequate to the love of a person, in particular to the love of a mother.[64]

The "ascending" entrustment is derived from the "descending" entrustment and necessitated by it. What Jesus has done for us in principle, we must ratify and appropriate both individually as well as collectively. On 12 May 1991, during a prayer vigil held in Fatima, Portugal, the Holy Father summarized his understanding of this exigency once again in a way that is particularly striking:

> During this journey [Mary's life on earth] of collaboration in the work of the redemption, her motherhood "itself underwent a singular transformation, becoming ever more imbued with 'burning charity', towards all those to whom Christ's mission was directed" (*Redemptoris Mater*, 39) and whose Mother he consecrated her at the foot of the cross: "Behold your son!" In fact, since she gave birth to Christ, the Head of the Mystical Body, she also had to have given birth to all the members of that one Body. Therefore, "Mary embraces each and every one *in* the Church, and embraces each and every one *through* the Church" (*Redemptoris Mater*, 47). *The Church, for her part does not cease consecrating herself to Mary.*[65]

63 *Inseg* III/1 (1980) 891–893 [*ORE* 629:2] (emphasis mine).

64 *Inseg* XI/1 (1988) 14 [*ORE* 1021:3].

65 *Inseg* XIV/1 (1991) 1217– 1218 [*ORE* 1191:5] (emphasis on last sentence mine).

The Church does not cease consecrating herself to Mary who was consecrated her Mother at the foot of the Cross, says John Paul II. And never, would it seem, has there been a Pope who has been so intrepid in giving voice to this ceaseless consecration.

Welcoming/Receiving Mary ("ascending" entrustment)

"Entrusting oneself totally to Mary," then, according to Pope John Paul II, means "accepting Mary into our lives." And, indeed, according to the best insights into the fourth gospel, this is precisely the response of the beloved disciple to his being entrusted by Jesus to Mary. "And from that hour the disciple took her to his own home" (Jn. 19:27): thus the rendition of the usually very dependable Revised Standard Version. "But," says Canon McHugh,

> if we take careful notice of John's vocabulary, a more meaningful rendering emerges. In the Fourth Gospel, the verb *lambáno* has two senses. When applied to material things, it means simply 'to take hold of,' 'to pick up,' 'to grasp,' etc. (*e.g.* 6:11; 12:13; 13:12; 19:23, 40); when applied to immaterial things, it means 'to accept' or 'to welcome,' usually as a gift from God (*e.g.* his witness, 3:11; his word, 17:8; his Spirit, 14:17; I Jn. 2:27). Secondly, the words *'eis tà 'ídia,* which certainly can mean 'to one's own home' (in a purely physical sense), can also mean 'among one's own spiritual possessions' (compare Jn. 8:44 and 15:19, in the Greek). The phrase is found in the prologue with this double meaning of 'physical home' and 'spiritual possession,' and in close conjunction with the verb 'to accept or welcome.' 'He came to *what was his own* … and to all who *accepted* him, he gave the power to become children of God' (Jn. 1:12–13). Jn. 19:27 seems to demand a translation which includes both the purely physical and the deeper, spiritual sense. 'And from that hour the disciple took her into his own home, and accepted her as his own

> mother, as part of the spiritual legacy bequeathed to him by his Lord.'[66]

"To receive Jesus and to receive his mother are, definitively, two equivalent gestures," said Father Ignace de la Potterie, S.J. (1914–2003), quoting Father André Feuillet, P.S.S. (1909–1998)[67] In another place he stated:

> This relation to Christ is prolonged now in a new relationship of the disciple to the mother of Jesus. In other words, the welcome which the disciple accords to the Mother of Jesus maintains a Christological significance.[68]

Father de la Potterie, an authority on the text of John 19:27b, traces the concept of receiving or welcoming Mary[69] through the Spanish Renaissance Cardinal Toleto back to Saint Ambrose,[70] and indicates that the Greek words *'eis tà 'ídia* were understood by the late Cardinal Charles Journet (1891–1975) in a manner similar to that expounded by Canon McHugh:

> "He took her [let us say rather: 'he welcomed her'] *into his intimacy*," into his interior life, *into his faith life*. This

66 McHugh 378 [in the eighth line of this quotation I have given the reference to John 17:8 rather than to 17:18, which seems to be a typographical error in the book]; Cf. also Braun 119–24; Aristide Serra, O.S.M., *Contributi dell'antica letteratura giudaica per l'esegesi di Giovanni 2, 1–12 e 19, 25–27* (Rome: Herder, 1977) 217, 226; *Maria a Cana e presso la croce: saggio di Mariologia Giovannea* (Rome: Centro di Cultura Mariana "Mater Ecclesiae," 1985) 106–115; *Maria secondo il Vangelo* (Brescia: Editrice Queriniana, 1988) 165–166.

67 Ignace de la Potterie, S.J., "La maternità spirituale di Maria e la fondazione della chiesa," *Gesù verità: Studi di cristologia giovannea* (Torino: Marietti, 1973) 160 (note 17, my translation).

68 Ignace de la Potterie, S.J., "La parole de Jésus 'Voici ta Mère' et l'accueil du Disciple (Jn. 19, 27b)," *Marianum* 36 (1974): 37–38 (my translation). Fr. de la Potterie further defended this position in the light of a controversy with F. Neirynck with, "'Et à partir de cette heure, le Disciple l'accueillit dans son intimité' (Jn. 19, 27b)," *Marianum* 42 (1980): 84–125.

69 Cf. Ignace de la Potterie, S.J., *Mary in the Mystery of the Covenant*, trans. Bertrand Buby, S.M., (Staten Island: Alba House, 1992) 226, in which he, like McHugh, makes an excellent case for translating the Greek verb *lambáno* in this instance by the Italian word *accogliere* (to receive, to accept, to welcome) or the French word *accueillir* (to receive, to receive graciously, to welcome).

70 Serra in *Maria a Cana e presso la croce* 111–12 provides brief texts on this topic from Saint Ambrose and Toleto.

> interiority of the disciple is none other than his availability to open himself in faith to the last words of Jesus and to carry out his spiritual testament, becoming the son of the mother of Jesus, welcoming her as his mother in his life as a disciple: the mother of Jesus, henceforth, is also *his mother*.[71]

Father Stefano De Fiores provided an appropriate practical summary of the exegetical positions which we have just presented with regard to the concept of "welcoming Mary," in his article on consecration in the *Nuovo Dizionario di Mariologia*[72] as well as in *Maria nella Teologia Contemporanea*.[73] We cited material from the latter source above together with the apposite comments of Bishop Franzi.[74]

In his constant and consistent treatment of John 19:25–27 the Holy Father has shown himself to be in complete accord with this exegetical position. Already in his first Encyclical, *Redemptor Hominis*, he said:

> Her Son [Jesus] explicitly extended His Mother's maternity in a way that could easily be understood by every soul and every heart by designating, when He was raised on the cross, His beloved disciple as her son … Later, all the generations of disciples, of those who confess and love Christ, like the apostle John, spiritually took this Mother to their own homes.[75]

In his homily at Fatima on 13 May 1982, which is a theological as well as pastoral masterpiece, he begins by citing John 19:27, developing first its literal meaning and then drawing out its "spiritual sense" with particular regard to Marian sanctuaries:

> The words "he took her to his own home" can be taken in the literal sense as referring to the place where he lived.

71 de la Potterie, *Maria nel mistero dell'alleanza* 245 (my translation).

72 "Cons" 398, 409, 410, 413.

73 326–328.

74 Cf. above 154-155.

75 *Inseg* II/1 (1979) 607 [St. Paul edition 56].

> Mary's motherhood in our regard is manifested in a particular way in the places where she meets us: her dwelling places; places in which a special presence of the mother is felt.
>
> There are many such dwelling places. They are of all kinds: from a special corner in the home or little wayside shrines adorned with an image of the Mother of God, to chapels and churches built in her honor. However, in certain places the Mother's presence is felt in a particularly vivid way. These places sometimes radiate their light over a great distance and draw people from afar. Their radiance may extend over a diocese, a whole nation, or at times over several countries and even continents. These places are the Marian sanctuaries or shrines.
>
> In all these places that unique testament of the crucified Lord is wonderfully actualized: in them man feels that he is entrusted and confided to Mary; he goes there in order to be with her, as with his Mother; he opens his heart to her and speaks to her about everything: *he "takes her to his own home," that is to say, he brings her into all his problems, which at times are difficult. His own problems and those of others. The problems of the family, of societies, of nations, and of the whole of humanity.*[76]

Just two weeks earlier, he developed this same theme with a large group of priests who work with the Focolari Movement (also known as "Opera di Maria"). This time he drew out the meaning of John 19:27 with particular reference to priests.

> The Gospel text just cited offers us the model for our devotion to Mary. "And from that hour the disciple took her to his own home" (Jn. 19:27). Can the same be said of us? *Do we also welcome Mary into our homes? Indeed, we should grant her full rights in the home of our lives, of our*

76 *Inseg* V/2 (1982) 1568, 1578 [*Portugal* 73] (emphasis mine). In his Letter to the Bishop of Leiria of 16 April 1983 he took up the theme again of Marian sanctuaries as special places of encounter with Our Lady, but expanded also on the need of each pilgrim to open his heart to her, to receive her even into his problems and preoccupations. Cf. *Inseg* VI/1 (1983) 968.

> *faith, of our affections, of our commitments, and acknowledge the maternal role that is hers, that is to say, her function as guide, as adviser, as encourager, or even merely as a silent presence which at times may of itself be enough to infuse us with strength and courage.* On the other hand, the first Scripture reading reminded us that the first disciples, after Jesus' ascension, were gathered with "Mary, the Mother of Jesus" (Acts 1:14). She was, therefore, also a part of their community; in fact, perhaps it was she who gave it cohesion. And the fact that she is specified as "the Mother of Jesus" shows how closely she was linked to the figure of her son; it tells us that Mary recalls always and only the salvific value of what Jesus did, our only Saviour, and on the other hand *it likewise tells us that to believe in Jesus Christ cannot dispense us from including also in our act of faith the one who was his mother.* In God's family, and so much more in the priestly family, Mary watches over the diversity of each one within the communion of all. *And at the same time she can teach us to be open to the Holy Spirit, to share anxiously Christ's total dedication to the will of the Father; above all she can teach us to participate deeply in the passion of the Son and carry out our ministry with assured spiritual fruitfulness. "Behold, your mother!" (Jn. 19:27). Everyone feels that these words are addressed to him, and therefore draws faith and enthusiasm from them for an always more determined and serene journey along the committed road of his priestly life.*[77]

To welcome, to receive Mary "as guide, as adviser, as encourager, or even merely as a silent presence" is a concrete translation of what the text *'élaben autèn ho mathètes 'eis tà 'ídia*, "to receive Mary as one of his spiritual goods," (Jn. 19:27) means. It is an exhortation to which the Holy Father liked to return, especially with priests, since the "beloved disciple" represents not only all the faithful but—as a member of the Apostolic

77 *Inseg* V/1 (1982) 1370–71 [*ORE* 736:12] (emphases mine).

College—priests in a special way.[78] To ordinands in Valencia on 8 November 1982, he said, "Welcome her [Mary] as a Mother as John welcomed her at the foot of the Cross";[79] and he took up the theme explicitly in his Holy Thursday Letter to Priests of 25 March 1988.[80]

On 8 May 1983, at the Marian Shrine of Suyapa, Honduras, Pope John Paul II even more explicitly made his own the interpretation of *'eis tà 'ídia* proposed by the exegetes cited above. Here is what he said on that occasion:

> In the hour of Jesus, of his Mother and of the Church, the words of the Redeemer are solemn and they make real what they proclaim: Mary is made the mother of Christ's disciples, of all men. Whoever welcomes in faith the doctrine of the Teacher has the privilege, the fortune, of welcoming the virgin as mother, *of receiving her with faith and love among his most beloved goods*, with the security that she who has faithfully carried out the word of the Lord has lovingly accepted the task of always being the mother of whoever follows Christ. Thus, from the dawn of faith and at every stage in the preaching of the Gospel, in the birth of every particular Church, the Virgin occupies the place which belongs to her as mother of the imitators of Jesus who make up the Church …
>
> "Behold your mother;" the pilgrim Pope repeats Jesus' words to you. Welcome her into your home: accept her as

78 While there continues to be a great deal of speculation in certain scholarly circles on the identity of the "beloved disciple" as to whether he is John, the son of Zebedee, and also the author of the fourth gospel [cf. Raymond E. Brown, S.S., *The Gospel According to John, I–XII*. Anchor Bible 29 (Garden City, N. Y.: Doubleday & Co., Inc. 1966) lxxxvii–cii], John Paul II continued to follow the tradition in assuming him to be John the Apostle, cf. *Inseg* X/3 (1987) 1377 [*ORE* 1020:11]; *Inseg* XI/1 (1988) 724, 736 [*ORE* 1032:6] – and Evangelist, cf. *Inseg* X/1 (1987) 735 [St. Paul edition 64]. Pope Benedict XVI, even as a great scripture scholar, followed in the same way; cf. Pope Benedict XVI, *Jesus, The Apostles, and the Early Church* (San Francisco: Ignatius Press, 2007) 71–80.

79 *Inseg* V/3 (1983) 1224 (my translation).

80 *Inseg* XI/1 (1988) 726–727 [*ORE* 1032:6–7]. He also quoted from the section of this letter on the welcoming of Mary at an Ordination Mass in Florida, Uruguay. Cf. *Inseg* XI/2 (1988) 1224 [*ORE* 1041:5–6].

> mother and model. She will make you know Christ and love the Church; she will show you the path of life; she will encourage you during difficulties. In her the Church and the Christian find reason for consolation and hope, because she "shines forth on earth, until the day of the Lord shall come, as a sign of sure hope and solace for the pilgrim People of God" (*Lumen Gentium*, #68).[81]

He continued to preach the importance and necessity of welcoming Mary into our lives with great conviction. There need be no hesitation about Mary ever usurping the place of Christ, he told a Neo-catechumenal group from Madrid in March of 1984: "Welcome her as a true mother, as a teacher, as a guide and example in your entire life because far from eclipsing the necessary Christological orientation of your life, she will facilitate it."[82]

In the context of the Consecration of Togo to Our Lady he prayed:

> We feel the need to receive you—still more—as our Mother. To take you with us down the days and down the years in a deeper way! In order that you may keep us close, ever closer to Jesus the Saviour, ever more faithful in the service of all his brethren.[83]

As we have already noted with regard to other themes, which had previously characterized the Pope's Marian catechesis, so here also he presented the theme of "welcoming Mary" with particular solemnity and clarity in *Redemptoris Mater*, in the context of his teaching on entrusting as "the response to the love of a mother":

---

81 *Inseg* VI/1 (1983) 649, 653 [*ORE* 781:9–10] (emphasis mine). Father Ignazio Calabuig Adan, O.S.M., made explicit recognition of the Pope's adoption in this homily of the exegesis of de la Potterie, Serra *et alii* in a 1985 typescript publication of the Congregation for Divine Worship, which was preparing for the publication of the *Collectio Missarum Beatæ Mariae Virginis*. This appropriation was likewise acknowledged by Father de la Potterie in a conversation with the writer on 14 October 1985.

82 *Inseg* VII/1 (1984) 750 (my translation).

83 *Inseg* VIII/2 (1985) 265 [*ORE* 901:2].

> The Marian dimension of the life of a disciple of Christ is expressed in a special way precisely through this filial entrusting to the Mother of Christ, which began with the testament of the Redeemer on Golgotha. Entrusting himself to Mary in a filial manner, the Christian, like the Apostle John, "welcomes" the Mother of Christ "into his own home" and brings her into everything that makes up his inner life, that is to say into his human and Christian "I": he *"took her to his own home."* Thus the Christian seeks to be taken into that "maternal charity" with which the Redeemer's Mother "cares for the brethren of her Son," "in whose birth and development she cooperates" in the measure of the gift proper to each one through the power of Christ's Spirit. Thus also is exercised that motherhood in the Spirit which became Mary's role at the foot of the Cross and in the Upper Room.[84]

Let us conclude the treatment of this rich theme of the "welcome" of Mary with the conclusion of the magnificent catechesis on the words of Christ, "Behold your Mother," which the Pope gave on 23 November 1988.

> John's action [of taking Mary into his own home] was the execution of Jesus' testament in regard to Mary; but it had a symbolic value for each one of Christ's disciples, who are asked to make room for Mary in their lives, to take her into their own homes. By virtue of these words of the dying Christ, every Christian life must offer a "space" to Mary and provide for her presence.
>
> We can then conclude this reflection on the message of the Cross with an invitation which I address to each one, namely, to ask oneself how one accepts Mary into one's home, into one's life; and with an exhortation to appreciate to an ever greater extent the gift which Christ Crucified made to us by leaving us his own Mother as our mother.[85]

84 *Inseg* X/1 (1987) 735–736 [St. Paul edition 64–65].

85 *Inseg* XI/4 (1988) 1638 [*ORE* 1066:16].

Remarkably, his variations on the theme continued to offer new insights and provide an indication of the on-going development of the doctrine of Marian consecration in the life of the Church.

Why to Mary's Immaculate Heart?

Shortly before the visit of Pope John Paul II to France in October of 1986, an excellent article appeared in the Belgian Jesuit theological journal, *Nouvelle Revue Théologique*, entitled "John Paul II at Paray-le-Monial or why the 'Heart'?"[86] The question was raised with regard to the cultus of the Sacred Heart of Jesus and its meaning since the Pope was scheduled to visit the sanctuary of Paray-le-Monial, the site of the apparitions to Saint Margaret Mary Alacoque, and the question was answered largely in terms of the history of seventeenth century French spirituality, particularly the seldom recognized link between Saint Margaret Mary Alacoque and Saint John Eudes.

In our particular context we might raise the query "Why the Heart?" from the perspective of the papal magisterium of Pope John Paul II, since many of his acts of consecration and entrustment to Mary are addressed to her Immaculate Heart. We have already treated the magisterial development of the theology of the Hearts of Jesus and Mary as it pertains to the history of consecration and the specific questions about the objects of these devotions.[87] Now let us examine briefly some of the particular nuances and developments, which he has contributed to the magisterium on the Hearts of Jesus and Mary.[88]

86 Édouard Glotin, S.J. "Jean-Paul à Paray-le-Monial ou Pourquoi le 'Cœur'?" *Nouvelle Revue Théologique* 108 (1986) 685–714. This is condensed from a larger study by the same author which appeared in *Jésus-Christ Rédempteur de l'Homme* (Venasque: Éditions du Carmel, 1986) under the title "Le centre de l'âme et l'Icône sacrée du Cœur. De Thérèse d'Avila à Marguerite-Marie" 103–154.

87 Cf. above (chapter 2) 75-113.

88 Canon Laurentin treated this matter briefly from the perspective of the "alliance of the two Hearts" in his paper, "The Magisterium of the Church on the Alliance of the Hearts of Jesus and Mary," in *The Alliance of the Hearts of Jesus and Mary* 169–84. I have also considered some of the Pope's fundamental

We have already briefly noted the basis for the Holy Father's "theology of the heart" as he gave expression to it in the extraordinarily insightful homily, which he gave in Rome on 28 June 1984 to the associated Faculty of Medicine at the Gemelli Polyclinic.[89] Here, I would like to return to another passage of it:

> We know the richness of anthropological resonance which in biblical language the word "heart" awakens. This word evokes not only sentiments proper to the affective sphere, but also all those memories, thoughts, reasonings, plans, that make up man's innermost world. The heart in biblical culture, and also in a large part of other cultures, is that essential center of the personality in which man stands before God as the totality of body and soul, as I who am thinking, willing and loving, as the center in which the memory of the past opens up to the planning of the future.[90]

From the anthropological exposition contained in that highly significant and concentrated discourse, as well as from other statements of a phenomenological nature which he has made on this topic, Paul L. Peeters does not hesitate to speak of "the Pope's theology of the heart."[91] The first thing to be noted in the above passage is that the heart stands for the whole person, but particularly "the essential center of the personality." In this he certainly stands in the Church's great tradition, which has been brought into ever clearer focus by the Holy Spirit as the magisterium has had to deal with the development of the *cultus* of the Hearts of Jesus and Mary.

---

contributions in my article, "Why the Heart?" *Homiletic & Pastoral Review* 89:9 (June 1989) 18–23. Perhaps the most detailed treatment of John Paul II's Sacred Heart doctrine in English remains that in Dr. Timothy O'Donnell's *Heart of the Redeemer* 225–255.

89 Cf. above (chapter 2, footnotes 8–10) 76-79.

90 *Inseg* VII/1 (1984) 1974 [*ORE* 843:9].

91 Paul L. Peeters, "*Dominum et Vivificantem*: The Conscience and the Heart," *Communio* 15 (1988) 148.

Very significantly, in fact, in the pages of the Gospels the word "heart" is used quite often, but in only two cases is the heart of a particular person indicated: Jesus (Mt. 11:29) and Mary (Lk. 2:19, 51).[92] Surely this is not without import. In both cases this usage constitutes an invitation to ponder a profound mystery. In the Gemelli homily the Pope said that

> In the Heart of Christ, therefore, there meet divine richness and human poverty, the power of grace and the frailty of nature, an appeal from God and a response from man. In the Heart of Christ the history of mankind has its definitive place of arrival, because "the Father has assigned all judgment to the Son" (Jn. 5:22). *Therefore, willing or not, every human heart must refer to the Heart of Christ.*[93]

In the Heart of the God-Man there is simultaneously present, according to the words of the Pope, "an appeal from God and a response from man." This is a wonderful way of describing the unique mediation of Jesus (cf. I Tim. 2:5–6) who in His divinity presents the call from God to mankind and in His humanity makes the perfect response to God in His earthly life and the sacrifice thereof.

All of this is symbolized in His pierced Heart. Every disposition of His human soul, every state through which He passed in His earthly life is encapsulated in His Heart. This was explicitly synthesized and clarified in the great Sacred Heart Encyclical of the Venerable Pius XII, *Haurietis Aquas*, as we have already seen in chapter two.[94]

> The Heart of the Incarnate Word is deservedly and rightly considered the chief sign and symbol of that threefold love with which the divine Redeemer unceasingly loves

92 Cf. Ignace de la Potterie, S.J., "L'Alleanza dei Cuori di Gesù e di Maria," *Il Mistero del Cuore Trafitto: Fondamenti biblici della spiritualità del Cuore di Gesù* (Bologna: Edizioni Dehoniane, 1988) 159; "The Alliance of the Hearts of Jesus and Mary: A Biblical Approach," trans. Sr. Rosario de Veyra, R.A. *The Alliance of the Hearts of Jesus and Mary* 85.

93 *Inseg* VII/1 (1984) 1976 [*ORE* 843:9] (final emphasis my own).

94 Cf. above (chapter 2, footnote 9) 77-78.

> his eternal Father and all mankind. It is a symbol of that divine love which he shares with the Father and the Holy Spirit but which he, the Word made flesh, alone manifests through a weak and perishable body ...
>
> It is, besides, the symbol of that burning love which, infused into his soul, enriches the human will of Christ and enlightens and governs its acts by the most perfect knowledge derived both from the beatific vision and that which is directly infused.
>
> And finally—and this in a more natural and direct way—it is the symbol also of sensible love, since the body of Jesus Christ, formed by the Holy Spirit in the womb of the Virgin Mary, possesses full powers of feelings and perception, in fact more so than any other human body.[95]

To speak, then, of the Heart of Jesus is to speak of His entire divine person, but particularly with regard to His divine-human love. In this regard John Paul II loved to make reference to *Gaudium et Spes*, #22: "He [Christ] loved with a human heart [*humano corde dilexit*]."

By way of analogy, one can say that the Heart of Mary is the chief sign and symbol of her person. In fact, as we have seen, the Congregation of Rites under Pius XII also clarified the cultus of the Immaculate Heart of Mary in this way:

> With this devotion the Church renders the honor due to the Immaculate Heart of the Blessed Virgin Mary, since under the symbol of this heart she venerates with reverence the eminent and singular holiness of the Mother of God and especially her most ardent love for God and Jesus her Son and moreover her maternal compassion for all those redeemed by the divine Blood.[96]

While Mary's is a human heart, not hypostatically united to a divine person, it is the human heart most similar to the Heart of Jesus. It is the Heart of the creature most eminent and singular in holiness.

95 *D-H* #3924.

96 Decree of 4 May 1944, *AAS* 37 (1945) 50 [English translation in *ORE* 959:12].

The theology of the "states" or "mysteries" of Jesus and Mary, as comprised of the interior dispositions of their souls and most perfectly represented by their Hearts, is a major contribution of the "French School" of spirituality, which developed under the impetus of the illustrious Cardinal Pierre de Bérulle (1575–1629).[97] The insights of Bérulle and his disciples, Charles de Condren (1588–1641), the Venerable Jean-Jacques Olier (1608–1657), St. John Eudes (1601–1680), together with the doctrine of St. Francis de Sales (1567–1622), set the stage for the revelations to St. Margaret Mary (1647–1690).[98]

So devoted was Pope John Paul II to this mystery of the Heart of Jesus that, besides numerous other references to the Sacred Heart, in 1985 he gave twelve Angelus addresses on the Heart of Jesus (and virtually always with reference to Mary and her Heart),[99] culminating in a marvelous exhortation inviting his hearers to unite with the "admirable alliance" of the Hearts of Jesus and Mary.[100] In 1986, he dedicated the same number of Angelus messages to this theme[101] and concluded a third cycle

97 Cf. above (chapter 1, footnotes 101–118) 43-47.

98 Cf. Marie-Odile e Jean-Hughes Marquis, *Spiritualità del Cuore di Cristo* trad. Sr. Clemente Moro (Milan: Editrice Ancora, 1986) 55–95. On Margaret Mary's relationship to the French School; cf. Glotin, "Le 'centre de l'âme'" 110–136.

99 *Inseg* VIII/1 (1985) 1703–1704, 1758–1759, 1856–1857; 1951–1952; 2037–2038; *Inseg* VIII/2 (1985) 125–126; 146–147; 169–171; 195–196; 526–527; 545–46; 670–671 [*ORE* 889:1; 890:1; 891:1; 892:1; 893:7; 895:1; 896:2; 897:2; 898:2; 901:9; 902:8; 904:1].

100 Angelus Address of 15 September 1985, *Inseg* VIII/2 (1985) 670–671 [*ORE* 904:1]. It should be noted that this was on the traditional date of the Feast of Our Lady of Sorrows, but since the date occurred on a Sunday there was no liturgical observance. The Pope, however, did not wish to let the date pass unobserved.

101 *Inseg* IX/1 (1986) 1788–1789; 1839–40; 1904–05; *Inseg* IX/2 (1986) 253–254; 277–278; 294–295; 315–316; 358–359; 391–392; 4054–06; 501–502; 836–837 [*ORE* 941:5; 942:11; 943:12; 946:2; 947:5; 948:1; 949:11; 950:2; 951:2; 952:2; 953:2; 960:4]. It might be noted that the last of these addresses was not a part of the series, but an Angelus message given at Paray-le-Monial with the Hearts of Jesus and Mary as major points of reference.

of eleven such reflections in 1989.[102] In 1991, he devoted two Angelus addresses to the Heart of Jesus in the month of June.[103]

On the occasion of his visit to Paray-le-Monial on 5 October 1986, site of the apparitions of the Lord to Saint Margaret Mary, he personally presented a letter to Father Peter-Hans Kolvenbach, the Superior General of the Jesuits, expressing his specific "desire that you pursue with persevering action the spread of the genuine cultus of the Heart of Christ," asking the entire Society of Jesus "to do everything that is possible to accomplish ever better this mission that Christ himself has entrusted to you, the spread of devotion to his divine Heart." I believe that the dogmatic core of that letter is this:

> If the Lord in his providence wished that a powerful drive in favour of the devotion to the Heart of Christ, under the forms indicated in the revelations received by St. Margaret Mary, should go forth from Paray-le-Monial in the seventeenth century, at the threshold of modern times, the essential elements of this devotion belong in a permanent fashion to the spirituality of the Church throughout her history; for since the beginning, the Church has looked to the Heart of Christ pierced on the Cross, from which blood and water flowed forth as symbols of the sacraments that constitute the Church; and, in the Heart of the Incarnate Word, the Fathers of the Christian East and West saw the beginning of all the work of our salvation, fruit of the love of the divine Redeemer. This pierced Heart is a particularly expressive symbol of that love.[104]

If His Heart synthesizes the Redemptive sacrifice, man's perfect reparation to God, it is nonetheless also "an appeal from God." In fact, this is precisely what John Paul II chose to underscore in Vancouver when he said: *"The Heart of Jesus Christ*

102 *Inseg* XII/2 (1989) 8–9; 60–61; 138–40; 159–60; 192–94; 393–95; 430–31; 498–99; 534–35; 1159–61; 1224–25 [*ORE* 1097:12; 1098:12; 1100:1; 1101:2; 1103:7; 1105:8; 1106:8; 1107:1; 1108:1; 1115:11; 1116:1].

103 *Inseg* XIV/1 (1991) 1679-1680 [*ORE* 1196:11]; *Inseg* XIV/1 (1991)1840-1841 [*ORE* 1198:10].

104 *Inseg* IX/2 (1986) 843 [*ORE* 960:7].

is a great and unceasing call from God, addressed to humanity, to each human heart!"[105] Obviously, the first human heart to respond fully to this call was Mary's. Her *fiat* at Nazareth (Lk. 1:38) made possible the formation of His human Heart (and all that it represented) beneath hers, a theme to which the Pope never tired of alluding.[106]

Mary's Heart, by virtue of her Immaculate Conception, is from the first moment of her existence, totally open to the call of God; and from the moment of her *fiat* she is in communion with the "forming" Heart of Jesus. Her Heart is the first to enter into the dialogue of salvation—that "alliance of hearts"[107] to which we are all called. Here is how the Pope put it in a letter addressed to the late Cardinal Jaime Sin (1928–2005) of Manila:

> We can say that just as the mystery of Redemption began in the womb of the Virgin of Nazareth, so did that splendid union of the hearts of Christ and his Mother. From the very moment when the Word was made flesh beneath the heart of Mary, there has existed, under the influence of the Holy Spirit, an enduring relationship of love between them. The heart of the Mother has always followed the redemptive mission of her Son. As Jesus hung on the Cross in completion of his salvific work, Simeon's prophecy foretelling the definitive alliance of the hearts of the Son and of the Mother was fulfilled: "And a sword will pierce your own soul too" (Lk. 2:25). Indeed the centurion's lance that pierced the side of Christ also penetrated the heart of his sorrowful Mother and sealed it in sacrificial love.[108]

If Jesus' Heart "is a great and unceasing call from God, addressed to humanity," then Mary's Heart is the perfect

105 *Inseg* VII/2 (1984) 603 [*ORE* 855:17].

106 Cf. *Redemptor Hominis* #22: *Inseg* II/1 (1979) 608 [St. Paul edition 57].

107 Cf. Angelus address of 15 September 1985: *Inseg* VIII/2 (1985) 671 [*ORE* 904:1].

108 8 September 1986, from Letter to Cardinal Jaime L. Sin, President of the International Symposium on the Alliance of the Hearts of Jesus and Mary, *Miles Immaculatæ* 23 (1987) 42–43.

response of humanity to the "call from God." If, "when we say 'Heart of Jesus Christ,' we address ourselves in faith to the whole Christological mystery: the mystery of the God-Man," as the Holy Father asserted at Vancouver's Abbotsford Airport on 18 September 1984,[109] then by analogy when we say "Heart of Mary," we might say that we address ourselves to the whole Mariological *and* ecclesiological mystery. For as the perfect human response to the "call from God," as that powerful symbol which evokes the whole mystery of Mary, especially with reference to her spiritual maternity,[110] it also summarizes all that the Church is meant to be in responding to the "call from God" which the Vatican Council refers to as "the universal call to holiness."[111]

Hence, when in his exceptional Angelus address of 15 September 1985, the Pope spoke of "that admirable alliance of" the Hearts of Jesus and Mary, he was speaking of the union of the Hearts of Jesus and Mary as paradigmatic of the synergy of the divine and human, grace and nature, salvific initiative of God and cooperative response of man, redemption by the God-Man and "coredemption" by Mary in the sense of St. Paul's words to the Colossians: "in my flesh I complete what is lacking in Christ's afflictions for the sake of his body, that is, the Church" (Col. 1:24). The response of Mary's Heart became the first answer of the Church to the "call from God" and remains its most perfect reply. It also becomes the model for our response.[112]

109 *Inseg* VII/2 (1984) 600. It should be noted that John Paul's insight is in total harmony with the French School on this point.

110 We recall again the Decree of the Sacred Congregation of Rites in the Decree establishing the Feast of the Immaculate Heart of Mary: "With this devotion the Church renders the honor due to the Immaculate Heart of the Blessed Virgin Mary, since under the symbol of this heart she venerates with reverence the eminent and singular holiness of the *Mother of God* and especially her most ardent love for God and Jesus her Son and moreover *her maternal compassion for all those redeemed by the divine Blood*": Decree of 4 May 1944, *AAS* 37 (1945) 50 [*ORE* 959:12] (emphasis mine).

111 *LG* #39–42. This theme was singled out for special attention at the Extraordinary Synod of 1985, cf. *Relatio Finalis (Final Report)* II.A.4.

112 I have written at some length on this admirable "Alliance of the Hearts of Jesus and Mary." Cf. "The Union of the Hearts of Jesus and Mary in St. Francis

de Sales and St. John Eudes" presented in Fatima, Portugal at the International Theological Symposium on the Alliance of the Hearts of Jesus and Mary, 14 – 19 September 1986, published in *Miles Immaculatae* 25 (1989) 472–512; "The Alliance of the Hearts of Jesus and Mary: A Theological Sounding," *Queen of All Hearts* Vol. 44, No. 6 (March–April 1994) 5–8; Vol. 45, No. 1 (May–June 1994) 28–30; Vol. 45, No. 2 (July–August 1994) 28–29, 45; Vol. 45, No. 3 (September–October 1994) 29–31; "The Alliance of the Hearts of Jesus and Mary: Our Share in Their Work of Reparation," in *1994 International Holy Family Year: Theological-Pastoral Framework* (Manila: Two Hearts Media Organization, Inc., 1994) 49–59; "The Alliance of the Two Hearts and Consecration," *Miles Immaculatæ* XXXI (Luglio/Dicembre 1995) 389–407; "The Alliance of the Two Hearts and Mariology," in *The Theology of the Alliance of the Two Hearts: Documents of the 1997 International Theological Pastoral Symposium on the Alliance of the Hearts of Jesus and Mary*, Book 1 (Rome: Two Hearts Media Organization, 1997) 229–252; "The Theology of the Alliance of the Hearts of Jesus and Mary – The Mystery of Iniquity," Part 1, *Missio Immaculatæ International* (English Edition) Year III, N° 4 (May 2007) 20–21; "The Theology of the Alliance of the Hearts of Jesus and Mary – The Mystery of Mediation," Part 2, *Missio Immaculatæ International* (English Edition) Year III, N° 5 (June 2007) 20–21; "The Theology of the Alliance of the Hearts of Jesus and Mary – Collaboration in Jesus' Mediation," Part 3, *Missio Immaculatæ International* (English Edition) Year III, N° 6 (July–August 2007) 24–25; "The Theology of the Alliance of the Hearts of Jesus and Mary – Mary's Collaboration in Jesus' Mediation," Part 4, *Missio Immaculatæ International* (English Edition) Year III, N° 7 (September 2007) 24–25; "The Theology of the Alliance of the Hearts of Jesus and Mary – Mary Coredemptrix," Part 5, *Missio Immaculatæ International* (English Edition) Year III, N° 8 (October 2007) 20–21; "The Theology of the Alliance of the Hearts of Jesus and Mary – Mary Coredemptrix," Part 6, *Missio Immaculatæ International* (English Edition) Year III, N° 9 (November 2007) 20–21; "The Theology of the Alliance of the Hearts of Jesus and Mary – Opposition," Part 7, *Missio Immaculatæ International* (English Edition) Year III, N° 10 (December 2007) 20–21; "The Theology of the Alliance of the Hearts of Jesus and Mary – Opposition," Part 8, *Missio Immaculatæ International* (English Edition) Year IV, N° 1 (January 2008) 20–21; "The Theology of the Alliance of the Hearts of Jesus and Mary," Part 9, *Missio Immaculatæ International* (English Edition) Year IV, N° 3 (March 2008) 20–21; "The Alliance of the Sacred Hearts and the Fatima Message – Maternal Love," Part 1, *Missio Immaculatæ International* (English Edition) Year IV, N° 5 (May 2008) 20–21; "The Alliance of the Sacred Hearts and the Fatima Message – The Apparitions of the Angel," Part 2, *Missio Immaculatæ International* (English Edition) Year IV, N° 6 (June/July 2008) 21; "The Alliance of the Sacred Hearts and the Fatima Message – Icons of Redemption and Coredemption," *Missio Immaculatæ International* (English Edition) Year IV, N° 7 (August/September 2008) 20–21; "The Alliance of the Sacred Hearts and the Fatima Message – Coredemption and the Magisterium," *Missio Immaculatæ International* (English Edition) Year IV, N° 8 (October 2008) 20–21; "The Alliance of the Sacred Hearts and the Fatima Message – Our Share in the Work of Redemption," *Missio Immaculatæ International* (English Edition) Year IV, N° 9 (November/December 2008) 28–29; "The Alliance of the Sacred Hearts and the Fatima Message – The Mediation of the Immaculate Heart of Mary," *Missio Immaculatæ International* (English Edition) Year V, N° 1 (January/February 2009) 12–13; "The Alliance of

In this sense, then, it is not surprising that on at least two occasions the Pope indicated that consecrating the world to the Immaculate Heart of Mary means effectively consecrating it to the pierced Heart of the Savior. Here, then, is a highly significant passage, which he spoke in Fatima on 13 May 1982, as a prelude to consecration of the world to the Immaculate Heart of Mary:

> On the cross Christ said: "Woman, behold your son!" With these words He opened in a new way His Mother's heart. A little later, the Roman soldier's spear pierced the side of the Crucified One. That pierced heart became a sign of redemption achieved through the death of the Lamb of God.
>
> The Immaculate Heart of Mary opened with the words "Woman, behold, your son!" is spiritually united with the heart of her Son opened by the soldier's spear. Mary's heart was opened by the same love for man and for the world with which Christ loved man and the world, offering Himself for them on the cross, until the soldier's spear struck that blow.
>
> **Consecrating the world to the Immaculate Heart of Mary means drawing near, through the Mother's intercession, to the very Fountain of life that sprang up from Golgotha.** This Fountain pours forth unceasingly

the Sacred Hearts and the Fatima Message – Her Immaculate Heart is our Way to God," *Missio Immaculatæ International* (English Edition) Year V, N° 2 (March/April 2009) 16–18; "The Alliance of the Sacred Hearts and the Fatima Message – Participating in Mary's Mediation," *Missio Immaculatæ International* (English Edition) Year V, N° 3 (May/June 2009) 19–21; "The Alliance of the Sacred Hearts and the Fatima Message – To Jesus through Mary: the Analogy of the Two Hearts," *Missio Immaculatæ International* (English Edition) Year V, N° 4 (July/August 2009) 13–15; "The Alliance of the Hearts of Jesus and Mary and the Fatima Message – The Triumph of the Immaculate Heart," *Missio Immaculatæ International* (English Edition) Year V, N° 5 (September/October 2009) 21–23; "The Alliance of the Two Hearts and the Magisterium," in *The Theology of the Alliance of the Two Hearts: Documents of the 2007 Asia-Pacific Theological and Pastoral Symposium on the Alliance of the Hearts of Jesus and Mary* (Manila: Two Hearts Media Organization, Inc., 2008) 51–85; "The Alliance of the Two Hearts and Mariology," in *The Theology of the Alliance of the Two Hearts: Documents of the 2007 Asia-Pacific Theological and Pastoral Symposium on the Alliance of the Hearts of Jesus and Mary* (Manila: Two Hearts Media Organization, Inc., 2008) 173–195.

> redemption and grace. In it reparation is made continually for the sins of the world. It is a ceaseless source of new life and holiness.
>
> Consecrating the world to the Immaculate Heart of the Mother means returning beneath the cross of the Son. It means consecrating this world to the pierced heart of the Savior, bringing it back to the very source of its redemption.[113]

Again, on 22 September 1986, he said of this act carried out most solemnly on 13 May 1982 and 25 March 1984:

> Our act of consecration refers ultimately to the Heart of her son, for as the Mother of Christ she is wholly united to his redemptive mission. As at the marriage feast of Cana, when she said 'Do whatever he tells you', Mary directs all things to her Son, who answers our prayers and forgives our sins. Thus ***by dedicating ourselves to the Heart of Mary we discover a sure way to the Sacred Heart of Jesus, symbol of the merciful love of our Savior***.
>
> The act of entrusting ourselves to the Heart of Our Lady establishes a relationship of love with her in which we dedicate to her all that we have and are. This consecration is practiced essentially by a life of grace, of purity, of prayer, of penance that is joined to the fulfillment of all the duties of a Christian, and of reparation for our sins and the sins of the world.[114]

There is a profound inner logic to all of this, which may well escape the worldly-wise (cf. I Cor. 1:18–2:16). **To respond to the "call from God" symbolized in the pierced Heart of Jesus, we must belong to Mary that she might teach us the dispositions of her Heart and become our tutor in the spiritual life.** As we learn from her, we take on her characteristics and become ever more perfectly that immaculate spouse "without spot or

113 *Inseg* V/2 (1982) 1573 [*Portugal* 79–80].

114 From address to participants in the International Theological Symposium on the Alliance of the Hearts of Jesus and Mary, held in Fatima under the patronage of Cardinal Jaime L. Sin, Archbishop of Manila, from 14 to 19 September 1986: *Inseg* IX/2 (1986) 700.

wrinkle" (Eph. 5:27) which the Church has already become in the person of Mary.[115]

[115] *LG* #65.

CHAPTER EIGHT

Pope Saint John Paul II's Thought in Perspective

Recapitulation

In the first part of this study we considered Pope John Paul's "program of Marian consecration and entrustment" in the context of the evolution of the ancient practice of the giving of oneself into the protection of Mary as this tradition has continued to flourish in every era of the Church's life. We have also noted the development of the concomitant theology implied in this praxis, especially as it has reached its highest dogmatic expression in the various acts of the pontifical magisterium. We have further taken account of the unique flowering of this custom as it has unfolded in twentieth century Poland, the providential matrix of Karol Wojtyła. We have observed how thoroughly all of the various elements of the tradition—ecclesial, pontifical and specifically Polish—have been integrated into the "program" of John Paul as it was manifested in the course of his long pontificate of more than twenty-six years. Finally, we have considered various representative strains of contemporary thought on the question of "the total gift of oneself [to Mary] for life and for eternity"[1] as this topic has continued to be deliberated subsequent to the Second Vatican Council's monumental eighth chapter of *Lumen Gentium* and the guidelines of *Marialis Cultus*. We have seen that the sometimes vexing and occasionally heated debate over the terminology of "consecration" as opposed to "entrustment"

1 This is the classic definition of Marian consecration given by the Venerable Pius XII on 21 January 1945; cf. above (chapter 4, footnote 11) 144.

does not seem to be envisioned as a matter of opposition in the thought of the Pope, but that he rather employs both terms as well as many others in order to draw out the various nuances of what it means to belong to Mary.

In the second part we carried out an extended analysis of the thought of Pope John Paul II on the question of Marian consecration. Although he never presented a fully developed treatise on this issue as a bishop or as pope, he did treat the subject and its ramifications with sufficient frequency and depth to make it possible for one to follow the major outlines of his thought.

We began our analysis by asking the classical question: "how can consecration to Mary be legitimated in light of the fact that consecration in the strict sense pertains only to God?" We presented the classical response to this query by having recourse to the principle of analogy and noted the frequently implicit analogous use of the term "to entrust" by the Pope which fully respects the distinction between *latria* and *hyperdulia*. We further noted that, in his own usage of the terms "consecration," "entrustment" and their cognates, he effectively takes the position that consecration is, in the first instance, an elicit act of religion (*latria*) directed to God or Christ without ceasing to be an act of *hyperdulia* directed to Mary.

The Holy Father, in effect, frequently spoke of consecrating or entrusting oneself to Christ through Mary. This, again, is in accord with the classical theological treatment of the matter. For example, it underlies the entire theology of Saint Louis-Marie Grignion de Montfort,[2] whose influence on his own spiritual formation the Pope readily acknowledged; and, moreover, it found its most developed explanation in the section on "Mary's Maternal Mediation" in *Redemptoris Mater* #38–41 and in his Letter to the Men and Women Religious of the Montfort Families

2 Cf. above (chapter 5, footnotes 28–30) 176-178; *Treatise on True Devotion* #121 [*God Alone* 327]; "Cons" 404–405.

for the 160th Anniversary of the Publication of *Treatise on True Devotion to Mary* of 8 December 2003.[3] The principle of Mary's secondary and subordinate but, nonetheless, real mediation is neatly synthesized in his endorsement in that same Encyclical of "the figure of Saint Louis-Marie Grignion de Montfort, who proposes consecration to Christ through the hands of Mary, as an effective means for Christians to live faithfully their baptismal commitments."[4]

Next we came to examine a question fundamental to our study: the Christological foundation of the two great public consecrations of the world to the Immaculate Heart of Mary and, in effect, of the Pope's whole program of entrustment. We noted that the core of the acts of 1982 and 1984 is the reference to the self-consecration of Christ (Jn. 17:19) as victim, which further implies His prior consecration as priest by the Father in the Incarnation (Jn. 10:36). Jesus' self-consecration becomes paradigmatic of the Christian's desire to unite himself with the sacrifice of Jesus for the sake of His Body, the Church (Col. 1:24) and as a ratification of the fundamental consecration accomplished in him by God in Baptism. This desire to be united with the redemptive consecration of Christ is then *entrusted* by the Pope to Our Lady along with the whole world, a further emphasis on the crucial role of her maternal mediation.

Then we further focused on the way the Pope linked Mary with Christ's consecration by describing her as "wholly united to the redeeming consecration of her Son." We also noticed

3 *Inseg* XXVI/2 (2003) 917–920 [*ORE* 1829:3]. In #4 of that notable document the Pope wrote: "'*All our perfection,*' St Louis Marie Grignion de Montfort writes, '*consists in being conformed, united and consecrated to Jesus Christ*; and therefore, the most perfect of all devotions is, without any doubt, that which most perfectly conforms, unites and consecrates us to Jesus Christ. Now, Mary being the most conformed of all creatures to Jesus Christ, it follows that, of all devotions, that which most consecrates and conforms the soul to Our Lord is devotion to his holy Mother, and that *the more a soul is consecrated to Mary, the more it is consecrated to Jesus*' (*Treatise on True Devotion*, n. 120)." Final emphasis mine.

4 Cf. above (chapter 5, footnote 84) 198.

how the Pope's emphasis on Mary as a "co-victim" with Christ, consecrated under Him, with Him and for the sake of the redemption, is deeply rooted in the eighth chapter of *Lumen Gentium*.[5] This recognition of Mary as the human being most "wholly united to the redeeming consecration of Christ" readily leads to her being proposed as the model of consecrated souls. This, we noted, is a special emphasis made by the Holy Father in his exhortations to religious.

After the establishment of this Christological foundation of John Paul's two great acts of consecration, we asked, "Why, then, should there be explicit entrustment to Mary?" The Pope's constant and consistent response was to cite "the entrustment scene" on Calvary (Jn. 19:25–27). He taught that Mary's spiritual maternity was confirmed by the dying Christ as the fruit of His sacrifice and the final consequence of Mary's cooperation in it. He pointed to her maternal mediation as deepening, but never interfering with or inhibiting, one's relationship with Christ. We also noted in this regard his continuity with the teaching of the Popes since Benedict XIV on Mary's spiritual maternity.

If his predecessors have invoked John 19:25–27 as a principal scriptural basis for Mary's spiritual maternity, John Paul II further found in the episode of Christ's entrustment of John to Mary the rationale for the entrustment of all of Christ's disciples to her. The Pope's thought in this area is particularly rich and deep.

The word "trust" is linguistically associated with the word "entrust" (at least in Italian and English), and so it is in the Pope's mind. Children are entrusted by God to mothers even more than to fathers in the sense that, in the ordinary course of events, mothers are the first objects of their children's trust and become bridges by which their children can learn to trust their

5 Cf. *LG* #56–58, 61. As we have seen in passing and will continue to see, the classical theological description of Mary's active but subordinate collaboration in the work of the redemption is described as coredemption.

fathers and the world outside of themselves. It is in this sense that Mary is both the Mother of our trust in God and also intended by him as the Mother of his trust in us. The unique linking of a mother to her child is implied in the word "entrusting," which is in a special way the response to a mother's love.[6]

Without using the terminology proposed by Father Bertetto, John Paul effectively upheld the principle that the "descending" entrustment to Mary, which was accomplished by Christ on Calvary, should be ratified by the Church's and our own "ascending" acts of entrustment. This understanding is further complemented by the exegesis of John 19:27b by de la Potterie, McHugh, Serra and others on the meaning of the beloved disciple's "welcome" or "reception" of Mary. It confirms the profound intuition of Origen, the first of the Fathers to speak of the "receiving" or "acceptance" of Mary by John, and was readily appropriated by the Holy Father who speaks of welcoming Mary "among our most beloved goods" and "as guide, adviser, encourager, or even merely as a silent presence which at times may be enough to infuse us with strength and courage."[7]

Finally, we pondered the unique relationship between Jesus and Mary in terms of John Paul's "theology of the heart" which builds upon the accumulated pontifical magisterium on this subject while developing his own theological and anthropological insights. Here Mary's subordinate, but nonetheless very real, cooperation in the work of our redemption is described as an "admirable alliance" with the Heart of Jesus.[8] Because of the singular nature of this "alliance" or "covenant" specifically willed by God, consecration to the Immaculate Heart of Mary is the chosen means of approaching the Heart of the Savior, the "Fountain of Salvation." Hence, the Pope could declare the

6 Cf. *Redemptoris Mater* #45.

7 Cf. above (chapter 7, footnote 77) 262.

8 Cf. above (chapter 7, footnote 100) 270.

ultimate equivalence of "consecration to the Immaculate Heart of Mary" and "consecration to the pierced Heart of the Savior."[9]

The Pope's Contributions to the Theology of Marian Consecration

At first sight it might appear that Pope John Paul II simply consolidated the teaching of his predecessors on the question of Marian consecration. Indeed, it is an important function of the office of Peter to hand on intact the teachings of the *depositum fidei* to the next generation and, given the tendencies toward "revisionism" which are present in every era, this in itself would constitute no small blessing. But John Paul did much more than this. He made his own significant contributions to the development of the body of doctrine on this subject, which was so obviously close to his heart; and now, looking back on his extraordinarily rich teaching, we are at a good vantage point to assess his distinctive contributions to the subject.

Unique emphasis on Christ's self-Consecration

The first of these, his unique emphasis on Christ's self-consecration (Jn. 17:19), was well signaled in the theological world after his Act of Consecration to the Immaculate Heart of Mary in Fatima on 13 May 1982 and in Rome on 25 March 1984.[10] It was a reaffirmation in an original way that all consecration is ultimately accomplished by and oriented to the Father.[11] Christ, consecrated by the Father at the moment of His conception, when His supreme sacrifice becomes imminent,

---

9 Cf. above (chapter 7, footnote 113) 276.

10 Cf. J. Patrick Gaffney, S.M.M., "Changing the I to We," *Queen of All Hearts* 35 (September–October 1984) 19; Eamon R. Carroll, O.Carm., "A Survey of Recent Mariology," *Marian Studies* 35 (1984) 167–169; "Mary, the Woman Come of Age," *Marian Studies* 36 (1985) 150–155; "The New Testament Charisms of the Blessed Virgin Mary," *One in Christ* 22 (1986) 361; Alfredo Marranzini, S.J., 'L'Atto di Affidamento e Consacrazione' a Maria," *Civiltà Cattolica* (1984) 12–17.

11 Cf. René Laurentin, "Bulletin sur la Vierge Marie," *Revue des Sciences Philosophiques et Théologiques* 70 (1986) 115–117.

consecrates Himself to the Father for the sake of humanity. The consecration of Christians, then, must be a participation in the self-consecration of Jesus, their Head.

Invocation of Mary as "wholly united to the redeeming consecration of your Son"

Intimately related to the self-consecration of Christ in those acts of 1982 and 1984 is his identification of Mary and calling upon her as "wholly united to the redeeming consecration of your Son." By virtue of her Immaculate Conception Mary is the most perfectly consecrated human being, consecrated by the Holy Spirit, as was Christ, from the first moment of her conception. She who had been predestined in the same divine decree with her Son,[12] was to associate herself freely with His redemptive sacrifice.[13]

The Theology of Entrustment – a Development of Doctrine

Perhaps the major contribution by John Paul II to the discussion of Marian consecration is what I have characterized as his "theology of entrustment." While it is true that the term was in use much earlier,[14] he has made it his own with all of its Polish resonances[15] and has used it consistently in interpreting the text of John 19:25–27.[16] It might well be argued that the applications which he has drawn from this text constitute a genuine development of doctrine which flows from the teaching on Mary's spiritual maternity.

12 Cf. above (chapter 6, footnotes 44–46) 214.

13 Cf. *LG* #56–58, 61.

14 Cf. above (chapter 2, footnote 93) 100, where Pius XII uses the terms *confiamos, entregamos, consagramos*; *affidiamo, rimettiamo, consacriamo* in his famous Act of Consecration to the Immaculate Heart of 31 October 1942, renewed on 8 December 1942 in the Vatican Basilica.

15 Cf. above (chapter 4, footnotes 41–45) 152-154.

16 Cf. above (chapter 6, footnote 64 - chapter 7, footnote 65) 220-257.

Having established the will of Christ with regard to every Christian's being entrusted to Mary with such emphasis, he never fails to point to the exigency on the part of the Christian to appropriate that entrustment by one's own deliberate act and to welcome her into one's own life with all its implications.[17] If de Montfort argues in favor of Marian consecration that Mary is the most direct way to Jesus, and Kolbe argues that going through Mary maximizes the value of all our acts, John Paul continues the argument by insisting that this is expressly the will of Christ.

On 19 July 1987, in the course of an Angelus address in the sanctuary at Lourdes, the Pope said:

> Mary is ... an excellent and unique vehicle of Christ's redemption. She is a most privileged channel of his grace, a chosen path by means of which grace comes to mankind with an extraordinary and marvellous abundance. Where Mary is present, grace abounds and people are healed both in body and soul.[18]

Without even a further word about the desirability of entrustment or consecration to her, he has said enough for the discerning listener. Mary shares in Jesus' mediation to the greatest extent possible for a creature, and He desires that we belong to her. To go to Jesus through Mary, then, is not to take a roundabout route, but the one that He has ordained. To consecrate ourselves to her is to consecrate ourselves to Him by the means which He has designated.

The "Why" of Consecration to Mary

One might well wonder why the Pope has made the subject of consecration/entrustment to Mary such a consistent point of reference in his ordinary magisterium. I believe that he has given the explanation for this preoccupation of his in the retreat,

17 Cf. above (chapter 7, footnotes 66–85) 258-265.

18 *Inseg* X/3 (1987) 98 [*ORE* 998:2].

which he preached for Pope Paul VI and the members of the Roman Curia in Lent of 1976:

> Both holy scripture, so rich in metaphor as we have just found, and the experience of the faithful see the Mother of God as the one who in a very special way is united with the Church at the most difficult moments in her history, when the attacks on her become most threatening. And this is in full accord with the vision of the woman revealed in Genesis and Revelation. Precisely in periods when Christ, and therefore his Church, Pope, bishops, priests, religious and all the faithful become the sign which provokes the most implacable and premeditated contradiction, Mary appears particularly close to the Church, because the Church is always in a way her Christ, first the Christ-child and then the crucified and risen Christ.
>
> If in such periods, such times in history, there arises a particular need to entrust oneself to Mary—as the Holy Father did on 8th December 1975, the 10th anniversary of the end of the Council—that need flows directly from the integral logic of the faith, from rediscovery of the whole divine economy and from understanding of its mysteries.
>
> The Father in heaven demonstrated the greatest trust in mankind by giving mankind his Son (cf. Jn. 3:16). The human creature to whom he first entrusted him was Mary, the woman of the *proto-evangelium* (cf. Gen. 3:15), then Mary of Nazareth and Bethlehem. And until the end of time she will remain the one to whom God entrusts the whole of his mystery of salvation.[19]

A Need flowing "from the integral logic of the faith"

The answer, then, is quite simply that even before, as well as during his pontificate, John Paul II saw a great need at this particular moment in her life to entrust the Church to Mary. She, "the woman of the proto-evangelium" (Gen. 3:15) and "the woman clothed with the sun" (Rev. 12:1) is involved by God's will in all the struggles of the Church against the powers

19 *Sign of Contradiction* 205.

of darkness. This is part of "the integral logic of the faith." The more the Church belongs to her and is conformed to her, the more it will belong to Christ and be conformed to Him; and the more it is conformed to Christ in His humiliation, the more it will be conformed to Christ in His victory. In his general audience address of 29 May 1996, he offered this commentary on these two highly significant scriptural passages:

> Along with Luke's account of the annunciation, tradition and the magisterium have seen in the so-called proto-evangelium (Gen. 3:15) a scriptural source for the truth of Mary's Immaculate Conception. On the basis of the ancient Latin version: "She will crush your head,"[20] this text inspired many depictions of the Immaculata crushing the serpent under her feet. … Since the biblical concept establishes a profound solidarity between the parent and the offspring, the depiction of the Immaculata crushing the serpent, not by her own power but through the grace of her Son, is consistent with the original meaning of the passage.
>
> The same biblical text also proclaims the enmity between the woman and her offspring on the one hand, and the serpent and his offspring on the other. This is a hostility expressly established by God, which has a unique importance, if we consider the problem of the Virgin's personal holiness. In order to be the irreconcilable enemy of the serpent and his offspring, Mary had to be free from all power of sin, and to be so from the first moment of her existence. In this regard, the Encyclical *Fulgens Corona*, published by Pope Pius XII in 1953 to commemorate the centenary of the definition of the dogma of the Immaculate Conception, reasons thus: "If at a given moment the Blessed Virgin Mary had been left without divine grace, because she was defiled at her conception by the hereditary stain of sin,

---

20 For an excellent treatment on the translation of Gen. 3:15, cf. Settimio M. Manelli, FI, "Genesis 3:15 and the Immaculate Coredemptrix," in *Mary at the Foot of the Cross – V: Redemption and Coredemption under the Sign of the Immaculate Conception. Acts of the Fifth International Symposium on Marian Coredemption* (New Bedford, MA: Academy of the Immaculate, 2005) 263–322.

between her and the serpent there would no longer have been—at least during this period of time, however brief—that eternal enmity spoken of in the earliest tradition up to the definition of the Immaculate Conception, but rather a certain enslavement" (AAS 45 [1953], 579).

The absolute hostility put between the woman and the devil thus demands in Mary the Immaculate Conception, that is, a total absence of sin, from the very beginning of her life. The Son of Mary won the definitive victory over Satan and enabled his Mother to receive its benefits in advance by preserving her from sin. As a result, the Son granted her the power to resist the devil, thus achieving in the mystery of the Immaculate Conception the most notable effect of his redeeming work. By drawing our attention to Mary's special holiness and her complete removal from Satan's influence, the title "full of grace" and the Protoevangelium enable us to perceive, in the unique privilege the Lord granted to Mary, the beginning of a new order which is the result of friendship with God and which, as a consequence, entails a profound enmity between the serpent and men.

The 12th chapter of Revelation, which speaks of the "woman clothed with the sun" (12:1), is often cited too as biblical testimony on behalf of the Immaculate Conception. Current exegesis agrees in seeing in this woman the Community of God's People, giving birth in pain to the risen Messiah. Along with the collective interpretation, however, the text suggests an individual one in the statement: "She brought forth a male child, one who is to rule all the nations with a rod of iron" (12:5). With this reference to child-birth, it is acknowledged that the woman clothed with the sun is in a certain sense identified with Mary, the woman who gave birth to the messiah. The woman-community is actually described with the features of the woman-Mother of Jesus.

Characterized by her motherhood, the woman "was with child and she cried out in her pangs of birth, in anguish for her delivery" (12:2). This note refers to the

Mother of Jesus at the Cross (cf. Jn. 19:25), where she shares in anguish for the delivery of the community of disciples with a soul pierced by the sword (cf. Lk. 2:35). Despite her sufferings, she is "clothed with the sun"—that is, she reflects the divine splendour—and appears as a "great sign" of God's spousal relationship with his people.[21]

Enmity between the World and "the Woman"

The very "framework" of *Redemptoris Mater*, in effect, says this. At the beginning of the Encyclical with bold and deliberate strokes the Pope presents Mary as "the woman of Genesis" and "the woman of the Apocalypse":

> In the salvific design of the Most Holy Trinity, the mystery of the Incarnation constitutes the superabundant *fulfillment of the promise* made by God to man *after original sin*, after that first sin whose effects oppress the whole earthly history of man (cf. Gen. 3:15). And so, there comes into the world a Son, "the seed of the woman" who will crush the evil of sin in its very origins: "he will crush the head of the serpent." As we see from the words of the Protogospel, the victory of the woman's Son will not take place without a hard struggle, a struggle that is to extend through the whole of human history. The "enmity," foretold at the beginning, is confirmed in the Apocalypse (the book of the final events of the Church and the world), in which there recurs the sign of the "woman," this time "clothed with the sun" (Rev. 12:1).
>
> Mary, Mother of the Incarnate Word, is placed *at the very center of that enmity*, that struggle which accompanies the history of humanity on earth and the history of salvation itself. In this central place, she who belongs to the "weak and poor of the Lord" bears in herself, like no other member of the human race, that "glory of grace" which the Father "has bestowed on us in his beloved Son," and this *grace determines the extraordinary greatness and beauty* of her whole being. Mary thus remains before God, and also

21 *Inseg* XIX/1 (1996) 1389–1391 [*ORE* 1444:11].

> before the whole of humanity, as the unchangeable and inviolable sign of God's election, spoken of in Paul's letter: "in Christ … he chose us … before the foundation of the world … he destined us … to be his sons" (Eph. 1:4, 5). *This election is more powerful than any experience of evil and sin, than all that "enmity" which marks the history of man.* In this history Mary remains a sign of sure hope.[22]

At the end of this Marian Encyclical, he presents Mary in the same way.

> Thanks to this special bond linking the Mother of Christ with the Church, there is further *clarified the mystery of that "woman"* who, from the first chapters of the Book of *Genesis* until the Book of *Revelation*, accompanies the revelation of God's salvific plan for humanity. For Mary, present in the Church as the Mother of the Redeemer, takes part, as a mother, in that "monumental struggle against the powers of darkness" which continues throughout human history. And by her ecclesial identification as the "woman clothed with the sun" (Rev. 12:1), it can be said that "in the Most Holy Virgin the Church has already reached that perfection whereby she exists without spot or wrinkle." Hence, as Christians raise their eyes with faith to Mary in the course of their earthly pilgrimage, they "strive to increase in holiness." Mary, the exalted Daughter of Sion, helps all her children, wherever they may be and whatever their condition, *to find in Christ the path to the Father's house.*[23]

Both of these splendid passages which "frame" the Encyclical speak of the struggle, "the hard struggle … that is to extend through the whole of human history," "that 'monumental struggle against the powers of darkness' which continues throughout human history."

22 *Inseg* X/1 (1987) 689–690 [St. Paul edition 16] (final emphasis mine).

23 *Inseg* X/1 (1987) 738 [St. Paul edition 66].

According to God's eternal Plan

In the first of the above quotations Mary is portrayed as "at the very center of that enmity ... which accompanies the history of humanity on earth and the history of salvation itself," but her election by God (which implies her Immaculate Conception) "is more powerful than any experience of evil and sin, than all that 'enmity' which marks the history of man." Hence, in the two most solemn Acts of Consecration to the Immaculate Heart of Mary, John Paul says that

> The power of this consecration [which is meant to be an identification with the self-consecration of Christ and entrusted to Mary] lasts for all time and embraces all individuals, peoples and nations. It overcomes every evil that the spirit of darkness is able to awaken, and has in fact awakened in our times, in the heart of man and in his history.[24]

Mary—as the "woman of the Apocalypse" in whom "the salvific power of the Redemption" has already triumphed, wrote John Paul to his brother bishops on the Solemnity of the Immaculate Conception in 1983, in preparation for the second of these solemn acts—is the one through whose Immaculate Heart he wished to profess this "power of the Redemption" again with the entire Church.[25] He spoke similarly on 17 March 1984 at the close of his annual retreat[26] and on the Solemnity of the Immaculate Conception in 1985 at the conclusion of the Extraordinary Synod.[27] Clearly, in his mind consecration/entrustment to her is intended by God and necessary in the struggle against the evils threatening to engulf the world.

The second text from *Redemptoris Mater* cited above might be said to speak in terms of that "integral logic of the faith"

24 *Inseg* V/2 (1982) 1588 [*ORE* 735:12]; *Inseg* VII/1 (1984) 776 [*ORE* 828:9].

25 *Inseg* VII/1 (1984) 417 [*ORE* 823:2].

26 *Inseg* VII/1 (1984) 691 [*ORE* 827:5].

27 *Inseg* VIII/2 (1985) 1460 [*ORE* 917:10].

which holds that consecration to Mary is necessary in order to be ever more fully consecrated to Christ in order to belong ever more completely to the Father. This is a manifestation of God's eternal plan (cf. Eph. 1:10–11) and Mary's place in it, which the Pope so beautifully considers in the first part of the Encyclical.[28]

The Teaching of *Ecclesia de Eucharistia*

Above I indicated that Saint John Paul II's statements about Marian consecration/entrustment in the Encyclicals *Redemptoris Mater* and *Ecclesia de Eucharistia* occurred at the highest level of his papal magisterium. I would like now to consider more carefully the statement in his last Encyclical:

> "Do this in remembrance of me" (Lk. 22:19). In the "memorial" of Calvary all that Christ accomplished by his passion and his death is present. Consequently *all that Christ did with regard to his Mother* for our sake is also present. To her he gave the beloved disciple and, in him, each of us: "Behold, your Son!." To each of us he also says: "Behold your mother!" (cf. Jn. 19: 26–27).
>
> Experiencing the memorial of Christ's death in the Eucharist also means continually receiving this gift. It means accepting—like John—the one who is given to us anew as our Mother. It also means taking on a commitment to be conformed to Christ, putting ourselves at the school of his Mother and allowing her to accompany us. Mary is present, with the Church and as the Mother of the Church, at each of our celebrations of the Eucharist. If the Church and the Eucharist are inseparably united, the same ought to be said of Mary and the Eucharist. This is one reason why, since ancient times, the commemoration of Mary has always been part of the Eucharistic celebrations of the Churches of East and West.[29]

With regard to this passage, it may be said once again, without any exaggeration, that Saint John Paul II broke new

28 *Inseg* X/1 (1987) 684–685 [St. Paul edition 12–13].

29 *AAS* 95 (2003) 471; *Inseg* XXVI/1 (2003) 508 [*ORE* 1790:IX–X].

ground in making explicit the link between Mary and the Mass, and between receiving the Eucharistic Jesus and receiving Mary in the Mass. Here it must be specified that, by virtue of the transubstantiation which takes place in the sacred species, one receives the Body, Blood, Soul and Divinity of Jesus Christ.[30] Clearly, the presence of Mary is not at the same level; rather, it is a mystical presence of Our Lady which accompanies the sacrifice of Christ.[31] It remains for theologians to try to specify this mode of presence. It is analogous to, but obviously not on the same level as the real presence of Jesus.[32]

Nonetheless, according to Saint John Paul II, our living the total experience of the Eucharistic memorial of Christ's death and resurrection also effectively means continually receiving the gift of His Mother, of being entrusted to her anew and of welcoming her into our lives. This is a dimension of his teaching, which, up to now, has barely been taken seriously, much less incorporated into catechesis, preaching, teaching and the piety of the faithful. In this, however, one might say that John Paul was following and developing in his own way the final teaching found in St. Louis de Montfort's *Treatise on True Devotion*.[33]

Continuing His Program

While it is not within the scope of this study to present an exhaustive analysis of all of the texts which present the saintly

30 Cf. *D-H* #1651; *CCC* #1374.

31 Cf. Severino M. Ragazzini, O.F.M. Conv., *Maria Vita dell'Anima: Itinerario Mariano alla SS. Trinità* (Frigento (AV): "Casa Mariana," 1984) 207–257; René Laurentin, *Présence de Marie: Histoire, Spiritualité, Fondements Doctrinaux* (Paris: Éditions Salvator, 2011).

32 I have dealt with this topic in much more detail in my essays, each one in a more fully developed manner: "Mary's Presence in the Mass," *Homiletic & Pastoral Review* XCVII, No. 10 (July 1997) 8–15; "Mary's Presence in the Mass according to Pope John Paul II," in *Mary at the Foot of the Cross* – VI: *Marian Coredemption in the Eucharistic Mystery. Acts of the Sixth International Symposium on Marian Coredemption* (New Bedford, MA: Academy of the Immaculate, 2007) 11–38.; "Mary's Presence in the Mass: The Teaching of Pope John Paul II," in *Antiphon: A Journal for Liturgical Renewal* Vol. 10, N° 2 (2006) 132–158.

33 Cf. *Treatise on True Devotion* #266–273.

Pope's teaching on Marian consecration/entrustment, I believe it is important to indicate how he continued on this path which he set out upon on the Solemnity of the Immaculate Conception in 1978. I will now present some major statements from the latter part of his pontificate indicating how he continued to develop with remarkable consistency and depth his teaching on putting oneself in Mary's hands and receiving her into one's life.

On 12 May 1991, in the homily which he gave at the prayer vigil in Fatima, John Paul II made a restatement of a very fundamental principle of his program as Pope. He began by quoting from his Marian Encyclical: "Mary embraces each and every one *in* the Church, and embraces each and every one *through* the Church" (*Redemptoris Mater*, 47). Then he went on to state: "The Church for her part, does not cease consecrating herself to Mary";[34] and that is exactly what he continued to do as her chief pastor. His constant concluding remarks in homilies, addresses, letters and more solemn documents virtually always ended with, "I entrust you all to the care of the Blessed Virgin Mary," with many variations in many different languages, but with extraordinary consistency. I have collected hundreds of these.

But beyond those all but innumerable references, he continued teaching—"in season and out of season,"[35] even into his final years, marked by his own ever greater physical weakness and suffering—the importance of consecration/entrustment to Mary and taking her into one's own home.[36] I offer here a few further examples among many. It will be noted that every one of these exhortations is unique. There are themes that are constantly reiterated, but no carbon copies. On 21 April 2000, the Year of the Great Jubilee, in the text he prepared for the Way of the Cross at the Coliseum, he put it this way:

34 *Inseg* XIV/1 (1991) 1217–1218 [*ORE* 1191:5].

35 Cf. 2 Tim. 4:2.

36 Cf. Jn. 19:27.

> "And from that moment the disciple took her to his own home" (Jn. 19:27). This is his bequest to those dearest to his heart. *His legacy to the Church.* The desire of Jesus as he dies is that the maternal love of Mary should embrace all those for whom he is giving his life, the whole of humanity.[37]

On 13 October of that same Jubilee Year, he addressed the Eighth Mariological Theological Colloquium on St. Louis Marie Grignion de Montfort and said:

> For me, St. Louis Marie Grignion de Montfort is a significant person of reference who has enlightened me at important moments in life. When I was working as a clandestine seminarian at the Solvay factory in Kraków, my spiritual director advised me to meditate on the *True Devotion to the Blessed Virgin.* Many times and with great spiritual profit I read and reread this precious little ascetical book with the blue, soda-stained cover. By relating the Mother of Christ to the Trinitarian mystery, Montfort helped me to understand that *the Virgin belongs to the plan of salvation*, by the *Father's* will, as the Mother of the *incarnate Word*, who was conceived by her through the power of the *Holy Spirit.* Mary's every intervention in the work of the regeneration of the faithful is not in competition with Christ, but derives *from* him and is *at* his service. Mary's action in the plan of salvation is always Christocentric, that is, it is directly related to a mediation that takes place in Christ. I then realized that I could not exclude the Mother of the Lord from my life without disregarding the will of God-the-Trinity, who wanted to "begin and complete" the great mysteries of salvation history with the responsible and faithful collaboration of the humble Handmaid of Nazareth. …
>
> Mary therefore appears as the place of the love and action of the Persons of the Trinity, and Montfort presents her in a relational perspective: "Mary is entirely relative to God. Indeed, I might well call her the relation to God. She

37 *Inseg* XXIII/1 (2000) 652 [*ORE* 1642:7].

> exists only with reference to God" (*True Devotion to the Blessed Virgin*, n. 225). For this reason, the All-Holy One leads us to the Trinity. By repeating *"Totus tuus"* to her every day and living in harmony with her, we can attain an experience of the Father in confidence and boundless love (cf. ibid., nn. 169, 215), docility to the Spirit (cf. ibid., n. 258) and transformation of self into the likeness of Christ (cf. ibid., nn. 218–221).[38]

On 24 February 2001, the Feast of Our Lady of Confidence, he addressed the seminarians at the Roman Major Seminary as follows:

> We learn from the pages of his diary [the Venerable Bruno Marchesini] that in 1936, at the end of May during his second year of philosophical studies, he consecrated himself to the Immaculate Heart of Mary. Solemnly repeating the offering of his chastity, he wrote: "Through you, O Mary, today I have dared to present the flowering lily of my purity to Jesus, truly present in my heart under the Eucharistic veil. You inspired me to do this, you will help me preserve it with all the fervour of this day." He added, as if clearly to emphasize his thought, that this consecration expressed his intention of a "supreme dedication of love to Jesus Christ."
>
> Bruno Marchesini understood that Our Lady is the surest way to reach Jesus and to belong to him totally and for ever. This has also been my personal experience. Welcome the Blessed Virgin into your lives as your Mother, dear seminarians. May each of you have a loving knowledge of Mary's role, especially during the valuable years of formation when you are preparing to become a priest, that is, an *"alter Christus."*
>
> In the seminary chapel you venerate the Blessed Virgin with the title *"Our Lady of Trust."* I urge you to come and visit her often and to open your heart to her: Mary is "the radiant dawn and sure guide for our steps" (*Nono millennio ineunte*, n. 58).[39]

38 *Inseg* XXIII/2 (2000) 593, 594 [*ORE* 1665:5].

39 *Inseg* XXIV/1 (2001) 445 [*ORE* 1686:8].

We note again here how he did not hesitate to use the term consecration while returning to the theme of accepting Mary's role in one's life.

On 16 October 2002, the twenty-fourth anniversary of his papal election, he clarified once again the difference between the roles of Jesus and Mary in the work of our salvation and yet their union in that work:

> During my recent trip to Poland, I prayed to Our Lady: "Most Holy Mother, ... obtain also for me strength in body and spirit, so that I may carry out to the end the mission given me by the Risen Lord. To you I give back all the fruits of my life and my ministry; to you I entrust the future of the Church ... in you do I trust and once more to you I declare: *Totus Tuus, Maria! Totus tuus*. Amen."[40]
>
> Today I repeat the same words giving thanks to God for the twenty-four years of my service to the Church in the Chair of Peter. On this special day, I entrust anew into the hands of the Mother of God the life of the Church and that so sorely tried of humanity. To her I entrust my future. I put everything in her hands so that with a Mother's love she may present it to her Son, "for the praise of his glory" (Eph. 1,12).
>
> The centre of our faith is Christ, Redeemer of the human person. Mary does not detract from him nor does she detract from his saving work. Assumed into heaven in body and soul, the Virgin Mary, the first to enjoy the fruits of the Passion and Resurrection of her own Son, is the One who in a sure way leads us to Christ, the final goal of our deeds and of our entire life. For this reason, in the Apostolic Letter *Novo Millennio ineunte*, directing to the entire Church the exhortation of Christ to "launch out into the deep," I added that "on this path the Blessed Virgin accompanies us to whom ... together with many bishops ... I entrusted the third millennium" (n. 58). Inviting believers to contemplate unceasingly the face

40 Cf. *Inseg* XXV/2 (2002) 193 [*ORE* 1756:7].

> of Christ, I desired that for everyone the teacher of such contemplation be Mary his Mother.[41]

On 8 March 2003, he released this beautiful Message for the 18th World Youth Day:

> For the 18th World Youth Day that will be celebrated in dioceses all over the world, I have chosen a theme related to the Year of the Rosary: "Behold, your mother!" (Jn. 19:27). Before his death, Jesus entrusted to the apostle John what was most precious to him: his Mother, Mary. These are the final words of the Redeemer, and therefore they take on a solemn nature and could be regarded as his spiritual testimony.
>
> The angel Gabriel's words in Nazareth: "Hail, full of grace" (Lk. 1:28) also cast light on the scene at Calvary. The Annunciation comes at the beginning, the Cross signals the fulfillment. At the Annunciation, Mary gives human nature to the Son of God within her womb; at the foot of the Cross, she welcomes the whole of humanity within her heart in the person of John. She was Mother of God from the first moments of the Incarnation, and she became the Mother of humanity during the final moments of the life of her Son Jesus on earth. She, who was without sin, on Calvary "experienced" within her own being the suffering of sin that her Son had taken upon himself to save humankind. At the foot of the Cross on which was dying the One whom she had conceived at the moment of her "yes" at the Annunciation, Mary received, as it were, a "second annunciation": "Woman, behold, your son!" (Jn.19:26).
>
> The Son upon the Cross can pour out his suffering into his Mother's heart. Every child who suffers experiences that need. You too, my dear young people, are faced with suffering: loneliness, failures and disappointments in your personal lives; difficulties in inserting yourselves in the adult world and in professional life; the separations and losses in your families; the violence of war and the death

41 *Inseg* XXV/2 (2002) 478–479 [*ORE* 1765:7].

of the innocent. Know, however, that in difficult times, which everyone experiences, you are not alone: like John at the foot of the Cross, Jesus also gives his Mother to you so that she will comfort you with her tenderness.

It says in the Gospel that "from that hour the disciple took her to his own home" (Jn. 19:27). This statement, the subject of many commentaries since early Christian times, does not simply point out the place where John lived. Beyond the material aspect, it evokes the spiritual dimension of this welcome and of the new bond established between Mary and John.

My dear young people, you are more or less the same age as John and you have the same desire to be with Jesus. Today, it is you whom Jesus expressly asks to receive Mary "into your home" and to welcome her "as one of yours"; to learn from her the one who "kept all these things, pondering them in her heart" (Lk. 2:19) that inner disposition to listen and the attitude of humility and generosity that singled her out as God's first collaborator in the work of salvation. She will discharge her ministry as a mother and train you and mould you until Christ is fully formed in you (cf. *Rosarium Virginis Mariæ*, n. 15).

This is why I now wish to repeat the motto of my episcopal and pontifical service: "*Totus tuus.*" Throughout my life I have experienced the loving and forceful presence of the Mother of Our Lord. Mary accompanies me every day in the fulfillment of my mission as Successor of Peter.

Mary is Mother of divine grace, because she is the Mother of the Author of grace. Entrust yourselves to her with complete confidence! You will be radiant with the beauty of Christ. Open up to the breath of the Spirit, and you will become courageous apostles, capable of spreading the fire of charity and the light of truth all around you. In Mary's school, you will discover the specific commitment that Christ expects of you, and you will learn to put Christ first in your lives, and to direct your thoughts and actions to him.[42]

---

42 *Inseg* XXVI/1 (2003) 327–328 [ORE 1785:6, 7].

Note the Pope's evocative reference to Jesus' pouring out "his suffering into his Mother's heart" and relating it to how "every child who suffers experiences that [same] need" and how "Jesus also gives his Mother to you so that she will comfort you with her tenderness." On 10 April 2003, the Thursday before Palm Sunday, which had been designated as the 18th World Youth Day, he spoke to the young people of Rome and Lazio preparing for the celebration on the following Sunday:

> "*Behold your Mother!*" (Jn. 19: 27). I chose these words of Jesus as the theme for this 18th World Youth Day.
>
> When his "hour" had come, Jesus from the cross gave Mary his Mother to the disciple John, making her, through the disciple he loved, *Mother of all believers*, Mother of us all. Behold, Jesus says *to each one of us*, Behold Mary, my Mother, who from this day becomes your Mother too!
>
> Let us ask ourselves: who is this Mother? To understand this better, I recommend, in this *Year of the Rosary*, that you re-read the entire marvelous chapter VIII of the dogmatic Constitution *Lumen Gentium* of the Second Vatican Council. Mary, "in an utterly singular way … cooperated by her obedience, faith, hope and burning charity in the Saviour's work of restoring supernatural life to souls. For this reason she is a mother to us in the order of grace."[43] And this supernatural motherhood will continue until the glorious coming of Christ.
>
> Of course, he, Jesus Christ, is the *only Redeemer*. He is the one Mediator between God and man! However—as the Council teaches—Mary cooperates and takes part in his work of salvation. Thus, she is a Mother for whom we must have a deep and true devotion, a *profoundly Christocentric* devotion, indeed, rooted in the Trinitarian Mystery of God himself.
>
> "'*Behold, your mother!*'. *And from that hour*," the Gospel continues, "the disciple took her into his own home" (Jn. 19: 27).

43 Cf. *LG* #61.

Welcoming Mary into their home, into their life, is the privilege of every one of the faithful. This is especially true in difficult moments, such as those that you young people also have to live through at times in this period of your life. I remember this moment for me, when I was young and worked at the chemical factory, and I discovered these words: *Totus Tuus*. And with the power of these words I was able to get through the terrible war, the terrible Nazi occupation, and then through the other difficult experiences after the war. The possibility of taking Mary into our own home, into our own life, is offered to us all.

This is why today *I want to entrust you to Mary*. Dear friends, and I tell you from experience, open the doors of your life to her! Do not be afraid *to open wide the doors of your hearts to Christ* through the One who wants to bring you to him, so that you may be saved from sin and death! She will help you to listen to his voice and say "yes" to every plan that God conceives for you, for your good and for that of all humanity.

I entrust you to Mary while in spirit you are already on your way towards the *World Youth Day in Cologne*. The young people from Toronto have just brought here *the Holy Year Cross*. From Toronto to Cologne the Cross that next Sunday, Palm Sunday, they will present to their friends from Cologne. On the other hand, two youth from Rome have set under the Cross *the Icon of Mary* which stood guard over the "dawn watchmen" at Tor Vergata on the unforgettable World Youth Day in the Year 2000. Tor Vergata! So that it will always be clearly visible that Mary is a very powerful Mother who leads us to Christ, I would also like *this Icon of Mary to be presented* to the young people from Cologne next Sunday, along with the Cross and from now on, to be taken on pilgrimage round the world in preparation for World Youth Days. …

"*Behold your Mother!*" (Jn. 19: 27), *Regina Pacis!* Responding to this invitation and taking Mary into your home will also mean *working for peace*. Mary, *Regina Pacis* (Queen of Peace), is indeed a Mother, and like

> every mother all she wants for her children is to see them living peacefully and in agreement with one another. In this tormented time in history, while terrorism and wars are threatening peace between men and women and religions, I would like to entrust you to Mary so that you may become *champions of the culture of peace*, today more necessary than ever.[44]

After that marvelous discourse, he then recited an Act of Entrustment which he had composed for the occasion.[45] On the day of Palm Sunday itself, he continued this catechesis, which he obviously considered of fundamental importance, in his homily:

> Peace is the gift of Christ, which he obtained for us with the sacrifice of the Cross. To achieve it effectively it is necessary to climb with the divine Teacher up to Calvary. And who can guide us better in this ascent than Mary who, as she stood at the foot of the Cross, was given to us as our mother through the faithful apostle, St John? To help the young discover this marvelous spiritual reality, I chose as the *theme of my Message* for World Youth Day this year the words of the dying Christ: *"Behold, your mother!"* (Jn. 19: 27). Accepting this testament of love, John opened his home to Mary (cf. Jn. 19: 27), that is, he welcomed her into his life, sharing with her a completely new spiritual closeness. The *intimate bond with the Mother of the Lord* will lead the "beloved disciple" to become the apostle of that Love that he drew from the Heart of Christ through the Immaculate Heart of Mary.
>
> "*Behold, your mother!*" Jesus addresses these words to each of you, dear friends. He also asks you to take Mary as your mother "into your home," to welcome her "as one of yours," because "she will discharge her ministry as a mother and train you and mould you until Christ is fully formed in you." May Mary make it so that you respond

44 *Inseg* XXVI/1 (2003) 441–443 [*ORE* 1789:5].

45 *Inseg* XXVI/1 (2003) 444–445 [*ORE* 1789:5].

> generously to the Lord's call, and persevere with joy and fidelity in the Christian mission![46]

What should not be missed is that the message, the discourse and the homily for World Youth Day were beautifully coordinated, each commenting on John 19:25–27, each shedding a slightly different light on the reality of Marian entrustment—and this during the last active Holy Week in John Paul's life. His final Holy Week in 2005 was spent in his apartment in the Vatican Apostolic Palace as he was dying.[47]

In his Post-Synodal Apostolic Exhortation, *Ecclesia in Europa*, of 28 June 2003, he spoke with prophetic foresight about why Europe needed to be entrusted to Mary.

> This is the certainty which heartens the Church on her pilgrim way; in the story of the woman and the dragon she reads her own history ever anew. The woman who gives birth to her son also brings to mind *the Virgin Mary*, especially at that moment when, transfixed by suffering at the foot of the Cross, she begets her Son anew as the victor over the prince of this world. She is then entrusted to John who in turn is entrusted to her (cf. Jn. 19:26–27), and thus she becomes the Mother of the Church. Thanks to the bond uniting Mary to the Church and the Church to Mary, the mystery of the woman becomes clearer: "Mary, present in the Church as the Mother of the Redeemer, takes part, as a mother, in that 'monumental struggle against the powers of darkness,' which continues throughout human history. And by her ecclesial identification as the 'woman clothed with the sun' (*Rev.* 12:1), it can be said that 'in the Most Holy Virgin the Church has already reached the perfection whereby she exists without spot or wrinkle.' "
>
> The whole Church, then, *looks to Mary*. Thanks to the countless Marian shrines dotting the nations of the

46 *Inseg* XXVI/1 (2003) 453 [*ORE* 1789:7].

47 Cf. George Weigel, *The End and the Beginning: Pope John Paul II – The Victory of Freedom, the Last Years, the Legacy* (NY: Doubleday, 2010) 383–384.

> continent, devotion to Mary is very strong and widespread among the peoples of Europe.
>
> *Church in Europe! Continue to contemplate Mary*, in the knowledge that she is "maternally present and sharing in the many complicated problems which today beset the lives of individuals, families, and nations" and is "helping the Christian people in the constant struggle between good and evil, to ensure that it 'does not fall,' or, if it has fallen, that it 'rises again.' "
>
> ***Prayer to Mary, Mother of Hope***
>
> In this contemplation, inspired by genuine love, Mary appears to us as a figure of the Church which, nourished by hope, acknowledges the saving and merciful action of God, in whose light she reads her own journey and all of history. Today too Mary helps us to interpret all that happens to us in the light of Jesus her Son. As a new creation moulded by the Holy Spirit, *Mary causes the virtue of hope to grow within us.*
>
> *To her*, Mother of hope and consolation, *we confidently lift up our prayer*: to her we entrust the future of the Church in Europe and the future of all the women and men of this continent.[48]

Once again, the rest of the Act of Entrustment follows, which he had composed as the conclusion of the exhortation.[49]

In his Letter of 8 September 2004 to the Bishop of Adria-Rovigo, on the occasion of the 17th International Marian Colloquium in Rovigo, he wrote about his theology of entrustment in this way:

> The theme chosen, "*Mary's gaze on the contemporary world*," is as it were an invitation to see with the eyes of the Blessed Virgin the happy and sorrowful events of our time. Mary's eyes are fixed first and foremost on the Most Holy Trinity, on the mystery of ineffable love that indissolubly unites the three divine Persons. Contemplating the Father,

48 *Inseg* XXVI/1 (2003) 1081–1082 [*ORE* 1800:XIV–XV].

49 *Inseg* XXVI/1 (2003) 1082–1083 [*ORE* 1800:XIV–XV].

> the Word and the Holy Spirit, the Virgin feels as though she were being directed to humanity to carry out for every human being the maternal mission entrusted to her by the crucified Son (cf. Jn. 19: 25–27). Mary watches over the world, where her children on their way towards the blessed homeland travel the path of faith, "surrounded by dangers and difficulties" (cf. *Lumen Gentium*, n. 62).
>
> The Blessed Virgin is present as a caring mother "in this ecclesial journey or pilgrimage through space and time, and even more through the history of souls" (*Redemptoris Mater*, n. 25). No situation escapes her motherly gaze, neither in the Church, nor of any individual member of the faithful or of the entire human family.
>
> Commemorating the coronation of the image of the Sorrowful Mother, it was natural to reflect in a special way on the "*gaze*" that the Virgin on Calvary turned upon the Crucified Christ, who from the Cross invited her to open her motherly heart to his beloved disciple: "*Woman, behold, your son*" (Jn. 19: 26). At that moment, after sharing in the passion of the Only-begotten Son, the Mother of God becomes the Mother of John, hence, the Mother of the entire human race (cf. Jn. 19: 26–27).[50]

In his homily on his last participation in the Solemnity of the Immaculate Conception, which corresponded to the 150th Anniversary of the proclamation of the dogma of the Immaculate Conception, he renewed the first solemn Act of Entrustment, which he had made on his first celebration of the Solemnity of the Immaculate Conception as pope in 1978:

> To you, Virgin Immaculate, predestined by God above every other creature to be the advocate of grace and model of holiness for his people, today in a special way I renew *the entrustment of the whole Church.*
>
> May you guide your children on their pilgrimage of faith, making them *ever more obedient and faithful to the Word of God.*

50 *Inseg* XXVII/2 (2004) 220–221 [*ORE* 1862:9].

> May you accompany every Christian on the path of conversion and holiness, in the fight against sin and in the search for *true beauty* that is always an impression and a reflection of divine Beauty.
>
> May you obtain *peace and salvation for all the peoples*. May the eternal Father, who desired you to be the Immaculate Mother of the Redeemer, also renew in our time through you, the miracles of his merciful love. Amen![51]

On 24 January 2005, the last year of his pontificate, he spoke thus to Spanish Bishops on the "ad limina" visit, with reference to the 150th Anniversary of the dogma of the Immaculate Conception:

> Dear Brothers, you have taken the initiative of dedicating a special year to the Immaculate Virgin, Patroness of Spain, to commemorate the 150th anniversary of the proclamation of the Marian Dogma of the Immaculate Conception. This is an invitation to the faithful to renew their consecration to our Mother, personally and as a community, and to accept my invitation to the whole Church to "listen to Mary Most Holy, in whom the mystery of the Eucharist appears, more than in anyone else, as a *mystery of light*" (*Ecclesia de Eucharistia*, n. 62).
>
> In Spain, evangelization and religious practice have always gone hand in hand with special love for the Virgin Mary. This is demonstrated by the many churches, shrines and monuments that dot the whole of your countryside; and by the confraternities, congregations, university corporations and councils that persist in defending her privileges as well as the practices of popular piety and celebrations in honour of the Mother of God. Moreover, she has also been a source of inspiration to many artists, celebrated painters and famous sculptors.
>
> Spain is Mary's Land. To her I commend your pastoral intentions. I place all priests, men and women religious,

51 *Inseg* XXVII/2 (2004) 670–671 [*ORE* 1873:3].

seminarians, children, young people and the elderly, families, the sick and the needy under her protection.[52]

Let it be noted that on this occasion, the last time that he received Bishops on the "ad limina" visit, he did not hesitate to speak of consecration to Our Lady, as we will note repeatedly in the concluding chapter.

The Final ***Totus Tuus***

The final days of the great Pontiff were painful for him, for those who assisted him and for all who watched—even from a distance. But the clandestine seminarian in Krakow who had learned from Saint Louis-Marie Grignion de Montfort to say *Totus tuus* continued to do so all his life, even to the end. The phrase, constantly used all his life, as we have seen, was abbreviated, transposed and excerpted from the Latin prayer *Tuus totus ego sum, et omnia mea tua sunt. Accipio te in mea omnia. Præbe mihi cor tuum, Maria* ["I belong entirely to you, and all that I have is yours; I take you for my all. O Mary, give me your heart"].[53] The first sentence is attributed to Saint Bonaventure.[54] The last two sentences are adaptations of John 19:27 and Proverbs 23:26. He took *Totus tuus* as his motto as bishop and pope.

In the first version of his last testament, dated 6 March 1979, to which he would refer yearly during his Lenten retreat as pope, he wrote

Totus Tuus ego sum

In the Name of the Most Holy Trinity. Amen.

52 *Inseg* XXVIII (2005) 89–90 [*ORE* 1880:5].

53 These Latin sentences come from the beginning and the last sentence of #266 in the *Treatise on True Devotion*. Cf. *Œuvres complètes de saint Louis-Marie Grignion de Montfort* (Paris: Éditions du Seuil, 1982) 666–667. *God Alone: The Collected Writings of St. Louis Mary de Montfort* (Bay Shore, N. Y.: Montfort Publications, 1987) 375–376. He explained his adoption of this terminology in *Gift and Mystery: On the 50th Anniversary of My Priestly Ordination* (Nairobi, Kenya: Paulines Publications, Africa, 1996) 42–43.

54 *Psalt. Majus, cant. Ad instar illius Moïsis*, Ex. 15 (Opera Omnia, Vivès, Parisiis 1868, 221 b).

> "Watch, therefore, for you do not know on what day your Lord is coming" (Mt. 24:42)—these words remind me of the last call that will come at whatever time the Lord desires. I want to follow Him and I want all that is part of my earthly life to prepare me for this moment. I do not know when it will come but I place this moment, like all other things, in the hands of the Mother of my Master: *Totus Tuus*. In these same motherly hands I leave everything and Everyone with whom my life and my vocation have brought me into contact. In these Hands I above all leave the Church, and also my Nation and all humankind.[55]

The following year during his Lenten retreat, he wrote further:

> Today, I would like to add just this: that everyone keep the prospect of death in mind and be ready to go before the Lord and Judge—and at the same time Redeemer and Father. So I keep this continuously in my mind, entrusting that decisive moment to the Mother of Christ and of the Church—to the Mother of my hope. …
>
> I would like once again to entrust myself entirely to the Lord's grace. He Himself will decide when and how I am to end my earthly life and my pastoral ministry. In life and in death [I am] *Totus Tuus* through Mary Immaculate.[56]

On 5 March 1982, less than a year after the attempt on his life, he added:

> I feel so much more deeply that I am totally in God's Hands—and I remain continuously available to my Lord, entrusting myself to Him through His Immaculate Mother (*Totus Tuus*).[57]

Finally, during the Lenten retreat of the Jubilee Year 2000, he added his final remarks to his testament:

> When, on 16 October 1978, the Conclave of Cardinals chose John Paul II, Cardinal Stefan Wyszynski, the Primate of Poland, said to me: "*The task of the new Pope* will be *to*

55 *Inseg* XXVIII (2005) 251 [*Testament* 5].

56 *Inseg* XXVIII (2005) 253 [*Testament* 8, 9].

57 *Inseg* XXVIII (2005) 254 [*Testament* 10].

> *lead the Church into the Third Millennium.*" I do not know if I am repeating the sentence exactly as he said it, but this was at least the sense of what I heard him say at the time. These words were spoken by the Man who went down in history as the Primate of the Millennium: a great Primate. I witnessed his mission, his total confidence, his struggles and his triumph. "When victory is won, it will be a victory through Mary": The Primate of the Millennium was fond of repeating these words of his Predecessor, Cardinal August Hlond.[58]

Thus, he had consistently prepared himself for the reality of death, and always as he had lived, putting himself entirely in the hands of Mary, his Mother and Mediatrix with Jesus.

One of his last recorded uses of the much-prayed phrase *Totus tuus* was as he returned to consciousness after his tracheotomy on 24 February 2005. Here is how George Weigel reports it:

> The tracheotomy was performed successfully, but it was only afterward, [Archbishop] Dziwisz remembered, that John Paul "concretely realized" what the doctors had meant when they had told him that the operation would render him mute for a time. The Pope signaled to Dziwisz that he wanted something on which to write, and then scrawled, "What have they done to me?! But … *totus tuus*"—chagrin combined with yet another sign of Karol Wojtyła's determination to bend his will to God's under the protection of the Virgin Mary.[59]

Cardinal Dziwisz commented thus on that incident: "He was trying to express both all the regret he felt at no longer being able to speak and his resolute, total self-abandonment into Our Lady's hands"—indeed, the perfect description of his consecration/entrustment to Mary.[60]

58 *Inseg* XXVIII (2005) 254–255 [*Testament* 11].

59 Weigel 381–382. This is also commented on in Stanisław Dziwisz, Czelas Drazek, S.J., Renato Buzzonetti, Angelo Comastri, *Let Me Go to the Father's House: John Paul II's Strength in Weakness* (Boston: Pauline Books and Media, 2006) 32, 68.

60 Cardinal Stanisław Dziwisz in Conversation with Gian Franco Svidercoschi, *A Life with Karol: My Forty-Year Friendship with the Man Who Became Pope*, trans.

Perhaps one of the saddest and most touching moments as his life was ebbing away was his attempt to give the *Urbi et Orbi* blessing on Easter Sunday, 27 March 2005, from the window of his study. He had appeared there hundreds of times to speak to the faithful and give his blessing. On that Easter day, thousands were assembled in Saint Peter's Square and millions were watching on television.

> He had practiced speaking for days beforehand, but when the moment came, nothing would come out. Stanisław Dziwisz recalled the drama of the moment:
>
> The Pope stood motionless in the window, as if frozen. He must have been overwhelmed by a combination of emotion and pain. In any case, he couldn't give the blessing. He whispered, "My voice is gone." Then, still silent, he made the sign of the cross three times, waved to the crowd, and gestured that he wanted to withdraw.
>
> He was deeply shaken and saddened. He also seemed exhausted by his unsuccessful attempt to speak. The people in the square were full of emotion; they were applauding him and calling out his name, but he felt the whole weight of the powerlessness and suffering he had displayed. He looked into my eyes and said, "Maybe it would be better for me to die if I can't fulfill the mission that has been entrusted to me." Before I could answer, he added, "Thy will be done. … *Totus tuus.*"[61]

Again, Cardinal Dziwisz would comment: "He wasn't expressing depression, but submission to God's will."[62]

Clearly, John Paul could not separate God's will from his belonging to Mary; for him it was the same thing. God was his Father; Mary was his Mother. No human being had fulfilled the Father's will as Mary had; no human being was as indissolubly united to Jesus as Mary was; no human being was more docile to the Holy Spirit than Mary was. She would help him to fulfill

Adrian J. Walker (NY: Doubleday, 2008) 254.

61 Weigel 384. Cf. *Let Me Go* 36.

62 Dziwisz 255.

God's will to the bitter end. In his general audience address of 23 November 1988 he had made one of his many insightful comments on John 19:25–27, touching on what is called "the joint predestination of Jesus and Mary." On that occasion he had said

> In this gift made to John and, through him, to Christ's followers and to all mankind, there is as it were a completion of the gift, which Jesus made of himself to humanity by his death on the Cross. Mary is as it were "entirely one" with him [Jesus], not only because they are mother and son "according to the flesh," but because in God's eternal plan they are contemplated, predestined and situated together at the center of the history of salvation.[63]

His own predestination in Christ would be linked to hers. She would take care of him and present him to her Son. And so it was. At about 9:00 P.M. that Saturday night, 2 April 2005, the then Archbishop Dziwisz suddenly felt "a kind of imperative command inside me" and began to celebrate in the Pope's bedroom the Mass of the Vigil of Divine Mercy Sunday, an observance officially established by John Paul II during the Jubilee Year 2000,[64] and was able to give him a few drops of the Precious Blood of Jesus as Viaticum, the "food for the journey."[65] Mary was surely present there as the Pope had taught. A few moments later the Pope's heart stopped beating. It was not only the Vigil of Mercy Sunday, but also the First Saturday of the month of April, Our Lady's day.

---

63 *Inseg* XI/4 (1988) 1636 [*ORE* 1061:16]. Cf. my study entitled "The Franciscan Thesis as Presented by Father Peter Damian Fehlner and the Magisterium," to be published by Pickwick Publications.

64 *Inseg* XXIII/1 (2000) 705 [*ORE* 1640:1]. Cf. George W. Kosicki, C.S.B., *John Paul II: The Great Mercy Pope* (Stockbridge, MA: Marian Press, Beatification edition, 2011) 233–237 and *passim*.

65 Dziwisz 258. Cf. Weigel 386.

CHAPTER NINE

Pope Saint John Paul's Magisterial Teaching Vis-à-vis Current Proponents

Magisterial Value of his Teaching

It will have been noted that there is a profound continuity between what Karol Wojtyła taught as Archbishop of Krakow and what he continued to teach as Pope with regard to consecration/entrustment to Our Lady. His commentaries on the various Acts of Consecration of Poland to the Mother of God bear this out. Nevertheless, what merits our particular attention is what he presented as Supreme Pontiff and, therefore, as chief teacher of the Church. While it is true that he presented nothing about consecration/entrustment to Mary in terms of a solemn *ex cathedra* definition on the level of the proclamation of Mary's Immaculate Conception by the Blessed Pius IX or the definition of her corporeal Assumption into Heaven by the Venerable Pius XII, it can certainly be argued that his "habitual acts of entrustment," his more solemn consecrations of the world and of individual nations to Our Lady, his frequent commentaries expounding the "theology of entrustment," especially his authoritative presentations on this matter in his Encyclical Letters, *Redemptoris Mater* and *Ecclesia de Eucharistia*, constituted an authentic exercise of the "ordinary magisterium" of the Roman Pontiff.

Here is what the Dogmatic Constitution on the Church, *Lumen Gentium*, says about such an exercise in its twenty-fifth article:

> In matters of faith and morals, the bishops speak in the name of Christ and the faithful are to accept their teaching and adhere to it with a religious assent [*religioso animi obsequio*]. This religious submission of mind and will must be shown in a special way to the authentic magisterium of the Roman Pontiff, even when he is not speaking ex cathedra [*Hoc vero religiosum voluntatis et intellectus obsequium singulari ratione praestandum est Romani Pontificis authentico magisterio etiam cum non ex cathedra loquitur*]; that is, it must be shown in such a way that his supreme magisterium is acknowledged with reverence, the judgments made by him are sincerely adhered to, according to his manifest mind and will. His mind and will in the matter may be known either from the character of the documents, from his frequent repetition of the same doctrine, or from his manner of speaking [*sive indole documentorum, sive ex frequenti propositione eiusdem doctrinae, sive ex dicendi ratione*].[1]

In this exposition the Fathers of the Council were making more explicit what Pius XII had already taught in his Encyclical Letter, *Humani Generis*, on the "ordinary magisterium" of the Roman Pontiff.[2]

The Character of the Documents

The first of the three criteria offered by *Lumen Gentium* has to do with the nature of the documents themselves. Clearly, an encyclical is near the highest levels of papal teaching. Thus the most solemn and explicit teaching of John Paul II on the matter of Marian consecration/entrustment may be found in his Encyclical, *Redemptoris Mater* #45–46 and 48, which we have already analyzed in some detail, and in his last Encyclical, *Ecclesia de Eucharistia* #57:

> "Do this in remembrance of me" (Lk. 22:19). In the "memorial" of Calvary all that Christ accomplished by

1 N.C.W.C. trans. (St. Paul edition, 1965) 24.

2 *AAS* 42 (1950) 568–569.

> his passion and his death is present. Consequently *all that Christ did with regard to his Mother* for our sake is also present. To her he gave the beloved disciple and, in him, each of us: "Behold, your Son!" To each of us he also says: "Behold your mother!" (cf. Jn. 19: 26–27).
>
> Experiencing the memorial of Christ's death in the Eucharist also means continually receiving this gift. It means accepting—like John—the one who is given to us anew as our Mother. It also means taking on a commitment to be conformed to Christ, putting ourselves at the school of his Mother and allowing her to accompany us. Mary is present, with the Church and as the Mother of the Church, at each of our celebrations of the Eucharist. If the Church and the Eucharist are inseparably united, the same ought to be said of Mary and the Eucharist. This is one reason why, since ancient times, the commemoration of Mary has always been part of the Eucharistic celebrations of the Churches of East and West.[3]

According to Pope John Paul II, then, our living the total experience of the Eucharistic memorial of Christ's death effectively requires that we should accept Mary as Mother and welcome her into our lives.[4] From this datum he underscores once again that "Mary is present, with the Church and as the Mother of the Church, at each of our celebrations of the Eucharist" [*Maria præsens est, cum Ecclesia et uti Mater Ecclesiæ, in singulis nostris celebrationibus eucharisticis*].

Further, it would seem that the Act of Consecration and Entrustment of 25 March 1984 would be equally on the most solemn level of the "ordinary magisterium" as a text of the *Ecclesia orans* used throughout the entire Catholic world and promulgated by the Supreme Pontiff in his capacity as Universal Bishop and not only of the Diocese of Rome [*in quantum Orbis*

3 *AAS* 95 (2003) 471; *Inseg* XXVI/1 (2003) 508 [*ORE* 1790:IX–X].

4 On the concept of receiving/welcoming Mary, cf. above (chapter 4, footnotes 46–48) 154-155; (chapter 7, footnotes 66–85) 258-265.

et non tantum Urbis Episcopus].[5] Although this latter text was not explicitly proposed as an instrument of teaching, it may certainly be taken as an instance of the axiom that the faith of the Church may be ascertained by its prayer [*Lex orandi statuat legem credendi*];[6] and surely many of the Church's beliefs about Mary, such as her spiritual maternity, her active collaboration in the work of redemption and her mediation, may be deduced from this prayer.

Frequent Repetition of the same Doctrine

The second of the criteria proposed by *Lumen Gentium* is the "frequent repetition of the same doctrine." So frequent were the major and minor instances of entrustment to Mary on the part of the Pope that they occurred regularly and predictably in his speeches, Angelus addresses, homilies and prayers several times in a given week.[7] Every time the Pope addressed a group, whether a small gathering of bishops on the "ad limina" visit or an assembly of thousands of the faithful in Saint Peter's Square, or anywhere throughout Italy or the world and simply said: "I entrust you to the Mother of God," this surely constituted an exercise of his "ordinary magisterium" and is thus a powerful reinforcement of the importance of the Christian's putting

5 Conradus M. Berti, Salvator M. Meo, Hermannus M. Toniolo, O.S.M., *De Ratione Ponderandi Documenta Magisterii Ecclesiastici* (Rome: Edizioni Marianum, 1961) 42.

6 I have treated this principle with regard to Marian doctrine in my article "Mary as Coredemptrix, Mediatrix and Advocate in the Contemporary Roman Liturgy," in Mark I. Miravalle, S.T.D., (ed.), *Mary Coredemptrix, Mediatrix, Advocate, Theological Foundations: Towards a Papal Definition?* (Santa Barbara, CA: Queenship Publishing Company, 1995) 46–49.

7 For instance, for the fifth year of his pontificate (22 October 1982 to 21 October 1983), I count 116 references to entrustment to Mary in the "log" of papal statements on Mary chronicled by Don Domenico Bertetto, S.D.B., in *Maria nel Magistero di Giovanni Paolo II: Quinto Anno* (Rome: Libreria Ateneo Salesiano, 1986) and have found six others for that year myself. That averages a reference to Marian entrustment about every third day. This continued up until the end of the pontificate. Even in 2004, his last full year as Pope and bowed down under Parkinson's disease, I counted over 90 occasions when he entrusted his hearers to Our Lady.

his life in Mary's hands. If the Montfort Fathers were able to put together an anthology of texts from Pius XII on Marian consecration,[8] I have the files from which to make a similar and immensely larger compilation from the texts of Saint John Paul II.

The Manner of Speaking

The third criterion presented in *Lumen Gentium* for recognizing the mind and will of the Pontiff is his manner of speaking [*ratio dicendi*]. Very frequently these acts of commendation take place within the context of prayer, an obvious indication of the great seriousness with which they are made. References to the "theology of entrustment" were often also found in homilies, general audiences and Angelus addresses where the Pope was always careful to present the doctrine of the Church in an unadulterated and integral form as an explicit exercise of his pastoral office. Here are just a few from literally hundreds of examples in which he expounded the theology of entrustment to Mary. In his general audience of 23 April 1997, he stated:

> The words of the dying Jesus actually show that his first intention was not to entrust his Mother to John, but to entrust the disciple to Mary and to give her a new maternal role. Moreover, the epithet "woman," also used by Jesus at the wedding in Cana to lead Mary to a new dimension of her existence as Mother, shows how the Saviour's words are not the fruit of a simple sentiment of filial affection but are meant to be put at a higher level. …
>
> Jesus' words acquire their most authentic meaning in the context of his saving mission. Spoken at the moment of the redemptive sacrifice, they draw their loftiest value precisely from this sublime circumstance. In fact, after Jesus' statements to his Mother, the Evangelist adds a significant clause: "Jesus, knowing that all was now finished …" (Jn. 19:28), as if he wished to stress that he

8 Cf. Pocock, *Pius XII on Consecration to Mary*.

> had brought his sacrifice to completion by entrusting his Mother to John, and in him to all men, whose Mother she becomes in the work of salvation. …
>
> On the Cross Jesus did not proclaim Mary's universal motherhood formally, but established a concrete maternal relationship between her and the beloved disciple. In the Lord's choice we can see his concern that this motherhood should not be interpreted in a vague way, but should point to Mary's intense, personal relationship with individual Christians.
>
> May each one of us, precisely through the concrete reality of Mary's universal motherhood, fully acknowledge her as our own Mother, and trustingly commend ourselves to her maternal love.[9]

On 7 May 1997, in another general audience address he spoke thus:

> In the light of this entrustment to his beloved disciple, one can understand the authentic meaning of Marian devotion in the ecclesial community. In fact, it places Christians in Jesus' filial relationship to his mother, putting them in a condition to grow in intimacy with both of them.
>
> The Church's devotion to the Virgin is not only the fruit of a spontaneous response to the exceptional value of her person and the importance of her role in the work of salvation, but is based on Christ's will.
>
> The words "Behold, your mother!" express Jesus' intention to inspire in his disciples an attitude of love for and trust in Mary, leading them to recognize her as their mother, the mother of every believer.
>
> At the school of the Virgin, the disciples learn to know the Lord deeply, as John did, and to have an intimate and lasting relationship of love with him. They also discover the joy of entrusting themselves to the Mother's maternal love, living like affectionate and docile children.
>
> The history of Christian piety teaches that Mary is the way which leads to Christ and that filial devotion to

9 *Inseg* XX/1 (1997) 749–751 [*ORE* 1489:11].

her takes nothing from intimacy with Jesus; indeed, it increases it and leads to the highest levels of perfection. …

According to the original Greek, the Gospel text continues: "From that hour the disciple took her among his possessions" (Jn. 19:27), thus stressing John's ready and generous adherence to Jesus' words and informing us about his behaviour for the whole of his life as the faithful guardian and docile son of the Virgin.

The hour of acceptance is that of the fulfillment of the work of salvation. Mary's spiritual motherhood and the first manifestation of the new link between her and the Lord's disciples begins precisely in this context.

John took the Mother "among his possessions." These rather general words seem to highlight his initiative, full of respect and love, not only in taking Mary to his house but also in living his spiritual life in communion with her.

In fact, a literal translation of the Greek expression "among his possessions" does not so much refer to material possessions since John—as St. Augustine observes (*In Ioan. Evang. tract.* 119, 3)—"possessed nothing of his own," but rather to the spiritual goods of gifts received from Christ: grace (Jn. 1:16), the Word (Jn. 12:48; 17:8), the Spirit (Jn. 7:39; 14:17), the Eucharist (Jn. 6:32–58) … Among these gifts which come to him from the fact that he is loved by Jesus, the disciple accepts Mary as his mother, establishing a profound communion of life with her (cf. *Redemptoris Mater*, n. 45, note 130).

May every Christian, after the beloved disciple's example, "take Mary into his house" and make room for her in his own daily life, recognizing her providential role in the journey of salvation.[10]

Here is a portion of the Act of Entrustment of the New Millennium, which he made on 8 October 2000 during the Jubilee Mass for Bishops, with a large number of Bishops from throughout the world joining with him:

10 *Inseg* XX/1 (1997) 903–904 [*ORE* 1491:11].

"Woman, behold your son!" (Jn. 19:26). As we near the end of this Jubilee Year, when you, O Mother, have offered us Jesus anew, the blessed fruit of your womb most pure, the Word made flesh, the world's Redeemer, we hear more clearly the sweet echo of his words entrusting us to you, making you our Mother: "Woman, behold your son!" When he entrusted to you the Apostle John, and with him the children of the Church and all people, Christ did not diminish but affirmed anew the role which is his alone as the Saviour of the world. You are the splendour which in no way dims the light of Christ, for you exist in him and through him. Everything in you is *fiat*: you are the Immaculate One, through you there shines the fullness of grace. Here, then, are your children, gathered before you at the dawn of the new millennium. The Church today, through the voice of the Successor Peter, in union with so many Pastors assembled here from every corner of the world, seeks refuge in your motherly protection and trustingly begs your intercession as she faces the challenges which lie hidden in the future. ...

Therefore, O Mother, like the Apostle John, we wish to take you into our home (cf. Jn. 19:27), that we may learn from you to become like your Son. "Woman, behold your sons!" Here we stand before you to entrust to your maternal care ourselves, the Church, the entire world. Plead for us with your beloved Son that he may give us in abundance the Holy Spirit, the Spirit of truth which is the fountain of life. Receive the Spirit for us and with us, as happened in the first community gathered round you in Jerusalem on the day of Pentecost (cf. Acts 1:14). May the Spirit open our hearts to justice and love, and guide people and nations to mutual understanding and a firm desire for peace. We entrust to you all people, beginning with the weakest: the babies yet unborn, and those born into poverty and suffering, the young in search of meaning, the unemployed, and those suffering hunger and disease. We entrust to you all troubled families, the elderly with no one to help them, and all who are alone and without hope.

> O Mother, you know the sufferings and hopes of the Church and the world: come to the aid of your children in the daily trials which life brings to each one, and grant that, thanks to the efforts of all, the darkness will not prevail over the light. To you, Dawn of Salvation, we commit our journey through the new millennium, so that with you as guide all people may know Christ, the light of the world and its only Saviour, who reigns with the Father and the Holy Spirit for ever and ever. Amen.[11]

Clarifications from the Magisterium of John Paul II about Marian Consecration

In his noted Encyclical Letter, *Humani Generis*, of 12 August 1950, the Venerable Pope Pius XII spoke with precision on the value of the "ordinary magisterium" of the Supreme Pontiff:

> It is true that Popes generally leave theologians free in those matters which are disputed in various ways by men of very high authority in this field; but history teaches that many matters that formerly were open to discussion, no longer now admit of discussion.
>
> Nor must it be thought that what is expounded in Encyclical Letters does not of itself demand consent, since in writing such Letters the Popes do not exercise the supreme power of their Teaching Authority. For these matters are taught with the ordinary teaching authority [*Magisterio enim ordinario haec docentur*], of which it is true to say: "He who hears you, hears me"; and generally what is expounded and inculcated in Encyclical Letters already for other reasons appertains to Catholic doctrine.
>
> But if the Supreme Pontiffs in their official documents purposely pass judgment on a matter up to that time under dispute, it is obvious that that matter, according to the mind and will of the same Pontiffs, cannot be any longer considered a question open to discussion among theologians.[12]

11 *Inseg* XXIII/2 (2000) 563, 565–566 [*ORE* 1663:7].

12 *AAS* 42 (1950) 568 [N.C.W.C. trans. 9–10]; *D-H* #3885.

We have already considered how John Paul II's teaching on Marian consecration/entrustment fulfills the criteria laid down in *Lumen Gentium* #25 for being considered part of his ordinary magisterium. I believe that this same teaching—at least in its broad outlines—also fulfills the above-stated teaching of *Humani Generis*.

While contemporary theologians, especially mariologists, have espoused various contrary opinions on the question of Marian consecration[13] and Our Lady's active collaboration in the work of the redemption—and thus her mediation of grace and spiritual maternity—it would be virtually untenable to state *prima facie* that the Pope took note of all of these and wished to settle various of these theological disputes [such as to whether one should employ the term "entrust" instead of "consecrate"] definitively. This is so especially because when Pius XII, the formulator of this principle, wished to settle matters which had previously been *quaestiones disputatæ*, he did so in such a way that his magisterial intervention could be readily acknowledged and adhered to, as, in fact, he did in *Humani Generis* and on other issues. The style or *modus operandi* of John Paul II tended to differ from that of his predecessor, and it is not terribly likely that he kept up with what many modern mariologists were writing.

On the other hand, even if he had not specifically intended to settle disputes among theologians on matters pertaining to Marian consecration/entrustment, I submit that by his consistent teaching, which was also an exercise of his ordinary magisterium, he nonetheless did so. Let us consider the questions to which he brought clarification.

The Question of Terminology

Here I would like to present a work published by the Pontifical International Marian Academy entitled *The Mother of*

13 Cf. above (chapter 4, footnotes 16–45) 145-154.

the Lord: Memory, Presence, Hope.[14] It was intended as a document offering guidelines to all who would undertake the study of Mariology. After a discursus of several pages on the history of Marian consecration[15] and admitting at the very beginning that the term can be traced back to St. John Damascene,[16] the last of the Eastern Fathers of the Church, we find these exhortations in #58:

> – We wish to encourage the efforts made, frequently by institutions which are directly involved, *to avoid the danger of certain expressions which cast a negative light on some forms of Marian spirituality, for example, the term 'slavery,' used to indicate a total dedication of the faithful to Mary, or words such as 'thing,' 'property,' 'instrument' to indicate, in some contexts, men and women who have become slaves of Mary. These terms are hard to reconcile with contemporary culture and hardly consonant with human dignity*;
>
> – *We encourage the request which many theologians have made for the last several years for a more careful use of the expression "consecration to Mary."* Strictly speaking, consecration, inasmuch as it is a free, total, irrevocable, and perpetual donation, is directed toward God alone. The expression 'consecrated to Mary' is, however, acceptable in reference of the institutes of consecrated life or of approved pontifical ecclesial movements when their dedication is an integral part of their formula of membership or profession. However, the term *consecration* appears 'inappropriate' in other situations, for example, those in which children and families are entrusted to Mary's protection.[17]

---

14 Pontifical International Marian Academy, *The Mother of the Lord: Memory, Presence, Hope*, trans. Thomas A. Thompson, S.M. (Staten Island, NY: St Pauls, 2007) [= *MotL*]. This is a translation of Pontificia Academia Mariana Internationalis, *La Madre del Signore Memoria Presenza Speranza. Alcune questioni attuali sulla figura e la missione della b. Vergine Maria* (Vatican City State, 2000).

15 *MotL* 76–85.

16 *MotL* 76.

17 *MotL* 86 (emphasis my own).

First, a word about authorship. The Preface of the original Italian edition bears the signatures of the then President of the Pontifical International Marian Academy (known by its Latin and Italian acronym, PAMI),[18] Fra Gaspar Calvo Moralejo, O.F.M., and the Secretary, Fra Stefano Cecchin, O.F.M. The Preface to the French edition, reproduced in the English edition, bears the signature of Vincenzo Battaglia, O.F.M., the then President of the Academy. The document was evidently drafted by the Academy's council, many of whom are professors of the Pontifical Faculty of the Marianum in Rome, and their colleagues.

1. Let us deal now with the first paragraph. The concept of Marian slavery, as we may recall, is already found in the language of Saint Ephrem the Syrian (+ 373), Pope John VII (+ 707) and most consistently developed by Saint Ildephonsus of Toledo (+ 667).[19] St. Odilo, Abbot of Cluny (+1049), also spoke of giving himself to Our Lady as her "slave" or "bondsman" [*tanquam proprium servum, tuo mancipatui trado*].[20] In the sixteenth century, confraternities of the Holy Slavery of Mary were germinating in the soil of Spain, promoted by Sister Agnes of St. Paul at the convent of the Franciscan Conceptionists at Alcalá de Henares, by the Franciscan Melchior de Cetina, by the Trinitarian, Saint Simon de Rojas (1552–1624), and by the Augustinian, Bartolomé de los Rios (1580–1652).[21]

This terminology of Marian slavery was further enriched and developed in seventeenth century France by the great Cardinal Pierre de Bérulle (1575–1629), the Founder of the French School of spirituality.[22] Of course, the greatest to popularize the concept of being a "slave of Jesus in Mary," or simply being a

18 Like other pontifical academies, like the Pontifical Academy of Sciences and the Pontifical Academy of Theology, it is not an academic institution, but rather a consultative body to which one may be named as a corresponding member or a full member and which the Holy See may consult on Marian matters.

19 Cf. above (chapter 1, footnotes 34–38) 26-27.

20 Cf. above (chapter 1, footnotes 48–49) 30.

21 Cf. above (chapter 1, footnotes 94–100) 41-42.

22 Cf. above (chapter 1, footnotes 101–114) 43-46.

"slave of Mary," was Saint Louis-Marie Grignion de Montfort (1673–1716).[23] As we have seen above, Pope Saint John Paul II, who often admitted that he was a disciple of Saint Louis-Marie, frequently and brilliantly defended the use of this terminology.[24]

The next *caveat* takes up the use of "words such as 'thing,' 'property,' 'instrument' to indicate, in some contexts, men and women who have become slaves of Mary." This, in fact, is very much the terminology of Saint Maximilian-Maria Kolbe, fully accepted and endorsed by Pope John Paul II.[25]

How does this hortatory paragraph conclude? "These terms are hard to reconcile with contemporary culture and hardly consonant with human dignity." This conclusion is nothing short of amazing. The "experts" of the Academy simply decided that classical concepts and terminology should be discarded in favor of being in tune with "contemporary culture," whatever that may mean. The Gospel, however, is counter-cultural, as was Jesus, who took on the form of a slave[26] for us and whose Mother, the purest of creatures, called herself the slave or handmaid of the Lord.[27] Jesus did not cling to His "equality with God," but "took on the form of a slave," thereby lifting us up to a higher dignity.

2. We turn our attention now to the second paragraph. According to the "experts" of the Academy, the term "*consecration* to Mary" should be practically limited to references to institutes of consecrated life and societies of apostolic life wherein this terminology has been canonically approved. They further state: "At the present, the concept of consecration to the Blessed Virgin has been an object of an ongoing analysis and reflection. Here we note that there appears in the texts of John Paul II

23 Cf. above (chapter 1, footnotes 125–132) 49-51.

24 Cf. above (chapter 1, footnotes 133–146) 52-56.

25 Cf. above (chapter 1, footnotes 175–193) 63-71.

26 Cf. Phil. 2:7. The Greek word used is δουλος, which may be rendered as servant or slave.

27 Cf. Lk. 1:38. The Greek word δουλη, the feminine form of δουλος, is used.

an increasing preference for the term *entrustment*."[28] As I have repeatedly indicated, John Paul II never limited himself in such a rigid way to this use of terminology.[29] Neither does this narrow use of language, which these "experts" try to impose, take into consideration the insights of Fathers Domański and Kosicki regarding the underlying Polish resonances, which we have cited above,[30] nor—even more importantly—does it do justice to the whole tradition of papal and national acts of consecration to the Hearts of Jesus and Mary, which we treated in the first three chapters of this book. Effectively these "experts" want to recast the whole tradition of Marian consecration in terms of their own agenda, and they have been doing this for years.

John Paul's Effective Response

Here are some further examples of Saint John Paul's use of the classical terminology the year of the publication of *The Mother of the Lord* in the original Italian edition and subsequently. From the Basilica of the Annunciation in Nazareth on 25 March 2000 he said: "To Mary, the *Theotókos*, the great Mother of God, I consecrate the families of the Holy Land, the families of the world."[31] In his Message to the General Chapter of the Immaculatine Franciscan Sisters of 17 June 2000 he wrote:

> The other fundamental element of your religious identity is Marian spirituality. As your rule recalls, Fr. Lodovico Acernese was distinguished by his extraordinary love of the Immaculate Virgin and, for this reason, he wanted to consecrate the institute he founded to Mary Most Holy as a "new homage to her Immaculate Conception" (*Constitutions*, n. 4).

---

28 *MotL* 77. We may note, too, that the "ongoing analysis and reflection" always took place in the same small circle.

29 Cf. above (chapter 1, paragraph immediately following footnote 193) 71; (chapter 4, footnotes 16–39) 145-151; (chapter 5, footnotes 32–59) 178-184.

30 Cf. above (chapter 4, footnote 40–45) 152-154.

31 *Inseg* XXIII/1 (2000) 457 [*ORE* 1636:10].

> Your Constitutions also indicate the most suitable way to show the institute's Marian face: "We will make that 'homage' shine in the congregation and in each one of us by a life of total consecration to the Immaculate Virgin. . . ."[32]

On the Solemnity of the Immaculate Conception in the Jubilee Year, he addressed the members of the Academy of the Immaculate: "I know that this is the day when you renew your consecration to Mary, and for this I assure you of a special remembrance in my prayer."[33]

The next year, on 24 February 2001, on the Feast of Our Lady of Confidence, Patroness of the Roman Major Seminary, he addressed the faculty and seminarians regarding the Venerable Bruno Marchesini (1915–1938):[34]

> We learn from the pages of his diary that in 1936, at the end of May during his second year of philosophical studies, he consecrated himself to the Immaculate Heart of Mary. Solemnly repeating the offering of his chastity, he wrote: "Through you, O Mary, today I have dared to present the flowering lily of my purity to Jesus, truly present in my heart under the Eucharistic veil. You inspired me to do this, you will help me preserve it with all the fervour of this day." He added, as if clearly to emphasize his thought, that this consecration expressed his intention of a "supreme dedication of love to Jesus Christ."
>
> Bruno Marchesini understood that Our Lady is the surest way to reach Jesus and to belong to him totally and for ever. This has also been my personal experience. Welcome the Blessed Virgin into your lives as your Mother, dear seminarians. May each of you have a loving knowledge of Mary's role, especially during the valuable

32 *Inseg* XXIII/1 (2000) 1116 [*ORE* 1651:5].

33 *Inseg* XXIII/2 (2000) 1055 [*ORE* 1672:3].

34 He was a seminarian from Bologna who studied at the Roman Seminary and died of meningitis before he could be ordained. On 20 December 2001, John Paul II signed the decree recognizing the heroicity of his virtues.

years of formation when you are preparing to become a priest, that is, an *"alter Christus."*[35]

In his Message to the Prior General of Carmelites of the Ancient Observance and the Superior General of the Discalced Carmelites on the Solemnity of the Annunciation 2001, commemorating the 750th Anniversary of the Scapular of Our Lady of Mount Carmel, he declared:

> This intense Marian life, which is expressed in trusting prayer, enthusiastic praise and diligent imitation, enables us to understand how the most genuine form of devotion to the Blessed Virgin, expressed by the humble sign of the Scapular, is consecration to her Immaculate Heart.[36]

In #15 of his Apostolic Letter, *Rosarium Virginis Mariæ*, of 16 October 2002, the 24th anniversary of his election to the See of Peter, he wrote:

> The Rosary mystically transports us to Mary's side as she is busy watching over the human growth of Christ in the home of Nazareth. This enables her to train us and to mold us with the same care, until Christ is "fully formed" in us (cf. Gal. 4:19). This role of Mary, totally grounded in that of Christ and radically subordinated to it, "in no way obscures or diminishes the unique mediation of Christ, but rather shows its power." This is the luminous principle expressed by the Second Vatican Council which I have so powerfully experienced in my own life and have made the basis of my episcopal motto: *Totus Tuus*. The motto is of course inspired by the teaching of Saint Louis Marie Grignion de Montfort, who explained in the following words Mary's role in the process of our configuration to Christ: *"Our entire perfection consists in being conformed, united and consecrated to Jesus Christ.* Hence the most perfect of all devotions is undoubtedly that which conforms, unites and consecrates us most perfectly to

35 *Inseg* XXIV/1 (2001) 445 [*ORE* 1686:8].

36 *Inseg* XXIV/1 (2001) 600 [*ORE* 1687:5]. He was specifically referring to the Venerable Pius XII's Letter, *Neminem profecto latet*, of 11 February 1950 [*AAS* 42 (1950) 390–391].

> Jesus Christ. Now, since Mary is of all creatures the one most conformed to Jesus Christ, it follows that among all devotions that which most consecrates and conforms a soul to our Lord is devotion to Mary, his Holy Mother, and that the more a soul is consecrated to her the more will it be consecrated to Jesus Christ." Never as in the Rosary do the life of Jesus and that of Mary appear so deeply joined. Mary lives only in Christ and for Christ![37]

Here he deliberately quoted from Saint Louis-Marie de Montfort's *Treatise on True Devotion* #120, as he would do again in his Letter of 8 December 2003 to the Men and Women Religious of the Montfort Families for the 160th Anniversary of the Publication of *Treatise on True Devotion to Mary*:

> "*All our perfection,*" St. Louis Marie Grignion de Montfort writes, "*consists in being conformed, united and consecrated to Jesus Christ*; and therefore, the most perfect of all devotions is, without any doubt, that which most perfectly conforms, unites and consecrates us to Jesus Christ. Now, Mary being the most conformed of all creatures to Jesus Christ, it follows that, of all devotions, that which most consecrates and conforms the soul to Our Lord is devotion to his holy Mother, and that the more a soul is consecrated to Mary, the more it is consecrated to Jesus" (*Treatise on True Devotion*, n. 120).[38]

In his Message of 30 July 2003 to Guides and Scouts of Europe for the Sixth European Jamboree Meeting, he wrote:

> At the Shrine of Jasna Góra, particularly dear to me, you will renew your baptismal commitment in front of Our Lady of Częstochowa, together with your scout promise and your desire to be true apostles for the love of Christ. You will renew the act of consecration to Our Lady of the Annunciation which you pronounced nearly 20 years ago in the Cathedral of Notre-Dame in Paris, on the occasion of your first European meeting. Since then, the *fiat* of

37 *Inseg* XXV/2 (2002) 497–498 [*ORE* III].

38 *Inseg* XXVI/2 (2003) 920 [*ORE* 1829:3].

> Mary in response to God's will has become a core element of the spirituality of the Guides and Scouts of Europe, especially through the *Angelus* prayer and the Rosary. May these moments of Marian prayer in this year consecrated to Our Lady of the Rosary continue to fill your days, reviving in your hearts the memory of the marvelous Redemption Christ won for us.[39]

On 15 May 2004, the day before the canonization of Don Luigi Orione (1872–1940),[40] founder of the Little Work of Divine Providence, John Paul II made an "Act of Consecration to the Virgin Mary" at the audience for pilgrims who had come to Rome for the canonization ceremonies. It began thus:

> Mary, Mother of Christ and of the Church, as we contemplate next to you in glory Luigi Orione, father of the poor and benefactor of suffering and abandoned humanity, we consecrate to you the Little Work of Divine Providence, your "work" from the beginning.
>
> Give to your little sons and daughters, O Mother, that unfailing capacity to love, which flows from the pierced Heart of the Crucified One.
>
> Give them hunger and thirst for apostolic charity after the example of their Founder, who sighed: Souls, souls![41]

On 5 November 2004, John Paul addressed the General Chapter of Augustinian Recollects with these words:

> As a little more than 75 years have passed since the Order's solemn consecration to the Most Holy Virgin Mary, I place in her hands the Chapter as it unfolds and the spiritual progress of all of your confreres. At the same time, I cordially bless everyone.[42]

39 *Inseg* XXVI/2 (2003) 95–96 [*ORE* 1808:2].

40 Cf. *John Paul II's Book of Saints* 99–101.

41 *OR* 17–18 maggio 2004, p. 6 [*ORE* 1844:7]. Curiously, this prayer is not found in the *Insegnamenti*, but was reported in the Italian daily edition of *L'Osservatore Romano* and in the weekly English edition. It is also found on the Vatican website for the date of 15 May 2004.

42 *Inseg* XXVII/2 (2004) 507 [*ORE* 1870:8].

On 13 December 2004, he addressed the Sons and Daughters of the Cross in this way:

> Dear Sons and Daughters of the Cross! Your spirituality is steeped in devotion to and love for the Virgin Mother of God.
>
> Love Our Lady, to whom you are totally consecrated, and like her, be faithful disciples of Christ. Serve the Church with enthusiasm, fostering unity and perfect harmony with the Pastors of the Christian Communities to whom you offer your pastoral cooperation. This will make you effective witnesses of the One who, from high on the Cross, entrusted us all as children to his sweetest Mother.
>
> May the Immaculate Conception continue to guide your steps and make you conform ever more closely to Jesus, who in a few days we will contemplate as a Child in the mystery of Holy Christmas. I express my fervent good wishes to you for the Christmas celebrations, and I cordially bless you all.[43]

The Rationale of the "Experts"

I have supplied all these examples to prove that, up until the end of his days, Saint John Paul II was not at all influenced by the dictates of the Pontifical International Marian Academy and, in all likelihood, was totally unaware of them. Nonetheless the "experts" were zealously promoting their policy. One can easily date this agenda as far back as 1984 with the publication of a work edited by the late Don Domenico Bertetto, S.D.B. (1914–1988).[44] The reader may recall him as one who proposed the distinction between "descending" and "ascending" consecration.[45] In that volume Don Egidio Viganò, S.D.B. (1920–1995), the then Rector Major of the Salesians of Don

43 *Inseg* XXVII/2 (2004) 698[*ORE* 1874:2].

44 Domenico Bertetto ed., *L'Affidamento a Maria* (Roma: Libreria Ateneo Salesiano, 1984).

45 Cf. above (chapter 7, footnote 30) 243-244.

Bosco, gave what he purported to be the authentic interpretation of #5 of the Second Vatican Council's Decree on the Renewal of Religious Life, *Perfectæ Caritatis*, which states that members of religious institutes

> have dedicated their lives to his [God's] service. This constitutes a special consecration, which is deeply rooted in their baptismal consecration and is a fuller expression of it. [*Totam enim vitam suam Eius famulatui mancipaverunt, quod quidem constituit peculiarem quamdam consecrationem, quae in baptismatis consecratione intime radicatur eamque plenius exprimit.*][46]

Don Viganò went on to say

> Before Vatican II one was used to speaking of an *act of consecration* to Our Lady. The Council specified the real theological meaning of the term *consecration*, even if it couldn't change the current use of this word proposed with other less exact theological meanings. From then on one began to have a concern for greater precision in the ecclesial use of such a term. The present Pope, John Paul II, has favored the use of another word, *entrustment*, to indicate better the relationship of affection, of donation, of putting oneself at the disposition, of belonging, of free "servitude," of trust of support with regard to the maternal patronage of Mary, the collaborator of Christ for the Kingdom. …
>
> Someone may ask what the difference is between an *act of consecration* and an *act of entrustment*. It does not refer merely to a change of terms, but to a deepening of concepts. For Vatican II *consecration* is an act carried out by God: a dynamism which descends from above to seal a divine plan assigned to one who is called: man "is consecrated" by God through the ministry of the Church. Speaking, then, of the personal act of response to consecration, the Council prefers to speak of the consecrated that they "have offered

46 *PC* #5; *Sacrosanctum Oecumenicum Concilium Vaticanum II: Constitutiones, Decreta, Declarationes* (Vatican City: Typis Polyglottis Vaticanis, 1974) 333; *Flan* 614.

> their lives totally to the service of God" (*mancipaverunt*), and that they pledge themselves in the Church with an "offering of self" (*suipsius donatio*). …
>
> It is good to have this clear theological vision of "consecration," which comes from above, and that of "donation" or "self-offering" or of "entrustment" which comes from us. God accomplished consecration by means of the Church; this is basically that of Baptism, of Confirmation, of Holy Orders (for deacons and priests), and that of religious profession.[47]

Frankly, I find it difficult to grasp how any supposed "expert" could take one text of the Second Vatican Council that has to do with consecrated persons and make an arbitrary application of it in the field of Mariology to which the text itself does not refer! Since chapter five I have been stressing that the theological justification for consecration to Our Lady is based on the two fundamental principles of the concept of analogy and that of Marian mediation. I have amply illustrated both of these from the entire tradition and specifically from the teaching of Saint John Paul II. Now we find a supposedly newly discovered principle from Vatican II, which purportedly provides a deeper insight into putting one's life into the hands of Our Lady and is thus meant to transform mariological terminology. Sadly, it is not a revolutionary new insight, but an instance of the fundamental ignorance of basic metaphysics as understood in Catholic philosophy and theology for millennia.[48] What is even more, it undermines and effectively negates the terminology employed by the magisterium itself.

Not surprisingly, the late Stefano De Fiores found this "Salesian solution" highly acceptable and promoted it in articles

47 Egidio Viganò, S.D.B., "Atto di Affidamento della Congregazione Salesiana a Maria Ausiliatrice – Madre della Chiesa," in Domenico Bertetto ed., *L'Affidamento a Maria* (Roma: Libreria Ateneo Salesiano, 1984) 19–20 (my translation).

48 Cf. John P. Noonan, S.J., *General Metaphysics* (Chicago: Loyola University Press, 1957) 91–104; Enrico Zoffoli, *Principi di Filosofia* (Cipi: Edizioni "Fonti Vivere," 1988) 84–87.

in his *Maria – Nuovissimo Dizionario*.[49] I have not found specific references to the "Salesian solution" in Laurentin's book, *The Meaning of Consecration Today*,[50] because it lacks almost all scholarly apparatus and has only very few footnotes, but the book does show itself to be in complete agreement with it.[51] The book clearly manifests Laurentin's all but complete refusal to take the concept of analogy seriously,[52] his misrepresentation and over-simplification of many of the great moments in the history of Marian consecration[53] and his insistence of the need for "purification of vocabulary."[54]

More nuanced is the treatment of Marian consecration in #204 of the *Directory on Popular Piety and the Liturgy: Principles and Guidelines*, published by the Congregation for Divine Worship and the Discipline of the Sacraments:

> The history of Marian devotion contains many examples of personal or collective acts of "consecration or entrustment to the Blessed Virgin Mary" (*oblatio, servitus, commendatio, dedicatio*). They are reflected in the prayer manuals and statutes of many associations where the formulas and prayers of consecration, or its remembrance, are used.
>
> The Roman Pontiffs have frequently expressed appreciation for the pious practice of "consecration to the Blessed Virgin Mary" and the formulas publicly used by them are well known.
>
> Louis Grignion de Montfort is one of the great masters of the spirituality underlying the act of "consecration to Mary." He "proposed to the faithful consecration to

49 Stefano De Fiores, *Maria – Nuovissimo Dizionario* 1 (Bologna: Edizioni Dehoniane Bologna, 2006) 7–8; 388–389.

50 René Laurentin, *The Meaning of Consecration Today: A Marian Model for a Secularized Age*, trans. Kenneth D. Whitehead (San Francisco: Ignatius Press, 1992). Cf. my review of this book in *Divinitas* XXXVII (1993) 304–308.

51 *The Meaning of Consecration Today* 92–108.

52 *The Meaning of Consecration Today* 50, 118, 128, 133, 134, 160, 202.

53 *The Meaning of Consecration Today* 47–90; 106–117; 191–193.

54 *The Meaning of Consecration Today* 118–122.

Jesus through Mary, as an effective way of living out their baptismal commitment."

Seen in the light of Christ's words (cf. John 19, 25–27), the act of consecration is a conscious recognition of the singular role of Mary in the Mystery of Christ and of the Church, of the universal and exemplary importance of her witness to the Gospel, of trust in her intercession, and of the efficacy of her patronage, of the many maternal functions she has, since she is a true mother in the order of grace to each and every one of her children.

It should be recalled, however, that the term "consecration" is used here in a broad and non-technical sense: "the expression is used of 'consecrating children to Our Lady', by which is intended placing children under her protection and asking her maternal blessing for them." Some suggest the use of the alternative terms "entrustment" or "gift." Liturgical theology and the consequent rigorous use of terminology would suggest reserving the term *consecration* for those self-offerings which have God as their object, and which are characterized by totality and perpetuity, which are guaranteed by the Church's intervention and have as their basis the Sacraments of Baptism and Confirmation.

The faithful should be carefully instructed about the practice of consecration to the Blessed Virgin Mary. While such can give the impression of being a solemn and perpetual act, it is, in reality, only analogously a "consecration to God." It springs from a free, personal, mature, decision taken in relation to the operation of grace and not from a fleeting emotion. It should be expressed in a correct liturgical manner: to the Father, through Christ in the Holy Spirit, imploring the intercession of the Blessed Virgin Mary, to whom we entrust ourselves completely, so as to keep our baptismal commitments and live as her children. The act of consecration should take place outside of the celebration of the Eucharistic Sacrifice, since it is a devotional act which cannot be assimilated to the Liturgy. It should also be borne in mind that the act

> of consecration to Mary differs substantially from other forms of liturgical consecration.[55]

Since this is an official document of the Holy See, approved by the Supreme Pontiff, it should be treated and received with respect, but I believe that it is not beyond critique. First of all—and happily—it does not rule out the use of the term "consecration to the Blessed Virgin Mary" and, in fact, "Consecration and Entrustment to Mary" is its heading. Hence, it does not subscribe to the "Salesian solution." On the other hand, I believe that saying "that the term 'consecration' is used here in a broad and non-technical sense" is not exactly in accord with the definition of the Venerable Pius XII,[56] with the great tradition which I have outlined in the first three chapters of this work, or with the use of this term and analogous terms in the pastoral practice of Saint John Paul II. Again, saying that "the practice of consecration to the Blessed Virgin" is "only analogously a 'consecration to God'" does not seem to me a very accurate use of terminology, nor to appreciate the depth of the concept of analogy. Quoting from Saint Louis-Marie de Montfort, however, does help to clarify the concept along with the statement about "imploring the intercession of the Blessed Virgin Mary, to whom we entrust ourselves completely, so as to keep our baptismal commitments and live as her children."

---

55 Congregation for Divine Worship and the Discipline of the Sacraments, *Directory on Popular Piety and the Liturgy: Principles and Guidelines* (Boston: Pauline Books & Media, 2002) 144–145.

56 Cf. above (chapter 4, footnote 11) 144. This is the description of Marian consecration made by the Venerable Pius XII in his allocution to representatives of the Marian Congregations on 21 January 1945 that has since become a classic definition: "Consecration to the Mother of God in the Marian Congregation is a total gift of oneself, for life and for eternity; it is not just a mere matter of form nor a gift of mere sentiment, but it is an effective gift, fulfilled in an intensity of Christian and Marian life, in the apostolic life, making the member of the Congregation a minister of Mary and, as it were, her hands visible on earth through the spontaneous flow of a superabundant interior life which overflows in all the exterior works of deep devotion, of worship, of charity, of zeal." Cf. Domenico Bertetto, S.D.B., *Il Magistero Mariano di Pio XII* (Rome: Edizioni Paoline, 1956) #136 [*OL* #389].

Mary's Maternal Mediation

Now let us turn again to the guidelines and exhortations of the Pontifical International Marian Academy's *The Mother of the Lord: Memory, Presence, Hope*, with regard to "Mary's Mediation," in #52.

> Today, many theologians, with a commendable intention of deepening and making this doctrine more precise, speak of the mediation of Mary from different points of view and in new terms. *Many of the aspects of the doctrine of Mary's mediation—its nature, its scope, and its relation with other forms of subordinate mediation—are disputed among theologians*, for which reason a renewed and more profound study of these questions is necessary.[57] *We believe that such a study should not be undertaken with the intention, terminology and images used by many theologians before Vatican II, but rather that the orientation and directives outlined in Lumen Gentium be followed.* John Paul II has often considered the cooperation of the Virgin in the Trinitarian salvific plan under the terms "the mediation of Christ" and "maternal mediation," that is, as one aspect of Mary's universal motherhood in the order of grace. Many theologians regard this context for studying Mary's mediation as a profitable one, based on sound biblical foundations (cf. Jn. 19:26–27), in accord with the *sensus fidelium*, and less subject to controversy.[58]

One immediately notices here the statement that Our Lady's mediation is disputed among theologians. The question, of course, is "Who are these theologians?" And the obvious answer is the drafters of this document. We know it from their writings.

---

57 In this regard, the Pontifical International Marian Academy published the following statement in The Declaration of the Theological Commission of the Pontifical International Marian Academy (August 1996): "Even if the titles were assigned a content and could be accepted as belonging to the deposit of faith, the definition of these titles, however, in the present situation would be lacking in theological clarity, as such titles and doctrines inherent in them still require further study in a renewed Trinitarian, ecclesiological, and anthropological perspective" (*OR* 4 giugno 1997, p. 12 [*ORE* 1494:12]).

58 *MotL* 68–69 (emphasis my own).

One has only to consult Stefano De Fiores' article on "Mediatrix" to discover virtually all the objectors to the traditional language of Marian mediation, their objections, their refusal to give a serious hearing to those who argue in favor of the millennial tradition and language, and his conclusion that a future doctrinal definition could only be based on agreement among all Christian ecclesial bodies.[59] One can only ask: "Since when is the deposit of faith established by those outside of the household of Catholic faith?" The footnote appended to this statement is a declaration drawn up in Częstochowa, Poland in August of 1996 and released almost a year later, in June of 1997. Instead of presenting the question to a study group well informed on the topic, it was presented, with no previous notice, to most of the participants, at an "ecumenical round table," consisting of 18 Catholics, 3 Orthodox, 1 Anglican and 1 Lutheran. Should their statement surprise anyone? All of this was carefully orchestrated and published in *L'Osservatore Romano*, the Vatican daily newspaper of 4 June 1997, while Pope John Paul II was on an apostolic visit to Poland.

The Predecessors of the "Experts"

Now we must take a step back in order to grasp fully the prehistory of the position of the "experts." First of all, the controversy about Mary's active collaboration in the work of the redemption has been a bone of contention among theologians of the twentieth century at least since Cardinal Alexis M. Lépicier, O.S.M. (1863–1936),[60] gave his noteworthy discourse on "Mary, Immaculate and Coredemptrix"[61] in 1904, commemorating the

59 Stefano De Fiores, *Maria - Nuovissimo Dizionario* 2 (Bologna: Edizioni Dehoniane Bologna, 2006) 1082–1141.

60 Cf. Angelo M. Tentori, O.S.M., "Mary Coredemptress in the Writings of Cardinal Alexis Henry Mary Lépicier, O.S.M.," in *Mary at the Foot of the Cross – II: Acts of the Second International Symposium on Marian Coredemption* (New Bedford, MA: Academy of the Immaculate, 2002) 361–379.

61 He developed it and published it as *L'Immaculée Mère de Dieu, corédemptrice du genre humain* (Tournhut, Belgium, 1906).

50th anniversary of the dogmatic definition of the Immaculate Conception.[62] Despite the movement of the papal magisterium in favor of Mary's active collaboration in the work of the redemption, the successors of the opponents and the proponents took up their positions during the Second Vatican Council. The opponents, seemingly primarily for ecumenical reasons,[63] wished to avoid any statement on Mary's mediation,[64] even though in a pre-conciliar consultation 382 bishops asked for a statement on Mary's mediation and 266 of them expressed a desire that the matter be defined.[65] The statement which did emerge in #60–62 of *Lumen Gentium*, while theologically sound, did not advance the question as far as the previous papal magisterium had done,[66] and reference to Mary as mediatrix was deliberately attenuated by apposition with more indeterminate titles such as advocate, helper and benefactress [*advocata, auxiliatrix, adiutrix*]. On the other hand, it was the last of the four titles listed, and to it was appended footnote 16 referring to four very strong statements about Mary's mediation from Pope Leo XIII, Pope Saint Pius X, Pope Pius XI and the Venerable Pope Pius XII. Further, this text of the Council has very often been subject to a "minimizing" interpretation.

62 Cf. Brunero Gherardini, *La Corredentrice nel mistero di Cristo e della Chiesa* (Rome: Edizioni Vivere In, 1998). Monsignor Gherardini discussed the positions of the opponents from pp. 40 to 65 and of the proponents from pp. 65 to 78.

63 Cf. René Laurentin, *The Question of Mary*, trans. I. G. Pidoux (New York: Holt, Rinehart and Winston, 1965) 138; Salvatore Meo, O.S.M., "La 'Mediazione materna' di Maria nell'Enciclica Redemptoris Mater," *Redemptoris Mater: Contenuti e Prospettive Dottrinali e Pastorali* (Rome: Pontificia Accademia Mariana Internazionale, 1988) 150, 154.

64 The titles "Mediatrix" and "Mother of the Church" effectively constituted the most contested matters and heated battles during the Council. Cf. Wiltgen, *The Rhine Flows into the Tiber* 91–95, 155, 156, 157, 158–159; *Theotokos* 242–245, 251–253; Arthur Burton Calkins, "Mary and the Church in the Papal Magisterium Before and After the Second Vatican Council," in *Mary at the Foot of the Cross – IX: Mary: Spouse of the Holy Spirit, Coredemptrix and Mother of the Church* (New Bedford, MA: Academy of the Immaculate, 2010) 31–38.

65 Cf. O'Carroll, "Still Mediatress?" 122.

66 Cf. above (chapter 5, footnote 77) 195.

With the publication of his book, *Mary: Coredemptrix, Mediatrix, Advocate*,[67] Dr. Mark I. Miravalle, a professor of the Franciscan University of Steubenville, launched a movement in favor of a papal definition of Mary as Coredemptrix, Mediatrix and Advocate. The movement quickly ignited a furor among those who considered themselves the official guardians and arbiters of Marian theology. In 1995, Miravalle published the first of a number of books of theological essays expounding on Our Lady's active collaboration in the work of redemption and immediately related issues.[68] This book was duly reviewed in the pages of *Marianum*, the journal of the Pontifical Faculty of the same name, by the then Don Angelo Amato, S.D.B.[69] As a contributor to the volume of 1995, I felt that the treatment in that article was rather demeaning, so I asked and was granted the opportunity to write a rebuttal, which was also published in *Marianum*.[70] In the midst of my exchange with Don Amato, the Częstochowa declaration was signed in 1996 and subsequently published on 4 June 1997 in *L'Osservatore Romano*, along with two other articles strongly critical of the movement for a definition.[71]

67 Mark I. Miravalle, *Mary: Coredemptrix, Mediatrix, Advocate* (Santa Barbara, CA: Queenship Publishing, 1993).

68 Mark I. Miravalle, S.T.D., (ed.), *Mary Coredemptrix, Mediatrix, Advocate, Theological Foundations: Towards a Papal Definition?* (Santa Barbara, CA: Queenship Publishing, 1995).

69 Angelo Amato, S.D.B., "Verso un Altro Dogma Mariano?" *Marianum* LVIII (1996) 229–232.

70 Arthur Burton Calkins, "'Towards Another Marian Dogma?' A Response to Father Angelo Amato, S.D.B." *Marianum* LIX (1997) 159–167.

71 "Richiesta della definizione del dogma di Maria Mediatrice, Corredentrice e Avvocata: Dichiarazione della Commissione teologica del Congresso del Częstochowa"; "Un nuovo dogma mariano?" Salvatore Perrella, O.S.M., "La cooperazione di Maria all'opera della Redenzione: Attualità di una questione," *OR* 4 June 1997 pp. 10–11. These were duly published in the English edition as well: "Declaration of the Theological Commission of the Pontifical International Marian Academy: Request for the definition of the dogma of Mary as Mediatrix, Coredemptrix and Advocate," *ORE* 1494:12; "A new Marian dogma?" *ORE* 1497:10; Salvatore M. Perrella, O.S.M., "Mary's Co-operation in Work of Redemption: Present State of a Question," *ORE* 1498:9–10.

René Laurentin also weighed in with highly critical articles discouraging any petitions to the Holy See for such a definition.[72] Clearly, the "experts," who were in charge, did not take kindly to this challenge to their authority. Furthermore they enjoyed the full confidence and support of the organisms of the Holy See. In 1998, a dossier was published in *Marianum*[73] stemming from a consultation, which I attended and at which I was the only one who spoke in favor of the proposed dogma. Here, I must pay homage to the late Ignazio M. Calabuig Adan, O.S.M. (1931–2005),[74] a Catalan Servite, who served in various capacities at the Pontifical Faculty Marianum from 1958 until his death. He was the editor of the journal *Marianum* at the time that I asked to respond to Don Amato's review, and he graciously consented. He invited me to attend the study day at the Marianum on 28 May 1998, and in a footnote in his article in that dossier he said of my published article on this matter in Italian:[75]

> With commendable precision the list of the usage of the title *Coredemptrix* in the magisterium of the Supreme Pontiffs was traced: A. BURTON CALKINS. *Il mistero di Maria Coredenrice nel magistero pontificio*, in A.A.V.V. *Maria Corredentrice*, I (cit. nota 4), pp. 141–220. The accurate and exhaustive study confirms what I have written: on the one hand *Coredemptrix* is not a proscribed title; it is susceptible to being correctly understood, which nonetheless requires some previous explanations of a linguistic and theological nature; on the other hand,

72 "Pétitions internationales pour une définition dogmatique de la médiation et la corédemption," *Marianum* LVIII (1996) 429–446; "Something to Consider Before you Sign," *Marian Library Newsletter*, No. 36 (new series), Summer 1998, 4.

73 "Dossier di una Giornata Teologica sulla Richiesta di Definizione Dogmatica di 'Maria Corredentrice Mediatrice Avvocata,' 28 Maggio 1998: Nota Introduttiva, Relazione Base di Ignazio M. Calabuig, Repertorio Bibliografico di Antonio Escudero Cabello" *Marianum* LXI (1999) 123–211.

74 Cf. "In Memoriam Prof. Ignacio (Rafael) M. Calabuig Adán, OSM." *Marianum* LXVII (2005) 551–589.

75 "Il Mistero di Maria Corredentrice nel Magistero Pontificio," in Autori Vari, *Maria Corredentrice: Storia e Teologia I* (Frigento [AV]: Casa Mariana Editrice "Bibliotheca Corredemptionis B. V. Mariae" Studi e Richerche 1, 1998) 141–220.

> such a title was rarely used by Supreme Pontiffs and in documents not of a magisterial character.[76]

All of these proceedings led up to the guidelines and exhortations in *The Mother of the Lord*. An earlier movement in favor of a definition of Marian mediation launched by Cardinal Désiré-Joseph Mercier (1851–1926) has been chronicled by Manfred Hauke[77] and Gloria Falcão Dodd.[78] This is only a partial and personal account, but by one who was involved from the beginning and remains involved as a protagonist of the movement launched by Miravalle.

All of this provides the necessary background for understanding the principle of Mary's mediation, which flows from her active collaboration in the work of the redemption, commonly referred to as Marian coredemption. This is not to say that Mary redeemed the world as an equal of Jesus, but that He redeemed the world in union with her, that He was the new Adam and she the new Eve, always secondary and subordinate to Him and totally dependent on Him, but nonetheless His helpmate.[79] This is also clearly taught in the *Catechism of the Catholic Church*:

---

76 Ignazio M. Calabuig e il Comitato di redazione della rivista "Marianum," "Riflessione sulla richiesta della definizione dogmatica di 'Maria corredentrice, mediatrice avvocata,'" *Marianum* LXI (1999) 157 (my translation). I would simply add that once the linguistic and theological precision is understood, there is no better word to describe Mary's unique position in the work of redemption. Words such as "cooperator," "collaborator," "co-worker," "partner," "ally," "associate," "sharer" may be affirmed of all of us. If a better word can be proposed, let it be proposed.

77 Manfred Hauke, *Mary, "Mediatress of Grace": Mary's Universal Mediation of Grace in the Theological and Pastoral Works of Cardinal Mercier*. Supplement to *Mary at the Foot of the Cross – IV: Mater Viventium (Gen. 3:20). Acts of the Fourth International Symposium on Marian Coredemption* (New Bedford, MA: Academy of the Immaculate, 2004).

78 Gloria Falcão Dodd, *The Virgin Mary, Mediatrix of All Grace: History and Theology of the Movement for a Dogmatic Definition from 1896 to 1964* (New Bedford, MA: Academy of the Immaculate, 2012).

79 Cf. Arthur Burton Calkins, "Mary Coredemptrix: The Beloved Associate of Christ," in Mark Miravalle (ed.), *Mariology: A Guide for Priests, Deacons, Seminarians, and Consecrated Persons* (Goleta, CA: Seat of Wisdom Books, 2007) 349–356 and passim to 409.

> In fact Jesus desires to associate with his redeeming sacrifice those who were to be its first beneficiaries. This is achieved supremely in the case of his mother, who was associated more intimately than any other person in the mystery of his redemptive suffering.[80]

Perhaps the single text of the papal magisterium that best illustrates how Mary's mediation and spiritual maternity flow from her participation in the work of redemption comes from Pope Saint Pius X's Encyclical, *Ad Diem Illum*:

> When the supreme hour of the Son came, beside the cross of Jesus there stood Mary, His Mother, not merely occupied in contemplating the cruel spectacle, but rejoicing that her only Son was offered for the salvation of mankind; and so entirely participating in His Passion that, if it had been possible "she would have gladly borne all the torments that her Son underwent" [St. Bonaventure, *I Sent*, d. 48, ad Litt. dub. 4].
>
> From this community of will and suffering between Christ and Mary "she merited to become most worthily the reparatrix of the lost world" (Eadmer, *De Excellentia Virg. Mariæ*, c. 9) and dispensatrix of all the gifts that our Savior purchased for us by his death and by his blood.
>
> It cannot of course be denied that the dispensing of these treasures is the particular and supreme right of Jesus Christ, for they are the exclusive fruit of His death, who by His Nature is the Mediator between God and man. Nevertheless, by this union in sorrow and suffering, We have said, which existed between the Mother and the Son, it has been allowed to the August Virgin "to be the most powerful Mediatrix and advocate of the whole world, with her Divine Son" (cf. *Ineffabilis Deus* [*OL* #64]).
>
> The source, then, is Jesus Christ, "and of his fullness we have all received" (Jn. 1:16); "from him the whole body (being closely joined and knit together through every joint of the system according to the functioning in due measure of each single part) derives its increase to the building up

80 *CCC* #618.

> of itself in love." But Mary, as St. Bernard justly remarks, is the "aqueduct," or if you will, the neck by which the body is joined to the head and the head transmits to the body its power and virtue: "For she is the neck of our Head, by which he communicated to his mystical Body all spiritual gifts" (St. Bern. Sen., *Quadrag. de Evangelio æterno*, Serm. X, a. 3, c. 3).
>
> We are thus, it will be seen, very far from declaring the Mother of God to be the authoress of supernatural grace. Grace comes from God alone. But since she surpassed all in holiness and union with Christ, and has been associated with Christ in the work of redemption, she, as the expression is, merits *de congruo* what Christ merits *de condigno*, and is the principal minister in the distribution of grace. He sits at the right hand of the Majesty on high (Heb. 1:3); but Mary sits as a Queen on His right hand, the securest refuge of those who are in peril, as well as the most faithful of helpers, so that we have naught to fear or despair of, as long as she is our guide and our patroness, she is our defender and our protector (cf. *Ineffabilis Deus* [*OL* #65]).
>
> With these principles laid down and returning to our subject, will it not appear to all that it is right and proper to affirm that Mary, whom Jesus made His constant companion from the house of Nazareth to the place of Calvary, knew, as no other knew, the secrets of His heart, distributes as by a mother's right the treasures of His merits, and is the surest help to the knowledge and love of Christ? They prove it only too truly who, by their deplorable manner of life, deceived by false teaching, or the wiles of the devil, fancy they can dispense with the aid of the Virgin Mother. Miserable and unhappy are they who neglect her under pretense that thus they honor Christ. They forget that the "Child is not found without Mary His Mother" (cf. Mt. 2:11; Lk. 2:16).[81]

What the Pope says with Latin phrases is this: what Jesus does *de condigno* as the God-man, Mary does *de congruo* as being

81 *ASS* 36 (1903–1904) 451–457 [*OL* #232–235]; *D-H* #3370.

entirely appropriate. Further, this text is referred in footnote 16 of *Lumen Gentium* #62.

The trick for the "experts" was to present what had been well established in the papal magisterium, including that of John Paul II, on Marian coredemption and mediation, delineated by Brunero Gherardini as *proxima fidei* (close to faith)[82] and, therefore, capable of being defined, as merely a matter of unedifying theological argumentation and not sufficiently ecumenical. Here is how they attempted to impose their position in #69 and 70 of *The Mother of the Lord*:

> Genuine ecumenism does not compromise or change the *depositum fidei* on the Blessed Virgin Mary, but proposes, through shared and sincere study and dialog, to help the brothers and sisters of other Christian confessions to know the full revelation concerning Mary of Nazareth and to ponder their situation in view of our historical and cultural explanation of the image of the Virgin Mary. *We believe that it would be a serious disappointment if the current discussions on the Mother of God would be an obstacle to rather than a factor for promoting Christian unity.*
>
> Relying on the teaching of John Paul II, we believe it opportune to recall some principles and norms which should guide theologians in mariological questions. They should follow the lines traced out in Vatican II's decree *Unitatis redintegratio* and the constitution *Lumen Gentium*, which urge theologians to "carefully refrain from whatever might by word or deed lead the separated brethren or any others whatsoever into error about the true doctrine of the Church." …
>
> This requires that Marian studies:
> – avoid long-standing prejudices (through *a purification of the historical memory*) and eliminate "expressions,

82 Cf. Brunero Gherardini, "The Coredemption of Mary: Doctrine of the Church," in *Mary at the Foot of the Cross – II: Acts of the Second International Symposium on Marian Coredemption* (New Bedford, MA: Academy of the Immaculate, 2002) 43. "This means it belongs to Revelation, and even if not explicit, it is beyond doubt. It is not *de fide,* because there is lacking the relative ecclesiastical definition." Cf. entire article *passim*.

> judgments and actions which do not represent the condition of our separated brethren with truth and fairness and so make mutual relations with them more difficult";...
> – refrain from imposing on brothers and sisters not in full communion with the Catholic Church "any burden beyond that which is strictly necessary (cf. Acts 15:28), *a counsel especially applicable to doctrinal matters concerning Mary which are disputed even among Catholic theologians themselves.*
> – use carefully, with great surveillance, terms and formulas related to the Virgin Mary (*purification of language*). *Words or formulas which are not of ancient provenance or are not accepted by a great number of Catholic theologians do not promote mutual understanding*; moreover, they arouse grave uneasiness among our brothers and sisters who are not in full communion with the Church; it is best to use terms which express the doctrine precisely and effectively without allowing the possibility of false interpretations.[83]

Of course, "Genuine ecumenism does not compromise or change the *depositum fidei* on the Blessed Virgin Mary," but the "experts" effectively go on to imply that any teaching on Mary's active collaboration in the work of the redemption and mediation of grace is merely an in-house dispute and would be upsetting to our separated brethren. First of all, a clear distinction needs to be made between "development of doctrine" in the Catholic Church and ecumenical dialogue. John Paul himself would point out that speaking of Mary's active collaboration in the work of the redemption is not a new concept, but deeply rooted in the tradition and has been developing for at least a millennium:

> At the end of the second century, St. Irenaeus, a disciple of Polycarp, already pointed out Mary's contribution to the work of salvation. He understood the value of Mary's consent at the time of the Annunciation, recognizing in the Virgin of Nazareth's obedience to and faith in the angel's message the perfect antithesis of Eve's disobedience

83 *MotL* 104–106 (emphasis my own).

and disbelief, with a beneficial effect on humanity's destiny. In fact, just as Eve caused death, so Mary, with her "yes," became "a cause of salvation" for herself and for all mankind (cf. *Adv. Haer.*, III, 22, 4; *SC* 211, 441). But this affirmation was not developed in a consistent and systematic way by the other Fathers of the Church.

Instead, this doctrine was systematically worked out for the first time at the end of the 10th century in the *Life of Mary* by a Byzantine monk, John the Geometer. Here Mary is united to Christ in the whole work of Redemption, sharing, according to God's plan, in the Cross and suffering for our salvation. She remained united to the Son "in every deed, attitude and wish" (cf. *Life of Mary*, Bol. 196, f. 123 v.).

In the West St. Bernard, who died in 1153, turns to Mary and comments on the presentation of Jesus in the temple: "Offer your Son, sacrosanct Virgin, and present the fruit of your womb to the Lord. For our reconciliation with all, offer the heavenly victim pleasing to God" (*Serm. 3 in Purif.*, 2: *PL* 183, 370).

A disciple and friend of St. Bernard, Arnold of Chartres, shed light particularly on Mary's offering in the sacrifice of Calvary. He distinguished in the Cross "two altars: one in Mary's heart, the other in Christ's body. Christ sacrificed his flesh, Mary her soul." Mary sacrificed herself spiritually in deep communion with Christ, and implored the world's salvation: "What the mother asks, the Son approves and the Father grants" (cf. *De septem verbis Domini in cruce*, 3: *PL* 189, 1694).

From this age on other authors explain the doctrine of Mary's special cooperation in the redemptive sacrifice.

At the same time, in Christian worship and piety contemplative reflection on Mary's "compassion" developed, poignantly depicted in images of the *Pietà*. Mary's sharing in the drama of the Cross makes this event more deeply human and helps the faithful to enter into the mystery: the Mother's compassion more clearly reveals the Passion of the Son.

> By sharing in Christ's redemptive work, Mary's spiritual and universal motherhood is also recognized. In the East, John the Geometer told Mary: "You are our mother." Giving Mary thanks "for the sorrow and suffering she bore for us," he sheds light on her maternal affection and motherly regard for all those who receive salvation (cf. Farewell Discourse on the Dormition of Our Most Glorious Lady, Mother of God, in A. Wenger, *L'Assomption de la Très Sainte Vierge dans la tradition byzantine*, p. 407). …
>
> The Second Vatican Council, after stating that Mary "in a wholly singular way cooperated in the work of the Saviour," concludes: "for this reason she is a mother to us in the order of grace" (*Lumen Gentium*, n. 61), thus confirming the Church's perception that Mary is at the side of her Son as the spiritual Mother of all humanity.[84]

The question as to whether one calls Mary's "sharing in Christ's redemptive work" coredemption or something else is quite secondary. The approach of the "experts" would have effectively stifled any of the Marian dogmas already defined: Mother of God, Ever Virgin, Immaculate Conception and Assumption.

The "experts" were also clever in their selective citing of John Paul II. For instance, the International Theological Commission, under the guidance of the then Cardinal Ratzinger, produced a document in 1999 entitled *Memory and Reconciliation: The Church and the Faults of the Past*, as a preparation for the Jubilee Year of 2000; and it was followed up by John Paul II, who openly confessed the faults of the Church in the past and asked forgiveness for them. The "experts" seized upon this terminology and proposed "a purification of the historical memory" and, even more specifically, a "purification of language," i.e., "words or formulas which are not of ancient provenance or are not accepted by a great number of Catholic theologians" and which obviously "do not promote mutual understanding." They had already stated that "terminology and images used by many theologians

84 *Inseg* XVIII/2 (1995) 934–937 [*ORE* 1414:11].

before Vatican II" should be eschewed. Then they went a step further and implied that such terminology as coredemption and mediation should be avoided as a "purification of language," as if it were sinful. We have already noted Laurentin's proposal of "purification of vocabulary."[85] The fact is that John Paul II promoted none of this abandonment of classical mariological vocabulary in any way.

John Paul's Effective Response

The genius of John Paul II's treatment of Mary's maternal mediation in *Redemptoris Mater* #21–22 and 38–41 is that it gave the Council's handling of the matter a "maximizing" interpretation; it was a veritable *tour de force*.[86] This matter is crucial because the Pope, as well as all reputable theologians before him, readily admitted that Mary is not the *terminus ad quem* of consecration;[87] rather, she is the one *through whom* (*per manus Mariae*) we may renew our consecration to Christ.[88] Now, without a doubt the theology of Mary's mediation had already been firmly established in the magisterium from the middle of the eighteenth century up until the Second Vatican Council.[89] While his treatment of the matter in *Redemptoris Mater* did not represent a specific advance on the part of the magisterium, it was a salutary reaffirmation of the Church's teaching after more than twenty years of hesitancy on this issue among theologians,

85 Cf. above (footnote 54) 336.

86 Cf. the interesting conclusions drawn about John Paul's development and deepening of the Council's teaching in Meo, "La 'Mediazione materna'" 155–157.

87 *Redemptoris Mater* #46: "This filial relationship, this self-entrusting of a child to its mother, not only has its *beginning in Christ* but can also be said to be *definitively directed towards him*." *Inseg* X/1 (1987) 736 [St. Paul edition 65].

88 *Redemptoris Mater* #47: "I would like to recall, among the many witnesses and teachers of this spirituality, the figure of Saint Louis-Marie Grignion de Montfort, who proposes consecration to Christ through the hands of Mary, as an effective means for Christians to live faithfully their baptismal commitments." *Inseg* X/1 (1987) 739 [St. Paul edition 68].

89 Cf. above (chapter 5, footnote 77) 195.

although it did not stop the march of many of them in the opposite direction.[90] I have treated this matter at some length in chapter five.[91]

Mary Coredemptrix

I have also treated John Paul II's teaching about Mary's active collaboration in the work of redemption, also known as Marian coredemption, at notable length,[92] and can only do so briefly here with one extraordinary text from his Apostolic Letter, *Salvifici Doloris*, of 11 February 1984, "On the Christian Meaning of Human Suffering." In #24 of that profoundly insightful document he declared: "The sufferings of Christ created the good of the world's Redemption. This good in itself is inexhaustible and infinite. No man can add anything to it."[93] Then he went on to state in #25:

> It is especially consoling to note—and also accurate in accordance with the Gospel and history—that at the side of Christ, in the first and most exalted place, there is always His Mother through the exemplary testimony that she bears *by her whole life* to this particular Gospel of suffering. In her, the many and intense sufferings were amassed in such an interconnected way that they were not

90 Cf. René Laurentin, *Queen of Heaven: A Short Treatise on Marian Theology*, trans. Gordon Smith (Dublin: Clonmore & Reynolds Ltd.; London: Burns Oates & Washbourne Ltd., 1956) 123–24; *The Question of Mary* 43–46; *A Year of Grace with Mary* 154–155; De Fiores, *Maria nella Teologia Contemporanea 248–250.*

91 Cf. above (chapter 5, footnotes 65–86) 187-199.

92 Cf. Arthur Burton Calkins, "Pope John Paul II's Ordinary Magisterium on Marian Coredemption: Consistent Teaching and More Recent Perspectives," in *Mary at the Foot of the Cross – II: Acts of the Second International Symposium on Marian Coredemption* (New Bedford, MA: Academy of the Immaculate, 2002) 1–36; also published in Divinitas XLV "Nova Series" (2002) 153–185; ibid., "Marian Coredemption and the Contemporary Papal Magisterium: The Truth of Marian Coredemption, the Papal Magisterium and the Present Situation," in *Maria "Unica Cooperatrice alla Redenzione." Atti del Simposio sul Mistero della Corredenzione Mariana, Fatima, Portogallo 3–7 Maggio 2005* (New Bedford, MA: Academy of the Immaculate, 2005) 147–158; ibid., "Mary Coredemptrix: The Beloved Associate of Christ," in Miravalle (ed.), *Mariology* 392–398.

93 *Inseg* VII/1 (1984) 307 [St. Paul Editions 37].

> only a proof of her unshakable faith but also a contribution to the Redemption of all. In reality, from the time of her secret conversation with the angel, she began to see in her mission as a mother her "destiny" to share, in a singular and unrepeatable way, in the very mission of her Son …
>
> It was on Calvary that Mary's suffering, beside the suffering of Jesus, reached an intensity which can hardly be imagined from a human point of view but which was mysteriously and supernaturally fruitful for the Redemption of the world. Her ascent of Calvary and her standing at the foot of the cross together with the beloved disciple were a special sort of sharing in the redeeming death of her Son. And the words which she heard from His lips were a kind of solemn handing-over of this Gospel of suffering so that it could be proclaimed to the whole community of believers.
>
> As a witness to her Son's passion by her *presence*, and as a sharer in it by her *compassion*, Mary offered a unique contribution to the Gospel of suffering, by embodying in anticipation the expression of St. Paul which was quoted at the beginning. She truly has a special title to be able to claim that she "completes in her flesh"—as already in her heart—"what is lacking in Christ's afflictions."[94]

These two citations from *Salvifici Doloris* help us to hold in tension the dynamic truths which underlie Marian coredemption. On the one hand: "The sufferings of Christ created the good of the world's Redemption, This good in itself is inexhaustible and infinite. No man can add anything to it." On the other hand: "Mary's suffering [on Calvary], beside the suffering of Jesus, reached an intensity which can hardly be imagined from a human point of view but which was mysteriously and supernaturally fruitful for the Redemption of the world." Thus, the Pope strikes that careful balance which is always a hallmark of Catholic truth: he upholds the principle that the sufferings of Christ were all-sufficient for the salvation of the world, while maintaining that Mary's suffering "was mysteriously and supernaturally fruitful for

94 *Inseg* VII/1 (1984) 307 [St. Paul Editions 37].

the Redemption of the world." Is this a contradiction? No. It is a mystery. The sacrifice of Jesus is all-sufficient, but God wished the suffering of the "New Eve," the only perfect human creature, to be united to the suffering of the "New Adam." Does that mean that Mary could redeem us by herself? By no means. But it does mean that she could make her own unique contribution to the sacrifice of Jesus as the "New Eve," the "Mother of the living."

Mary Mediatrix

From Mary's role as Coredemptrix flows her role as Mediatrix. Again, I have dealt with Saint John Paul's treatment of this topic both in chapter five[95] and elsewhere,[96] whereas here I can only indicate a few major texts, but they are sufficient to indicate his consistency and ever-new insights. In a general audience address of 12 January 2000, the Holy Father stated:

> Completing our reflection on Mary at the end of the series of catecheses devoted to the Father, today we want to stress *her role in our journey to the Father.*
>
> *He himself willed Mary's presence in salvation history.* When he decided to send his Son into the world, he wanted him to come to us by being born of a woman (cf. Gal. 4:4). *Thus he willed that this woman, the first to receive his Son, should communicate him to all humanity.*
>
> Mary is therefore found on the path that leads from the Father to humanity as the mother who gives the Saviour Son to all. At the same time, *she is on the path that men must take in order to go to the Father through Christ in the Spirit* (cf. Eph. 2:18).
>
> To understand Mary's presence on our journey to the Father, we must recognize with all the Churches that

95 Cf. above (chapter 5, footnotes 65–86) 187-199.

96 Arthur Burton Calkins, "Mary, Mediatrix of All Graces, in the Papal Magisterium of Pope John Paul II," in *Mary at the Foot of the Cross – VII: Coredemptrix, Therefore Mediatrix of All Graces. Acts of the Seventh International Symposium on Marian Coredemption* (New Bedford, MA: Academy of the Immaculate, 2008) 17–63.

> Christ is "the way, and the truth, and the life"(Jn. 14:6) and the only Mediator between God and men (cf. 1 Tm. 2:5). Mary is involved in Christ's unique mediation and is totally at its service. ...
>
> Viewed in this way, *Mary's mediation appears as the most sublime fruit of Christ's mediation and is essentially directed to bringing us into a more intimate and profound encounter with him.*[97]

Now let us summarize the salient points found here. (1) The Father "himself willed Mary's presence in salvation history." (2) The Father specifically willed her "role in our journey to him." (3) The Father "willed that this woman, the first to receive his Son, should communicate him to all humanity." Here let us note that, according to the Pope, Mary's mediatorial role is willed by the Father so that Mary "should communicate Jesus to all humanity." (4) Just as Mary is "found on the path that leads from the Father to humanity," so at the same time "she is *on the path that men must take* in order to go to the Father through Christ in the Spirit." (5) Since "she is *on the path that men must take* in order to go to the Father through Christ," she can certainly be called a "Mediatrix with the Mediator," as the Pope himself, citing Saint Bernard of Clairvaux, had already pointed out in a footnote in *Redemptoris Mater*.[98] (6) The goal of Mary's mediation "is essentially directed to bringing us into a more intimate and profound encounter with him." (7) This text in a certain sense continues to develop those Marian passages pregnant with meaning, which we have already cited from *Redemptor Hominis* #22 and *Dives in Misericordia* #9.[99]

John Paul continued to reflect on the correlation between Marian coredemption and mediation in #120 of his Encyclical, *Veritatis Splendor*, of 6 August 1993, in this way:

97 *Inseg* XXIII/1 (2000) 53–54 [*ORE* 1626:11 (alt.)] (emphasis my own).

98 *Inseg* X/1 (1987) 725, note 237 [St. Paul Editions 78, note 96]. The formula used is *Mediatrix "ad Mediatorem."*

99 Cf. above (chapter 5, footnotes 69–75) 189-194.

> Mary is also Mother of Mercy because it is to her that Jesus entrusts his Church and all humanity. At the foot of the Cross, when she accepts John as her son, when she asks, together with Christ, forgiveness from the Father for those who do not know what they do (cf. Lk. 23:34), Mary experiences, in perfect docility to the Spirit, the richness and the universality of God's love, which opens her heart and enables it to embrace the entire human race. Thus *Mary becomes Mother of each and every one of us, the Mother who obtains for us divine mercy.* …
>
> Until the time of his birth, she sheltered in her womb the Son of God who became man; she raised him and enabled him to grow, and *she accompanied him in that supreme act of freedom which is the complete sacrifice of his own life. By the gift of herself, Mary entered fully into the plan of God who gives himself to the world.* …
>
> Mary shares our human condition, but in complete openness to the grace of God. Not having known sin, *she is able to have compassion on every kind of weakness.* She understands sinful man and loves him with a Mother's love.[100]

In effect, the Pope says that in accepting John, Mary becomes a Mother to each of us and "obtains for us divine mercy" and "is able to have compassion on every kind of weakness."

Again, I will limit myself to underscoring what I see as the major points here. (1) Mary accompanied Jesus "in that supreme act of freedom which is the complete sacrifice of his own life" and thus "By the gift of herself, she entered fully into the plan of God who gives himself to the world." This echoes the classic formulation of Marian coredemption that she offered Jesus and offered herself in union with Him for the redemption of the world, but it does so in a very graceful way, emphasizing that this was a part of God's divine plan. (2) Because of this cooperation, Mary is "the Mother who obtains for us divine mercy," and "she is able to have compassion on every kind of weakness." Clearly,

100 *Inseg* XVI/2 (1993) 273, 274 [*ORE* 1310:XVIII–XIX] (emphasis my own).

this declaration that she obtains mercy for us is simply another way of saying that she obtains grace for us.

Some Conclusions about John Paul's Teaching on Mary's Mediation

I trust that I have made my point with sufficient clarity regarding Saint John Paul's treatment of Our Lady's Mediation. For those who seek further information about this, I refer to my extensive study, "Mary, Mediatrix of All Graces, in the Papal Magisterium of Pope John Paul II," in *Mary at the Foot of the Cross* – VII, and herewith share the conclusions, which I drew at the end of that essay.

1. Even from what has been presented here, it should now be apparent that Pope John Paul II has left us a remarkably coherent body of teaching on Mary's maternal mediation in the course of his long pontificate of over twenty-six years.

2. His most recognized contribution on this topic is his treatment in *Redemptoris Mater* which effectively re-launched discussion of Mary's mediation in academic and mariological circles. It was conducted with exclusive reference to the pronouncements of the Second Vatican Council's chapter 8 of *Lumen Gentium*, but with great care to insist on Mary's mediation as being "mediation in Christ" and uniquely "maternal mediation." It was, in effect, a maximalist interpretation of the conciliar teaching, and it also developed the concept of mediation on the "ontological level" flowing from God's eternal designs, a new acquisition in terms of magisterial teaching, at least insofar as I am aware.

3. Over and above, anterior and subsequent to his treatment of Marian mediation in *Redemptoris Mater*, however, John Paul II consistently made frequent reference to Mary's mediation in speeches, homilies and in all forms of papal documents. These references—often passing, but of notable depth and beauty—are

seen to be fully consonant with the tradition and the magisterium of his predecessors and shed unexpected light on the mystery of Marian mediation. They are not *obiter dicta*, but form part of his ordinary magisterium.

4. More than any of his predecessors, John Paul II has contextualized Mary's presence in the mystery of Christ. This is particularly true of his treatment of Our Lady in the brief, but profoundly rich passages about her in his Encyclicals, *Redemptor Hominis* and *Dives in Misericordia*. These also help to orient what he presented at greater length in *Redemptoris Mater* and to provide a truly valuable point of entrance into the mystery of Marian mediation.

5. Likewise, closely allied to his thought on Mary's presence in the mystery of Christ is his meditation on Mary's role in the Father's plan and what he had described in *Redemptoris Mater* as her belonging to the "ontological level" of mediation. All of these are different facets of the same mystery.

6. His development of what I have characterized as Mary's role as "Reverser of the Curse" proceeds from the classic formulation of Mary as the "New Eve" presented by Saint Irenaeus. In doing so, he emphasizes Mary as the one through whom the grace of God reaches man.

7. The great majority of those who have gained prominence as the major arbiters of the discipline of Mariology since the Council and up to the present hold for a "minimalist" interpretation of the Second Vatican Council's teaching on Marian mediation. They thus want to proscribe the use of the classical terminology of Marian mediation by mandating a methodology which is an effective break with the Roman Catholic tradition—and they enlist Pope John Paul II as upholding their position.

8. From what I have presented here, it should be apparent that the late Pope did not follow their prescriptions. While "Mediatrix of all graces" has effectively become prohibited

terminology in academic mariological circles, we see that the Pope used the expression at least nine times; and he gave many other indications that he firmly believed that, according to the divine plan, Mary is truly the "Mediatrix of all graces." At the very least, we can say that his teaching clearly demonstrates that the term is not forbidden and that there need be no "rupture" with the pre-conciliar understanding and use of this title.

9. I already know the sort of evaluation the Marian minimalists will make of my presentation here. Just as was the case with the Pope's use of the term "Coredemptrix," which I have carefully documented,[101] they will readily dismiss the Pope's usage of the title "Mediatrix of all graces" as "marginal and therefore devoid of doctrinal weight"[102] because it does not occur in papal documents of the highest level of importance. My response is that these papal statements, nonetheless, constitute a fundamental component of the ordinary magisterium of the Roman Pontiff, and this is so precisely in view of the frequency with which he returned to this theme,[103] revealing ever new facets of unexpected beauty.

10. In further responding to the inevitable attempts to undervalue the teaching of Pope John Paul II on Mary as Mediatrix of all graces, I am pleased to quote Pope Benedict XVI again, who specifically tells us: "We know that the Pope was a man of the Council, that he internalized the spirit and the word of the Council. Through these writings he helps us understand what the Council wanted and what it didn't."

11. While I am convinced that the doctrine on Mary as Mediatrix of all graces is the very heart of Pope John Paul

101 Arthur Burton Calkins, "The Mystery of Mary the Coredemptrix in the Papal Magisterium," in Mark I. Miravalle, S.T.D. (ed.), *Mary Co-redemptrix: Doctrinal Issues Today* (Goleta, CA: Queenship Publishing Company, 2002) 41–44.

102 *Documenti pontifici secondari, e quindi senza peso dottrinale* is the phrase which occurs in the unsigned commentary on the Declaration of the Theological Commission of the 1996 Częstochowa Mariological Congress in *OR* 4 giugno 1997, p. 10 [*ORE* 1497:10].

103 Cf. *LG* #25.

II's teaching on Marian mediation, I make no pretense here of having covered or even alluded to all of the aspects of his teaching on this vast topic. I have been primarily interested in establishing the truth of Mary's distribution of graces (the second phase of Marian mediation or the application of the fruits of the redemption, or "descending" mediation—all terms which we have been enjoined to avoid) in the magisterium of Pope John Paul II, precisely because this is under attack. Dr. Manfred Hauke has already provided an excellent introduction to Mary's maternal mediation in the cycle of the seventy Marian catecheses given at general audiences from 6 September 1995 to 19 November 1997.[104] There remains much more to delineate in terms of "ascending" Marian mediation, i.e., of going "to Jesus through Mary," which is another major element in the Pope's magisterium on this topic and which I have barely been able to touch upon in this presentation. I have not presented his exegesis of the Visitation (Lk. 1:39–56) or the Cana narratives (Jn. 2:1–11) or of Mary's presence in the Upper Room (Acts 1:14), which certainly bear on Mary's role as Mediatrix. Nor have I analyzed the topic of Mary's mediation as intercession—not that this is of no interest, but rather because Marian minimalists would prefer to reduce Marian mediation to this dimension alone.

12. While it is apparent that the thought of John Paul II cannot be described as fitting into the classic scholastic mold, neither does it contradict the great insights of the scholastics. His approach is uniquely his own and it is obvious that, especially from the time he discovered Louis de Montfort, he never stopped pondering on Mary's place in his life, in the life of his country and in the life of the Church. The result of this pondering (cf. Lk. 2:19, 51) is an immense enrichment of Marian doctrine for the entire Church. Much still remains to be explored, but I am convinced that what I have presented here is

104 Cf. Manfred Hauke, "La Mediazione materna di Maria secondo papa Giovanni Paolo II," *Maria Corredentrice: Storia e Teologia* VII (Frigento: Casa Mariana Editrice, 2005) 46–52.

a further enhancement and refinement of the Church's doctrine on Marian mediation.[105]

My Final Conclusion

In the course of this study I have striven to respond to the question of how one may justify the practice of consecration to the Mother of God, of entrusting oneself to her, of putting one's life in her hands according to the teaching of Pope Saint John Paul II. At the same time, I had to recognize that there is a body of "experts" in the field of Mariology who inform us—to employ an American idiom—that after the Second Vatican Council, "It's a whole new ballgame," that the rules in the study of Mariology have changed, and that they will instruct us on the new rules. They assert that, in setting forth these new rules, they are but following the lead of John Paul II; but, in fact, they cite him very selectively and mostly with vague references. I have documented this book meticulously, not only for the edification of readers who may wish to delve more deeply into the Marian writings of this great Pope, but also to respond to the "experts."

My response from chapter five onwards is that Marian consecration can be justified by the two principles of analogy and, even more, by Mary's unique position of mediation in God's plan. The "experts" tell us that these principles are no longer sufficient, especially in the light of what I call "lowest common denominator" ecumenism. In this regard, I recall a comment made during the Council by the late Cardinal Francis Spellman (1889–1967) of New York precisely regarding titles of Our Lady like Coredemptrix and Mediatrix: "The task of the Ecumenical Council is to teach the members of the Church, rather than those outside of it."[106] In saying this, of course, I am not discounting the importance of genuine ecumenism, but

105 "Mary, Mediatrix of All Graces, in the Papal Magisterium of Pope John Paul II," in *Mary at the Foot of the Cross* - VII. *Acts of the Seventh International Symposium on Marian Coredemption* 59–63.

106 Wiltgen, *The Rhine Flows into the Tiber* 94.

the danger of the "lowest common denominator" type. Pope Benedict XVI approached this matter in a more generic way in speaking about the interpretation of the Second Vatican Council in his Address to the Roman Curia on 22 December 2005:

> The question arises: Why has the implementation of the Council, in large parts of the Church, thus far been so difficult?
>
> Well, it all depends on the correct interpretation of the Council or—as we would say today—on its proper hermeneutics, the correct key to its interpretation and application. The problems in its implementation arose from the fact that two contrary hermeneutics came face-to-face and quarreled with each other. One caused confusion, the other, silently but more and more visibly, bore and is bearing fruit.
>
> On the one hand, there is an interpretation that I would call "a hermeneutic of discontinuity and rupture"; it has frequently availed itself of the sympathies of the mass media, and also one trend of modern theology. On the other, there is the "hermeneutic of reform," of renewal in the continuity of the one subject-Church which the Lord has given to us. She is a subject which increases in time and develops, yet always remaining the same, the one subject of the journeying People of God.
>
> The hermeneutic of discontinuity risks ending in a split between the pre-conciliar Church and the post-conciliar Church.[107]

I don't honestly see how the "experts" can be seen in any other light other than as promoters of discontinuity. John Paul could never be pegged as a "scholastic," but neither did he ever come into conflict with that noble body of teaching. He did his first doctorate, after all, under the great Thomist, Réginald Garrigou-Lagrange (1877–1964).[108] His approach to Marian doctrine was *sui generis*, but still in the great line of his

107 *AAS* 98 (2006) 45–46 [*ORE* 1925:5–6].

108 Cf. George Weigel, *Witness to Hope: The Biography of Pope John Paul II* (NY: HarperCollins Publishers,1999) 85–87; English edition: Karol Wojtyła, *Doctrina*

predecessors and remarkable for the development of doctrine. Further, what I have presented here meets all the requirements of *Lumen Gentium* #25 to be recognized as his ordinary magisterium. I still marvel at the effrontery of the comment by the Pontifical International Marian Academy with regard to the use of the title Coredemptrix that

> here and there, in papal writings which are marginal and therefore devoid of doctrinal weight, one can find such a title, be it very rarely. In substantial documents, however, and in those of some doctrinal importance, this term is absolutely avoided. [*in documenti pontifici secondari, e quindi senza peso dottrinale, si può trovare, sia pure molto raramente tale titolo. Nei documenti fondamentali invece in quelli di qualche rilievo dottrinale esso è accuratamente evitato.*][109]

Compare that statement by the "experts" of the Pontifical International Marian Academy founded by Father Karlo Balić, O.F.M. (1899–1977), to this statement redacted by the same Balić as *Prænotanda*,[110] to the first draft of what would eventually become chapter eight of *Lumen Gentium*:

> Certain expressions and words used by Supreme Pontiffs have been omitted, which, in themselves are absolutely true, but which may only be understood with difficulty by separated brethren (in this case Protestants). Among such words may be numbered the following: "Coredemptrix of the human race" [Pius X, Pius XI]; "Reparatrix [or Repairer] of the whole world" [Leo XIII]; "she renounced her motherly rights over her Son for the salvation of mankind" [Benedict XV, Pius XII], "we may well say that she with Christ redeemed mankind" [Benedict XV], etc. … [*Omissæ sunt expressiones et vocabula quædam a Summis Pontificibus adhibita, quæ, licet in se verissima, possent difficilius intelligi*

de fide apud S. Ioannem a Cruce. English edition: *Faith According to St. John of the Cross* trans. Jordan Aumann, OP (San Francisco: Ignatius Press, 1981).

109 *OR* 4 June 1997, p. 10 [*ORE* 1497:10].

110 Cf. Dinko Aračic, *La Dottrina Mariologica negli Scritti di Carlo Balić* (Rome: Pontificia Academia Mariana Internationalis, 1980) 100–101.

> *a fratribus separatis (in casu a protestantibus). Inter alia vocabula adnumerari queunt sequentia: "Corredemptrix humani generis" [S. PIUS X, PIUS XI]; "Reparatrix totius orbis" [LEO XIII]; "materna in Filium iura pro hominum salute abdicavit" [BENEDICTUS XV, PIUS XII], "merito dici queat Ipsam cum Christo humanum genus redemisse" [BENEDICTUS XV], etc.*][111]

Clearly, Balić understood and favored these titles, but was already under constraint in terms of ecumenical preoccupations.[112] However, he did manage to cite many of these pontifical documents in the footnotes of chapter eight of *Lumen Gentium*.[113]

Comparing the text of the founder of the Academy, which at the time remained undisputed, with the present approach of *The Mother of the Lord*, one can readily see the evolution of an agenda at work. The founder insisted that the title Coredemptrix and similar ones are "absolutely true" [*in se verissima*], whereas the "experts" are only too ready to jettison them.

Agreed Ecumenical Statements on Mary's Role

Without attempting to be exhaustive, let us look now at the results of various agreed ecumenical statements on Mary that might shed some light on the subject of this book and indicate the direction which our "experts" would lead us in. First, let us consider the widely hailed *Mary in the New Testament: A Collaborative Assessment by Protestant and Roman Catholic Scholars*, sponsored by the United States Lutheran-Roman Catholic Dialogue. Here is a section of the analysis by

111 *Acta Synodalia Sacrosancti Concilii Oecumenici Vaticani Secundi*, Vol. I, Pt. VI (Typis Polyglottis Vaticanis, 1971) 99; Giuseppe Besutti, O.S.M., *Lo schema mariano al Concilio Vaticano II* (Rome: Edizione Marianum-Desclée, 1966) 41; cf. also Ermanno M. Toniolo, O.S.M., *La Beata Vergine Maria nel Concilio Vaticano II* (Rome: Centro di Cultura Mariana "Madre della Chiesa," 2004) 98–99 (my translation).

112 Cf. Aračic 111, 116–133; 203–226.

113 Cf. footnotes 11, 12, 13, 14, 16, 23 and 24, which make reference to the papal magisterium from Blessed Pius IX to the Venerable Pius XII in which these very titles occur.

those scholars of Mary at the foot of the Cross (John 19:25–27), so fundamental to the Marian magisterium of the Popes and particularly of Saint John Paul II:

> In later church writing and continuing into modern Roman Catholicism this scene has been invoked as a basis for the spiritual motherhood of Mary or for the picture of Mary as the mother of Christians.[114] At Cana Mary was denied a salvific role in the ministry, but now in the hour of Jesus' glorification she is given her place in salvation history. This interpretation faces the added difficulty that it requires the mother of Jesus in 19:25–27 to be treated as an individual (Mary) while the beloved disciple is treated as a general symbol of every Christian. An ordinary symbolic pattern would treat both as individuals or both as general. …
>
> The majority of the task force was willing to settle for a primary symbolism in 19:25–27 based on a new eschatological family relationship to Jesus stemming from discipleship, without any clear commitment toward a symbolism for the mother of Jesus as Israel, or Zion, or the New Eve.[115]

Let us listen now to another highly praised Marian ecumenical venture by the Dombes Group, a group of theologians from the Reformed Church of France and the Catholic Church who dealt with the matter of Mary's cooperation in the work of our salvation, so central to our theme:

> First of all Mary was chosen to be the mother of the Lord: the term of being chosen indicates the absolute divine priority. This is why she was justified by grace only and in the faith that Mary could be associated in the work of God

114 See, for instance, D. Unger, "The Meaning of John 19, 26–27 in the Light of Papal Documents," *Marianum* 21 (1959), 188–221. Today, Roman Catholics would make a greater distinction between the Church teaching on this question and the teaching of Scripture. They may accept the spiritual motherhood of Mary without claiming that it is taught by the Scriptures.

115 Raymond E. Brown, Karl P. Donfried, Joseph A. Firzmyer, and John Reumann (eds.), *Mary in the New Testament: A Collaborative Assessment by Protestant and Roman Catholic Scholars* (Philadelphia: Fortress Press; New York/Ramsey/Toronto, 1978) 216–218.

> in Christ. Her "cooperation" was unique regarding the nature of that which she accomplished, because she was the mother of Jesus and brought him up. She cooperated in the unique and universal event of salvation. But, from the structural point of view, or in terms of her role, her "cooperation" did not differ from that of every person justified by grace. It was totally the fruit of the grace of God.[116]

Finally, let us take note of this declaration from the Agreed Statement of the Anglican-Roman Catholic International Commission, *Mary: Grace and Hope in Christ*:

> As a result of our study, the Commission offers the following agreements, which we believe significantly advance our consensus regarding Mary. We affirm together…
>
> - That Mary has a continuing ministry which serves the ministry of Christ, our unique mediator, that Mary and the saints pray for the whole Church and that the practice of asking Mary and the saints to pray for us is not communion dividing (paragraphs 64–75).[117]

The statement by the United States Lutheran-Roman Catholic Dialogue leaves us in a quandary. It says nothing definite and settles by offering us the position of the majority of the task force. There is no clarity about Mary's position at the foot of the Cross. The statement of the Dombes Group is pure Lutheranism: Mary's cooperation—insofar as one can speak of cooperation in the work of redemption—is no different from ours. The Anglican-Roman Catholic statement manifests that unique Anglican capacity for "comprehensiveness": one may pray to Our Lady or not, but this need not cause division.

116 Gruppo di Dombes, *Maria nel disegno di Dio e nella comunione dei santi* (Magnano (BI) Comunità di Bose: Edizioni Qiqajon, 1998) 111 (my translation from the Italian). The original French edition is *Marie dans le dessein de Dieu et la communion des saints. I. Une lecture œcuménique de l'histoire et de l'Écriture. II. Controverse et conversion* (Paris: Bayard Éditions, 1997, 1998).

117 The Anglican-Roman Catholic International Commission, *Mary: Grace and Hope in Christ, An Agreed Statement* (Harrisburg, London: Morehouse Publishing, 2005) 78–80.

One common theme in all of these statements is that they are based on the Lutheran principle of *sola scriptura* (scripture alone), which has never been a Catholic principle and is the result of Martin Luther's rejection of Catholic teaching.[118] It seems evident that all of the Catholic participants in these ecumenical agreed statements have simply accepted *sola scriptura* as a foundation upon which to work without any preoccupation about the living tradition of the Catholic Church and its magisterium.[119] What is the position of the Catholic Church in this regard? It is clearly enunciated in *Dei Verbum*, the Dogmatic Constitution on Divine Revelation of the Second Vatican Council, the very Council to which the "experts" constantly appeal:

> Sacred Tradition and Sacred Scripture make up a single sacred deposit of the Word of God, which is entrusted to the Church. …
>
> But the task of giving an authentic interpretation of the Word of God, whether in its written form or in the form of Tradition, has been entrusted to the living teaching office of the Church alone. Its authority in this matter is exercised in the name of Jesus Christ. Yet this Magisterium is not superior to the Word of God, but is its servant. It teaches only what has been handed on to it. At the divine command and with the help of the Holy Spirit, it listens to this devotedly, guards it with dedication and expounds it faithfully. All that it proposes for belief as being divinely revealed is drawn from this single deposit of faith.
>
> It is clear, therefore, that sacred Tradition, Sacred Scripture and the teaching authority [magisterium] of the Church, in accord with God's most wise design, are so linked and joined together that one cannot stand without the others, and that all together and each in its own

118 Cf. the excellent analysis of this matter by Monsignor Brunero Gherardini, "Unity and Coredemption," in *Mary at the Foot of the Cross – III: Maria, Mater Unitatis. Acts of the Third International Symposium on Marian Coredemption* (New Bedford, MA: Academy of the Immaculate, 2003) 54–69.

119 *CCC* #80–100.

> way under the action of the one Holy Spirit contribute effectively to the salvation of souls.[120]

I submit once again that what I have been presenting in this book is the ordinary magisterium of Saint John Paul II. It meets all of the requirements of *Lumen Gentium* #25. It developed in an extraordinary, but orderly and consistent way in the course of his long pontificate. It is not my invention, but what I have discovered after years of patient chronicling and research. Those "experts" and their disciples who would disprove what I have presented must do so with as much rigor and careful scholarship as that with which I have set it forth. Their vague and generalized assertions are not sufficient except to mislead the uninformed. This is a book for theologians, but above all, it is also a book for the faithful. Those who love Our Lady will find much for their nourishment by reading and pondering over and over again these magnificent papal texts that are otherwise not readily available.

A final Reflection

One might be tempted to ask: How conscious was Pope Saint John Paul II of being an agent in the development of Marian doctrine? How did this doctrine come to him? Was he aware of the Marian gems that he was lavishly scattering in the course of his daily teaching? Why did he make some of his most beautiful statements on Our Lady's role in some of the most unexpected places? We will most probably never know in this life, but I suspect all of this was the work of the Holy Spirit and Our Lady. What is really important, however, is the great patrimony of Marian teaching which he has left us and which still needs to be discovered, analyzed, assimilated and handed on. I believe that his Marian magisterium was his greatest single gift to the Church. For this and for my role as one who has uncovered and shared this magisterium I give thanks to the Lord Jesus Christ, to the Most Blessed Virgin Mary, His Mother, and to Pope Saint John Paul II!

120 *DV* #10.

Afterword

None who have carefully pondered the purpose of this study, as explained in its first edition by Msgr. Calkins, will think that this second edition consists merely of minor corrections and additions. It is far more: it is a definitive presentation of Pope St. John Paul II's goals in stressing—not only early in his pontificate, but throughout its entirety—the great importance of total consecration to the Immaculate Heart, i.e., the Triumph of the Immaculate Heart in our hearts and in the Church, so that Jesus can triumph there. The importance of this triumph lies in this, that love of the Immaculate Heart is the condition laid down by Jesus for loving His Sacred Heart as His Mother loves His Heart. Jesus requires such love, not only of a privileged few, but of every member of the Church: every church, every diocese, every bishop and priest and pastor of souls in the work of salvation and renewal of the Church.

In a word, the teaching of Pope John Paul II on this point is not merely sound theological opinion or optional devotion. This consecration to Mary is an indispensable condition for realizing consecration to the Sacred Heart of Jesus and everlasting joy in the company of Jesus. Because this is so, and because so many endanger their salvation and the salvation of others by downplaying or rejecting this truth, he thought it necessary to proclaim this as a truth of the ordinary Magisterium.

Msgr. Calkins has clearly formulated the central question of this study: "Why is the Pope so doggedly persistent in entrusting every local church, country, and the universal Church to the Mother of God? Is there a Christological perspective which justifies such deportment?"

The Holy Father set forth his teaching in numberless documents of all kinds, but especially one: *Redemptoris Mater*. In all of them the answer is a resounding "YES," an answer given first of all by Jesus Himself as He was about to die on the Cross (cf. Jn 19:25-27). This consecration complements the consecration or sanctification of Jesus' own self sacrifice, made the night before at the Last Supper (cf. Jn 17:17,19). It reveals how, just as the beginning of Jesus' saving ministry involves Jesus as Son and Mary as Mother, so the completion of that work of salvation also involves the divine Mother as Coredemptrix, Mother of the mystical Body, and Mediatrix of all graces. The response of the beloved Disciple to the command of Jesus to love His Mother and take her into his heart is a response for us as well, for without that response the Church cannot survive. And so, from its beginning, the Church has always taken Mary into her midst as her principal member: Mother of the Church's Head and Mother of the members of Christ's mystical Body.

Msgr. Calkins continues: "Hence, the explicit purpose of this study is to analyze the act of consecration or entrustment to Mary in order to discover its basis in the mystery of Christ the Incarnate Word and in the eternal plan of God—and to do so explicitly in terms of the teaching and practice of one of the Church's supreme pastors, Pope Saint John Paul II."

Those readers familiar with the first edition of this study will be aware of the author's success in accomplishing this objective with the abundant documentation already then available. The eight chapters in that first edition show consistently how the Holy Father links his program and the traditional exposition of this theme in the teaching of the Church, not excluding that of Vatican II, above all in *Lumen Gentium*, nos. 60-62.

This is precisely the passage cited most often, not only a quarter century ago, but now even more subtly, by those who wish to dispense everywhere with any unique Marian maternal mediation on Calvary, to dispense with needed "go-betweens" to reach Jesus, and to reject such apt terminology as coredemption and joint predestination of Jesus and Mary—a terminology reflecting a union that, once opened, is never to be terminated, even on Calvary (cf. Pius IX, *Ineffabilis Deus*; Vatican II, *Lumen Gentium*, nn. 56-59).

It is evident from the teaching of Pope John Paul II that the Pontiff's plan is exactly the opposite: not only do we need Mary for Christ to be present to us; we need Mary to find Jesus and to consecrate ourselves to Him through her. Both of these involvements in the work of salvation by Mary—first as divine Mother at the Annunciation and then as Coredemptrix on Calvary—are, above all, maternal. Christ might have come as Savior in many ways. In fact, however, there is only one way He deigns to come: as the Child conceived by Mary to be our Savior. And He could have completed His saving work on Calvary in far different ways but, in fact, He completes it through the unique maternal mediation of Mary. She is Coredemptrix because she is the divine Mother; and she is the divine Mother because she is the Immaculate Conception. To be wholly hers requires that we cooperate in some way with the graces won for us by Jesus.

We can only be disposed for this as the Father wishes by being born again of Mary and the Holy Spirit, and enjoying her maternal mediation which renders possible our consecration to Christ through her. We can only be happy for all eternity by loving Mary as Jesus does and with Jesus, as Savior of His Mother and of all whom she has begotten spiritually. The old saying goes thus: no Mary, no Jesus. This is true not merely at the first moment of the Incarnation, but at every moment thereafter. For, Mary is active as Coredemptrix on Calvary and, thereafter, as spiritual Mother of the Church and of her members. Unless we love Mary as Jesus does, He will not be pleased with us. Likewise, if we do not love Jesus as Mary does, especially if we go so far as to exclude Mary from our lives, we will not please Jesus or the Father.

But what is still more evident is the manner in which the Holy Father not only reaffirmed the past teaching, but made it possible to see how his position—and not that of his critics of today and yesterday—is the true reading of Vatican II on Marian mediation. No matter who the promoters for changing this terminology from clear to vague might be, what they are doing is sinful. They are rejecting the teaching of the Church and placing themselves in danger of losing the blessings of the Cross. And they are doing so by the use of cheap arguments, such as claiming that cooperation with Jesus under His direction detracts from His glory in saving souls. Quite the opposite is true: the cooperation of men with the Creator in perfecting the world in no way detracts from the perfect glory of that dear Creator, but enables the creature to praise God and share in his glory. Our collaboration in the work of redemption in one way or another—rendered possible by the perfect collaboration of Mary as maternal Mediatrix—is surely the most exalted of ways in which we can and, indeed, are called to cooperate with Jesus through Mary, in union with her and with the Holy Spirit.

A considerable amount of new material available only after 1991 has been added to the first eight chapters of this second edition to show how Pope John Paul II has finalized rather than modified his teaching in the face of these challenges. One new chapter, the ninth, has been added to answer the question of whether or not the persistent practice of total consecration, wherever the Pope found himself, represents an exercise of the ordinary Magisterium of the Church—that is to say, whether the formulation of this doctrine on total consecration to Christ represents not merely a laudable personal position of the Pope, but also one to be accepted as part of the deposit of faith and an indispensable instrument in the renewal of the Church and its members, the baptized, as well as those yet to be converted.

There is no question about the author's position. The ninth chapter in this second edition of *Totus Tuus* is a definitive chapter, a chapter in which to recognize, not simply the teaching of one document such as *Redemptoris Mater*, but of innumerable documents—pre-pontifical and pontifical—insistently repeating the same great truths in thousands of formulations. This chapter is the confirmation of the very motto, *Totus Tuus*, underscoring the importance of total consecration to the Immaculate Heart in order to know and love Jesus, especially today. John Paul tells us unequivocally and repeatedly that entrustment or consecration to Mary has a Christological foundation as well as finality. It is truly a golden thread running throughout his papal teaching. *Totus Tuus* is truly an appropriate motto, a summation of the convictions of the Pope—and not only of the Pope alone, but of all creatures. We must all be totally Mary's, or we will never know the salvation and love of Jesus and, through and in Jesus, the salvation and love of the Father.

May the Immaculate Virgin be pleased with these efforts to promote her cause. May she deign to use them as instruments for the salvation of souls, for the ever greater incorporation of the mystery of her Immaculate Conception into the fabric of human life: in every person, in every community, for the greater glory of her Son and Savior and for the triumph of His Kingdom.

Fr. Peter Damian M. Fehlner

Bibliography

I. Works of Pope John Paul II (Karol Wojtyła)

A. Pre-Papal Works

Il Buon Pastore: Scritti, Discorsi e Lettere Pastorali. Trans. Elzbieta Cywiak e Renzo Panzone. Rome: Edizioni Logos, 1978.

Chiamati all'Amore: Itinerari di Santità. Trans. Aldo Cantarini. Rome: Edizioni Logos, 1980.

Doctrina de fide apud S. Ioannem a Cruce. English edition. *Faith According to St. John of the Cross.* Trans. Jordan Aumann, O.P. (San Francisco: Ignatius Press, 1981).

"Inspiracja Maryjna Vaticanum II." *W Kierunku prawdy.* Ed. Bohdan Bejze. Warsaw Catholic Academy of Theology, 1976. 112–121.

"Komentarz teologiczno-diszpasterski do aktu dokonanego na Jasnej Gorze dnia 3 maja 1966 R." *Ateneum Kapłanskie* (Wokławek) 79 (1972): 5–21.

Maria: Omelie. Prefazione di Stefan Card. Wyszyński. Trans. Janina Korzeniewska. Vatican City: Libreria Editrice Vaticana, 1982.

Maximilien Kolbe, Patron de notre siecle difficile. Paris: Lethielleux 1982.

"Oddanie Bogurodzicy w swietle nauki Soboru." *Przewodnnik Katolicki* 26 (1972) 228.

Sign of Contradiction. New York: Crossroad-Seabury Press, 1979.

Sources of Renewal: The implementation of the Second Vatican Council. Trans. P. S. Falla. San Francisco: Harper & Row, Publishers, 1980.

"Tysiacleci chrztu a oddanie Matce Boskiej." *Notificationes e Curia Metropolitana Cracoviensi* 1965: 189–195.

The Word Made Flesh: The Meaning of the Christmas Season. Trans. Leslie Wearne. San Francisco: Harper & Row Publishers, 1985.

"Znaczenie Wyszyłskiego dla wspolczesnego Kosciofa." *Zeszyty Naukowe* 3 (1971): 19–37.

B. Papal works

Insegnamenti di Giovanni Paolo II, I–XXVIII (1978–2005). Vatican City: Libreria Editrice Vaticana, 1979–2006.

L'Osservatore Romano, daily edition in Italian.

L'Osservatore Romano, weekly edition in English.

Affido a Te, O Maria. A cura di Sergio Trasatti e Arturo Mari. Bergamo: Editrice Velar, 1982.

Talks of John Paul II. Boston: St. Paul Editions, 1979.

Messages of John Paul II: Servant of Truth. Boston: St. Paul Editions, 1979.

The Redeemer of Man [*Redemptor Hominis*]. Boston: St. Paul Editions, 1979.

Pilgrim to Poland. Boston: St. Paul Editions, 1979.

Ireland "In the Footsteps of St. Patrick." Boston: St. Paul Editions, 1979.

U.S.A . – The Message of Justice, Peace and Love. Boston: St. Paul Editions, 1979.

Africa: Apostolic Pilgrimage. Boston: St. Paul Editions, 1980.

France: Message of Peace, Trust, Love and Faith. Boston: St. Paul Editions, 1980.

Brazil: Journey in the Light of the Eucharist. Boston: St. Paul Editions, 1980.

Germany: Pilgrimage of Unity and Peace. Boston: St. Paul Editions, 1981.

The Far East: Journey of Peace and Brotherhood. Boston: St. Paul Editions, 1981.

Africa: Land of Promise, Land of Hope. Boston: St. Paul Editions, 1982.

Portugal: Message of Fatima. Boston: St. Paul Editions, 1983.

Pope John Paul II in Argentina. Boston: St. Paul Editions, 1983.

Mother of the Redeemer [*Redemptoris Mater*]. Boston: St. Paul Editions, 1987.

Gift and Mystery: On the 50th Anniversary of My Priestly Ordination. Vatican City: Libreria Editrice Vaticana. 1996.

Rise, Let Us Be On Our Way. Trans. Walter Ziębma. Vatican City: Libreria Editrice Vaticana, 2004; Milan: Arnaldo Mondadori Editore S.p.A., 2004.

Memory and Identity: Personal Reflections. London: Weidenfeld & Nicholson, 2005.

Testament of the Holy Father John Paul II. Vatican City: Libreria Editrice Vaticana, 2005.

C. Biographical Works

Boniecki, Adam, M.I.C., *The Making of the Pope of the Millennium: Kalendarium of the Life of Karol Wojtyła*. Stockbridge, MA: Marian Press, 2000.

Williams, George Huntston. *The Mind of John Paul II: Origins of His Thought and Action.* New York: The Seabury Press, 1981.

Frossard, André. *"Be Not Afraid!": Pope John Paul II Speaks Out on his Life, his Beliefs and his Inspiring Vision for Humanity.* Trans. J. R. Foster. NY: St. Martin's Press, 1984.

Crossing the Threshold of Hope. Ed. Vittorio Messori and Trans. Jenny and Martha McPhee. London: Jonathan Cape, 1994.

Weigel, George. *Witness to Hope: The Biography of Pope John Paul II.* NY: Harper Collins Publishers, 1999.

———, *The End and the Beginning: Pope John Paul II – The Victory of Freedom, the Last Years, the Legacy.* NY: Doubleday, 2010.

Comastri, Angelo. *Let Me Go to the Father's House: John Paul II's Strength in Weakness.* Boston: Pauline Books and Media, 2006.

Dziwisz, Cardinal Stanisław, in Conversation with Svidercoschi, Gian Franco. *A Life of Karol: My Forty-Year Friendship with the Man Who Became Pope* Trans. Adrian J. Walker. NY: Doubleday, 2008.

The Story of My Life: Collected Memories. Compiled by Saverio Gaeta. Boston: Pauline Books & Media, 2011.

II. Magisterial Documents

Acta Apostolicæ Sedis I (1909 –).

Acta Sanctæ Sedis (1865–1908).

Acta Synodalia Sacrosancti Concilii Oecumenici Vaticani Secundi, Vol. I, Pt. VI. Vatican City: Typis Polyglottis Vaticanis, 1971.

Bertetto, Domenico, S.D.B., ed. *La Madonna nella Parola di Paolo VI*. Seconda edizione. Rome: Libreria Ateneo Salesiano, 1980.

———, *Il Magistero Mariano di Pio XII*. Roma: Edizioni Paoline, 1956.

Catechism of the Catholic Church second edition. Washington, D.C.: United States Conference of Catholic Bishops, 1997.

Carlen, Claudia, I.H.M. *The Papal Encyclicals 1878–1903*. Raleigh, NC: McGrath Publishing Co., 1981.

———, *The Papal Encyclicals 1903–1939*. Raleigh, NC: McGrath Publishing Co., 1981.

Congregation for Divine Worship and the Discipline of the Sacraments. *Directory on Popular Piety and the Liturgy: Principles and Guidelines*. Boston: Pauline Books & Media, 2002.

Denzinger, Heinrich. *Compendium of Creeds, Definitions, and Declarations on Matters of Faith and Morals*, 43rd Edition edited by Peter Hünermann for the bilingual edition and for the English edition by Robert Fastiggi and Anne Englund Nash. San Francisco: Ignatius Press, 2012.

Dogmatic Constitution on the Church [*Lumen Gentium*]. Boston: St. Paul Editions, 1964.

Enchiridion Indulgentiarum – Preces et Pia Opera – Versio Anglica [*The Raccolta*]. NY: Benziger Brothers, Inc., 1957.

Flannery, Austin, O.P. ed. *Vatican Council II: The Conciliar and Post Conciliar Documents*. Collegeville, Minnesota: Liturgical Press, 1975.

Humani Generis: Encyclical Letter of Pope Pius XII. Washington, D. C.: National Catholic Welfare Conference, 1950.

Insegnamenti di Paolo VI, I–XV (1963–78). Vatican City: Libreria Editrice Vaticana, 1965–79.

Larkin, Francis, SS.CC. ed. *Haurietis Aquas: The Sacred Heart Encyclical of Pope Pius XII*. Orlando, Florida: Sacred Heart Publication Center, 1974.

Neuner, J., S.J., and J. Dupuis, S.J., eds. *The Christian Faith in the Doctrinal Documents of the Catholic Church*. New York: Alba House, 1982.

Paul VI. *Mary – God's Mother and Ours*. Boston: St. Paul Editions, 1979.

Pocock, Hubert M., S.M.M. *Pius XII on Consecration to Mary*. Bay Shore, N. Y.: Montfort Publications, 1956.

The Pope Speaks, 1 (1954 –).

Secretaria Generalis Concilii Oecumenici Vaticani II: *Constitutiones, Decreta, Declarationes Sacrosanctum Oecumenicum Concilium Vaticanum II*. Città del Vaticano: Typis Polyglottis Vaticanis, 1974.

Solesmes, Benedictine Monks of, eds. *Our Lady: Papal Teachings*. Trans. Daughters of St. Paul. Boston: St. Paul Editions, 1961.

Synod of 1985, Extraordinary. Boston: St. Paul Editions, 1986.

Synodus Extraordinaria. *Relatio Finalis*. *L'Osservatore Romano*. 10 dicembre 1985, supplemento.

Unger, Dominic J., O.F.M. Cap. ed. *Mary, Christ and the Church*. Bayshore, NY: Montfort Publications, 1979.

III. Scriptural Studies

The Anglican-Roman Catholic International Commission, *Mary: Grace and Hope in Christ, An Agreed Statement* (Harrisburg, London: Morehouse Publishing, 2005).

Braun, F.M., O.P. *Mother of God's People.* Trans. John Clarke, O.C.D. New York: Alba House, 1967.

Brown, Raymond E., S.S. *The Gospel According to John, I–XII.* Anchor Bible 29. Garden City, New York: Doubleday & Co., Inc. 1966.

———, *The Gospel According to John, XIII–XXI.* Anchor Bible 29A. Garden City, New York: Doubleday & Co., Inc. 1970.

Brown, Raymond E., S.S., Donfried, Karl P., Fitzmyer, Joseph A., and Reumann, John, eds. *Mary in the New Testament.* Philadelphia: Fortress Press; NY: Paulist Press, 1978.

Cazelles, Henri, P.S.S. "Consécration du Christ et consécration de l'homme." *Cahiers Marials* #86 (1973) 5–13.

———, "L'Esprit qui consacre le Christ, Marie, l'Eglise." *Cahiers Marials* #133 (1982) 131–45.

———, "Note sur le ministère apostolique de consécration." *Bulletin de Saint-Sulpice* 1 (1975): 302–07.

Deiss, Lucien, C.S.Sp. *Mary, Daughter of Sion.* Trans. Barbara T. Blair. Collegeville, Minnesota: The Liturgical Press, 1972.

de la Potterie, Ignace, S.J. "L'Alleanza dei Cuori di Gesù e di Maria." *Il Mistero del Cuore Trafitto.* Bologna: Edizioni Dehoniane, 1988. 137–80.

———, "The Alliance of the Hearts of Jesus and Mary: A Biblical Approach." Trans. Sr. Rosario de Veyra, R.A. *The Alliance of the Hearts of Jesus and Mary: The International Theological/Pastoral Conference, Manila, Philippines, 30 November – December 1987, Texts and Documents.* Manila: Bahay Maria, 1988. 68–117.

———, "'Et à partir de cette heure, le Disciple l'accueillit dans son intimité' (Jn. 19, 27b)." *Marianum* 42 (1980): 84–125.

———, *Mary in the Mystery of the Covenant.* Trans. Bertrand Buby, SM. Staten Island: Alba House, 1992.

———, "La maternità spirituale di Maria e la fondazione della chiesa." Gesù verità: Studi di cristologia giovannea. Torino: Marietti, 1973. 158–64.

———, "La parole de Jésus 'Voici ta Mère' et l'accueil du Disciple (Jn. 19, 27b)." *Marianum* 36 (1974): 1–39.

———, *La Verité dans Saint Jean* 2. Analecta Biblica 74. Rome: Pontificium Institutum Biblicum, 1977.

Delorme, Jean. "Sacerdoce du Christ et Ministère (A propos de Jean 17): Sémantique et théologie biblique." *Recherches de Science Religieuse* 62 (1974): 199–219.

———, "Sacrifice, sacerdoce, consécration." *Recherches de Science Religieuse* 63 (1975): 343–66.

Feuillet, André, P.S.S. "De muliere parturiente et de maternitate spirituali Mariae secundum evangelium sancti Johannis (16, 21; 19, 25–27)." *Acta Congressus Mariologici-Mariani in Republica Dominicana Anno 1965 Celebrati* 5: *De Beata Virgine Maria in Evangelio S. Ioannis et in Apocalypsi*. Rome: Pontificia Academia Mariana Internationalis, 1967. 111–22.

———, *The Priesthood of Christ and His Ministers*. Trans. Matthew J. O'Connell. Garden City, New York: Doubleday & Co., Inc., 1975.

Groupe de Dombes. *Marie dans le dessein de Dieu et la communion des saints. I. Une lecture œcuménique de l'histoire et de l'Écriture. II. Controverse et conversion*. Paris: Bayard Éditions, 1997, 1998.

Gruppo di Dombes, *Maria nel disegno di Dio e nella comunione dei santi*. Magnano (BI) Comunità di Bose: Edizioni Qiqajon, 1998.

Koester, Helmut. "*splángchnon, splangchnízomai, 'eúsplangchnos*." Gerhard Friedrich ed. *Theological Dictionary of the New Testament*. Grand Rapids, Michigan: Wm. B. Eerdmans Publishing Company, 1971. 548–559.

Lagrange, M.-J., O.P. *L'Évangile selon Saint Jean*. Paris: Gabalda et Cie., 1936.

Manelli, Settimio M., F.I. "Genesis 3:15 and the Immaculate Coredemptrix," in *Mary at the Foot of the Cross* – V: *Redemption and Coredemption under the Sign of the Immaculate Conception. Acts of the Fifth International Symposium on Marian Coredemption* (New Bedford, MA: Academy of the Immaculate, 2005. 263–322.

Manelli, Stefano M. F.I. *All Generations Shall Call Me Blessed: Biblical Mariology* Revised and Enlarged Second Edition Trans. Peter Damian Fehlner, F.I. New Bedford, MA: Academy of the Immaculate, 2005.

McHugh, John. *The Mother of Jesus in the New Testament*. Garden City, NY: Doubleday & Co., Inc., 1975.

Serra, Aristide, O.S.M. *Contributi dell'antica letteratura giudaica per l'esegesi di Giovanni 2, 1–12 e 19, 25–27*. Roma: Herder, 1977.

———, *Maria a Cana e presso la croce: saggio di Mariologia Giovannea*. Rome: Centro di Cultura Mariana "Mater Ecclesiae," 1985.

———, *Maria secondo il Vangelo*. Brescia: Editrice Queriniana, 1988.

IV. Theological Works Consulted

Alonso, Joaquin Maria, C.M.F. "Her Own Words." *A Heart for All: The Immaculate Heart of Mary in the Apparitions of Fatima*. Washington, N. J.: A.M.I. Press, 1972. 23–72.

Amato, Angelo S.D.B. "Verso un Altro Dogma Mariano?" *Marianum* LVIII (1996) 229–232.

Amorth, Gabriele, S.S.P. *Dialoghi su Maria*. Padua: Edizioni Messaggero Padova, 1987.

———, *Dietro un sorriso. Alessandrina Maria da Costa*. Cinisello Balsamo: Edizioni Paoline, 1992.

Anderson, Robin. *Between Two Wars: The Story of Pius XI*. Chicago: Franciscan Herald Press, 1977.

Apollonio, Alessandro M., F.I. "La consacrazione a Maria," *Immaculata Mediatrix* I:3 (2001) 49–101.

———, *Mariologia Francescana: Da san Francesco d'Assisi ai Francescani dell'Immacolata*. Rome: Dissertationes ad Lauream in Pontificia Facultate Theologica "Marianum," 1997.

Aračic, Dinko. *La Dottrina Mariologica negli Scritti di Carlo Balić*. Rome: Pontificia Academia Mariana Internationalis, 1980.

Armbruster, J.-B., S.M. *G.-J. Chaminade: Ecrits Marials* Vols. 1 & 2. Fribourg, Switzerland: Séminaire Marianiste, 1966.

Barré, Henri, C.S.Sp. "Exégèse de Jean 19, 25–27 et développement doctrinal." *Acta Congressus Mariologici-Mariani in Republica Dominicana Anno 1965 Celebrati* 5: *De Beata Virginia Maria in Evangelio S. Ioannis et in Apocalypsi*. Rome: Pontificia Academia Mariana Internationalis, 1967. 161–71.

———, *Prières Anciennes de L'Occident à la Mère du Sauveur: Des origènes à Saint Anselme*. Paris: Lethielleux, 1963.

Barré, Jean-Louis S.M. *La Mission de la Vierge Marie d'après les Écrits d'Émile Neubert Sm. (1878–1967)*. Rome: Dissertationes ad Lauream in Pontificia Facultate Theologica "Marianum," 2007.

Barres, John O. *Jean-Jacques Olier's Priestly Spirituality: Mental Prayer and Virtue as the Foundation for the Direction of Souls*. Rome: Pontificia Universitas Sanctæ Crucis, Thesis ad Doctoratum in Theologia, 1999.

Becker, Constantin. "Marie du Divin Cœur." M. Viller et al. *Dictionnaire de Spiritualité Ascétique et Mystique* 10. Paris: Beauchesne, 1980. 485–86.

Bengoechea, I., O.C.D. "Un precursor de la consagración a Maria en el siglo XV: Arnoldo Bostio (1445–1499)." *Estudios Marianos* 51 (1986) 215–29.

Bertetto, Domenico, S.D.B., "Beata Virgo Maria et testamentum Domini in cruce." *Acta Congressus Mariologici-Mariani in Republica Dominicana Anno 1965 Celebrati* 5: *De Beata Virgine Maria in Evangelio S. Ioannis et in Apocalypsi*. Rome: Pontificia Academia Mariana Internationalis, 1967. 181–99.

———, "Consacrazione e affidamento: Senso ed esigenze dell'affidamento a Maria." Domenico Bertetto, S.D.B. ed. *L'Affidamento a Maria*. Rome: Libreria Ateneo Salesiano, 1984. 75–85.

———, *Maria nel Magistero di Giovanni Paolo II; Primo Anno di Pontificato, 16 ottobre 1978 – 21 ottobre 1979*. Roma: Libreria Ateneo Salesiano, 1980.

———, *Maria nel Magistero di Giovanni Paolo II; Secondo Anno di Pontificato, 22 ottobre 1979 – 21 ottobre 1980*. Roma: Libreria Ateneo Salesiano, 1981.

———, *Maria nel Magistero di Giovanni Paolo II; Terzo Anno di Pontificato, 22 ottobre 1980 – 21 ottobre 1981*. Roma: Libreria Ateneo Salesiano, 1983.

———, *Maria nel Magistero di Giovanni Paolo II; Quarto Anno di Pontificato, 22 ottobre 1981 – 21 ottobre 1982*. Roma: Libreria Ateneo Salesiano, 1984.

———, *Maria nel Magistero di Giovanni Paolo II; Quinto Anno di Pontificato, 22 ottobre 1982 – 21 ottobre 1983*. Roma: Libreria Ateneo Salesiano, 1986.

———, *Maria nel Magistero di Giovanni Paolo II; Sesto Anno di Pontificato, 22 ottobre 1983 – 21 ottobre 1984*. Roma: Libreria Ateneo Salesiano, 1986.

Berti, Conradus M., Salvator M. Meo, Hermannus M. Toniolo, O.S.M. De Ratione Ponderandi Documenta Magisterii Ecclesiastici. Rome: Edizioni Marianum, 1961.

Bérulle, Pierre de. Œuvres Complètes, 8 volumes (Paris: Oratoire de Jésus, Éditions du Cerf) 1995–1996.

Besutti, Giuseppe, O.S.M. *Bibliografia Mariana 1967–1972*. Rome: Edizioni Marianum, 1974.

———, *Bibliografia Mariana 1973–1977*. Rome: Edizioni Marianum, 1980.

———, *Bibliografia Mariana 1978–1984*. Rome: Edizioni Marianum, 1988.

———, *Lo schema mariano al Concilio Vaticano II*. Rome: Edizione Marianum-Desclée, 1966.

Bittremieux, J. "Consecratio Mundi Immaculato Cordi B. Mariae Virginis." *Ephemerides Theologicae Lovanienses* 20 (1943) 99–103.

Bremond, Henri. *Histoire Littéraire du Sentiment Religieux en France depuis la Fin de Guerres de Religion jusqu'a Nos Jours*, Vol. IX: *La Vie Chrétienne sous l'Ancien Régime*. Paris: Librairie Bloud et Gay, 1932.

Boaga, O.Carm., Emanuele. *Con Maria sulle vie di Dio: Antologia dellamarianità carmelitana*. Rome: Edizioni Carmelitane, 2000. 82–87.

Bossard, Alphonse, S.M.M. "Le don total au Christ par Marie selon Montfort." *Cahiers Marials* #86 (1973) 29–48.

———, "Se consacrer à Marie." *Cahiers Marials* #137 (1983): 95–106.

Bover, José M., S.J. "El Principio Mariologico de Analogia." *Acta Congressus Mariologici-Mariani Romae Anno Sancto MCML Celebrati* 11: *De Mariologia in Genere Nonnullisque Privilegiis ac Muneribus Almae Sociae Christi*. Rome: Pontificia Academia Mariana Internationalis, 1953. 1–13.

Bradshaw, Robert. *Frank Duff: Founder of the Legion of Mary*. Bay Shore, N. Y.: Montfort Publications, 1985.

Brogan, Cuthbert, O.S.B. "Mary and the Eucharist in the Syriac Fathers," in *Mary at the Foot of the Cross – VI: Marian Coredemption in the Eucharistic Mystery. Acts of the Sixth International Symposium on Marian Coredemption*. New Bedford, MA: Academy of the Immaculate, 2007) 95–113.

Bunson, Matthew and Margaret. *John Paul II's Book of Saints*. Huntington, IN: Our Sunday Visitor Publishing Division, 2007.

Buono, A. "Hyperdulia." *Dictionary of Mary*. New York: Catholic Book Publishing Co., 1985. 129–30.

Calabuig Adan, Ignazio M., O.S.M. "In Memoriam Prof. Ignacio (Rafael) M. Calabuig Adán, OSM." *Marianum* LXVII (2005). 551–589.

———, "Liturgia." *Nuovo Dizionario di Mariologia*. Milan: Edizioni Paoline, 1985. 767–87.

———, "Tre Messe in onore della Beata Vergine *Madre della Chiesa*." *Marianum* 36 (1974): 70–78.

Calabuig, Ignazio M. e il Comitato di redazione della rivista "Marianum." "Riflessione sulla richiesta della definizione dogmatica di 'Maria corredentrice, mediatrice avvocata.'" *Marianum* LXI (1999) 157.

Calkins, Arthur Burton. "The Alliance of the Hearts of Jesus and Mary: A Theological Sounding, Part 1." *Queen of All Hearts* Vol. 44, No. 6 (March–April 1994) 5–8.

———, "The Alliance of the Hearts of Jesus and Mary: A Theological Sounding, Part 2." *Queen of All Hearts* Vol. 45, No. 1 (May–June 1994) 28–30.

———, "The Alliance of the Hearts of Jesus and Mary: A Theological Sounding, Part 3." *Queen of All Hearts* Vol. 45, No. 2 (July–August 1994) 28–29, 45.

———, "The Alliance of the Hearts of Jesus and Mary: A Theological Sounding, Part 4." *Queen of All Hearts* Vol. 45, No. 3 (September–October 1994) 29–31.

———, "The Alliance of the Hearts of Jesus and Mary: Our Share in Their Work of Reparation." *1994 International Holy Family Year: Theological-Pastoral Framework*. Manila: Two Hearts Media Organization, Inc., 1994. 49–59.

———, "The Alliance of the Sacred Hearts and the Fatima Message – Maternal Love," Part 1. *Missio Immaculatæ International* (English Edition) Year IV, N° 5 (May 2008). 20–21.

———, "The Alliance of the Sacred Hearts and the Fatima Message – The Apparitions of the Angel," Part 2. *Missio Immaculatæ International* (English Edition) Year IV, N° 6 (June/July 2008). 21.

———, "The Alliance of the Sacred Hearts and the Fatima Message – Icons of Redemption and Coredemption." *Missio Immaculatæ International* (English Edition) Year IV, N° 7 (August/September 2008). 20–21.

———, "The Alliance of the Sacred Hearts and the Fatima Message – Coredemption andthe Magisterium." *Missio Immaculatæ International* (English Edition) Year IV, N° 8 (October 2008). 20–21.

———, "The Alliance of the Sacred Hearts and the Fatima Message – Our Share in the Work of Redemption." *Missio*

Immaculatæ International (English Edition) Year IV, N° 9 (November/December 2008). 28–29.

———, "The Alliance of the Sacred Hearts and the Fatima Message – The Mediation of the Immaculate Heart of Mary." *Missio Immaculatæ International* (English Edition) Year V, N° 1 (January/February 2009). 12–13.

———, "The Alliance of the Sacred Hearts and the Fatima Message – Her Immaculate Heart is our Way to God." *Missio Immaculatæ International* (English Edition) Year V, N° 2 (March/April 2009). 16–18.

———, "The Alliance of the Sacred Hearts and the Fatima Message – Participating in Mary's Mediation." *Missio Immaculatæ International* (English Edition) Year V, N° 3 (May/June 2009). 19–21.

———, "The Alliance of the Sacred Hearts and the Fatima Message – To Jesus through Mary: the Analogy of the Two Hearts." *Missio Immaculatæ International* (English Edition) Year V, N° 4 (July/August 2009). 13–15.

———, "The Alliance of the Hearts of Jesus and Mary and the Fatima Message – The Triumph of the Immaculate Heart." *Missio Immaculatæ International* (English Edition) Year V, N° 5 (September/October 2009). 21–23.

———, "The Alliance of the Two Hearts and Consecration." *Miles Immaculatæ* XXXI (Luglio/Dicembre 1995) 389–407.

———, "The Alliance of the Two Hearts and Mariology." *The Theology of the Alliance of the Two Hearts: Documents of the 1997 International Theological Pastoral Symposium on the Alliance of the Hearts of Jesus and Mary*, Book 1. Rome: Two Hearts Media Organization, 1997. 229–252.

———, "The Alliance of the Two Hearts and Mariology." *The Theology of the Alliance of the Two Hearts: Documents of the 2007 Asia-Pacific Theological and Pastoral Symposium on the*

Alliance of the Hearts of Jesus and Mary. Manila: Two Hearts Media Organization, Inc., 2008. 173–195.

———, "The Alliance of the Two Hearts and the Magisterium." *The Theology of the Alliance of the Two Hearts: Documents of the 2007 Asia-Pacific Theological and Pastoral Symposium on the Alliance of the Hearts of Jesus and Mary*. Manila: Two Hearts Media Organization, Inc., 2008. 51–85.

———, "The Cultus of the Hearts of Jesus and Mary in the Papal Magisterium from Pius IX to Pius XII." *Acta Congressus Mariologici-Mariani Internationalis in Sanctuario Mariano Kevelaer (Germania) Anno 1987 Celebrati* II: *De Cultu Mariano Saeculis XIX et XX usque ad Concilium Vaticanum II Studia Indolis Generalioris*. Rome: Pontificia Academia Mariana Internationalis, 1991. 355–392.

———, "The Hearts of Jesus and Mary in the Magisterium of Pope John Paul II." *Acta Congressus Mariologic-Mariani Internationalis in Civitate Onubensi (Huelva - Hispania) Anno 1992 Celebrati* IV: *De Cultu Mariano Saeculo XX a Concilio Vaticano II usque ad Nostros Dies*. Vatican City: Pontificia Academia Mariana Internationalis, 1999. 147–167.

———, "John Paul II's Consecration to the Immaculate Heart of Mary: Christological Foundation." *Miles Immaculatae* 23 (1987) 88–115; 364–417.

———, "Mary as Coredemptrix, Mediatrix and Advocate in the Contemporary Roman Liturgy." Miravalle, Mark I. S.T.D., Ed. *Mary Coredemptrix, Mediatrix, Advocate, Theological Foundations: Towards a Papal Definition?* Santa Barbara, CA: Queenship Publishing Company, 1995. 45–118.

———, "Mary Coredemptrix: The Beloved Associate of Christ." Miravalle, Mark, Ed., *Mariology: A Guide for Priests, Deacons, Seminarians, and Consecrated Persons*. Goleta, CA: Seat of Wisdom Books, 2008. 349–409.

———, "Mary, Mediatrix of All Graces, in the Papal Magisterium of Pope John Paul II," in *Mary at the Foot of the Cross* – VII: *Coredemptrix, Therefore Mediatrix of All Graces. Acts of the Seventh International Symposium on Marian Coredemption.* New Bedford, MA: Academy of the Immaculate, 2008. 17–63.

———, "Marian Coredemption and the Contemporary Papal Magisterium: The Truth of Marian Coredemption, the Papal Magisterium and the Present Situation," in *Maria "Unica Cooperatrice alla Redenzione." Atti del Simposio sul Mistero della Corredenzione Mariana, Fatima, Portogallo 3–7 Maggio 2005.* New Bedford, MA: Academy of the Immaculate, 2005. 147–158.

———, "Mary's Presence in the Mass." *Homiletic & Pastoral Review* XCVII, No. 10 (July 1997). 8–15.

———, "Mary's Presence in the Mass according to Pope John Paul II," in *Mary at the Foot of the Cross* – VI: *Marian Coredemption in the Eucharistic Mystery. Acts of the Sixth International Symposium on Marian Coredemption.* New Bedford, MA: Academy of the Immaculate, 2007. 11–38.

———, "Mary's Presence in the Mass: The Teaching of Pope John Paul II," in *Antiphon: A Journal for Liturgical Renewal* Vol. 10, N° 2 (2006) 132–158.

———, "Pope John Paul II's Ordinary Magisterium on Marian Coredemption: Consistent Teaching and More Recent Perspectives," in *Mary at the Foot of the Cross* – II: *Acts of the Second International Symposium on Marian Coredemption.* New Bedford, MA: Academy of the Immaculate, 2002. 153–185.

———, "Mary and the Church in the Papal Magisterium Before and After the Second Vatican Council," in *Mary at the Foot of the Cross* – IX: *Mary: Spouse of the Holy Spirit, Coredemptrix and Mother of the Church.* (New Bedford, MA:

Academy of the Immaculate, 2010) 11–51. Also published in *Divinitas* XLV "Nova Series" (2002) 153–185.

———, "Pope John Paul II's Teaching on Marian Coredemption." Mark I. Miravalle, S.T.D., ed. *Mary Coredemptrix, Mediatrix, Advocate, Theological Foundations II: Papal, Pneumatological, Ecumenical.* Santa Barbara, CA: Queenship Publishing Company, 1997. 1–36.

———, "Mary and the Church in the Papal Magisterium Before and After the Second Vatican Council," in *Mary at the Foot of the Cross* – IX: *Mary: Spouse of the Holy Spirit, Coredemptrix and Mother of the Church. Acts of the Ninth International Symposium on Marian Coredemption.* New Bedford, MA: Academy of the Immaculate, 2010. 11–51.

———, "Mary, Mediatrix of All Graces in the Papal Magisterium of Pope John Paul II," in *Mary at the Foot of the Cross* – VII: *Coredemptrix, Therefore Mediatrix of All Graces. Acts of the Seventh International Symposium on Marian Coredemption.* New Bedford, MA: Academy of the Immaculate, 2008. 17–63.

———, "Mary 'Minister of Grace' in the Magisterium and in the Contemporary Roman Liturgy," in *Mary at the Foot of the Cross* – IV: *Mater Viventium (Gen. 3:20). Acts of the Fourth International Symposium on Marian Coredemption.* New Bedford, MA: Academy of the Academy of the Immaculate, 2004. 29–70.

– "Il Mistero di Maria Corredentrice nel Magistero Pontificio," in Autori Vari, *Maria Corredentrice: Storia e Teologia I* (Frigento [AV]: Casa Mariana Editrice "Bibliotheca Corredemptionis B. V. Mariae" Studi e Richerche 1, 1998) 141–220.

———, "The Theology of the Alliance of the Hearts of Jesus and Mary – The Mystery of Iniquity," Part 1. *Missio Immaculatæ International* (English Edition) Year III, N° 4 (May 2007). 20–21.

———, "The Theology of the Alliance of the Hearts of Jesus and Mary – The Mystery of Mediation," Part 2. *Missio Immaculatæ International* (English Edition) Year III, N° 5 (June 2007). 20–21.

———, "The Theology of the Alliance of the Hearts of Jesus and Mary – Collaboration in Jesus' Mediation," Part 3. *Missio Immaculatæ International* (English Edition) Year III, N° 6 (July–August 2007). 24–25.

———, "The Theology of the Alliance of the Hearts of Jesus and Mary – Mary's Collaboration in Jesus' Mediation," Part 4. *Missio Immaculatæ International* (English Edition) Year III, N° 7 (September 2007). 24–25.

———, "The Theology of the Alliance of the Hearts of Jesus and Mary – Mary Coredemptrix," Part 5. *Missio Immaculatæ International* (English Edition) Year III, N° 8 (October 2007). 20–21.

———, "The Theology of the Alliance of the Hearts of Jesus and Mary – Mary Coredemptrix," Part 6. *Missio Immaculatæ International* (English Edition) Year III, N° 9 (November 2007). 20–21.

———, "The Theology of the Alliance of the Hearts of Jesus and Mary – Opposition," Part 7. *Missio Immaculatæ International* (English Edition) Year III, N° 10 (December 2007). 20–21.

———, "The Theology of the Alliance of the Hearts of Jesus and Mary – Opposition," Part 8. *Missio Immaculatæ International* (English Edition) Year IV, N° 1 (January 2008). 20–21.

———, "The Theology of the Alliance of the Hearts of Jesus and Mary," Part 9. *Missio Immaculatæ International* (English Edition) Year IV, N° 3 (March 2008). 20–21.

———, "The Union of the Hearts of Jesus and Mary in St. Francis de Sales and St. John Eudes." *Miles Immaculatae* 25 (1989) 454–495.

———, "'Towards Another Marian Dogma?' A Response to Father Angelo Amato, S.D.B." *Marianum* LIX (1997) 159–167.

———, "Why the Heart?" *Homiletic & Pastoral Review* 89:9 (June 1989) 18–23.

Calvo Moralejo, Gaspar, O.F.M. "Fray Melchor de Cetina, O.F.M., el primer teólogo de la 'Esclavitud Mariana' (1618)." *Estudios Marianos* 51 (1986) 249–71.

Canal, José Maria, C.M.F. "La Consagración a la Virgen y a su Corazon Inmaculado." *Acta Congressus Mariologici-Mariani Romae Anno MCMLIV Celebrati* 12: *De Virginis Immaculatae Regalitate Eiusque Corde Materno*. Rome: Pontificia Academia Mariana Internationalis, 1956. 221–348.

Carroll, Eamon R., O. Carm. "Mary the Woman Come of Age." *Marian Studies* 36 (1985): 136–60.

———, "A Survey of Recent Mariology." *Marian Studies* 35 (1984): 157–87.

———, "The New Testament Charisms of the Blessed Virgin Mary." *One in Christ* 22 (1986) 356–64.

———, *Understanding the Mother of Jesus*. Wilmington, Delaware: Michael Glazier, Inc., 1979.

Chasle, Louis. *Sister Mary of the Divine Heart*. Trans. by a Member of the Order. London: Burns & Oates, Ltd., 1906.

Ciappi, Mario Luigi Cardinal, O.P. *The Heart of Christ the Centre of the Mystery of Salvation*. Trans. Leslie Wearne and Andrew Wade. Rome: Cuore di Cristo Publishers, 1983.

Cochois, Paul. *Bérulle et l'École française*. n. 31 de *"Maîtres Spirituels."* Paris: Editions du Seuil, 1963.

La Consacrazione nella Congregazione Mariana. Rome: Edizioni Stella Matutina, 1963.

Cras, Pierre. "Mother Mary of the Divine Heart: A Divine Messenger." John J. Sullivan, S.J. (ed. & translation) *Divine Masterpieces*. Paterson, N. J.: St. Anthony Guild Press, 1960.

Colin, Louis, C.Ss.R. *Berthe Petit Apôtre du Cœur douloureux et Immaculé de Marie*. Paris: Nouvelles Éditions Latines, 1967.

Daniel, Lázaro Ilzo. *La Mediazione Materna di Maria in Cristo negli Insegnamenti di Giovanni Paolo II*. Lugano: Europress FTL, 2011.

de Becker, Gérald, SS.CC. *Lexique Pour la Théologie du Cœur du Christ*. Paris: Téqui, 1975.

———, *Les Sacrés-Cœurs de Jésus et de Marie: Étude Doctrinale*. Rome: Etude Picpuciennes #5, 1959.

de Finance, Joseph, S.J. "Consécration." M. Viller et al. *Dictionnaire de Spiritualité Ascétique et Mystique* 2. Paris: Beauchesne, 1953. 1576–83.

De Fiores, Stefano, S.M.M. *Itinerario spirituale di S. Luigi Maria de Montfort (1673–1716) nel periodo fino al sacerdozio (5 giugno 1700). Marian Library Studies*, new series, 6. Dayton, Ohio: University of Dayton, 1974.

———, "Linee di Sviluppo della Riflessione Teologica sul Ruolo Storico di Maria." *Il ruolo di Maria nell'oggi della Chiesa e del Mondo*. Rome: Edizioni Marianum, 1979. 205–18.

———, *Maria nella Teologia Contemporanea*. seconda ed. Rome: Centro di Cultura Mariana "Mater Ecclesiae," 1987.

———, *Maria: presenza viva nel popolo di Dio*. Rome: Edizioni Monfortane, 1980.

———, *Maria, Nuovissimo Dizionario*, 1. Bologna; Edizioni Dehoniane, 2006.

———, *Maria: Nuovissimo Dizionario*, 2. Bologna: Edizioni Dehoniane, 2006.

———, *Maria: Nuovissimo Dizionario*, 3. Bologna: Edizioni Dehoniane, 2008.

———, "Proposte teologiche circa la consacrazione Mariana." *La Madonna* 30.3–4 (agosto 1982): 3–15.

———, "Questi tuoi figli o Madre." *L'Osservatore Romano* 9–10 dicembre 1981: 1–2.

De Fiores, Stefano, General Editor. *Jesus Living in Mary: Handbook of the Spirituality of St. Louis Marie de Montfort.* Bay Shore, NY: Montfort Publications, 1994.

De Fiores, Stefano, S.M.M., Santino Epis, S.M.M., and Gabriele Amorth S.S.P. *La consacrazione dell'Italia a Maria: Teologia, storia, cronaca.* Presentazione del card. Carlo Maria Martini. Rome: Edizioni Paoline, 1983.

De Fiores, Stefano, S.M.M., and Salvatore Meo, O.S.M., eds. *Nuovo Dizionario di Mariologia.* Milan: Edizioni Paoline, 1985.

Degli Esposti, Francesco. *La Teologia del Sacro Cuore di Gesù da Leone XIII a Pio XII.* Rome: Casa Editrice Herder, 1967.

Deville, Raymond, P.S.S. *L'école française de spiritualité.* n. 11 de la *Bibliothèque d'Histoire du Christianisme.* Paris: Desclée, 1987.

de los Angeles, Juan – de Cetina, Melchior. *Esortazione alla devozione della Vergine Madre di Dio: Alle origini della "schiavitù mariana."* Introduzione, traduzione e note di Stefano M. Cecchin, O.F.M. (Vatican City: Pontificia Academia Mariana Internationalis, 2003).

Dillenschneider, Clément, C.Ss.R. *La Mariologie de S. Alphonse de Liguori: Sources et Synthèse Doctrinale.* Fribourg: Studia Friburgensia, 1934.

Dodd, Gloria Falcão. *The Virgin Mary, Mediatrix of All Grace: History and Theology of the Movement for a Dogmatic*

Definition from 1896 to 1964. New Bedford, MA: Academy of the Immaculate, 2012.

Domański, Jerzy, O.F.M. Conv. *For the Life of the World: Saint Maximilian and the Eucharist*. New Bedford, MA: Academy of the Immaculate, 1993.

"Dossier di una Giornata Teologica sulla Richiesta di Definizione Dogmatica di 'Maria Corredentrice Mediatrice Avvocata,' 28 Maggio 1998: Nota Introduttiva, Relazione Base di Ignazio M. Calabuig, Repertorio Bibliografico di Antonio Escudero Cabello," *Marianum* LXI (1999) 123–211.

Duda, Bonaventura, O.F.M. "'Ecce mater tua' (Jo. 19, 26–27) in documentis Romanorum Pontificum." *Acta Congressus Mariologici-Mariani in Republica Dominicana Anno 1965 Celebrati* 5: *De Beata Virgine Maria in Evangelio S. Ioannis et in Apocalypsi*. Rome: Pontificia Academia Mariana Internationalis, 1967. 235–89.

Duff, Frank. *The Woman of Genesis*. Dublin: Praedicanda Publications, 1976.

Duffner, I. M.S.C. *Berthe Petit, Tertiaire franciscaine (1870–1943) et La Dévotion au Cœur Douloureux et Immaculé de Marie*. La Seyne-sur-Mer: Bénédictines Camaldules, 1955.

Durwell, F. X., C.Ss.R. *The Resurrection: A Biblical Study*. Trans. Rosemary Sheed. New York: Sheed and Ward, 1960.

Elvins, Mark. "The Origin of the Title 'Dowry of Mary' and the Shrines of Our Lady at Westminster." A paper given to the London branch of the Ecumenical Society of the Blessed Virgin Mary on 18 May 1989.

Epis, Santino, S.M.M. "La Consacrazione dell'Italia a Maria: Un Capitolo di Storia e un Impegno Permanente" De Fiores, Epis, Amorth (eds.) *La Consacrazione dell'Italia a Maria*. Rome: Edizioni Paoline, 1983. 65–88.

Études Carmélitaines: *Le Cœur*. Paris: Desclée de Brouwer, 1950.

Eudes, St. Jean. *Œuvres Complètes du Vénérable Jean Eudes*. 12 vols. Vannes: Imprimerie Lafoyle Frères, 1905–11.

———, *The Life and Kingdom of Jesus in Christian Souls*. Trans. Trappist Father. New York: P. J. Kenedy & Sons, 1946.

———, *Letters and Shorter Works*. Trans. Ruth Hauser. New York: P. J. Kenedy & Sons, 1948.

———, *The Sacred Heart of Jesus*. Trans. Richard Flower, O.S.B. New York: P. J. Kenedy & Sons, 1946.

Flynn, J. "Mazzella, Camillo." *New Catholic Encyclopedia* 9. New York: McGraw-Hill Book Co., 1967. 523–24.

Fehlner, Peter Damian, O.F.M. Conv. "The Immaculate and the Mystery of the Trinity in the Thought of St. Maximilian Kolbe." *La Mariologia di S. Massimiliano Kolbe*. Rome: Ed. Miscellanea Francescana, 1985. 382–416.

———, "Mary Immaculate and St. Francis." *Miscellanea Francescana* 82 (1982) 502–19.

———, "Mulieris Dignitatem." *Miles Immaculatae* 25 (1989) 6–9.

Fernandez, Quirino. "Los Rios y Alarcon, (Bartolomé de)." M. Viller et al. *Dictionnaire de Spiritualité Ascétique et Mystique* 9. Paris: Beauchesne et Ses Fils, 1976. 1013–18.

Franzi, Francesco M. "'Consacrazione' o 'affidamento'?" *Miles Immaculatae* 17 (1981) 216–28.

———, "Per un orientamento sul tema della 'consacrazione a Maria'." *Teologia e Pastorale della Consacrazione a Maria*. Padua: Edizioni Messagero, 1969. 7–12.

Frossard, André. *"Be Not Afraid!": Pope John Paul II Speaks out on his Life, his Beliefs, and his Inspiring Vision for Humanity*. Trans. J. R. Foster. New York: St. Martin's Press, 1984.

Gaffney, J. Patrick, S.M.M. "Changing the I to We." *Queen of All Hearts* 35 (Sept.–Oct. 1984) 18–19, 24.

———, “The Holy Slavery of Love.” Juniper B. Carol, O.F.M. ed. *Mariology* 3. Milwaukee: Bruce Publishing Co., 1961. 143–61.

———, “Saint Louis Mary Grignion de Montfort and the Marian Consecration.” *Marian Studies* 35 (1984) 111–156.

Galot, Jean, S.J. “The First Act of Consecration.” *Queen of All Hearts* 33.2 (July–August 1982): 12–13.

———, *Theology of the Priesthood.* Trans. Roger Balducelli, O.S.F.S. San Francisco: Ignatius Press, 1984.

Gambero Luigi (ed.). *Testi Mariani del Secondo Millennio*, 4: *Autori medievali dell'Occidente sec. XIII–XV* (Rome: Città Nuova, 1996) 678–683.

Gardeil, H. D., O.P. *Introduction to the Philosophy of St. Thomas Aquinas IV: Metaphysics.* Trans. John A. Otto. St. Louis: B. Herder Book Co., 1967.

Garrigou-Lagrange, Reginald, O.P. *The Mother of The Saviour and Our Interior Life.* Trans. Bernard J. Kelly, C.S.Sp. St. Louis: B. Herder Book Co., 1957.

———, *Our Savior and His Love for Us.* Trans. A. Bouchard. St. Louis: B. Herder Book Co., 1951.

———, *The Three Ages of the Interior Life* II. Trans. Sister Timothea Doyle, O.P. St. Louis: B. Herder Book Co., 1948.

Gauthey, Monseigneur François-Léon. Ed. *Vie et Œuvres de Sainte Marguerite-Marie Alocoque.* Paris: Ancienne Librairie Poussielgue, 1920. Vol. 2.

Gautier, Jean. *Some Schools of Catholic Spirituality.* Trans. Kathryn Sullivan, R.S.C.J. Tournai: Desclée Co., 1959.

Gharib, Georges. “La Madonna della Misericordia: ‘Sotto la tua protezione’.” *Madre di Dio* 59 (maggio 1991) 13–16.

Gharib, Georges, Ermanno M. Toniolo, Luigi Gambero, and Gerardo di Nola. eds. *Testi Mariani del Primo Millennio* Vol.

2: *Padri e altri autori bizantini*. Rome: Città Nuova Editrice, 1989.

Geagea, O.C.D., Nilo. *Maria, Madre e Decoro del Carmelo: La pietà mariana dei Carmelitani durante i primi tre secoli della loro storia*. Rome: Institutum Historicum Teresianum, 1988. 369–438.

Geenen, G., O.P. "Les Antécédents Doctrinaux et Historiques de la Consécration du Monde au Coeur Immaculé de Marie." Hubert du Manoir, S.J., ed. *Maria: Études sur la Sainte Vierge* I. Paris: Beauchesne et Ses Fils, 1949. 825–873.

Gherardini, Brunero. *La Corredentice nel mistero di Cristo e della Chiesa*. Rome: Edizioni Vivere In, 1998.

———, "The Coredemption of Mary: Doctrine of the Church," in *Mary at the Foot of the Cross* – II: *Acts of the Second International Symposium on Marian Coredemption*. New Bedford, MA: Academy of the Immaculate, 2002. 37–48.

———, *La Madre: Maria in una sintesi storico-teologica*. Seconda edizione riveduta eaggiornata. Frigento: Casa Mariana Editrice, 2007.

———, *Sta La Regina alla Tua Destra: Saggio storico-teologico sulla Regalità di Maria* Rome: Edizioni Vivere In, 2002.

———, "Unity and Coredemption," in *Mary at the Foot of the Cross* – III: *Maria, Mater Unitatis. Acts of the Third International Symposium on Marian Coredemption*. New Bedford, MA: Academy of the Immaculate, 2003. 54–69.

Giamberardini, Gabriele O.F.M. *Il culto mariano in Egitto*, Vol. I: *Secoli I–VI*. Jerusalem: Franciscan Printing Press, 1975.

Gila, Angelo. "'Maria Regina e Madre di Misericordia': Un Tema Tipico dell'Epoca Medioevale" in *Maria Madre di Misericordia: Monstra Te Esse Matrem* a cura di Piergiorgio Di Domenico e Elio Peretto (Padua: Messaggero di Sant'Antonio Editrice, 2003) 186–217.

Ginn, Roman, O.C.S.O. "Slave Talk in St. Paul and St. Louis de Montfort." *Queen of All Hearts* 39 (March–April 1989) 12–13.

Glotin, Edouard, S.J. "Le centre de l'âme et l'Icône sacrée du Cœur. De Thérèse d'Avila à Marguerite-Marie." *Jésus-Christ Rédempteur de l'Homme*. Venasque: Éditions de Carmel, 1986. 103–154.

———, "Jean-Paul à Paray-le-Monial ou Pourquoi le 'Cœur'." *Nouvelle Revue Théologique* 108 (1986) 685–714.

———, *La Bible du Cœur de Jésus*. Paris: Presses de la Renaissance, 2007.

Grignion de Montfort, St. Louis-Marie. *Œuvres complètes de saint Louis-Marie Grignion de Montfort*. Paris: Éditions du Seuil, 1982.

———, *God Alone: The Collected Writings of St. Louis Mary de Montfort*. Bay Shore, N. Y.: Montfort Publications, 1987.

Gutierrez Osorio, Pastor, S.I. "'Ecce Mater tua' (Jn. 19, 25–27): Maternitas spiritualis Mariae in luce exegeseos SS. Patrum et scriptorum posteriorum." *Acta Congressus Mariologici-Mariani in Republica Dominicana Anno 1965 Celebrati* 5: *De Beata Virgine Maria in Evangelio S. Ioannis et in Apocalypsi*. Rome: Pontificia Academia Mariana Internationalis, 1967. 151–60.

Hauke, Manfred. *Maria, "Mediatrice di Tutte le Grazie": La Mediazione Universale di Maria nell'Opera Teologica e Pastorale de Cardinale Mercier*. Lugano: Europress FTL, 2005.

———, *Mary, "Mediatress of Grace": Mary's Universal Mediation of Grace in the Theological and Pastoral Works of Cardinal Mercier*. Supplement to *Mary at the Foot of the Cross* – IV: *Mater Viventium (Gen. 3:20). Acts of the Fourth International*

Symposium on Marian Coredemption. New Bedford, MA: Academy of the Immaculate, 2004.

Iacoangeli, R. "*Sub tuum praesidium.* La più antica preghiera mariana: filologia e fede," Sergio Felici ed. *La mariologia nella catechesi dei Padri (età prenicena).* Roma: Libreria Ateneo Salesiano "Biblioteca di Scienza Religiosa" #88, 1989. 207–40.

"Il Papa Giovanni Paolo II tra gli 'apostoli degli ultimi tempi'," in *Spiritualità Monfortana* 6. Rome: Centre International Montfortain, 2006. 9–19.

Jelly, Frederick M., O.P. "The mystery of Mary's mediation." *Homiletic and Pastoral Review* 80:8 (May 1980) 11–20.

Johnston, Francis. *Alexandrina: The Agony and the Glory.* Rockford, Illinois: Tan Books and Publishers, 1982.

———, *Fatima: The Great Sign.* Washington, N.J.: A.M.I. Press, 1980.

Joseph de Sainte-Marie, O.C.D. "Réflexions sur un acte de consécration: Fatima, 13 mai 1982." *Marianum* 44 (1982) 88–142.

———, *Reflections on the Act of Consecration at Fatima of Pope John Paul II on 13th May 1982.* Trans. William Lawson, S.J. Chulmleigh, Devon.: Augustine Publishing Co.; Rockford, Ill.: Tan Books and Publishers, Inc., 1983.

———, *Teologia e Spiritualità della Consacrazione a Maria.* Rome: Pontificio Istituto di Spiritualità del Teresianum, n.d.

Jungmann, J. A., S.J. *Pastoral Liturgy.* New York: Herder and Herder, 1962.

Kiefer, William J., S.M. (ed.). *Mary in Our Christ-Life* (Milwaukee: Bruce Publishing Company, 1961).

Klubertanz, G. P. "Analogy." *New Catholic Encyclopedia* 1. New York: McGraw-Hill Book Co., 1967. 461–65.

Koehler, Theodore, S.M. "Maternité Spirituelle, Maternité Mystique." Hubert du Manoir, S.J. ed. *Maria: Études sur la Sainte Vierge* 6. Paris: Beauchesne et Ses Fils, 1961. 552–638.

———, "Mary's Spiritual Maternity after the Second Vatican Council." *Marian Studies* 23 (1972) 39–68.

———, "Les principales interpretations traditionelles de Jn. 19, 25–27 pendant les douze premiers siècles." *Études Mariales* 16 (1959): 119–55.

———, "Servitude (saint esclavage)." *M. Viller et al. Dictionnaire de Spiritualité Ascétique et Mystique* 14. Paris: Beauchesne et Ses Fils, 1990. 730–745.

Kolbe, St. Maximilian, O.F.M. Conv. *Scritti di Massimiliano Kolbe*. Trans. from the Polish by Cristoforo Zambelli. Rome: Editrice Nazionale M.I., 1997.

Kolbe, St. Maximilian Maria, *The Writings of St. Maximilian Maria Kolbe*, Lugano, Switzerland: Nerbini International, 2016. Volume I: *Letters*; Volume II: *Various Writings*.

Kondor, Louis, S.V.D., ed. *Fatima in Lucia's Own Words*. Trans. Dominican Nuns of Perpetual Rosary. Fatima, Portugal: Postulation Centre, 1976.

Kosicki, George W., C.S.B. *Born of Mary*. Stockbridge, MA: Marian Press, 1985.

———, *John Paul II: The Great Mercy Pope*. Stockbridge, MA: Marian Press, Beatification edition, 2011.

Larkin, Francis, SS.CC. "Crawley-Boevey, Mateo." *New Catholic Encyclopedia* 4. New York: McGraw-Hill Book Co., 1967. 16.

Laurenceau, J., O.P. "Aperçus sur l'histoire de la consécration à Marie." *Cahiers Marials* 137 (1983) 66–84.

Laurentin, René. "Bulletin sur la Vierge Marie." *Revue des Sciences Philosophiques et Théologiques* 70 (1986) 101–50.

———, "Consecration and Entrustment: A Commitment to the Hearts of Jesus and Mary – Its Meaning for Our Personal Lives and the Life of Our People." Trans. Srs. Edita Telan, M.I.C. and Rachel de Mars, M.I.C. *The Alliance of the Hearts of Jesus and Mary: The International Theological/Pastoral Conference, Manila, Philippines, 30 November – December 1987, Texts and Documents*. Manila: Bahay Maria, 1988. 231–59.

———, "The Magisterium of the Church on the Alliance of the Hearts of Jesus and Mary." Trans. Srs. Edita Telan, M.I.C. and Rachel de Mars, M.I.C. *The Alliance of the Hearts of Jesus and Mary: The International Theological/Pastoral Conference, Manila, Philippines, 30 November – December 1987, Texts and Documents*. Manila: Bahay Maria, 1988. 158–87.

———, *Marie, l'Église et Le Sacerdoce I: Essai sur le Développement d'une Idée Religieuse*. Paris: P. Lethielleux "Nouvelles Editions Latines," 1952. 422–467.

———, "Pétitions internationales pour une définition dogmatique de la médiation et la corédemption," *Marianum* LVIII (1996). 429–446.

———, *Présence de Marie: Histoire, Spiritualité, Fondements Doctrinaux*. Paris: Éditions Salvator. 2011.

———, *Queen of Heaven: A Short Treatise on Marian Theology*. Trans. Gordon Smith. Dublin: Clonmore & Reynolds; London: Burns Oates & Washbourne Ltd., 1956.

———, *The Question of Mary*. Trans. I. G. Pidoux. New York: Holt, Rinehart and Winston, 1965.

———, "Something to Consider Before you Sign." *Marian Library Newsletter*, No. 36 (new series), Summer 1998, 4.

———, *Le voeu de Louis XIII: Passé our avenir de la France 1638–1988*. Paris: O.E.I.L., 1988.

———, *A Year of Grace with Mary: Rediscovering Her Presence and Her Role in Our Consecration*. Trans. Msgr. Michael J. Wrenn. Dublin: Veritas, 1987.

Lebon, Henri S.M. "Chaminade (Guillaume-Joseph)." M. Viller et al. *Dictionnaire de Spiritualité Ascétique et Mystique* 2. Paris: Beauchesne et Ses Fils, 1990. 454–59.

Lebrun, Charles, C.J.M. *Le Bienheureux Jean Eudes et le Culte Public du Cœur de Jésus*. Paris: P. Lethielleux, 1918.

———, *The Spiritual Teaching of St. John Eudes*. Trans. Basil Whelan, O.S.B. London: Sands and Co., 1934.

Leeming, Bernard, S.J. "Consecration to the Sacred Heart." Augustinus Bea, S.J., Hugo Rahner, S.J., Henri Rondet, S.J. et Friedr. Schwendimann, S.J. eds. *Cor Jesu: Commentationes in Litteras Encyclicas Pii XII "Haurietis Aquas"* I: *Pars Theologica*. Roma: Casa Editrice Herder, 1959. 597–655.

Lépicier, Alexis M., O.S.M. *L'Immaculée Mère de Dieu, corédemptrice du genre humain*. Tournhut, Belgium. 1906.

Léthel, François-Marie, O.C.D. *L'Amour de Jésus en Marie: Le Traité de la vraie dévotion à la Sainte Vierge, Le Secret de Marie*. Geneva: Éditions Ad Solem, 2000. I:81–119.

———, *La Luce di Cristo nel Cuore della Chiesa: Giovanni Paolo II e la Teologia dei Santi. Esercizi Spirituali con Benedetto XVI*. Vatican City: Libreria Editrice Vaticana, 2011

———, "La Maternité de Marie dans le Mystère de l'Incarnation et de notre Divinisation selon saint Louis-Marie Grignion de Montfort et le Cardinal de Bérulle." Léthel, François-Marie O.C.D. *Théologie de l'Amour de Jésus: Écrits sur la théologie des saints*. Venasque: Editions du Carmel, 1996. 103–138.

Letourneur, Jean. "Dufriche-Desgenettes, Charles-Eléonor." M. Viller et al. *ictionnaire de Spiritualité Ascétique et Mystique* 3. Paris: Beauchesne et es Fils, 1957. 1757–1759.

Lewandowski, Bogumil. *Tutti consacrati alla Madonna.* Rome 1988.

Little, Joyce A. "*Redemptoris Mater*: The Significance of Mary for Women." *Marian Studies* 39 (1988) 136–58.

Lohkamp, N. "Consecration, Personal." *New Catholic Encyclopedia* 4. New York: McGraw-Hill Book Co., 1967. 209.

Lozano, Juan Maria, C.M.F. *Mystic and Man of Action: Saint Anthony Mary Claret.* Trans. Joseph Daries, C.M.F. Chicago: Claretian Publications, 1977.

Luis, Angel, C.Ss.R. "La consagración a Maria en la vida y doctrina de Juan Pablo II." *Estudios Marianos* 51 (1986) 77–112.

Mai, Angelo Cardinal ed. *Nova Patrum Bibliotheca*, Vol. VI, *Pars Secunda.* Rome: Typis Sacri Consilii Propagando Christiano Nomini, 1853.

Manteau-Bonamy, H., O.P. *La Doctrine Mariale du Père Kolbe: plein feu sur l'Immaculée.* Deuxieme édition remaniée. Paris: Lethielleux, 1979.

———, *Immaculate Conception and the Holy Spirit: The Marian Teachings of Father Kolbe.* Trans. Bro. Richard Arnandez, F.S.C. Kenosha, Wisconsin: Franciscan Marytown Press, 1977.

J. Marangos, S.J., "Le Culte Marial Populaire en Grèce." Hubert du Manoir, S.J. ed. *Maria: Études sur la Sainte Vierge* 4. Paris: Beauchesne et Ses Fils, 1956. 810–811.

Marranzini, Alfredo, S.I. "L' 'Atto di Affidamento e Consacrazione' a Maria: Significato teologico." *Civilta Cattolica* 135.2 (1984): 12–29.

———, "Consacrazione a Maria in Prospettiva Teologico-Antropologica." *Madonna: Rivista di Cultura Mariana* 27 (agosto 1979) 51–76.

Marquis, Marie-Odile e Jean-Hughes. *Spiritualità del Cuore di Cristo*. Trans. Sr. Clemente Moro. Milano: Editrice Ancora, 1986.

Martins, Antonio Maria, S.J. ed. and trans. *Memórias e Cartas de Irmã Lúcia*. Porto, Portugal: Simão Guimarães, Filhos, Lda., 1973.

Masson, Pierre-Reginald, O.P. "'Ecce mater tua' (Jn 19, 25–27) selon l'interpretation des théologiens." *Acta Congressus Mariologici-Mariani in Republica Dominicana Anno 1965 Celebrati* 5: *De Beata Virgine Maria in Evangelio S. Ioannis et in Apocalypsi*. Roma: Pontificia Academia Mariana Internationalis, 1967. 201–23.

Mathews, Stanley G., S.M. *Queen of the Universe: An Anthology on theAssumption and Queenship of Mary*. Saint Meinrad, Indiana: Grail Publications, 1957.

Meo, Salvatore, O.S.M. "La 'Mediazione materna' di Maria nell'Enciclica 'Redemptoris Mater.'" *Redemptoris Mater: Contenuti e Prospettive Dottrinali e Pastorali*. Rome: Pontificia Accademia Mariana Internazionale, 1988. 131–157.

Mercado, Alphonsus, O.F.M. "De verbis Jesu ad Matrem et Discipulum (Io. 19, 26–27a) iuxta genus ioanneum. Adnotationes." *Acta Congressus Mariologici-Mariani in Republica Dominicana Anno 1965 Celebrati* 5: *De Beata Virgine Maria in Evangelio S. Ioannis et in Apocalypsi*. Rome: Pontificia Academia Mariana Internationalis, 1967. 123–37.

Micewski, Andrzej. *Cardinal Wyszyński: A Biography*. Trans. William R. Brand and Katarzyna Mroczkowski-Brand. New York: Harcourt Brace Jovanovich, Publishers, 1984.

Michaud, J.-P., S.M.M. "Au service du Mystère de Dieu avec les Hommes." *Cahiers Marials* #86 (1973) 15–22.

Miller, Frederick L. *The Grace of Ars*. San Francisco: Ignatius Press, 2010.

Mitchell, Valentine Albert, S.M. *The Mariology of Saint John Damascene*. Kirkwood, MO: Maryhurst Normal Press, 1930.

Molien, A. "Bérulle." Marcel Viller, S.J., et al. *Dictionnaire de Spiritualité Ascétique et Mystique*. Paris: Gabriel Beauchesne et Ses Fils, 1937. 1539–1582.

Morgain, O.C.D., Stéphane-Marie. *Pierre de Bérulle et les Carmélites de France* (Paris: Éditions du Cerf, 1995).

Most, W. G. "Marian Consecration as Service: Historical, Theological and Spiritual Reflections." *Miles Immaculatae* 24 (1988) 441–63.

———, *Mary in Our Life: Our Lady in Doctrine and Devotion*. New York: P. J. Kenedy & Sons, 1955.

———, *Vatican II – Marian Council*. Athlone, Ireland: St. Paul Publications, 1972.

Murphy, John F. *Mary's Immaculate Heart: The Meaning of the Devotion to the Immaculate Heart of Mary*. Milwaukee: Bruce Publishing Company, 1951.

———, "Origin and Nature of Marian Cult." Juniper B. Carol, O.F.M. ed. *Mariology* 3. Milwaukee: Bruce Publishing Co., 1961. 1–21.

McCarthy, Msgr. John F. "An Assessment of the Recent Extraordinary Synod." *The Wanderer*, 119.11 (13 March 1986): 3.

McCurry, James, O.F.M. Conv. "Maximilian Kolbe and the Franciscan Marian Tradition." *The Cord* 33 (Sept. 1983): 227–38.

MacDonald, Donald, S.M.M. "From the Slavery of sin to the Total Consecration to Christ." *Queen of All Hearts* 40 (July–August 1989) 18–19.

McGratty, Arthur R., S.J. *The Sacred Heart Yesterday and Today.* New York: Benziger Brothers, Inc., 1951.

Nagyfalusy, Louis, S.J. "Le Culte de la Sainte Vierge en Hongrie, 'Regnum Marianum'," *Maria* 4:645–646, 649–650.

Neubert, Emile, S.M. *Autobiography of Father Emile Neubert, Marianist.* Trans. & Ed. Thomas A. Stanley, S.M. Dayton: North American Center for Marianist Studies. Monograph Series, no. 55, 2007.

———, *La Mission Apostolique de Marie et la Nôtre.* Paris: Alsatia, 1956.

———, *Mary in Doctrine.* Milwaukee: Bruce Publishing Co., 1954.

———, *My Ideal: Jesus Son of Mary.* Rockford, IL: Tan Books and Publishers, 1988.

———, *Queen of Militants.* St. Meinrad, IN: Grail Publications, 1947.

Noye, Irenée, P.S.S. "O Jesus Living in Mary." Trans. Roger M. Charest, S.M.M. *Queen of All Hearts* 32 (January–February 1982) 7–9, 36.

"O Matce i Krolowej Polakow" – Refleksje, modlitwy, piesni Jasna Gora. Rzym: Paulini, 1982. 263–66.

O'Carroll, Michael, C.S.Sp. "The Alliance of the Two Hearts." *Doctrine and Life* 38 (1988) 234–241.

———, *Mediatress of All Graces.* Westminster, MD: Newman Press, 1958.

———, "Still Mediatress of All Graces?" *Miles Immaculatae* 24 (1988) 114–33.

———, *Theotokos: A Theological Encyclopedia of the Blessed Virgin Mary*. Wilmington: Michael Glazier, Inc.; Dublin: Dominican Publications, 1982.

———, *Veni Creator Spiritus: A Theological Encyclopedia of the Holy Spirit*. Collegeville, Minnesota: The Liturgical Press "A Michael Glazier Book," 1990.

O'Connor, Edward D., C.S.C. "Mary and the Holy Spirit." *Homiletic & Pastoral Review* 90:8 (1990) 21–30.

———, *Pope Paul and the Spirit: Charisms and Church Renewal in the Teaching of Paul VI*. Notre Dame, Indiana: Ave Maria Press, 1978.

———, "The Roots of Pope John Paul II's Devotion to Mary." *Marian Studies* 39 (1988) 78–114.

O'Donnell, Timothy Terrance. *Heart of the Redeemer: An Apologia for the Contemporary and Perennial Value of the Devotion to the Sacred Heart of Jesus*. Manassas, Virginia: Trinity Communications, 1989.

Ong, Walter J., S.J. *Fighting for Life*. Ithaca, N.Y./ London: Cornell University Press, 1981.

The Official Handbook of the Legion of Mary. Dublin: Concilium Legionis Mariae, 1961.

Ordoñez Marquez, J. "La Cofradía de la Esclavitud en las Concepcionistas de Alcalá." *Estudios Marianos* 51 (1986) 231–48.

Pach, Jan, O.S.P.P.E. *Maria nell'Insegnamento del Cardinal Stefan Wyszyński*. Rome: Dissertationes ad Lauream in Pontificia Facultate Theologica "Marianum," 1989.

Papàsogli, Benedetta. *Montfort: A Prophet for our times*. Trans. Ann Nielsen, D.W. Roma: Edizioni Monfortane, 1991.

Pasquale, Umberto M., S.D.B. *Messaggera di Gesù per la Consacrazione del Mondoal Cuore Immacolato*. Rome: Postulazione Casa Generalizia Salesiana, n.d.

Peeters, Paul L. "*Dominum et Vivificantem*: The Conscience and the Heart." *Communio: International Catholic Review* 15 (1988) 148–55.

Pelletier, Joseph A., A.A. *The Immaculate Heart of Mary*. Worcester, MA: An Assumption Publication, 1976.

Perillo, Mother M. Francesca, F.I., "*Sub Tuum Præsidium*: Incomparable Marian Præconium," in *Mary at the Foot of the Cross – IV*: *Acts of the Fourth International Symposium on Marian Coredemption* (New Bedford, MA: Academy of the Immaculate, 2004) 138–69.

Perrella, Salvatore O.S.M. "La cooperazione di Maria all'opera della Redenzione: Attualità di una questione," *OR* 4 June 1997. 10–11.

———, "Mary's co-operation in work of Redemption: Present State of a Question." *ORE* 1498:9–10.

Philips, Gerard. "La Vierge au IIe Concile du Vatican et L'Avenir de la Mariologie." Hubert du Manoir, S.J. ed. *Maria: Études sur la Sainte Vierge* 8. Paris: Beauchesne et Ses Fils, 1971. 42–88.

Pontifical International Marian Academy. *The Mother of the Lord: Memory, Presence, Hope*. Trans. Thomas A. Thompson, SM. Staten Island, NY: St Pauls, 2007.

Pontificia Academia Mariana Internationalis. *La Madre del Signore Memoria Presenza Speranza. Alcune questioni attuali sulla figura e la missione della b. Vergine Maria*. Vatican City, 2000.

Pope Benedict XVI. *Jesus, The Apostles, and the Early Church*. San Francisco: Ignatius Press, 2007.

Poupon, M.-Th., O.P. *Le poème de la parfaite consécration à Marie.* Lyon: Librairie de Sacré-Cœur, 1947.

Pourat, Pierre, P.S.S. "Abandon." M. Viller, S.J. et al. *Dictionnaire de Spiritualité Ascétique et Mystique* 1. Paris: Gabriel Beauchesne et Ses Fils, 1937. 1–49.

———, *Christian Spirituality* 3. Trans. W. A. Mitchell. Westminister, Md.: Newman Press, 1953.

———, "La Dévotion à Marie dans la Compagnie de Saint-Sulpice," Maria III:153–162.

Prat, Ferdinand, S.J. *Jesus Christ: His Life, His Teaching, and His Work* 2. Trans. John J. Heenan, S.J. Milwaukee: Bruce Publishing Co., 1950.

Pujana, Juan. "Simon de Rojas." Marcel Viller, S.J., et al. *Dictionnaire de Spiritualité Ascétique et Mystique* 14. Paris: Gabriel Beauchesne et Ses Fils, 1990. 877–884.

Quéméneur, M., S.M.M. "La consécration de soi à la Vierge à travers l'histoire." *Cahiers Marials* 3 (1959) 119–28.

———, "Towards a History of Marian Consecration." Trans. *William Fackovec, S.M. Marian Library Studies* 122 (March 1966).

Ragazzini, Severino M. O.F.M. Conv. *Maria Vita dell'Anima: Itinerario Mariano alla SS. Trinità.* Frigento (AV): "Casa Mariana," 1984. 207–257.

Ratzinger, Joseph / Pope Benedict XVI. *Jesus of Nazareth* Part Two: *Holy Week – From the Entrance into Jerusalem to the Resurrection.* Trans. Vatican Secretariat of State. San Francisco: Ignatius Press, 2011.

Resch, Andreas C.Ss.R. *I Beati di Giovanni Paolo II*, Vol. II: 1986–1990. Vatican City: Libreria Editrice Vaticana, 2002.

———, *I Beati di Giovanni Paolo II*, Vol. III: 1991–1995. Vatican City: Libreria Editrice Vaticana, 2003.

———, *I Beati di Giovanni Paolo II*, Vol. IV: 1996–2000. Vatican City: Libreria Editrice Vaticana, 2004.

———, *I Beati di Giovanni Paolo II*, Vol. V: 2001–2004. Vatican City: Libreria Editrice Vaticana, 2004.

Rayez André, S.J. "La Dévotion Mariale chez Bérulle et ses Premiers Disciples" in *Maria* 3. 31–72.

Resch, Peter A., S.M. "Filial Piety." Juniper B. Carol, O.F.M., ed. *Mariology* 3 (Milwaukee: Bruce Publishing Co., 1961. 162–67.

Ricciardi, Antonio, O.F.M. Conv. *St. Maximilian Kolbe: Apostle of Our Difficult Age*. Trans. Daughters of St. Paul. Boston: St. Paul Editions, 1982.

Robichaud, Armand J., S.M. "Mary, Dispensatrix of All Graces." Juniper. B. Carol, O.F.M., ed. *Mariology* 2. Milwaukee: Bruce Publishing Co., 1957. 426–60.

Romb, Anselm, O.F.M. Conv., ed. *The Kolbe Reader*. Libertyville, IL: Franciscan Marytown Press, 1987.

Roschini, Gabriele M., O.S.M. "La Consacrazione del Mondo al Cuore Immacolato di Maria." *Il Cuore Immacolato di Maria, Settimana di Studi Mariani*. Rome: Edizioni Marianum, 1946. 55–78.

———, *Dizionario di Mariologia*. Roma: Editrice Studium, 1961.

———, *Maria Santissima nella Storia della Salvezza* 4 vols. Isola del Liri: Tipografia Editrice M. Pisani, 1969.

Salaville, S., A.A. "Marie dans la Liturgie Byzantine ou Gréco-Slave." Hubert du Manoir, S.J., ed. *Maria: Études sur la Sainte Vierge* 1. Paris: Beauchesne et Ses Fils, 1949. 249–326.

Salgado, Jean-Marie, O.M.I. "Les appropriations trinitaires et la théologie mariale." *Marianum* 49 (1987) 377–448.

———, "Aux Origines de la Découverte des Richesses duCœur Immaculé de Marie: du IIIè au XIIè Siècle." *Divinitas* 31 (1987) 186–232.

———, "La maternité spirituelle de la Sainte Vierge chez les Pères durant les quatre premiers siècles." *Divinitas* 30 (1986) 53–77.

———, *La Maternité Spirituelle de la Très Sainte Vierge Marie.* Vatican City: Libreria Editrice Vaticana "Studi Tomistici" #36, 1990.

———, "La Maternité Spirituelle de la très Sainte Vierge Marie: Bilan Actuel." *Divinitas* 16 (1972) 17–102.

———, "Mise à Jour d'un Bilan: La Maternité Spirituelle de la Sainte Vierge Marie dans l'Écriture Sainte." *Divus Thomas (Piacenza)* 87 (1984) 289–323.

———, "La Visitation de la Sainte Vierge Marie: Exercice de Sa Maternité Spirituelle." *Divinitas* 16 (1972) 445–52.

Schmidt, Firmin M., O.F.M. Cap. "Our Lady's Queenship in the Light of *Quas Primas.*" *Marian Studies* 4 (1953) 118–33.

———, "The Universal Queenship of Mary." Juniper B. Carol, O.F.M., ed. *Mariology* 2. Milwaukee: Bruce Publishing Co., 1957. 493–549.

Sebastian, Wenceslaus, O.F.M., "Mary's Spiritual Maternity." Juniper B. Carol, O.F.M., ed. *Mariology* 2. Milwaukee: Bruce Publishing Co., 1957. 325–76.

Segalla, Giuseppe, Luigi Gambero, S.M., e Théodore Koehler, S.M. *Maria ai piedi della Croce.* Casale Monferrato: Edizioni Piemme, 1989.

Semmelroth, Otto, S.J. *Mary, Archetype of the Church.* Trans. Maria von Eroes and John Devlin. New York: Sheed and Ward, 1963.

Sennott, Thomas Mary, O.S.B. "Mary, Mediatrix of All Graces, Vatican II and Ecumenism." *Miles Immaculatae* 24 (1988) 151–67.

Sigrist, Paul. "Libermann (François-Marie-Paul)." *M. Viller et al. Dictionnaire de Spiritualité Ascétique et Mystique* 9. Paris: Beauchesne et Ses Fils, 1976. 764–780.

Simón, Alfredo "La Presenza della Beata Vergine nel Rinnovamento Promosso da Cluny." Enrico Dal Covolo, S.D.B. e Aristide Serra, O.S.M. (eds.) *Storia della mariologia*, Vol. 1: *dal modello biblico al modello letterario* (Rome: Città Nuova Editrice, Marianum, 2009) 593–617.

Sloyan, Gerard S. "Marian Prayers." Juniper B. Carol, O.F.M. ed. *Mariology* 3. Milwaukee: Bruce Publishing Co., 1961. 64–68.

Sparks, T. M., O.P. *Summarium de Cultu Cordis Immaculati Beatae Mariae Virginis*. Roma: Marietti, 1951.

Stasiewski, B. "Hlond, Augustyn." *New Catholic Encyclopedia* 7. New York: McGraw-Hill Book Co., 1967. 41.

Stern, Karl. *The Flight from Woman*. New York: Farrar, Strauss and Giroux, 1965.

The Sorrowful and Immaculate Heart of Mary: Message of Berthe Petit, Franciscan Tertiary (1870–1943) Trans. Nun of Kylemore Abbey. Kenosha, Wisconsin: Franciscan Marytown Press, 1974.

Sulle Orme dei Santi. Il Santorale Cappucino: Santi, Beati, Venerabili, Servi di Dio. Rome: Istituto Storico dei Cappucini, Postulazione Generale, 2000.

Tambasco, Anthony J. *What are they saying about Mary?* New York: Paulist Press, 1984.

Teologia e Pastorale della Consacrazione a Maria. Padua: Edizioni Messagero, 1969.

Thompson, William M., ed. *Bérulle and the French School: Selected Writings*. New York: Paulist Press, 1989.

Toniolo, Ermanno M., O.S.M. *La Beata Vergine Maria nel Concilio Vaticano II*. Rome: Centro di Cultura Mariana "Madre della Chiesa," 2004.

Totus Tuus: attualità e significato della consacrazione a Maria. Rome: Santuario Madonna del Divino Amore, 1978.

The Treasury of the Sacred Heart. New York: D. J. Sadlier & Co., 1879.

Triacca, Achille M. "*Sub tuum praesidium*: nella *lex orandi* un'anticipata presenza della *lex credendi*. La *teotocologia* precede la *mariologia*?" Sergio Felici, ed. *La mariologia nella catechesi dei Padri (età prenicena)*. Rome: Libreria Ateneo Salesiano "Biblioteca di Scienza Religiosa" #88, 1989. 183–205.

Trochu, Francis. *The Curé of Ars: St. Jean-Marie-Baptiste Vianney*. Trans. Dom Ernest Graf, O.S.B. 1927. Rockford, IL: Tan Books and Publishers, Inc. 1977.

Urquia Barroso, Juan Ramon, S.M. *The Theological Content of Consecration to Mary*. Trans. Robert Wood, S.M. Marianist Resources Commission. n.d.

Vagaggini, Cipriano, O.S.B. *Maria nelle Opere di Origene*. Roma: Pont. Institutum Orientalium Studiorum "Orientalia Christiana Analecta" #31, 1962.

Valabek, Redemptus M., O.Carm. *Mary, Mother of Carmel: Our Lady and the Saints of Carmel* I. Rome: Institutum Carmelitanum, 1987.

Vandergheynst, Leon. *Le Pape et le Consécration du Monde à Marie*. Bruxelles: La Pensée Catholique; Paris: Office Général du Livre, 1968.

Vasey, Vincent, S.M. "Mary in the Doctrine of Bérulle on the Mysteries of Christ." *Marian Studies* 36 (1985): 60–80.

Villaret, E., S.J. "Marie et la Compagnie de Jésus." Hubert du Manoir, S.J. ed. *Maria: Études sur la Sainte Vierge* 2. Paris: Beauchesne et Ses Fils, 1952. 936–973.

Vallin, Pierre. "Ramière (Henri)." M. Viller et al. *Dictionnaire de Spiritualité Ascétique et Mystique* 13. Paris: Beauchesne et Ses Fils, 1988. 63–70.

Verheylezoon, Louis, S.J. *Devotion to the Sacred Heart: Object, Ends, Practice, Motives*, 1955. Rockford, IL: Tan Books and Publishers, Inc., 1978.

Vloberg, Maurice. "Le Voeu de Louis XIII." Hubert du Manoir, S.J. *Maria: Études sur la Sainte Vierge* V. Paris: Beauchesne et Ses Fils, 1958. 519–533.

Walsh, Eugene A., S.S. *The Priesthood in the Writings of the French School: Bérulle, De Condren, Olier*. Washington, D. C.: The Catholic University of America Press, 1949.

Ward, J. Neville. "Abandon." Gordon S. Wakefield ed. *The Westminster Dictionary of Christian Spirituality*. Philadelphia: The Westminster Press, 1983. 1–2.

Wenger, A., A.A. "L'Intercession de Marie en Orient du VIe au Xe siècle." *Bulletin de la Société française d'Études Mariales* 23 (1966) 51–75.

William Joseph Chaminade: Marian Writings. Trans. Henry Bradley, S.M., & Joseph H. Roy, S.M. Dayton: Marianist Resources Commission, 1980. Vols. 1 & 2.

Williams, Margaret, R.S.C.J. *The Sacred Heart in the Life of the Church*. NY: Sheed and Ward, 1957.

Wiltgen, Ralph M. S.V.D. *The Rhine Flows into the Tiber: A History of Vatican II*. Rockford, IL: Tan Books and Publishers, Inc., 1985.

Winowska, Maria. "Le Culte Marial en Pologne." Hubert du Manoir, S.J., ed. *Maria: Études sur la Sainte Vierge* 4. Paris: Beauchesne et Ses Fils, 1956. 684–709.

Wyszyński, Stefan Cardinal. "Oddanie Się Matce Boga Zywego." ts. 1 March 1961.

Załęcki, Marian, O.S.P. *Theology of a Marian Shrine: Our Lady of Częstochowa. Marian Library Studies*, new series, 8. Dayton, Ohio: University of Dayton, 1976.

Zoffoli, Enrico, CP. *Principi di Filosofia.* Cipi Edizioni "Fonti Vivere," 1988.

INDEX OF BIBLICAL REFERENCES

INDEX OF PERSONS

INDEX OF SUBJECTS

The Academy of the Immaculate

The Academy of the Immaculate, founded in 1992, is inspired by and based on a project of St. Maximilian M. Kolbe (never realized by the Saint because of his death by martyrdom at the age of 47, August 14, 1941). Among its goals the Academy seeks to promote at every level the study of the Mystery of the Immaculate Conception and the universal maternal mediation of the Virgin Mother of God, and to sponsor publication and dissemination of the fruits of this research in every way possible.

The Academy of the Immaculate is a non-profit religious-charitable organization of the Roman Catholic Church, incorporated under the laws of the Commonwealth of Massachusetts, with its central office at Our Lady's Chapel, POB 3003, New Bedford, MA 02741-3003.

Special rates are available with 25% to 50% discount depending on the number of books, plus postage. For ordering books and further information on rates to book stores, schools and parishes: *Academy of the Immaculate, P.O. Box 3003, New Bedford, MA 02741, Phone/FAX (888)90.MARIA [888.90.62742], E-mail academy@marymediatrix.com.* Quotations on bulk rates by the box, shipped directly from the printery, contact: *Franciscans of the Immaculate, P.O. Box 3003, New Bedford, MA 02741, (508)996-8274, E-mail: ffi@marymediatrix.com. Website: www.marymediatrix.com.*

Printed in the United States of America